THE DERVISH BOWL

First published in 2024 in the United Kingdom by
Haus Publishing Limited
4 Cinnamon Row
London SW11 3TW

A CIP catalogue for this book is available from the British Library

ISBN 978-1-913368-97-5
eISBN 978-1-913368-98-2

Typeset in Garamond by MacGuru Ltd

Printed in the United Kingdom by Clays Ltd, Elcograf S.p.A.

Images on pages 136, 193, and 270 courtesy of the Library and Information Centre of
the Hungarian Academy of Sciences

www.hauspublishing.com

THE DERVISH BOWL

The Many Lives of Arminius Vambéry

ANABEL LOYD

Some of Arminius' books were never translated into English; in others his story varies in translation. All unattributed quotations in the text are taken from Vambéry's accounts of himself and his travels, all available online at Project Gutenberg and elsewhere: *His Life and Adventures*; *The Story of My Struggles*; *Travels in Central Asia*; *Sketches of Central Asia*; and additional material written by Arminius in several publications.

Contents

Vambéry's Central Asian journey, 1862–4

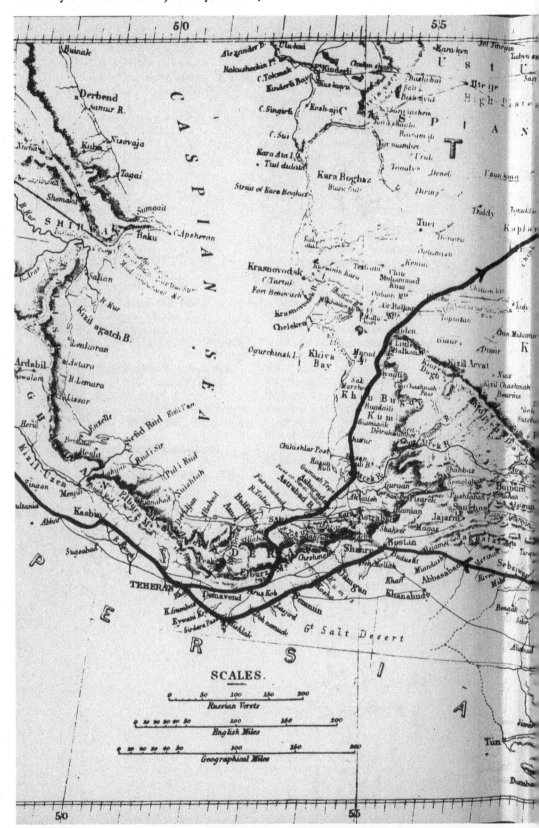

Acknowledgements

Anyone glancing through the pages of *The Dervish Bowl* will realise that my greatest thanks must be to the late Lory Alder and Richard Dalby, for their original research into Arminius Vambéry's remarkable life for *The Dervish of Windsor Castle*. I seem to have started a great many sentences with 'As Alder and Dalby said…' Richard Dalby was a bookseller and collector, with a passion for tales of the supernatural, who died in 2017, not long before I first came across Arminius. Lory Alder, Arminius' great niece, a screenwriter and otherwise author of a unique bilingual guide to Paris, is also dead, and I regret that I missed the chance to pick their brains for more of the first-hand knowledge they gleaned from Arminius' still-living relations and former pupils when they wrote their book.

Closer to hand, I would like to thank Dr Barbara Schwepcke for thinking this book was a good idea after she encountered Arminius Vambéry in Central Asia; Harry Hall of Haus Publishing for agreeing to publish it and putting up with one email after another whenever I had a new thought; and Jacky Colliss Harvey for taking the time and trouble to edit those thoughts, once on paper, into something that made a comprehensible narrative and had most of the right references in the right places, when she could instead have been fighting through the Thirty Years War beside her extraordinary hero, Jack Fiskardo, and his friends and enemies, in the wonderful historical fiction she writes herself. To Ed Doxey further thanks for dealing with the final details of the book.

There are others in the UK and Hungary who have been immensely helpful in getting Arminius Vambéry's story into print and to whom I owe my thanks. In London, Dr Rosemary Raza for introducing me to Paul Ambrus, who kindly translated a variety of Hungarian documents for me. In Budapest, Professor István Vásáry, of the Hungarian Academy of Sciences and Eötvös Loránd University, who answered a great many questions about Arminius when I visited Budapest at the end of 2019 for the temporary exhibition about his life. He gave me a tour of the city, which included Arminius' last home and his grave among the great Hungarians buried in Kerepesi Cemetery. He also took me into the wonderfully historic halls of the Hungarian Academy of Sciences. From that great institution I would like to thank Dr Nándor Erik Kovács, former curator of Turkish and Persian manuscripts, now teaching at Eötvös Loránd University, for finding documents and answering various queries; the head of the Oriental Collection, Dr Ágnes Kelecsényi, for her help in sourcing images from the Vambéry Bequest; and her colleague, János Boromisza, for sending them to me more than once when I lost the downloads. Katalin Pásztor persevered, resorting to using her personal email for better communication, to find digital images of Arminius held by the Hungarian National Museum and to arrange proper permissions for their use.

I should also like to thank David Mandler for the serious academic research that led to his excellent book, *Arminius Vambéry and the British Empire: Between East and West,* which has been of enormous help to me. Finally, I am very grateful too for the help of Aron Rimanyi and to Dr György Antall, whom I met during the final stages of the work on this book. Dr Antall provided another link with Arminius: he had known Arminius' last pupil, Gyula Germanus. Professor Germanus had taught Dr Antall's father, the Hungarian prime minister, József Tihamér Antall, at university. Dr Antall's memories of the eccentric Professor Germanus suggest that he was, in old age, a similar, rather curmudgeonly character to the teacher whose remarkable life is explored in the following pages.

The wandering Jew is a very real character in the great drama of history. From Ur of the Chaldees to Palestine and Egypt, back again to the Holy Land and then to Assyria and Babylon and the farthermost cities of the far-flung Roman Empire, he has travelled as a nomad and settler, as fugitive and conqueror, as exile and colonist, as merchant and scholar, as mendicant and pilgrim, as collector and as ambassador. His interest in foreign countries both near and far was fostered by Scripture, and the famous chapters of Isaiah and Jeremiah, among others, are a very mine of ancient geography. He was of necessity bilingual and could make himself master of many languages…

Sir Edward Denison Ross, *Jewish Travellers*, 1930

Introduction

If I had done my homework better, the dervish bowl in the museum at Baku would not have been a surprise. It was, however, no surprise that there, and in other museums on both sides of the Caspian Sea, one after another of the young tourist guides should misidentify the origin of so foreign an object. Born in a Soviet state, educated only as his or her newly independent country began the exhumation of its obliterated culture, dusting off the skeleton memories of regional and religious histories and affiliations, each had dutifully learned their multilingual museum lecture off pat. It was the usual monochrome chant of dates and conquests, warriors and kings, but missing the colour and romance of those small but irresistible details that, for me, bring all history alive. As the relics of Soviet housing and state control across the vast distances of the former USSR illustrate, grey drabness was the order of everyday Soviet life and the narrative of the people's republics, no matter that the bright residues and ruins of long-ago regimes still ornamented their ancient cities.

I recognised the dervish bowl on sight. A tourist curiosity now, it was made from a natural phenomenon that had once been the subject of mythology, and been believed to have magical properties. It was the forbidden fruit of the tree of life, adrift from Eden, found floating on the ocean or washed up on some deserted shore. Only a little more prosaically, it might instead be the extraordinary fruit of a submarine tree that fell upwards from its branch to the surface of the sea. After all, why not? If you have seen mermaids and sea monsters, travelled to lands where 'here be dragons', and others where the fantastic baobab tree grows, apparently upside down, anything might be possible. No wonder the rare and bizarre fruit of the female *Lodoicea maldivica*, the coco de mer, which grows only in two small areas of the Seychelles archipelago, should become the begging bowl or *kashkul* of a wandering holy man. Even if its erotic shape, in the round – so like the belly, buttocks, and thighs of a female torso – might raise the eyebrows of the more puritanical.

The young museum guides, however, had never heard of such a thing or seen it fully formed – only this polished bowl. The best *kashkuls*, found sometimes on the international art market, were intricately carved by Indian, Persian, or Turkish craftsmen with a variety of scripts, the name of Allah glorified in calligraphy for decorative and devotional effect. One such, perhaps of no great age, hangs now from its chain above my desk. The empty vessel signifies the emptying of the Sufi dervish's ego and the liberation of his soul through the renunciation of worldly goods and ties. It also embodies the idea of physical sustenance, to be filled by begging, being both food- and drinking-bowl for its owner. But what was it made of? The guides hypothesised, a nut perhaps? A coconut, as some indeed have been? Carved out of wood or, one suggested, shaped from camel leather? The description of its distant origins and true nature raised their eyebrows.

So, they and we may take the time to look a little closer at those curling photographs and prints of the dervish groups who tramped the dangerous routes of Turkestan in earlier centuries. There they are, gathered at the end or the beginning of a journey, in Bukhara or Khiva, best dressed for the camera in their embroidered patchwork coats and pointed, fur-fringed 'dunces' caps' (as they were described by Western observers of the period), their *kashkuls* – not always but often made from the coco de mer – strung on chains or leather straps and hanging from their shoulders. Look closer at this old lithograph, or that carefully posed early photograph, and glimpse one of the company, a little more evasive of the lens's searching eye than his fellows. The rest know their companion is unusual; he has come from Stamboul and is of great learning. They know him as 'Reshid Effendi', a highly educated man, light skinned (although the thick desert dust on his face makes an effective mask), and more travelled than they by far. They believe he is also a *Haji*, one who has made the pilgrimage to Mecca; but they do not know half the story of the effendi Arminius Vambéry. Were he not in fact (the poor, lame Hungarian Jew) an unbeliever of the very religion he seems here to espouse, a doubter, at the least, of any religious faith, he might himself believe that Allah in his wisdom has destined his safe path through this perilous adventure. Certainly he has, from birth it seems, been gifted with the remarkable memory and ear for language that works so well with the quick tongue of the mountebank to confound his questioners. Either that, or he has the luck of a *shaitan*, an evil spirit – the luck of the devil himself.

Arminius Vambéry's facility with languages and his ability to rise to an occasion were his greatest attributes. They were the best armour, he tells us, against the dangers of his extraordinary journey in the guise of a Sufi wanderer in Central Asia. This was the brief but perilous adventure that became his passport to international fame. The trappings of his dervish travels, in which he was much photographed, added to his celebrity as the false dervish in Britain, where he had his greatest success, and spread from there across Europe and America. In Hungary, his home country, Arminius never felt he received the recognition he deserved: the poor Jewish boy, forever at a disadvantage for his lack of formal academic credentials. In fact, the clever scholar was supported in his adventures by some of the most influential men of his day from among the membership of the famous Hungarian Academy of Sciences. More than a hundred years after his death, he has not been forgotten in those academic circles, and the Vambéry Bequest of rare Persian and Turkish documents has been preserved in the Academy throughout the vicissitudes faced by Hungary in the intervening years.

Recently, a Vambéry Civic Association has been founded in Dunaszerdahely, the town now in southern Slovakia where he was born. It is supported by Hungarian Orientalist specialists and academics and, in late 2019, an exhibition on Arminius Vambéry opened in the Ybl Buda Creative House in Budapest to bring his achievements to a wider audience. Arminius epitomised the spirit of his age in a Hungary searching for its unique national characteristics and looking towards the East to find them, with the exhibition being the sequel to another the year before, *Hungarians on the Silk Road*. Other Hungarian scholar-travellers who came before and behind Arminius included Alexander Csoma de Kőrös, who travelled as far as Ladakh in Kashmir in search of the elusive linguistic roots of Hungarian, and who became instead the founding father of Tibetan studies and librarian of the Asiatic Society of Bengal. Then there was Aurel Stein, the great archaeologist and cartographer, another Hungarian Jew, who became a British citizen and the recipient of high honours, and who was one of the best-known servants of the British Empire.[1]

---

1 Born in Budapest in 1862, Stein died in 1943 in Kabul, leaving a huge collection of artefacts

Arminius himself first visited Great Britain in 1864, shortly after his Central Asian travels, and found Victorian Britain highly receptive to Eastern adventurers and the whiff of oriental drama. It was there that he found the fame he thought he deserved as he was swiftly re-branded as the epitome of the Orientalist adventurer and lionised by fascinated London high society. As well as being an Orientalist, Arminius was a Russophobe; a zealous Anglophile imperialist; a bit-player in the Great Game between empires in Asia; a self-important master of self-publication; and a British secret agent of sorts, funded by the British government into his old age. He was also an established guest, confidante, and sometimes friend of monarchs in both East and West. Yet in the twenty-first century in the UK he has been almost entirely forgotten. There is a Vambéry Road in Woolwich (which it took a Hungarian member of the present-day Hungarian Academy to point out to me, and to send photographic proof). He occasionally turns up in accounts of nineteenth-century travellers on the Silk Road, or those of other players of the Great Game. And he is sometimes spotted *almost* paired with Joseph Wolff, the highly eccentric 'English Dervish', who was in fact no more a dervish than was Arminius – although he was a man of intense religious belief.[2]

In Hungary, where he felt so deprived of the plaudits of fame in his lifetime, Arminius is remembered today as a scholar, traveller, and friend of kings and emperors. His work is celebrated, though its academic value, beyond his legacy of old and rare manuscripts and books, is difficult to judge. The mass of his writing was journalism, but he also wrote books (generally biography or reportage), letters, and reports. His are not generally scholarly works but he is seen now, in Hungary, as one of the great Orientalists, as in a scholar of the East, of the nineteenth century. Arminius Vambéry was a remarkable linguist; a prolific writer; and, for his academic credentials, a professor of Asian languages. He was also an actor and a storyteller, and so fine a raconteur of baroque tales of the unknown East and of picturesque

and papers. These are now mainly in British institutions, or in Calcutta and Delhi, but with a considerable archive bequeathed to the Hungarian Academy.

2 Wolff was a German Jew born, coincidentally, not far from Bamberg, where the Vambéry or Wamberger family originated. He became a Christian missionary and travelled to forbidden Bukhara in 1843, where he so amazed and amused the psychotic Emir Nasrullah with his antics that he was one of the few who survived to tell the tale of their meeting (see page 89).

Hungarian history and folklore that he would even help, at one point, to conjure *Dracula* from the writer Bram Stoker's fertile gothic imagination.

Vambéry and Stoker first met at a theatrical performance in front of Queen Victoria at Sandringham, when Stoker was Henry Irving's stage manager and Arminius the guest of the prince of Wales. That prince, later Edward VII, remained a lifelong friend to Arminius and was godfather to his only son, Rustem. Stoker and Irving were fascinated by Arminius the storyteller, who was to be described by his friend, the Zionist leader Max Nordau, as 'Scheherazade translated into the masculine'. In *Dracula*, Professor Van Helsing shares his academic title and his foreignness with Vambéry, and even speaks of writing to his 'friend Arminius' of 'Buda-Pesth university' regarding Dracula's identity. Arminius was the perfect fit for the character of Professor Van Helsing's expert friend, and the use of his name a tribute from one teller of fantastical tales to another. By the time *Dracula* was published, in 1897, the name of Arminius Vambéry had also acquired the necessary academic dignity to lend a gloss of verisimilitude to Stoker's gothic horror.

All this was fame, the gilding of his *amour propre* that Arminius craved. In his decidedly hagiographical appreciation after Arminius' death, his one-time student Max Nordau denied any vanity in the great man: 'he was an *arrivé* not a *parvenu*... only conscious of his own worth'.[3] But reading his own autobiographical works and other less self-interested commentaries on Arminius' character in our more judgemental times, it is hard not to spot less attractive characteristics in the man. These seem to have stemmed from the eternal chip on the shoulder of Hermann or Chaim (Haschele in the family) Wamberger, the lame second child and only son of a poor, young, Hungarian Jewish couple. Arminius' over-sensitivity to any imagined slight was the result of his own early struggles and only grew with time and as his level of success never reached his own, self-appointed mark. He was overtly socially and financially grasping, and resented and denigrated any view dissenting from his own. Addressing his reflection in the looking-glass while staying at Windsor Castle in 1889 as a guest of the prince of Wales, Arminius is said to have declared 'Haschele Wamberger, du hast Du gut gemacht!' ('Haschele Wamberger, you have done well!'[4]), but it was never enough.

Arminius had a clever and elastic mind and would become a world-famous Orientalist scholar, but one wonders if the prickly self-regard of the old Professor Vambéry in Pest was a defence against his own realisation that he had only been acting a part all his life, whatever the success that had brought him. He had been born poor and Jewish in an intolerant society, and (more importantly for him) his formal education was never finished. He had no framed certificate to hang on the wall; he was a remarkable autodidact; and his learning experience included his travels and his surviving on his wits, but was that enough? He wrote that his journey in the role of the dervish was his best introduction to everything that came later, and it continued to be his calling card. Did that cast him permanently as not quite the real thing in his own mind – always the travelling player rather than the genuine academic? There were certainly those among his fellow Orientalists and elsewhere who considered him a fraud, but there were a few others (including in the British Foreign Office, who continued, until his death, to sign off on his annual payments) who could never quite resist him.

Arminius died in 1913, his love for Britain tempered by policies of which

3 Max Nordau, 'My Recollections of Vambéry', introduction to the posthumous 9th edition of the *Life and Adventures*.
4 Lory Alder and Richard Dalby, *The Dervish of Windsor Castle* (London, 1979), 318.

he disapproved, by changing times, and by ideas that he refused to accept. His detestation of Russia was exemplified by mutterings in print and in person almost to the end, although his attention had by then become more focused on Persia, Germany and, in particular, Turkey. It may be childish but is nevertheless irresistible for another keen, if less adventurous travel- ler, perforce in a time when fewer paths are left unbeaten, not to wonder what he would have thought of events in the century or so since his death. That more recent history, not least including a contemporary view of places visited and written about by Arminius, has played a part in the conception and inception of this book. The Russians never did get to India, at least not until new wealth took them as tourists to the fleshpots of Goan holiday resorts. Their excursions into Afghanistan were as disastrous as every other foreign adventure into that impossible country. The Soviet dream fruited and failed. Its tattered remains survive to mark or mar the lands of Central Asia, where Arminius found fame, beside the decoratively crumbling legacy of the earlier Tsarist Russian expansion and settlement that he railed against for so long.

Now there are other tyrants, both within the independent countries of Middle Asia and without. Chinese expansionism is more determined, more ambitious, faster and broader-cast than any past imperial power. Would Arminius Vambéry now substitute Sinophobia for Russophobia? Given his admiration for the British, imperialism was not his complaint, only the manner of its formation, and Chinese business and finance are potent seduc- ers. Moreover, any future hegemony in the lands of the silk routes may find itself threatened in the longer run by nature herself as much as by com- peting powers. Travellers have long since pointed at water shortages – an after-effect, not least, of intensive Russian cotton cultivation dating back to the Tsarist conquest and maximised in the Soviet era. The drying of the Aral Sea is catastrophic, and the waters of the legendary rivers the Amu Darya (the ancient Oxus) and the Syr Darya (or Jaxartes) have been up for grabs since the fall of the Soviet Union. This can be seen most clearly in Uzbekistan, where the increase in salinity can be measured by the fre- quent traveller to Samarkand, for example, in the salt that rises year by year, layer by layer, coating the bricks of historic monuments with a corro- sive crust and denying all efforts to stop its encroachment. Touch the earth almost anywhere across the deserts and into the oases of Central Asia, from

Turkmenbashi to Sary-Tash, on the Kyrgyz side of the border with China, and lick your finger. You will taste the salt.

Arminius Vambéry came to know the deserts of Turkestan all too well, so far as he was concerned, during the formative, if relatively brief, period in his life of his journey in dervish disguise. His accounts of the drama and fear of his meetings with rulers and their agents – who might, had they pierced that disguise, have put him to death by the most imaginatively painful means – stuck in the minds of his readers and made him famous. Nature at these extremes was, however, every bit as barbarous and might have killed him just as easily, whoever he was or was not. The nimble tongue of the storyteller and a quick change of coat was no insurance against the insentient elements, but Vambéry survived to tell his tales again and again, and to build a career on a foundation of disguise, chicanery, and words.

1

The Lame Boy

Arminius Vambéry's father had been a Talmudic scholar and failed business-man in the small town of St Georghen near Pressburg in Austria-Hungary.[1] He died of the cholera that was seasonally endemic in Hungary when his son was only months old, in either 1831 or 1832. (Ironically the cholera, like most unex-plained misfortunes, was generally blamed upon the Jews.) Nobody much cared in this anti-Semitic society that Jewish births were rarely registered and often inaccurately recorded, and Arminius was never sure of his exact age. In 1889, when he was invited to Windsor by Queen Victoria, he was required to enter his date of birth in the royal birthday book. Arminius wrote of his hesita-tion until, he reported to his readers, Sir Henry Ponsonby, the queen's private secretary, informed him that 'Her Majesty lays less weight upon the birth of her guests than upon their actions and merits'. His official birthday is generally given as 19 March 1832, the date written in the queen's book.

Mr Fleischman, Arminius' mother's second husband, proved a better provider of more children than of the wherewithal to feed and clothe their shared brood. He was 'kind-hearted' but 'by no means industrious or enter-prising', according to Arminius. Inn-keeping was a Jewish trade (*vide* Dr Demant's devout grandfather, in Joseph Roth's *The Radetzky March*, who 'sat outside his inn, like an ancient king among innkeepers'), and Arminius' mother (whose first name, sadly, has not come down to us) had set up as

---

1 Now Svätý Jur, a small town near Bratislava, capital of Slovakia. The Treaty of Trianon in 1920, after World War I, redefined the borders of Hungary and many place names were changed. In general, this book uses place names, including in Central Asia, Persia, or Turkey, that will be recognisable to the reader even if they are not in present use. Diacritic marks are also used judiciously.

an innkeeper while she was still married to her unworldly scholar. Now Mr Fleischman proceeded to spend the income from his wife's successful business. She was a resourceful woman who might have been better off without another feckless husband, but she had only been twenty-two when she was widowed, and who can tell what pressures she had to withstand alone, especially in her conventional Jewish community?

When Arminius was three, the Fleischmans moved to Mr Fleischman's hometown of Dunaszerdahely in southern Slovakia, and it was there that Arminius began his education. As the money from the sale of his mother's inn dwindled, one after another failed business venture of his stepfather's, including leech farming ('a sort of family trade' according to Arminius, who was disgusted by the leeches), left the family hungry if not actually starving. 'Inexorable poverty', however, was no bar to the basic religious education received by all Jewish boys, albeit at a 'third-rate school', where Arminius' 'inborn brightness of intellect' and remarkable memory soon allowed him to shine and to qualify for entry to the best Jewish school available in Dunaszerdahely at a reduced fee.

By his own description, he was not only a bright but an attractive child, in spite of the additional handicap to his future prospects caused by a severe limp. He described this as coxalgia, meaning hip pain, but it was probably due to some joint defect from birth, or an injury followed by infection, which came on when he was about three and set his left knee at a tight right angle. His mother's attempts to find a cure varied from quackish potions and treatments to magic charms, and included Arminius being laid out at a crossroads at midnight 'to fall under the spell of passing old gypsy women'; 'selling' her son to another woman 'in the hope that this would please God'; and allowing herself to be gulled by a venal Catholic priest in a distant village for an expensive 'prescription' from an equally dishonest local apothecary. Finally, she tried a more radically barbarous treatment at the hands of an illiterate peasant 'cureworker'. For five days the boy's leg was held over hot steam to loosen the sinews, after which he was held down on the floor while the 'doctor' threw all his weight onto the rigid knee, whereupon, unsurprisingly, Arminius lost consciousness. His leg was then tightly splinted, but when the splint was removed, his knee was no less affected, and he was forced to use a crutch – while still determined to compete with the other village children in the physical activities in which he was bound to fail.

To his readers, much later, Arminius marvelled that his common-sensical mother should be so 'desperately entangled in the meshes of superstition'. He quoted her saying, 'My child you will do better than any of them' – salving, one guesses, her own pain as well as her son's. It is worth remembering that these memories of childhood, less detailed in his earlier autobiographical works, were written in *The Story of My Struggles* when Arminius was seventy-four and approaching the end of a celebrated life. It would have been a pity for the difficulties of his early years not to have suited the reality of what came later and his almost legendary status in the eyes of his adherents. Nevertheless, he undoubtedly did have a limp all his life and those descriptions of horrible attempted cures are too graphic not to be believable in the context of time and place. Nor is it hard to imagine the clever child, less physically able than he would have wished, being encouraged by his mother to channel his energy towards more intellectual means of achievement in a community where, in any case, learning was traditionally highly valued. Arminius believed he had inherited his memory from his mother because she could remember the smallest details of her own childhood. Although illiterate, she clearly had high ambitions for her first-born son, keeping him 'rigorously at his lessons', and making him sleep with his books under his pillow so that knowledge should seep into his brain while he slept. He described her as a remarkable woman, a mix of great energy, good sense, and 'blind superstition'; 'a type of the Jewess of the Middle Ages, full of ancient principles and maxims, sometimes showing themselves in a tenacious clinging to the old faith, sometimes conforming to existing circumstances'.

In her determination to get the best possible education for Arminius, his mother was also unusually careless of existing conformity. Surprisingly, for her time and community, his mother removed him from his Jewish school to enter him into the local Protestant Christian elementary school when he was eight. Arminius was a voracious reader, as he remained throughout his life, and his non-Jewish schooling contributed to the fact that he could read and write German and Hungarian at a time when Yiddish was the lingua franca of the Jewish community, in which few would have had more than a smattering of the national language. He also knew much of the Torah by heart and could read and translate Hebrew, but these skills would not pay for his long-term education. Aged eleven, he was made apprentice to a Jewish tailoress, his board and lodging in her house paid for by tutoring her son of the same age in Hebrew. So began Arminius' peripatetic working career. It quickly became apparent to him that stitching was not his vocation, and he was next placed with an innkeeper, some distance from Dunaszerdahely, where he taught the son of the house for four hours a day and was unofficial waiter and boy of all work for the rest of his time. After six months of hard work and long hours he left, returning home with money in his pocket for the first time in his life. It was the means of paying for the next step of his mother's plan for his education: in the Catholic Piarist's college at St Georghen, near Bratislava (then Pressburg).[2]

First, Arminius had his bar mitzvah at home in Dunaszerdahely, a ceremony which he appears to have regarded with indifference but one his mother must have known was important if he was to have any chance of acceptance into the Jewish community in St Georghen. There, it was said, 'the poor, deserted and much-oppressed Jew was always delighted to share his hardly-earned crust of bread with those who thirsted for knowledge'. In Eastern and Central European Jewish communities, religious study continued until 1939 to be considered the highest calling. Mendele Mocher Sforim, the 'Grandfather of Yiddish Literature', spoke of the support for students of the Torah who came 'on foot, penniless. No sooner did they put their pack down – two worn, patched shirts, one pair of socks with dirty, much trodden heels – than they came under the town's care. The townspeople, poor as they were, supported these boys willingly. The poorest man in town shared his bread with a pious scholar'.[3] Arminius' unorthodox educational path did not, however, help his cause in the longer term, regardless of the bar mitzvah. He wrote that 'Jewish charity was not compatible with Christian education'. When starvation loomed, it was his Christian schoolmates, who had previously given him bread in exchange for help with their work, who unexpectedly took pity on him and invited him to eat in their homes.

---

2 Aurel Stein, the most famous Jewish Hungarian explorer of Central Asia, was also educated at a Piarist college, in his case in Pest. His biographer Annabel Walker noted that the Piarists were 'less dogmatic' than the Benedictines, the other Roman Catholic teaching order, and 'had many Jewish children in their classes'. See Annabel Walker, *Aurel Stein: Pioneer of the Silk Road* (London, 1995), 10.

3 Quoted in David Aberbach, 'Poverty and Mass Education: The Jews in the Roman Empire,' *Working Paper Series* (2019), 18–192, accessed online 2 Nov. 2023.

During his second year Arminius encountered anti-Semitism from the priest who was his new professor, and had stones thrown at him in the street. Under these circumstances it may not have been very 'extraordinary the change that took place in me as far as religion was concerned'. Jewish orthodoxy had been 'done away with'; kosher food rules 'seemed to me childish and ridiculous'. Arminius' indifference to religion, beyond his doubts about Judaism, was directly motivated by the behaviour of the inhabitants of the Piarist monastery, not least the carelessness of religious observance that made use of him, a despised Jew, as an altar boy when the designated Christian student failed to turn up. He 'knew the catechism by heart, they said, and was quite like a Catholic: there was no need to make any difficulty about it'. Arminius admitted he 'enjoyed the comedy very much', and wrote in his usual superior tone that he considered 'this and similar experiences were a good preparation for the role of Mohammedan priest [sic]'. Certainly, he learned to think nothing of chameleon-like changes in his professed religious affiliation when expedient. His religion, when he professed one at all, was questioned throughout his life and he encouraged his reputation as a free thinker. In their biography, Alder and Dalby recount an almost certainly apocryphal story of a friend calling unexpectedly on a Jewish holiday in his last years to find the old Arminius 'wrapped in his prayer shawl, the ritual phylacteries on his forehead and an open prayer-book on his knee'. Arminius was to be baptised on 30 December 1864 at the Calvin Square Reformed Church in Budapest by the Calvinist bishop Pál Török, but it is doubtful that his baptism made any more impact on him than his bar mitzvah, although he was buried under Protestant rites.[4] His simple gravestone may be seen among the trees and lawns and the massive mausolea of the great and good of Hungary in Kerepesi Cemetery in Budapest.

Arminius' summer holiday, at the end of his second year at St Georghen, was spent walking or hitching lifts with carters to explore Austria-Hungary. He stayed with local clergy, where his Latin conversation brought its rewards,[5] and he considered these travels, which fed his growing wanderlust,

---

4 In 1848, the then Pastor Török had stopped a mob attacking Jews near the Orczy House in the Jewish quarter of Pest with an unsheathed sword, and had previously protected the Jews of the city as an important part of society. See Gèza Komoróczy, ed., *Jewish Budapest: Monuments, Rites, and History* (Budapest, 1999).

5 Alder and Dalby note that 'Latin had survived in Hungary as a living language and a sign of

as early training for his dervish journey. At the end of the holiday, wearing
a new suit given to him by wealthier relatives in Lundenburg, he moved to
a school run by the Benedictines in Pressburg/Bratislava, home to the third
largest Jewish community in Hungary after those of Obuda and Pest.

Looking back, Arminius made it clear in his autobiographies that he
had early acquired the necessary mindset and actorly skills needed to make
his life easier during his youthful struggles, and which would stand him in
good stead in his later roles. He could play the starving student to get free
food, and the clever but pathetic lame boy when he had no money to buy
his train ticket to Lundenburg, just as he would one day play the dervish.
He had been funded for this train journey by other relatives in Pressburg,
but he was still only fourteen and spent too much of his windfall buying
'10 or 15 butter-cakes more than I should have done'. Always resourceful, he approached two other passengers and enquired politely: *'Domini
spectabilis rogo jumullime, dignemini mihi dare aliquanto cruciferos qui iter
ferrarium solvendi mihi carent'* ('Kind sirs, please give me the few pence I
lack for my fare'), which speech in Latin, from the little lame boy, 'had
its effect'.

Whether such a speech would have had a similar effect if delivered in
Lille or Leeds to a passing stranger is questionable, even in the days of classical education. In Hungary, however, Latin had long been the official and
living language of government, used to overcome the problem of a multi-
national and multilingual population. Now, in the era of reform of the 1830s
and 1840s, language had become a political and nationalist football, and it
was the political and cultural importance of the Magyar language and its
linguistic roots that was to be the official impetus for Arminius' journey to
Central Asia.

'Priestly animosity and disgraceful intolerance' from the Benedictines discouraged Arminius' interest in formal education in favour of reading and
studying on his own. He began to teach himself French, without which he
believed his education would not be complete in the eyes of society. Meanwhile his survival was ensured by giving reading and writing lessons to 'the
lower classes of Jewish society', where his skills writing billets-doux for cooks

---

education well into the nineteenth century and one is driven to speculate whether Vambéry's
Latinisation of his first name was not in some way connected with it'.

and maids were paid for in sustaining kind. They also led to his introduction into upstairs society, and his recommendation as a private tutor in Hungarian, French, and Latin to the Jewish community of Pressburg, which provided paid work for a few hours a day. It helped him survive, but left little time for his own studies on top of eight hours of school.

In 1848, the year of revolutions, when Arminius was sixteen, Hungary, inspired and led by the statesman and orator Lajos Kossuth (1802–94), rose up against Austrian rule and riots broke out across the country. In Pressburg, resentment against the expansion of Jewish businesses beyond the walls of the ghetto boiled over, and the life of the Jewish community was violently disrupted. Astonishingly no Jews were killed, but property was destroyed and people badly beaten.[6] Arminius had to get out. All schools in Hungary had closed with the outbreak of the Revolution, so his means of income had been destroyed, and he was appalled by the executions of Hungarian patriots with whom he strongly identified.

That Magyar patriotism has been regularly noted by historians of the period. The intense sense of encompassing Hungarian-ness, within which Jewishness might be no different to being Protestant or Roman Catholic, peaked within the Jewish community of Hungary during the second half of the nineteenth and early years of the twentieth century. It was this nationalism that created the dichotomy of a community that could produce the activist Theodor Herzl (1860–1904), 'the spiritual father of the Jewish State'[7] and creator of political Zionism, with whom Arminius was involved late in life, and at the same time 'its most fervent opposition'.[8] As an example of this nationalism, in the first comprehensive modern history of *The Jews of Hungary*, published only in 1996, the writer Raphael Patai, who was born in 1910, notes that the historian Samuel Kohn ends his *The History of the Jews of Hungary from Earliest Times to the Disaster of Mohacs* (1884), with the disastrous Battle of Mohacs in 1526, which marked the beginning of the Ottoman control of Hungary; and then never seems to have had the heart to complete a planned second volume. Patai writes that Kohn's early history

---

6 Michael K. Silber, 'Bratislava', *The YIVO Encyclopedia of Jews in Eastern Europe*, accessed online 8 Nov. 2023.

7 Taken from *The Declaration of the Establishment of the State of Israel*, 1948.

8 Raphael Patai, *The Jews of Hungary: History, Culture, Psychology* (Detroit, 1996), 12.

was coloured by the 'red, white and green' of nineteenth-century national-ism, which sought to show an affinity between Hungarians and Jews, 'even extending to a common origin and that the position of the Jews had always been better in Hungary than in any of the neighbouring countries'. Mohacs itself was still seen as an equal catastrophe by all Hungarians, no matter what their religious affiliation. Patai also suggests that Hungarian Jewish anti-Zionism was motivated by the conviction 'that the Jews, or at any rate the Hungarian Jews, were not a race, not a people, not an ethnic group, not a nationality, but purely and simply a religious denomination'.

Patai's argument, that 'it is in the fusion of autochthonous Jews with semi-Jewish Khazars and Kavars in the tenth century that we must seek the earliest demographic basis of the Jewish population of mediaeval Hungary', thus aligned the concept of Hungarian 'easternness' with the origins of Hun-garian Jews.[9] In his chapter on 'The origins of the Hungarians', in his highly nationalistic *The Story of Hungary* (which is filled with ripping yarns from Hungarian history and otherwise never mentions the Hungarian Jews), Arminius himself described the Khazars as 'the mightiest of the Turkish races of that time' who had 'embraced the Jewish religion'.[10] That would have suited his image of himself as a Hungarian with ties to the Orient, in particular to Turkey, and the thinking of his times in a community that was Hungarian first and Jewish second.

In 1860, the initial support by the Academy of Sciences in Budapest for Arminius' proposal of a journey into the regions of Central Asia in search of the linguistic origins of Hungarian, and its links with the East, was a fit with the zeitgeist. The belief in common Turkic origins and an all-encom-passing national pride made this Hungarian Jewish Orientalist a round peg in the round hole of contemporary academic study. The earliest 'Orientalists' were, for a start, Hebrew speakers who then learned Arabic, as did Armin-ius; Alexander Csoma de Kőrös (1784/8–1842), for example, also studied Hebrew at the same time as Latin and Greek – although in his case not as part of a traditional *yeshiva*, or orthodox Jewish religious school education

9 Ibid. In more recent years this hypothesis has been seen as anti-Zionist and has become known as the 'Khazar myth' of the origins of Eastern European Jews. Patai remarked the concern of more recent Hungarian Jewish historians about their Jewishness being 'less than complete – in fact, rather partial and superficial' and was himself convinced of the Khazar relationship.
10 Vambéry, *The Story of Hungary* (New York and London, 1889), 34.

for the reading of the Torah, but as a senior student at the charitable Beth-lenianum College of Nayenyed, a seminary for the Calvinist priesthood, in the expectation of a future focused on biblical Hebrew. Anti-Semitism notwithstanding, Hungarian Jews shared the national experience. During massacres of Jews throughout the Middle Ages, the darkest period in the history of European Jewry until the Holocaust, Hungary remained a haven when compared with almost anywhere else. Arminius and his community suffered discrimination, but his Jewishness was not seen as a handicap to those who would, in part, fund his travels in Central Asia. In any case, in the assimilated society of the Hungarian capital, many of the Budapest elite and Arminius' supporters were also Jewish. His linguistic skills were his selling point; the only question mark hung over his crippled leg and his physical ability to make the journey.

Work as a tutor to a family in a village in the Carpathians gave Arminius more time for study and enough income to be able to return to school at the Protestant Lyceum where prejudice was unusually absent. He was taught in German and the lectures were better but, aged eighteen, the struggle to support himself at the same time as attending school had become too much. He decided, to his regret, to leave school and go out into the world in the hope of finishing his formal education later. That would never happen, but his next employment, as language teacher to the sons of a small land-owner, had unexpected benefits for his future in glossier society. Mrs von Petrikovitch, his employer's wife, took it upon herself to add social polish to the young tutor's accomplishments. Arminius suggested he took these finishing-school lessons quite as seriously as – and to the detriment of – his more academic studies. He spent hours practising bows, table manners, and drawing-room elegancies while gazing into his looking-glass, and his vanity led to expenses that ate up his small income. He was unable to pay the sixteen florins required to gain his official school leaving certificate from the Lyceum, the lack of which was an obstacle in the first place to his academic career and, in the second, a lasting wound to his self-worth.

His engagement with the Petrikovitch family ended when the boys went to school in Pest. He had to find another post through the best medium available in the city to a Jewish tutor in search of work – the Café Orczy.[11]

---

11 Old photographs show the café at the front of the huge complex of the Orczy House at the

The café combined the roles of coffee house, complete with kosher food and Yiddish newspapers, with that of a commodity exchange for the grain business across several European countries, as well as being a location for the business transactions of wholesale merchants in other goods and an unofficial employment agency for cantors and Jewish teachers.[12] Years later Arminius compared it to the slave markets of Central Asia, a place where agents touted their human wares and took fees that were the lion's share of the 'earnest money' that changed hands to seal the deal on a new appointment.

His first job via the Café Orczy took Arminius far away from the Piarist college, where he had hoped to continue his interrupted schooling and thus by some means overcome the problem of the missing school certificate. Moreover his payment in board and lodging in this new post proved so mean that he decided once and for all to give up the chance of a definite profession and find a better job as a tutor in the country. By now he felt able to advertise himself – on the basis, he admitted, of 'slight acquaintance' – as a professor of seven languages. His next, well-paid, and considerably more comfortable employment with a family in Slavonia was curtailed when he suffered the fate of so many poor young tutors in nineteenth-century romances. Bewitched by 'the shining orbs of Miss Emily', the daughter of the house, he found himself dismissed after taking her hand a little too firmly while guiding her writing. All was not lost, however, as he had had plenty of time in his working day for his own studies. According to his own account, they ran to the acquisition of Spanish, Danish, and Swedish, not to mention the local Illyric (Serbian) to add to his store of Hungarian, Slav, German, French, Italian, Hebrew, and Russian; and he had also begun to learn Turkish and pursue his Oriental studies seriously. He went home to his mother who he knew would be less than impressed by such unprofitable achievements. He was right, and after a short visit Arminius left to 'throw himself once more on

---

centre of the Jewish quarter. The Orczy House, with its hundreds of apartments occupied by Jewish families, was demolished in 1936 to make way for modern housing. The writer József Kiss, in his 1874 novel *The Secrets of Budapest*, described the café, which had been in existence since 1825, as 'the nest of the proletariat and Judaism'. Here was 'oriental dirt, Constantinople din…'

12 See Andràs Koerner, *How They Lived: The Everyday Life of Hungarian Jews, 1867–1940* (Budapest, 2015) for more details of its history.

the world's turmoil', travelling to Vienna to look for the better employment as an interpreter that he believed his linguistic skills deserved.

Despite his poor background, lack of any introductions, and entire ignorance of the labyrinth of Austrian bureaucracy, Arminius managed to be in the right place at the right time to encounter some of the right people. They could not give him work, but Baron Joseph von Hammer-Purgstall (1774–1856; former diplomat, Orientalist, and founder-president of the Austrian Academy of Sciences) and his friend Franz Schlechta von Wschehrd (1796–1875), who were Jewish or had Jewish connections, both encouraged Arminius' study of 'Turkology'. Handily, both also believed that Hungarian speakers already had an advantage in the study of Eastern languages. Arminius also met the Serbian linguist Vuk Karadžić, who promoted further study of this language to Arminius, and the priest at the Russian Embassy, 'Mr' Rayewski, who encouraged him to visit St Petersburg and to learn Russian. Arminius' languages and unusual mixed career were opening doors, but for now he had to return to Pest to find work and new lodgings. His new landlady was a professional nurse with a house at 7, Three Drums Street, and a four-bed dormitory that slept eight. The benefit, he wrote, of his popularity with the nurse was a bedfellow who was a 'thin tailor-lad' and happily did not take up too much room in the bed.

This glimpse of higher society had not yet improved everyday existence for Arminius, and back he went to Mr Mayer at the Café Orczy in search of a better post. He kept body and soul together teaching for a few florins a month, and studied Russian for as many hours a day as possible with, he wrote, occasional excursions into German literature and the romance languages of southern Europe. He was cold and hungry. Breakfast, in exchange for a lesson to the son of a coffee-house proprietor, was coffee and a couple of rolls, when he could 'easily have demolished half a dozen'. At last Mayer found him an appointment with a wealthy family in Kecskemét, in central Hungary, where he stayed for the next year. He was now able to afford the necessary books to begin his study of Arabic and Turkish and to borrow others from Professor Môr Ballagi, the Hungarian linguist, who lived nearby and who had fought for the emancipation of Hungarian Jews. By this time the professor had converted to Protestantism and Magyarised his name, as Arminius was also shortly to do.

Arminius wrote that he could not remember why he had left so comfortable a job, but possibly it may have been because his students' general education 'left much to be desired', in spite of their progress in languages. He left with a good-enough reference to secure his next satisfactory job, out in the country on the edge of the Great Plain of Hungary. There, he assured his later readers, having somehow or somewhere picked up Greek, he lay in the shade of a haycock reciting the *Odyssey* to a nomadic audience of amazed shepherds and their flocks. A happy meeting with a fellow eccentric, the amateur meteorologist and landowner Karl Balla, who had been director of the Pest country prison, led to comfortable employment the following winter, in which he taught French and English to Balla's son while pursuing his own studies, which now included Persian. Unfortunately for him, Herr Balla's anti-Semitic wife created such a level of family uproar that Arminius was sent away but, back in Pest, he was able to find an equally good, and final, tutoring position in Hungary with the Grunfeld family.

It ended badly, as Arminius described it, with violence, drama and, on his part (as he assured his later readers), high heroics, when the family was robbed in a 'ghastly nocturnal scene'. According to him, the masked and armed robbers, to whom he had mistakenly opened the front door on 11 November 1856, were probably political fugitives on the run from the Austrian government. Unsatisfied by their haul of about 20,000 florins from the family, they threatened to shoot Herr Grunfeld. Arminius, who had learned the value of a good story by the time he offered his own to posterity, or had perhaps been leavening his study of the *Odyssey* with other tales of derring-do, leapt to his feet, grabbed the gun, and pointed it at his own heart, declaring 'If you must kill, kill me; I have neither wife nor child, it is better that I should die!' After that, the astonished robbers desisted from further violence, collected their loot (which included some 'volumes of Hungarian classics' belonging to our hero) and went on their way. Unfortunately, this eccentric haul not unreasonably strengthened police suspicion of Arminius' involvement with the criminals, since he had also let them into the house. Although his employer saved him from worse consequences, he had had enough, and with his mother's death at about the same time cutting his last ties to home, Arminius decided to follow his dreams eastwards. How he should achieve his goal of travel to Constantinople was another question.

69.

VÁMBÉRY ÁRMIN,

2

Constantinople

Probably through his various employers, possibly through wealthier relations and the networks of Jewish communities in Hungary and Austria, Arminius was beginning to gain useful contacts. His unusual linguistic talents too had propagated the seed of a reputation – undoubtedly, whatever their real scope, he knew enough of a wide range of languages to impress. But to get the required passport for travel to Constantinople, he now needed someone to vouchsafe that same reputation did not include revolutionary leanings. All Hungarian travellers to the Ottoman Empire, where leaders of the 1848 Revolution such as Lajos Kossuth had taken refuge, were suspect to the Austrian authorities. To Baron József Eötvös (1813–71),[1] the champion who came forward, this young man with his newly Hungarian name must have appeared the epitome of the transformed Hungary of which the reformist liberal statesman Eötvös dreamed: a multi-ethnic, multilingual country, coming together as the Hungarian national movement, post-Kossuth and the 1848 Revolution, bore fruit in a liberalised Magyarisation.

With some difficulty, Eötvös arranged the provision of a passport for Arminius. He also encouraged and supported his protégé's study of philology with an introduction to the library of the Hungarian Academy of Sciences, so he could borrow more books. Arminius' biographer David Mandler[2] has noted the great help given by Baron Eötvös to Arminius that

---

1 Eötvös was a novelist, poet, and reformist liberal statesman, part of the elite who wanted to assimilate the Jews, and notably supported young scholars like Arminius. Minister of education before 1848, he returned to the political field in the 1860s as minister of education and religion and led the bill for the Emancipation of the Jews in Hungary through the Diet in 1867.

2 David Mandler, *Arminius Vambéry and the British Empire: Between East and West* (Maryland,

is detailed in the Hungarian original, but absent from the English version, of Arminius' last autobiographical work, *The Story of My Struggles*. Eötvös' assistance included a German-language letter of appeal to the chief of the Pest Jewish Congregation, for support for this young scholar and linguistic prodigy. That appeal failed, but there were also introductions to other important scholars, researchers, and Orientalists who donated to Arminius' travel fund and are listed in the Hungarian original of his memoir. In addition, the Orientalist János Repiczky (1817–55) was persuaded to teach Arminius Turkish grammar in his own house and, more tellingly for expectations of future success, at Arminius' lowly rented accommodation. Mandler considers two possible reasons for the omissions in the English-language version of Arminius' book. The first, more charitably, is that British readers would be little interested in so much domestic detail; the second (more probable, given Arminius' constant careful crafting of his life story) is that an account of such real assistance might detract from his image as the Dick Whittington of Eastern scholarship.[3]

Baron Eötvös also gave Arminius money for his journey, new clothes, and a half-price ticket from Pest to Galatz (now Galati), the trading port on the Danube. The traveller packed up his books and, as he remembered fifty years later, some underclothes, and went aboard on a May morning in 1857, filled with 'joyful exultation and rapturous delight'. His departure got his name in the press for the first time. In *The Story of My Struggles*, Arminius regularly mentions his ability, especially for a man of small stature, to eat large quantities of food and of his sufferings when, as was often the case on his travels, there was little or no food to be found. On this first serious journey, but not for the first time in his life, he made sure of his internal comfort. He buttered up the ship's Italian cook, he reported, with recitations of Petrarch's sonnets from a seat outside the kitchen door, and spoke to all and sundry among the hospitable passengers in as many languages as they and he could muster. When the first Turks came on board at Widdin (now Vidin in Bulgaria), Arminius watched in fascination as an old man prayed, and then approached him. Mehemed Aga, he discovered, was on his way to visit his son, who was studying in Constantinople and would eventually

2016), 14.
3 Ibid.

become Ottoman Minister of Justice. Afterwards Mehemed Aga would con-tinue to Mecca. Arminius did not hesitate to demonstrate his Turkish skills, reading to Mehemed Aga in Turkish and taking the opportunity to pick the old man's brain for knowledge as well as make a useful friend for the remainder of this journey.

From Galatz, Arminius managed to get a cheap lower-deck ticket on the *Baron Eichhoff*, an Austrian steamer to Constantinople, one of those run by the Lloyd shipping company of Trieste. This was a journey, according to Murray's *Handbook* of a few years earlier, of fifty-one hours. One 'E.R.P', writing to the *Literary Gazette* in 1847, noted an eight-day journey from Pest to Galatz and took issue with Mr Murray's 'very terrible account of the insalubrity of the Danube, even in a late edition'. 'He evidently is under the impression that a voyage down the Danube is as bad as a residence at Sierra Leone', wrote E.R.P. whereas all that was needed was 'a determination not to be put out by little inconveniences', and to view everything as much as possible 'couleur de rose'. E.R.P. further recommended a supply of good wine and English porter (procurable in Vienna).[4] He, Murray, and Arminius may all have travelled on the same steamer, as the *Baron Eichhoff* remained in service from 1837 until 1852, then (re-named *Oriente* after a re-fit) ran until 1873.

A few years later Arminius would come to know that same John Murray very well indeed, when Murray published his *Travels in Central Asia* and Arminius became the sensation of the London season. However, as he boarded the Lloyd's steamer in a state of excitement at his first sight of the 'boundless watery expanse', familiar only from 'Byron's aquatic scenes', Murray's 1854 *Handbook for Travellers in Turkey* would have been an unlikely inclusion in Arminius' small stock of books. English was not then among his accomplishments so far as we know from the man himself. We may suppose he read Byron, one of Murray's most famous clients, in the earliest French translation by Amédée Pichot. This has been criticised as being 'neither romantic nor Byronic', but rather, in the case of *Childe Harold* at least, as 'a mawkish consolation for the disillusions of life'[5] in which case it sounds

---

4 *Literary Gazette & Journal, A Weekly Journal of Belles Lettres, Arts, Sciences &C for the Year 1848* (London, 1848).
5 Quoted in Peter Cochran, *Byron's European Impact* (Cambridge, 2015), 94.

perfectly pitched to have appealed to the youthful, struggling, romantically inclined Arminius. Or perhaps the mention of Byron just slipped into a rewrite of his memoirs when he came to present the manuscript of *Travels* to their shared publisher. Meanwhile his literary and linguistic talents continued to bring rewards on the ship. In the excitement of enjoying the 'terrible majesty of the Euxine in a real storm', while standing on the first-class deck close to the rail, he began to 'declaim a few stanzas of the *Henriade*', Voltaire's epic poem, in convenient earshot of the Secretary of the Belgian Legation at Constantinople. The ensuing conversation resulted in an invitation to a meeting in Pera, the European and diplomatic district of that city.

Carried away by his first sight of Constantinople, when the ship anchored at the Golden Horn, Arminius awoke to the fragility of his situation, with barely enough money for the ferry and no idea where to go in this completely foreign city. He fell on his feet, if not comfortably at least quickly, in the company of compatriots. He assured his later readers that his first new acquaintance, Mr Puspoki, an impoverished cook, greeted him with the question: 'Ah, perhaps you are the philologer of whose journey to the East we have read in the Hungarian papers?' Mr Puspoki was an habitué of the Café Flamm de Vienne and introduced Arminius into its society, where he found more of his fellow Hungarians. They were, by and large, the flotsam and jetsam of disappointed adventurers, bankrupts, former Hungarian army officers who had entered Ottoman service, and political exiles from the Revolution, few of whom would have met with the approval of the Austrian authorities.[6] They do, however, seem to have included the former lieutenant and 1849 emigrant to Constantinople Daniel Szilagi. He became a renowned antiquarian bookseller who may have been responsible for the acquisition of manuscripts later in Arminius' possession. When they could afford them, the group ate breakfasts of café au lait and the Vienna rolls provided at the café. Mr Puspoki also gave Arminius a place to stay, half of his own 'Turkish divan' in a single bare room with broken windows. Arminius claimed to have slept well, untroubled by the 'fiendish noise of the rats racing about' as they gnawed his boots and his clothes.

---

6 See Nándor Kovács, 'Hungarian Turkophiles in Nineteenth-Century Constantinople and Their Bequests in the Library of the Hungarian Academy of Sciences', *International Symposium on Ottoman Istanbul*, IV (2016), 453–72.

He set about exploring the city, talking to anyone he met, reading aloud from his Turkish books and, he told his later admirers, astonishing his audience with his ability to speak 'Turkish like an Effendi' after only a few days in the city. But when Mr Puspoki departed suddenly for employment on a French steamer, he left Arminius without a roof over his head. Resourceful as always, he persuaded the secretary of the Hungarian Association (the 'Magyar Egylet') to allow him to sleep in its council room. The Association had been founded by revolutionary emigrants in 1851 with seventy-eight regular and twenty-six honorary members, and was raided the same year by the Austrian Consulate, who confiscated the library and all the papers they could find. For a few years it had been part of the expatriate social life of Constantinople, giving balls, publishing its own literary paper ('Conversations') and subscribing to those of other European countries but, by the time Arminius washed up on the council room couch, the Association was disintegrating.[7] When he asked for some sort of covering to keep himself warm on a cold night, the secretary brought him an old, torn tricolour of the Revolution with the stirring words: 'Friend! This flag has fired the hearts of many in their heroic flights, it was itself once full of fire; wrap yourself up in it, dream of glorious battlefields, and maybe it will keep you warm too'.

Arminius realised quickly that tourism and the generous sharing of their meals by curious locals or fellow expatriates was not a long-term option. His written advertisements of his skills as a language instructor resulted in appointments to teach French and Danish to the Danish Consul. Despite his surname, Casimir Alphonse von Hübsch was actually an Ottoman citizen, with only the sketchiest knowledge of Danish. He desired to be able to read the Danish court circulars and, according to his teacher, by the end of eighteen months, the Consul could not only read Danish newspapers but, under Arminius' direction, a novel, *Kun en Spillemand* (*Only a Fiddler*) by Hans Christian Andersen. Mr Hübsch was all very well, but Arminius' next pupil was far more satisfactory from the point of view of his own learning. This was a young bey, who had come into a fortune and now wished to add a smattering of French conversation to the accepted trappings of class, wealth, and fashionable Westernisation he had already acquired. These included

---

7 György Csorba, 'Hungarian Emigrants of 1848–49 in the Ottoman Empire' in Celal Guzel Hasan (ed.), *The Turks*, 4, Ottomans (Ankara, 2002), 242–32.

tight patent-leather shoes, a fine suit of broadcloth cut in the latest fashion, gloves, and a fez 'rakishly worn on one side of the head'. Arminius discovered little interest in actual learning in his new student. The main point for the bey was to possess a French teacher, not to study French, although he was very keen to know more about life in the West. Arminius enjoyed the 'abundant breakfast' in the bey's house and was amused by the old mullah he found there, 'who fairly shuddered' when he heard the languages of infidels. Meanwhile, he felt he was gaining valuable understanding of Turkey from meeting the bey's acquaintants.

Eventually, through Ismail Pasha – otherwise known as the former Hungarian freedom fighter and ally of Kossuth, General György Kmety – Arminius found full-time work as tutor to the son of General Hussein Daim Pasha.[8] Arminius' new employer was Circassian by birth, probably from an important local tribe, and had either been sent by his parents to Constantinople as a boy or sold to be a page in the sultan's palace.[9] He lived in Kabatash, a strictly Muslim area of the city, where Arminius noted the 'weirdlike sounds' of the azan resounded from a nearby minaret. Here, Arminius' Eastern education was continued by the pasha's Anatolian major-domo, who taught him how to behave in Turkish society. The major-domo succeeded so well that Arminius became 'a regular Turk' and his employer insisted the household henceforth call him 'Reshid', meaning 'the brave or the discreet', with the title 'Effendi' in honour of his learning.

Arminius may well have needed to be discreet. It was a time of bubbling revolt against the state in Turkey, fertilised by the exiled European revolutionary population in the capital and by the exposure of the Turkish army to the ways of its Western allies during the Crimean War of 1853 to 1856. In his memoirs, Arminius covered what became known as the Kuleli Conspiracy of the Society of Martyrs, after army pay had been left in arrears. The plot, which was led by Hussein Daim Pasha, was the first political protest

---

8 General Kmety (1813–65) served with the Ottoman army and was a leading figure in its modernisation. After he retired to London in 1861, he once again came to Arminius' assistance, vouching for his Hungarian identity in London society when the 'dervish' arrived from his travels in 1864.

9 The system of *devşirme*, a levy on the Christian boys of the Ottoman Empire, in place since the fifteenth century, was a form of stylised semi-slavery. It carried no stigma but, on the contrary, offered education and the Islamisation necessary to reach high office.

against 'Tanzimat' (*Tanzimat-i-Hayriye*, or the 'Blessed Reforms'), advanced by Sultan Abdulmejid I (1823–61) in an attempt to modernise the Ottoman Empire. Tanzimat reforms were intended to bring greater equality to all the sultan's subjects and to create a sense of Ottoman nationality as a defence against separatist movements in other parts of the widely spread Turkish Empire.[10]

The Kuleli conspirators plotted to depose, replace, and possibly assassinate the sultan, and to impose their own reforms on the administration. Abdulmejid's reforms, including changes such as replacing the turban with the fez, were both too radical and not radical enough for the pasha and his adherents, while the sultan's efforts to Europeanise his capital, court, and state, and to reduce Islamic superiority, were unpopular with nationalist Muslim factions. In addition, Hussein Daim Pasha had seen the corruption in the royal court at first hand and was determined to bring change. The sultan, who had come to the throne aged only sixteen, was surrounded by a powerful coterie of family and ministers in an atmosphere of venality and corruption. The construction of the spectacularly expensive European-style Dolmabahçe Palace had been completed in 1856, more palace-building was in hand, and there were rumours of a spendthrift court being responsible for the arrears in army pay. Meanwhile the sultan took to drink. It might be charitable to imagine he was under the influence when he first met Arminius, then acting as interpreter for an Italian and an Englishman, who were trying to sell an autographed letter of the Prophet, brought from Upper Egypt. Arminius reported the sultan's payment of 'a large sum of money' for this 'questionable relic'.

Arminius commented that his own pupil, the bey, whose father was 'a notoriously pious Mussulman', was also usually suffering the effects of last night's debauch when his teacher arrived in the morning. It was said of Sultan Abdulmejid that spectators of his *selamlik*, or religious processions through the city, accompanied by a band playing Rossini or other European music, were concerned that he might fall off his horse when suffering similarly the morning after the night before.[11] Arminius merely noted that 'in his

---

10 The reforms permitted, for example, the ringing of church bells in Constantinople after 1856 for the first time since the fall of the Byzantine Empire in 1453.

11 See Philip Mansel, *Constantinople: City of the World's Desire, 1453–1924* (London, 1995).

simple black suit made by Dusetoy in Paris'[12] no one would have recognised the sultan as 'the earthly representative of Mohammed and the Khalif of all believers'. No indeed, and no great wonder, under such circumstances, that a religiously conservative, professional Ottoman army officer might lead a conspiracy to replace Abdulmejid with his reputedly more continent brother Abdulaziz. Arminius also gave a colourful description of the pasha's terrifying fellow-conspirator, Sheikh Ahmed, a fierce Naqshbandi Sufi from Baghdad. The sheikh was described by Arminius as a 'man of boundless fanaticism' and 'the life and soul of the whole conspiracy', whose sword and lance never left his side except when he prayed. He was a natural opponent to the sultan's reforms, and as Arminius pointed out 'it was quite natural that such a man should please Hussein Daim Pasha'. The sheikh and the pasha had met during the siege of Kars in the last stages of the Crimean War, where Ahmed had fought as a *ghazi* or holy warrior. The support of a holy warrior such as Sheikh Ahmed would add legitimacy to a sultanate of greater moral purity and stricter religious practice, one that espoused the popular promise of the clearing-out of a morally corrupt court and of protecting traditional laws. But there was also confusion over the restructuring of the highly complicated system of governance, evolved over centuries of Ottoman rule, and opposition to change in a system involving generational ties of family and patronage throughout the sultan's court and government. However, the plotters of the Society of Martyrs had Muslim public opinion on their side and whether because of that, or because they had friends in high places, or because Abdulmejid was notoriously reluctant to execute miscreants of any variety, when the plot failed the leaders suffered exile within the empire rather than imprisonment or death. Only two years later, after the sultan's death from tuberculosis, most of them returned to Constantinople.

Reshid Effendi the Discreet largely brushes over the details of the conspiracy, not least the involvement of his own pupil, the pasha's son. Perhaps he was indeed acquiring new habits of mind as he claimed in his memoirs, assisted in this by Sheikh Ahmed himself, who believed that in Arminius he might have a potential convert in his hands. For all his zealotry, Ahmed was a man of great learning, a consummate Persian and Arabic scholar with, Arminius said, an almost supernatural memory. It is reasonable to suppose

---

12 Auguste Dusautoy, also tailor to the emperors of France and Russia.

that Arminius' own later impersonation of a travelling dervish might have been influenced by his experience and observation of Sheikh Ahmed. Arminius himself would start the rumour that went rattling round the bazaars of the khanates of Central Asia a few years later that he, the unusually light-skinned holy man, was a Turkish Naqshbandi, a member of one of the most habitual Sufi travelling orders to visit the pilgrimage sites of Central Asia. Arminius was familiar with the Naqshbandi order of Sufism, with its roots in Bukhara, but even so, with an eye as usual on his Western audience, in his *Life and Adventures*, written in 1883 when his celebrity was well-established, Arminius also noted in his usual manner: 'the more I studied the civilisation of Islam and the views of the nations professing it, the higher rose, in my estimation, the value of Western civilisation.'

Arminius believed himself almost unique in Constantinople in having all doors open to him, both high and low, and he drank in the new sights and experiences. He described learning from Sheikh Ahmed as an 'unlocking, to my dazzled eyes in one moment, the whole of Mohammedan Asia'. That 'fairy key' added to his dreams of seeing more of the continent for himself. It's likely his curiosity would also have led him to visit the order of the Mevlevi dervishes, whose ceremonial whirling was already part of travellers' lore.

Even though they were not a mendicant order, the Mevlevi were wide-spread across the countries of the Ottoman Empire, into the Balkans and Greece and on to Egypt and Palestine. The Orientalist John P. Brown, writing in 1863, would also note the Naqshbandi as one of the most exten-sive dervish orders in the East, with a reputation for the strange spiritual, almost magical, powers of its sheikhs. They constantly called on God's name, as Arminius wrote that he also learned to do in his imitation of the dervish role. Brown also remarked, however, that the wandering dervishes found in Constantinople and all over the East, often with a tiger or leopard skin over their shoulders and with a *kashkul* begging bowl, might be merely fakirs from India and Bukhara.[13] But then he, Arminius, and other Orientalists were literary wanderers in the labyrinths of Asian religious belief and, with

---

13 It can be hard to clarify Brown's definitions. He also wrote that many of these 'fakirs' belonged to the actual dervish orders including the Naqshbandi; that they had abandoned the pleasures of the world for the love of God; and 'spend much of their time in prayer and meditation'.

Sufism in particular, hopelessly confused by possible ties between eastern Christianity, Hinduism, Islam, and other belief systems. Orthodox Sunni Muslims were also suspicious of the Bektasi and Mevlevi dervishes' Shiite leanings and laid-back 'pandering' to old Christian and pagan beliefs among ordinary people. A degree of confusion is perhaps understandable.[14]

Brown's description of the dervishes veers between the sensationalist and the prosaic. There were those, under the intoxication of the direct divine encounter at the core of Sufi mysticism, who engaged in extremes of self-mortification; and others, members of dervish *tekkes* – cloisters or monasteries – who had regular professions that reached across all layers of society. These Brown described (somewhat patronisingly) as 'liberal and sincere, intelligent and the most faithful friends'. Descriptions of the more fantastical dervish practices lost nothing in their telling by imaginative Orientalists, greatly influencing the British Romantics, weaving and re-weaving the magic carpet upon which the great Victorian explorers and, in due course, the remarkable dervish traveller Arminius Vambéry stood, to tell their own, first-hand, exotic tales to a transfixed London audience.[15] Brown's 'fakirs' sound like some of Arminius' later travelling companions and like the image he invented for himself, at least in printed memory. The model of Sheikh Ahmed, embellished with a patchwork of the practises Brown describes, would fit his dervish persona, and might also have suited circumstances where holy foolery and the pretence of extraordinary powers could be the best way out of a tricky situation. The dervish was, Arminius believed, 'the veritable personification of Eastern life', so seamless a fit into the puzzle of Central Asia that, as he 'represents the general character and so the different peoples of the East', he became almost invisible. There were also advantages 'in a country [sic] like the East', where 'the dervish or beggar, though placed at the very bottom of the social scale, often enjoys as much consideration as the prince who reigns over millions and disposes of immense treasures'.

The expected skills of a travelling dervish included the *nefes* or holy breath (blowing on the sick to cure them), continually crying out the name of

14 Bernard Lewis, *The Emergence of Modern Turkey* (Oxford, 2002), 406.
15 For more details see Meena Sharify-Funk, William Rory Dickson, and Merin Shobhana Xavier, *Contemporary Sufism: Piety, Politics and Popular Culture* (Abingdon, 2018).

God, and handing out amulets and charms with suitable incantations. These activities are ascribed by Brown to mere commercial 'Diviners', conjurors to the gullible faithful; but in the villages and caravanserai of Central Asia, innocent belief offered hope, the only available medicine, regardless of its true efficacy or the reliability of its purveyor. Colin Thubron described the theology of Sufism in twentieth-century Central Asia as 'belonging to a distant past, but the holy places were still crowded with devotees, chanting and swooning under matted hair and candle-snuffer hats, while hemp-crazed *kalender* went whirling and prostrating themselves through the streets'.[16] In that most recent past, the warrior dervishes fought again, first against the Bolshevik invasion and then to frustrate the grip of the communist fist. The shrines of Sufi saints became centres for secretly practised Islam, faith, and hope.

16 Colin Thubron, *The Lost Heart of Asia* (London, 1994), 91.

3

Reshid Effendi

The open doors of Constantinople society and a growing reputation for his learning and linguistic skills allowed this oddity, Arminius, to rise through Ottoman social circles and acquire an extraordinarily broad acquaintance-ship. It eventually included the teenage future sultan, Abdul Hamid, the last absolute ruler of the Ottoman Empire, who Arminius visited and cor-responded with regularly in their later lives. Arminius believed his Turkish acquaintances expected he would convert to Islam in due course, like other Europeans who had seen the material advantages of fully joining the ruling class in Constantinople and remaining there indefinitely. In *The Story of My Struggles,* with hindsight and with far longer experience and study of Asia and of Turkey, he wrote of the forbearance of the Turkish upper classes in politely accepting the hypocrisy of the *giaour*, the infidel or non-Muslim, when they 'did not pin the slightest faith to the conversion of Europeans'. He compared them favourably with the

> *soi-disant* cultured classes of European society. These latter high-born gentlemen, brought up in the trammels of prejudice, short-sightedness, and hypocrisy, presuppose in their converts the same lack of inner per-suasion, and consider conversion to their views quite a possible thing. The cultured, Turk, be he ever so religious, recognises in Islam a world of thought, born and bred in the blood, dependent upon education and mental development, and absolutely impossible of adoption by a man of Western training.

Did Arminius in his various memoirs invest his remarkable youth and his Turkish education with *couleur de rose*? Who knows. But by his own account, in the melting pot of Constantinople and in a society untrammelled by the social barriers and inequalities of Europe, the poor Jewish scholar and unappreciated multilingual prodigy felt more accepted than he had ever done before. He saw by the example of Hussein Daim Pasha, how the man with 'no aristocracy of birth; the man of obscure origin, can suddenly become Marshal and Grand-Vizier', and 'in the foreigner they do not so much consider his antecedents as his personal capabilities'. Never again would Arminius appear or describe himself as genuinely so at ease in a society where 'an obscure Jewish teacher became the confidential friend of the most distinguished and wealthiest dignitaries'. All the same, the opportunity of a career in the diplomatic service of the Sublime Porte, the Ottoman central government, where a foreigner could rise to be an ambassador, could not overcome his desire for adventure and freedom, nor (which was more) his frustration that his talents would never be enough to negate his background and allow him such a career in the service of a European country. His later letters exemplify the manners and customs he had absorbed in Constantinople; he might have made as good a fit into Turkish diplomatic or civil service life as into its society, but he could not shake the idea that it was too easy, in fact, too 'Oriental', as with other areas of Porte life that he disapproved of or disliked. As it was, for the rest of his life, Arminius played one role after another; from the scholar to the dervish; the literary lion to the spy; the Turcologist to the purveyor of folk tales; the royal friend; the freethinker; the Protestant; the renegade Jew or the Zionist and more. In his own country he was always the outsider and, finally, in his cantankerous old age, the not-quite-revered-enough academic, who may have been trying to find peace or redemption in the recapture of the faith of his birth – or some other.

Arminius wrote that it would be too much to name all the eminent Turks he met in Constantinople on his first long visit, but he tried. Many, like the five-times grand vizier, Mehmed Ali Pasha, the 'paragon of Oriental intriguers and dissimulators', who signed the Treaty of Paris at the conclusion of the Crimean War, or his successor Mehmed Fuad Pasha, and Mustafa Reshid Pasha, who wrote the edict of Tanzimat, are well-known historical figures. Others are not quite so easily identifiable due to the complications of official titles and the rare use of surnames before Ataturk's 1934 Surname Law but were diplomats, statesmen, and leaders of the Tanzimat reforms. Arminius was in a position of trust: Ali Pasha, for example, put him down as a scholar of philology, with no interest in politics, and trusted Arminius to keep quiet about the conversations he regularly overheard when he borrowed Chagataic[1] books from the pasha's library. He was witness to the transformation of Turkish high society under the influence of well-travelled statesmen, and an increasing number of hopeful young men who had been educated in Europe. However, he was unimpressed by these Europeanised men, such as Reouf Bey, his pupil in the wealthy household of the recently deceased Sadik Rifaat Pasha, a former Minister of Foreign Affairs. In his top hat and tails, the young bey was 'a complete European', but at home, 'he sits cross-legged on a divan, wears a fez and has learned only enough Arabic grammar and Persian at school to enable him to enter the civil service. He is usually totally ignorant of Turkish literature or history and has only a most superficial knowledge of French'. Under pressure to satisfy 'the craving impatience of the West', Arminius believed everything moved too fast towards reforms that were little more than skin deep. Anyone who was anyone had to speak French, but there was no commensurate understanding of an entirely alien form of culture, or of geography, history, science, or mathematics. The introduction of modern civilisation was being forced onward far too hastily.

From Daim Pasha, Arminius had moved to the house of the Chief Chancellor of the Imperial Divan Afif Bey, whose son-in-law, Kiamil Bey, he taught for about a year. It was there, and in the house of Rifaat Pasha, where he taught Reouf Bey history, geography, and French, that he met the leading intellectuals, writers, and politicians of the time. They included the notables of the Tanzimat reforms as well as many of the proponents of the Young Ottoman movement, forerunners to the Young Turks, who were opposed to Tanzimat. Reouf Bey, regardless of his tutor's low opinion of his learning, 'gathered round him in the evening the celebrated *kiatibs* [writers] of the day' and 'led the conversation to selections of Turkish authors'. Arminius 'revelled in the enjoyment of the marvellous metaphors and gems of oratory in the Osmanli language'. At these assemblies those in high office were criticised in 'witty epigrams' and 'elaborate flowery language'. Arminius enjoyed less the evenings where he, never much of a drinker, had to hang about

---

1 Chagatai was a 'dead' language of Central Asia that remained in literary use until the twentieth century.

hungry in a smoke-filled room while the 'grand Muslim gentlemen' got drunk on *mastika* or *raki*, which circumvented the Quranic ban on wine. Even when dinner was served, things did not improve. Arminius found it almost impossible to eat his fill of any dish before it was whisked away, as the Turks ate 'ten to fifteen dishes in a quarter of an hour'. Neither was the conversation on these evenings, 'coarse and vile in the extreme', to the prudish taste of the 'young European striving after higher ideals', and he was shocked that such conversation should take place in front of the very young.

The 'disgusting stories', and his regret over those uneaten delicacies, then inspired Arminius to discourse for his European readers on the beneficial effects of women on society. 'If our dear Orientals had a lady at their side, who would engage them in conversation, they would make longer pauses between their numerous dishes and realise that stimulating conversation increases the delights of the table.' He returned to similar themes later when writing of 'a certain vice' prevalent in Bukhara. There, he wrote, although, 'our pen refuses to describe this disgusting vice in its full extent', the law of the harem was so inviolable that 'marriages à la Tiberius' had become quite popular. Fathers were said to be introducing their sons to friends or acquaintances for an annual payment and 'this atrocious crime' had been declared 'no sin' by the religious. He continued in a similar vein on the subject of alcohol and drugs in Islam – the outraged moral high ground of the Orientalist interchangeable with that of a prim evangelical.

Disagreeable drunken parties aside, the greatest obstacles to Arminius' enjoyment of Constantinople were jealous servants and the inhabitants of the harem. He had a boot thrown at his head by one family retainer, and was astonished by the influence the most powerful servants held over their employers. On longer observation he was inclined to put this down also to the absence of intelligent female company, encouraging 'the unqualifiable vice' between men. There was the *kaftan-agasi*, the holder of coats, who snooped and spied, and the *kapidshi*, the keeper of shoes, who had learned to read footwear as the biography of its owner. The *tchibuktchi*, the pipe servant, was the highest-ranking of them all. He was his master's constant companion, in perpetual attendance to prepare and light his long-stemmed pipe and was also the messenger for important documents which were stored in the tobacco chest and often got lost. His role was, in reality, as much ritual – the essential symbol of his master's rank and wealth – as practical. Sultan Abdul Mejid was said never to have taken more than three puffs from a pipe, and Ali Pasha never to have smoked a pipe to its end.[2] But everyone smoked in Ottoman society. There is a view that cigarettes may have been invented by the Ottomans, although the evidence is uncertain, but they were undoubtedly popularised by Ottoman soldiers during the Crimean War and then travelled across the Atlantic to the armies of the American Civil War. Ottoman Turks even broke their Ramadan fast to smoke, and the tobacco monopoly of the Public Debt Administration (PDA) in the latter days of Abdul Hamid's reign brought in thirty-five per cent of all PDA revenues.[3] Arminius was particularly shocked by children smoking. The harem women had their own female pipe servants and, he wrote, by middle age, they 'spread so acrid a smell' around them that they could be smelt 'from afar like a weatherbeaten sailor'.

Arminius found the insults of the women of the harem far harder to bear than difficulties with the servants of the households where he lived. As a rule, they were highly conservative and detested everything Christian. Who knows what faith if any Arminius was espousing at the time, but one infidel was indistinguishable from another and none was to be trusted with the education of their children. Of the children themselves, Arminius had a high opinion of their natural intelligence but wrote that all his efforts to educate them in physics, history, and geography failed with pupils who had already been taught for several years by a *khodja,* one of the Muslim teachers Arminius considered fanatical. He was also saddened that their relationship to their parents, or rather to their father, was based more on respect than love. In addition, their imaginations were constantly influenced by the opinions emanating from the harem. To explain natural phenomena, Arminius used a French booklet entitled *Les Pourquois et les parceques* ('The Whys and the Wherefores') and wrote that no sooner had he explained thunder, lightning, and rainbows than the boys rushed off to the harem to tell their mothers. This resulted in the *Ferenghi-Khodja* (or 'foreign teacher') being damned as 'an ass born in the blackest belief', and entreaties to God that the sin of the father, in employing such a teacher, be forgiven.[4]

---

2 Alder and Dalby, op. cit., 52.
3 Douglas A. Howard, *A History of the Ottoman Empire* (Cambridge, 2017), 284.
4 Alder and Dalby, op. cit., 53–4.

Arminius made strenuous efforts to gain favour with these unseen women by paying them compliments, running errands, and regaling them with flattering speeches through the barrier of the *dolab*. This 'round, revolving sort of cupboard' was the means of interchange for objects, requests, or demands between the male *selamlik* and the female *haremlik*. Still aged only twenty-four, Arminius – in an echo of his unfortunate enchantment with Miss Emily – found it hard to maintain the correct harem etiquette, and to look away when faced with 'the fiery orbs of a beautiful Circassian'. Neither was he unaware of the 'naked foot in the tiny slipper', 'the exposed breasts', or the 'charms so justly sung by the poets'. At last, his 'youthful fire could not fail to take effect' among the women, 'most of them very beautiful Circassian slaves', who were neglected by their aging master, and there was a thaw in their attitude to him. The chief wife sent him to accompany an aging odalisque with toothache to the dentist in Pera (the European and diplomatic quarter of the city). On the way up one of the city's steepest hills, Arminius took the woman to the house of a Hungarian friend for a rest. She was so impressed by her hospitable reception that other women from the harem were also shortly stricken with toothache and required dental treatment.

Arminius described the entertainments laid on for the women, including the ritual of a picnic where all the wives, women, girls, and female slaves were driven to some satisfactory picnic spot in 'richly decorated carriages', guarded by the eunuchs. He observed a more covert purpose in this for the women. It was a chance to amuse themselves in distant flirtations with male admirers through a code using fingers, coloured handkerchiefs, a silk wrap, or their veils, just as nineteenth-century European society women were reputed to use their fans. He also wrote, rather disapprovingly, of the time spent by women in the *hammam*, where they would spend hours gossiping and were so well washed, 'using 4 pieces of soap for their hair', that they looked like 'overcooked fowl'. In winter, he wrote, the *hammam* replaced the opera and concerts of Europe as the chief form of entertainment. Nevertheless, Arminius enjoyed the baths himself, where 'the naked master is followed by the naked servant carrying the pipe and the cup'. Massages were given by beardless young boys, mostly Georgian slaves, and after their ministrations, the master would drink coffee, smoke, and play chess or Tric-Trac (backgammon). If he chose to sing, the architecture of the *hammams* gave an echo, 'which gives the singer the illusion of having a beautiful voice'.

Arminius was horrified by the institution of slavery but considered, in slight mitigation, that the young slaves he observed in the harem were at least given some level of education in singing, dancing, and embroidery, and might sometimes be treated as members of the family. Nevertheless, the trade in human beings was appalling and he saw how the harem women looked upon it as a means of making money, selling on child slaves as they reached puberty for vastly inflated prices.

At Afif Bey's house, Arminius met Midhat Effendi, recently returned from travels in western Europe and working as secretary to Afif Bey.[5] Midhat Effendi studied French with Arminius, and introduced his tutor to the *madrasa* where he was allowed to attend lectures with students of divinity. Arminius wrote that he was the first European to be educated in the religious school, and it was there he acquired the practical knowledge of Islam that was later to become the most potent part of his dervish disguise. He suggested he found the religious education easier because it was similar to that of the *yeshiva*, with which he was familiar from his earliest years. He understood the process where the minutest details of the law were discussed and argued and told his readers that he was soon the best scholar, or *mukht-edi* – one brought to the truth – and that 'all my remarks were applauded'. He was also drawn to the '*tekkes* of the Bokhariots', where he found a teacher from Central Asia. Mullah Khalmurad fuelled Arminius' imagination with the stories of his own travels in Bukhara and Samarkand, of the Oxus and Jaxartes rivers, and of the pilgrimage sites of Arabia.

By 1859, when he was twenty-seven, Arminius was part of Constantinople and familiar enough with Turkish language and custom that he was trusted to teach Fatma, the daughter of Sultan Abdul Mejid. It was at this time that he met her brother, later Sultan Abdul Hamid. The princess was married to the son of one of the viziers and lived in a white marble palace where Arminius went three times a week to teach her through a heavy curtain in her room where she was guarded by eunuchs. Princess and tutor never set

---

5 Later Midhat Pasha, Midhat Effendi (1822–83) was twice grand vizier and led the constitutional movement that bore fruit in the 1876 Ottoman constitution, at the end of the Tanzimat period. One of the most celebrated and cosmopolitan Turkish statesmen of his time, and particularly popular in England, he died in prison, probably murdered on Abdul Hamid's orders as the sultan reverted to a more despotic rule, incompatible with the pasha's lifelong reforming zeal.

eyes on each other. He had become well known in the Pera quarter of the city where he was recognised, he reported later, as 'the only foreigner familiarly acquainted with the Porte and with Turkish family life'. One might also surmise that he was already making himself useful to European diplomats by passing on details of the information and conversations he was party to in Ottoman households.

Discrepancies in names and dates, and the absence of a full name for this or that pasha or vizier mentioned by Arminius, create occasional doubts about the real extent of his acquaintanceship with the Ottoman great and good. He would hardly be the first memoirist to embellish his story with a few extra gems, reporting friendships that might not bear close examination, and we know he was an inveterate name-dropper. To muddy the waters further he wrote about his life, throughout his life, in Hungarian, English, or German. Memory is a tricky creature, and he was writing in those different languages for different audiences, always trying to maintain his image as the poor but brilliant Jewish boy who became the dervish traveller. Different translations of his work, by himself or by others, contemporaneously or later, may also have led to involuntary discrepancies in his biographical accounts, quite apart from those elaborations necessary to burnish his public image. Both before and since Arminius' death, other writers, and now myself, have written about or commented on his story, using one or another or several versions of his autobiographies as source material, and in one or another or several languages and/or translations. It is a game of Chinese whispers, and mistakes will happen. Nonetheless it is not possible to ignore the discrepancies in the stories he told and re-told over the years and not to begin to question truth or lie when the pieces of the jigsaw do not quite fit. It is, however, a pleasure when, unexpectedly, they do.

As an example of that jigsaw (or perhaps it is more akin to finding the path through a maze), Arminius wrote at this time of his experiences interpreting for Mahmud Nedim Pasha, the highly conservative Ottoman statesman and later grand vizier to Sultan Abdulaziz, who opposed reform and was nicknamed 'Nedimoff' for his close ties with Russia. It is perfectly possible that Arminius interpreted for Nedimoff (and thus discovered his 'boundless' ignorance of Western affairs); it is, however, highly unlikely that, despite his claim, he was interpreting Nedimoff to Lord Stratford de Redcliffe, previously Stratford Canning, the legendarily famous and long-serving British ambassador to the Sublime Porte, as Lord Stratford left Constantinople in late 1857, the year Arminius arrived, and retired entirely in 1858. During this period Arminius was teaching Danish to Mr Hübsch, was very new to Constantinople, and his Turkish was unlikely to have been up to interpreter standards. I still believe that to be the case. However, the search for another Arminius contact in Constantinople – one Baron von Schlechta, to whom he had an introduction and who he may have met previously in Vienna – produced an entirely unexpected story of interconnections that make credible Arminius' claim to have met Stratford Canning at least once before the latter returned to Britain for good. Baron von Schlechta was wrongly identified by Alder and Dalby as the Austrian ambassador, but, as the story turns out, was part of an extraordinary embassy network, at a completely different level of diplomatic life, and had better contacts and potentially more influence than any ambassador. The story is partly a sideline but gives breadth to the picture of Arminius, the known British go-between at a later date and by chance, if not design, part of the world of clandestine diplomatic information from this early stage in his career.

Arminius had built a reputation in Pera as someone who knew what was going on in Stamboul (as the old Turkish part of what is now known as Istanbul was referred to at the time) and in the Sublime Porte. Those he knew and to whom he may have passed on information were not so much the ambassadors, who came and went, but the dragomans, the interpreters and fixers for European embassies. As was the case with Baron von Schlechta, dragoman at the Austrian Embassy, they were posted by their home governments to Constantinople, although, at the time Arminius lived in Constantinople, they came more usually from the Levantine community of European families who had often lived for generations in the Ottoman Empire. They were Ottoman citizens, like Count Alexander Pisani, the head dragoman and interpreter during Stratford Canning's ambassadorship, and, of course, Arminius' pupil Mr Hübsch.

An account of the Pisani family perfectly demonstrates the connectedness of the family networks of these Western embassies in the Ottoman Empire, from which it is possible to look outwards to the wider network of global diplomacy of the period. There are several different versions of the Pisani family's origins,[6] in Pisa, Rome, and/or Venice, and there were other branches

---

6 All information on the Pisani family has come from the PhD dissertation of Frank

of the family, beyond that which served the British Embassy in Constantinople. We need to be aware of them so far as Arminius is concerned only in terms of the family's wide network across Pera and the other European embassies in the city. The story of the British branch of the Pisanis was given by Charles Pisani after the death of his brother, Count Alexander (the last Pisani to serve at the British Embassy), on the basis of the latter's own study of his family descent.

As the marriage merry-go-round and network of Levantine families continued to spread, Etienne-Stefano Pisani married Marie Hübsch in 1767. The Hübsch von Grossthal family were German merchants in Constantinople who had entered the diplomatic world when Friedrich Hübsch was appointed Court Councillor for Saxony in 1730 by the King of Poland, and rose to become the resident minister for Poland in the Sublime Porte. With this marriage we have more or less reached the end of this meander from the main path of Arminius' story. His pupil, Casimir Alphonse Hübsch, *chargé d'affaires* for Denmark in Constantinople, was a descendant of Pisan–Hübsch marriage.[7]

Regardless of his official role, Mr Hübsch had no reason to be able to speak Danish or French when he employed his polyglot Hungarian tutor. In exchange for teaching his pupil enough Danish to read Hans Christian

---

Castiglione, *Family of Empires: The Pisanis in the Ottoman and British Empires*, 2016. Charles Pisani's account had probably not been cited before Frank Castiglione used it in his fascinating dissertation on the family, which I found online by total chance. It confirms the family's origin in Pisa and their ancestor Domenico's capture by the Turks during the Ottoman-Venetian War in 1696. Domenico was brought as a prisoner to Constantinople where, in due course, he married the daughter of another Italian family. His wife was Victoria Bianchi, whose family was connected to the Navonis, another important Levantine family in Pera, with whom the Pisanis later also contracted a marriage. Of Domenico's two named sons, the first returned to Italy and was granted the title of count by Pope Clement XI; the second, Antonio, born in Pera, became head dragoman for the British Embassy sometime in the 1730s or 1740s. Other members of the family followed in that post and as dragomans in the Russian Embassy. As time went on, the Pisanis added to their networks through marriage into other Levantine families. These included the Testas, whose family members worked as dragomans or in other positions in the Austrian and Dutch embassies and in the governments or embassies of Venice, Genoa, Tuscany, Prussia, and Poland.

7 The Pisanis also married into British families. Beatrix, the daughter of Antonio Pisani, married Henry Adam Churchill, who had grown up in Constantinople and became British Consul General. He thereafter held diplomatic positions all over the Ottoman Empire from the middle of the nineteenth century, including in Persia.

Anderson, Arminius may have found with Mr Hübsch his passport into the spreading network of the Pera diplomatic community, with all its breadth of influence across the Ottoman Empire and into Persia and Europe. And in a community with all these familial connections it seems reasonable to suppose that Arminius also met Count Pisani through Mr Hübsch and, through Count Pisani, that he may have met the famous Stratford Canning, with or without the presence of Mahmud Nedim Pasha. He would also almost certainly have met at this time Charles Alison, the secretary of the British Embassy and a fellow linguist of note.[8]

It is perhaps no more than another footnote to Arminius' story, but Stratford Canning had been as anti-Semitic in his younger years as any of his background and education. By this stage of his career, however, long experience and broader horizons had entirely changed his views. On his return to London and the House of Lords, he demanded the removal of barriers to Jews entering parliament and remarked that for Britain not to have Jews sitting in parliament was the subject of 'remark in Turkey' where he had been influential in the institution of reforms for religious equality.[9] He might thus very well have been interested to meet the bright young Jewish linguist Vambéry during his last weeks in Constantinople. After Charles Alison was appointed minister plenipotentiary to Tehran in 1860, he likewise took up the cudgels on behalf of a Jewish population in Persia who

---

8 The gifted, eccentric, and wildly bearded Alison was appointed minister plenipotentiary to Tehran in 1860, was there when Arminius arrived in Persia, and remained there until his death from pneumonia in 1872. Abbas Amanat wrote of Alison's eccentricity and the drunkenness and promiscuity of which Edward Eastwick, the secretary to the British Legation from 1860 to 1863, formally accused him. Alison however was exonerated and Eastwick sent home, later to become private secretary to Lord Cranborne, secretary of state for India, and, thereafter, a member of parliament. Alison was noted for the brevity of his reports but his letters that have been preserved, while sometimes written in a hand as wild and extravagant as his famously outlandish beard, are not at all those of a man either mad, insensibly drunk, or disinterested. Alison's second wife, the beautiful Elizabeth Baltazzi, who died in 1863, not long after their marriage, also came from a Levantine family. Her father was Richard Sarell, a wealthy merchant of English extraction. She had been married in 1842, aged twenty, to her first husband, the Levantine banker Theodore Baltazzi, in the chapel of Her Majesty's Ambassador to the Sublime Porte.

9 Steven Richmond, *The Voice of England in the East: Stratford Canning and Diplomacy with the Ottoman Empire* (London, 2014), 234–5.

had been appallingly treated through forced conversions.[10] An improbable dispute over diplomatic seats at the Tehran racecourse gave Alison the excuse to suspend all social relations with the Persian prime minister and to cause such an uproar that the shah, the long-reigning Naser al-Din, agreed to settle all issues outstanding between the British mission and his government. This, one month later, included 'an autograph letter', from the shah, 'ordering his prime minister to treat the Jews with justice and kindness'.[11]

Von Schlecta (Baron Ottokar Maria Schlechta von Wschehrd, to give him his full name), the Austrian interpreter or dragoman, came from a very different background to the Levantines. He was one of the first European professionals to take over the almost dynastic embassy roles of those families as the decades moved on towards the twentieth century and the fall of the Ottoman sultanate. He might have been the role model for Arminius' ambition to become an interpreter for a European embassy, 'riding on a high horse, attended by servitors' in the Porte and 'enjoying a certain amount of distinction in the Pera circles'. But Von Schlechta had all the advantages Arminius lacked. His family was ennobled in Austria in the sixteenth century, and his father was section chief in the Ministry of Finance in Vienna, a privy councillor and a hereditary member of the House of Magnates, the upper house of the diet or parliament of the kingdom of Hungary.[12]

Arminius did not have the birth or education to become another Von Schlecta. Denied that fleeting dream, it was of his own choice that he decided against similar employment in the Ottoman diplomatic corps,

---

10 In 1839 the persecution of the Jewish population of Mashhad was followed by the flight of hundreds of families to Herat and their forced repatriation by the retreating Persian army during the Anglo-Persian War of 1856–7.

11 Abigail Green, *Moses Montefiore: Jewish Liberator, Imperial Hero* (Cambridge, MA, 2012), 789–90.

12 Mustafa Serdar Palabiyik, 'The Emergence of the Idea of "International Law" in the Ottoman Empire before the Treaty of Paris (1856)', *Middle Eastern Studies*, 50/2 (2014), accessed online 27 Sept. 2023. Von Schlecta was also a poet and friend of the composer Franz Schubert, had studied at the University and the Oriental Academy of Vienna and, while he was still a student or soon after, had compiled from European law treatises and translated into Turkish the *Kitab-i-Hukuk-u-Mile* (*The Book of Law of Nations*), to introduce Ottoman officialdom to an understanding of European law. After early service in the Austrian Foreign Ministry, he became the interpreter at the Austrian Embassy in Constantinople and was there for twelve years, continuing to study Turkish, Persian, and Arabic literature. In 1861 he returned to Vienna to become the director of the Oriental Academy and the Ottoman Railway Company.

despite spending time as a translator in the Correspondence Office of the Foreign Ministry and as a private secretary to Mehmed Fuad Pasha. The job of the dragomans was a lot more than 'riding on the high horse'. Dragomans were their ambassador's right hand, as well as being the advisors, intelligence gatherers, and mediators between embassies and Ottoman officialdom and society. In constant touch with everyone from the grand vizier downwards, their work was unending. They knew, or were expected to know, everyone's character, business, and intentions and, as links in an extraordinary network, were commensurately influential in all the international relationships of the Sublime Porte and between the representatives of European powers in Constantinople.[13] They were the people to know, with contacts throughout the Ottoman Empire and into Europe. The dragomans may have encouraged Arminius' dissemination of information from the Ottoman and Pera societies he frequented, and nurtured his abilities as an intelligence collector and the course he followed later as long-term informant and expert for the British. Their role might certainly have appealed to him on the face of it but if, as he suggested, wider travel and experience remained his goal in his twenties, the position of dragoman would not have been a good choice of career. It would never have satisfied his wanderlust or desire for freedom. Neither would it have suited what appeared later to be his inability to work collegiately.

Having risen in life through his own graft, Arminius was unimpressed by those who took their work more lightly. The scene he described in the Correspondence Office of the Foreign Ministry, as it filled up with workers towards eleven o'clock every morning, sounds remarkably like that in a workplace today. A group chatting in one place, one individual eating, another drinking coffee, others arguing, sharpening pencils, standing around, until the boss arrived and silence fell. Nor was that the end of it. Arminius did not think work there was taken seriously at all except at the highest level, where discussions were so secret that the pipe-servants were all deaf and dumb. At about two in the afternoon, the painted passages of the office filled with an extraordinary assortment of hopeful beggars and orphans, vendors of cheese, sherbet, or sweets, or of clothes, books, and writing materials, at

---

13 See Douglas A. Howard, *A History of the Ottoman Empire* (Cambridge, 2017) for more details of the dragomans.

the same time as clients, the curious, and the hangers-on. On the irregular paydays they became still more chaotic, turning into a sort of bazaar that encompassed entertainers, marriage brokers, and any passing layabout, who might also manage to get paid in a 'sorely misplaced' form of charity. Young beys stood about, theoretically absorbing the means by which they would, in due course, become civil servants, fledged in 'the official creche run by the State'. The criteria for civil service entrance were not high. If they could read enough French to decipher Fenelon's *Télémaque,* or the news from the *Journal de Constantinople*, they might dream of the highest civil office or the sort of post at an embassy that Arminius had imagined enhancing with his superior skills. Some of this 'mass of high-born young Beys lolling around' might go to Paris to improve their French, but Arminius believed that once there, 'they frequent the *Jardin Mabil* and the *Café Chantant* far more frequently than their college and bring home with them vices which do not honour us Europeans'.[14]

---

14 See Alder and Dalby, op. cit., 58–60, for the description of life in the Correspondence Office.

4

The Many Lives Begin

Arminius was ready to move on. In 1858, emboldened by his growing Turkish language skills, he had written a German–Turkish pocket dictionary as his first published book. He followed this by winning his 'first journalistic spurs', writing for the *Augsburger Allgemeine Zeitung*, and in letters for the Hungarian *Pesti Napló*, under the pen-name Reshid. He remarked that his only payment was in 'patriotic acknowledgements', but his correspondence led to a regular position with *Der Wanderer*, a journal published in Vienna. Meanwhile, through his continued study of Ottoman manuscripts and history, he had 'found so much that had reference to the history of Hungary'. As he studied possible links between the Magyars and Turkic peoples, his interest in their origins and in the relationship between the Hungarian language and Chagatai, the extinct Turkic language of Central Asia, continued to grow. Arminius maintained that his interest in the subject came from the folk tales and legends he had heard in his school days (echoing in this the experience of the earlier traveller Alexander Csoma de Kőrös, who came from a community, the Székelys, who believed they were descended from Attila the Hun, and who had heard the old stories of this ancestry as a boy in Transylvania). In particular, Arminius remembered a moment in 1849, as he and his schoolfellows watched defeated Hungarian soldiers making their way home after the War of Independence against Austria. An old peasant had remarked, 'Whenever our nation is in trouble, the old Magyars from Asia come to our rescue, they will not fail us this time'. The common legend of a metaphorical 'king under the mountain' ready to ride to his country's rescue, was a perfect fit with the early nineteenth-century nationalist construction of Hungarian singularity in Europe. Meanwhile, the quest for the roots of Hungarian language and culture were expressions of the desire for liberation from Austria, in turn inspired by the French Revolution, the American War of Independence, and the Enlightenment.

It does not take any great leap of understanding to see how the sheer uniqueness of the Hungarian language should lead to questions of its origins and, from there, to the ethnogenesis of the Magyar people. As Edward Fox wrote in his biography of Alexander Csoma de Kőrös,[1] in visiting Budapest, the tourist from any other European country (which should feel as familiar as Paris, given the *fin de siècle* ambiance of the city) 'feels he has been struck by total dyslexia. Even the ubiquitous police car, usually bearing its recognisable label, *polizei, polizia, polis*, or similar variants, has become the incomprehensible "*szobarend*"'. There are no discernible Latin, Greek, or Germanic roots to the language and, as the present writer can vouch, street signs in the city are as discombobulating as those Russian street signs in Tajikistan that turn out to be Persian written in Cyrillic. And so arose the unassailable fact for nineteenth-century Hungarian nationalists: *we are different.* Followed by the inevitable question, *then who are we?* It is now usually accepted that Hungarian belongs to the Finno-Ugric group of languages, with Finnish, Estonian, and others less known, but arguments continue. A Jesuit scholar, Janos Sajnovics, first posited the theory of a relationship with Finnish in 1769 after noticing similarities with Hungarian while travelling in Lapland,[2] but miserable peasant Finns from an outlandish northern outpost did not fit at all with the image the proud nationalist Hungarian nobility had of themselves. A suggestion of a closer relationship by geography with the Finno-Ugric Vokul and Otyak fishing communities of the Upper Volga was dismissed as *halszagft utyafisdg*, a 'kinship connection that smells of fish'.[3] The Hungarian nobles were as keen as Arminius would become to hear the hoofbeats of romantic swashbuckling horsemen echoing from their distant history and to look eastwards for that more glamorous origin. In 1725, the Hungarian aristocrat Samuel Turkoly had claimed to find a Hungarian-speaking race near the Caspian Sea, and then there were all those old legends…

1 Edward Fox, *The Hungarian who Walked to Heaven* (London, 2001), 20.
2 Ibid.
3 Susan Gal, 'Linguistic Theories and National Images in Nineteenth-Century Hungary', *Pragmatics*, 5/2 (1995), 155–66, 159.

In short, an Eastern origin for Hungarian did not appear to be an impossible theory and could even be supported with selective evidence. For example, 'Kipchak', or 'Cuman', the undoubtedly Turkic language of the shamanist Kipchak nomads, was spoken where they had settled in the Cumania region of Hungary until both it and they became extinct in the eighteenth century. Even in the late nineteenth century, the handbook of Hungarian literature then used in schools opened with a chapter entitled 'From the Banks of the Volga: A few ancient characteristics of the Magyar soul' and was illustrated with a single 'eagle-eyed horseman' in 'leopard-skin with Persian sword' calmly scanning the horizon, awaiting his enemy. 'If only a few of them come, he will fight them alone; if they come in a horde, he will call the others.' This image certainly suited the politics of the time regarding the Magyar soul, as Hungarian elites were attempting to recover from the defeat of 1848, re-establish a semi-independent state within the dual Austro-Hungarian monarchy, and continue to claim the moral right to rule over an ethnically diverse and increasingly restive population.

Arminius' interest in the East and in Hungary's Eastern origins flowered anew with his exposure in Ottoman Turkey to the exoticism of Asia and the 'proud, dignified bearing' of the people of the East, which 'must necessarily increase the desire to claim relationship with these old-world types'. He was determined to discover the secrets of the *terra incognita* of Central Asia, which might perhaps point to a real solution to the 'origin question' of the Magyars. At the same time, and as one or other theory of Hungarian ethnogenesis arose and was discredited, Arminius, throughout his life, maintained that language and ethnicity did not themselves always have the same origins, and that his own real interest was always in linguistics.[4]

In addition to his other endeavours, as his knowledge and interest grew, Arminius had made translations of Ottoman manuscripts that had come to the attention of the Hungarian Academy, the same to which he had been introduced originally by Baron Eötvös. In 1860 the Academy made him a corresponding member and, in 1861, he returned from Constantinople to

---

4 In the twenty-first century the rise of right-wing nationalism has, in some cases, seen a resurgence in political Turanism as a theory aiming to bring together a number of ethnic groups of the region. Theories on the linguistic heritage of and similarities between Hungarian and some other European languages with those of Central Asia still abound and are still argued in more or less scientific circles.

Pest to deliver his entrance address to the Academy. His friends in Constantinople thought him perfectly mad to want to explore the barbaric wilderness of Central Asia in pursuit of a bizarre fascination with a dead language, but luckily for him, the president of the Hungarian Academy of Sciences, Count Emil Dessewffy (1814–66), was a good deal more encouraging and steamrollered the naysayers who considered Arminius' lameness an insurmountable obstacle to his proposed journey. Arminius himself, in his account of the proceedings, remarked loftily that he paid very little attention to such remarks when, as he knew, travelling in Asia required 'neither legs nor money but a clever tongue'. He also reported that when a craniologist suggested he should carry back Tartar skulls to compare with Magyar skulls, Count Dessewffy had replied, 'Before all things we would ask our fellow-member to bring his own skull home again'. The Academy provided a travelling fund of a thousand florins in banknotes and a sort of *laissez-passer*, written in Latin and addressed to 'all the Sultans, Khans and Begs of Tartary' – a document which would in fact have been a guaranteed death sentence for the infidel traveller had he ever shown it to any of them. So armed, Arminius embarked once more for Constantinople to make final preparations for his journey.

By the time Arminius started for Trebizond on another Lloyd steamer, the *Progresso*, in the spring of 1862, his money had dwindled to barely enough to take him as far as Tehran. Reshid Effendi, as he had to remain for his own safety from then on, was better supported by the introductions and letters he carried from his exalted contacts in Constantinople to the Turkish ambassador to the court in Tehran. He wrote that he set off in a state of high excitement at the beginning of this realisation of his dreams, not forgetting to note that the hardships he had experienced in life and the goal of enriching humankind's knowledge added a sort of missionary zeal that he expected would ease the difficulties of his journey. Arminius could hardly have realised at the time that the chronicled hardships of his journey through Central Asia would become his most valuable calling-card. The fame he discovered on publication of his account of his journey informed the rest of his life although the journey itself only covered a few months in the relatively long span of his existence. What would he have been without it? A gifted linguist, an Orientalist academic in Budapest, always slightly at a disadvantage for his Jewishness and lack of formal certification? Or, in the end, a civil servant back in Constantinople?

The journey began easily enough. En route to Tehran, Arminius arrived at Trebizond on the Black Sea in the train of Emir Muhlis Pasha, his fellow passenger on the *Progresso* and the new Governor of Trebizond, who invited him to stay during his time in the city. Arminius was impressed by Trebizond but was there only long enough to buy the necessities for his onward journey to Tehran: a carpet bag to hold a couple of shirts, a few books, a kettle and tea service, and two carpets, one for use as a mattress. In addition, he hired a horse. This last became a source of extreme misery from his first day in the saddle. He had not had the practice of the dragomans he envied in Pera, and a hired baggage nag was not likely to be a comfortable ride in any case. With an Armenian companion, he joined a small trading caravan, and later remembered looking down from the hills above Trebizond after an hour's ride. When he spotted the Austrian ship on which he had arrived, now at anchor on the calm water of the harbour, he was suddenly overcome by a dawning realisation of the difficulties of his undertaking. After that short but stiff uphill ride he was already suffering, but this was as nothing to his misery that evening after six solid hours in the saddle. Extreme exhaustion could not overcome the hardness of the ground where he lay or the noise and constant activity in the *khan*, or inn for travellers, where he and his Armenian companion spent the night. On his first night on the road, he also made a horrible job of preparing his own dinner of burnt rice, rancid fat, and 'one of the worst kinds of bread' he had ever eaten in Turkey.

Arminius' account does not give the impression that he enjoyed much of the journey from Trebizond to the Persian border, although there were a few high spots. In Persia he found his vision of 'genuine Eastern life,' as opposed to the 'gaudily painted curtain of the Eastern world' of Constantinople, which, he now decided, 'presented a tame and lifeless and somewhat Europified [sic] picture of the Orient'. There were still plenty of faults to be found however, and he took careful note of dirt, discomfort, and the insults thrown at his Stamboul Sunni 'effendi' persona from a fanatical Shiite population. In fact, the discomforts of the journey were leavened by meetings with friends and former contacts from Constantinople, beginning in Erzurum where Arminius arrived on 28 May to stay with his former employer Hussein Daim Pasha who, after a period of exile in Rhodes, had become military governor in Erzurum. Arminius described him now as 'an enthusiastic religious mystic', and as an acknowledged member of the Naqshbandi dervish order, facts that the pasha had carefully hidden in Constantinople.

The pasha's initial efforts to dissuade Arminius from making the dangerous journey to Bukhara changed when he decided that its true purpose must be a pilgrimage to the famous shrine of the founder of his order, the fourteenth-century religious leader Bahauddin Naqshband. Alder and Dalby suggest that Hussein Daim Pasha also suspected Arminius of embarking on a secret mission for one or other European power, but I can find no evidence of this in Arminius' descriptions of his time in the pasha's Erzurum house. Then again, by the time Arminius had spent some months in Persia (his onward journey having been delayed by the war between Dost Mohammed Khan, emir of Afghanistan, and Ahmed Khan, ruler of Herat), he had undoubtedly made new acquaintances among the international diplomatic corps in Tehran and renewed many old friendships. If there was ever concrete evidence of Arminius' engagement in intelligence-gathering on his dervish journey it has disappeared, but there are plenty of pointers to that possibility. The historian Raphael Patai, for example, suggests that Arminius was spying for Britain,[5] and even though he does not provide evidence for this, it is a belief this writer shares simply because it is so credible in the context of time and place. Conversely, Professor Vásáry, present member of the Hungarian Academy and contemporary expert on Vambéry's life, remains positive that the dervish journey was, as advertised, purely of philological intent. Arminius, he believes, was a born traveller, an adventurer, passionate about the study of languages and keen to find their sources and the people who spoke those he did not know. Vasary describes Hungarian as 'a lonely language', its uniqueness part of nineteenth-century Hungarian nationalism and the impetus behind the adventurous journeys of several clever young scholars.

Tantalising tags to notes on Charles Alison's letters to Eastern colleagues or to the various foreign secretaries of his tenure concerning Russian plots and spies suggest he at least among Arminius' acquaintances shared our hero's distrust of Russian ambitions in Central Asia and India, which might in themselves have provided a further incentive for Arminius to involve himself in espionage. The problem is that what remains of Alison's communications

---

5 Patai, op. cit., 394.

makes a sparse archive, possibly because (as has also been suggested) the Foreign Office had every intention of ignoring Persia as much as possible after the 1856–7 Anglo-Persian War and the Treaty of Paris. Charles Alison was a noted Central Asian expert, but he would not have been an obvious candidate to head the British mission in Persia unless it had been some-what downgraded or unless, and perhaps in addition, what was needed in Tehran at the time was less the courtly ambassador and more a man whose 'orientalised mannerisms'[6] and extensive, if not always exalted, circle of acquaintances, plus his wide linguistic abilities, were a perfect fit in a fragile region where intelligence-gathering was the most important game afoot.[7]

Arminius' documented meetings with British diplomats and ambassa-dors make it clear that he knew Alison in Tehran, and his description of his friendly reception by Alison mentions the previous opportunities given him at Alison's 'hospitable table' of 'studying the question [of] why the English envoys everywhere distinguish themselves amongst their diplomatic brethren by the comfortableness and the splendour of their establishments'. It is easy enough to imagine that Arminius might have been requested by Alison to keep his eyes and ears open for information on his travels through a little-understood region of significant geopolitical importance. Such an arrangement, given Alison's character, might never have been formally reported to the Foreign Office and certainly not committed to a letter. It would have suited Arminius' own inclinations, even at this early stage of his career, to help British interests, to enable them to hinder Russian ambi-tions in the region and to cloud the lens of their view towards Afghanistan and India. There was also, as always, the question of funds: Arminius was perpetually short of money, or thought he was, even into his comfortable old age. He did not find his travelling stipend from the Hungarian Academy over-generous and had to use up a lot of his funds loitering in Persia, waiting for peace between Herat and Afghanistan, before he could start his journey

---

6 Abbas Amanat, *Pivot of the Universe: Nasir-al-Din Shah Qajar and the Iranian Monarchy, 1831–1896* (London, 1997), 377.

7 This would also accord with the contemporaneous travels and reports of Lewis Pelly, who went to Persia in 1859 to be secretary to the legation and then *chargé d'affaires*. In 1860 he made a highly dangerous fact-finding journey from eastern Persia, through Herat, Afghanistan, and Baluchistan, to India, reporting back both to Alison and to London. He later became political resident in Bushire, watching over the Persian Gulf, until 1872.

proper. As his later correspondence with the Foreign Office demonstrates, he was never backwards in coming forwards to ask for payment. Alison might easily have helped him out, to the tune of a few pounds from petty cash, for his anticipated services.

Arminius may have become the best-known of the 'false dervish' travellers, but there was at least one well-known *genuine* dervish informant to both the Turks and the British. Suleyman Effendi was a Bukharan, born in 1820, who had undertaken the hajj in 1844 and thereafter became Bukharan envoy to the Sublime Porte in Constantinople and *postnişin*, or sheikh, of one of the Uzbek dervish *tekkes*. He was also, like Arminius, a lexicographer and philologist; he published a Chagatai–Ottoman dictionary with the intention of proving the links between the languages of Central Asia and Turkish, and was the Ottoman delegate to the Pan-Turanian congress held in Budapest in 1877. Arminius may have met him there or already known him from visits to Constantinople. (He would also, much later, send a letter of introduction to Suleyman Effendi for Ignác Kúnos, one of his pupils and a famous Hungarian scholar of Turkish of the early twentieth century.[8])

Suleyman's scope, however, was much wider than lexicography or his role as a dervish. The extent of his travels in pursuit of information for the Turkish sultan puts Arminius' journey in the shade. Suleyman travelled to India, possibly by ship from Constantinople to Egypt and on to Bombay, went northwards to Delhi and Agra, Lahore, Rawalpindi, and Peshawar, and then, via the Khyber Pass, into Afghanistan. He was received by the emir in Kabul and went on to Bukhara, seeing the buddhas at Bamiyan on the way. After Bukhara he followed a route to Khiva, Merv, and back across the Oxus to Kabul and India once again. From Bombay, he took a ship to Basra and travelled from there to the pilgrimage cities of Mecca and Medina, followed by another stay in Cairo, before he at last returned to Constantinople to report to Sultan Abdul Hamid on everything he had observed.

Hamid Algar has suggested that Suleyman's association with the British was not only known to the sultan but positively encouraged by him, with

---

8 Ignác Kúnos (1860–1945) made a German translation of Suleyman Effendi's dictionary and other works. He complained to Arminius' sometime friend and academic rival, the German linguist Josef Budenz, about errors and inconsistencies in Suleyman's work due to his use of local dialect words.

the goal of persuading the British that he had far greater pan-Islamic appeal than was in fact the case. Algar additionally quotes the Turkish historian and Ottoman specialist Azmi Ozcan's view that 'parallels between the "true dervish" – Suleyman Effendi – and the "false dervish" – Arminius Vambéry – may not be coincidental'.[9] Arminius certainly had similar aims to Suleyman Effendi and both the British and the Ottomans were aware of the later relationship between them. From the time of Sir Henry Layard's arrival in Constantinople as British ambassador to the Sublime Porte in 1877, Suleyman was also reporting to him. Layard had initially suspected him of being a Russian spy; not unreasonably when the Russians were travelling widely in Asia and their use of foreign spies had been known to the British since the Crimean War. Indeed, in 1862 Charles Alison had reported to the foreign secretary, Lord John Russell, the discovery of a secret treaty made between Persia and Russia in 1854, in which 'the most salient point is the invasion of India, which, it is clear, was seriously contemplated, a scheme not without plausible features, considering how disaffected the Great Bengal Army then were',[10] as the Sepoy Mutiny of 1857 loomed.

Alison was well aware of 'the superiority of Russian diplomacy' over that of England and the 'designs of Russia on India and Central Asia' after the Crimean War,[11] designs led by a vanguard of clever young Poles and Lithuanians who had learned 'several Asiatic languages' while exiled in Siberia for plotting against the tsar. They had been pardoned, pragmatically, by Nicholas I when he saw a good use for their skills; some were 'loaded with honours' by their former enemy, and they were all immediately put to work in the East as 'conspirators' on a variety of missions for the Russian state, including to China, Bukhara, Herat, Kabul, and Kandahar. One, 'the mysterious Vitkevich',[12] had only been about sixteen years old when he was taken in 1824 from Vilna (Vilnius) 'loaded with chains', which made him lame for life, and transported to central Russia. He had then, unexpectedly, 'addicted

---

9 Hamid Algar, '*Tarīqat* and *Tarīq*: Central Asian Naqshbandīs on the Roads to the Haramayn', in *Central Asian Pilgrims: Hajj Routes and Pious Visits between Central Asia and the Hijaz*, Alexandre Papas, Thomas Welsford, and Thierry Zarcone (eds.) (Berlin, 2012), 81, n.

10 'Russo-Persian Relations, 1854–1875' [36r] (80/356), *Qatar Digital Library*, accessed online 27 Sept. 2023.

11 Ibid., [22r] (52/356).

12 Peter Hopkirk, *The Great Game: On Secret Service in High Asia* (London, 1990), 165–74.

---

himself to the study of languages spoken in India', and was despatched to Calcutta, where, 'being of a very enterprising and vivacious character, during a couple of years, he extended considerably the ramifications of Muscovite doctrines, amongst the Sepoys, Mahrattas and Sikhs'.[13] The British authori- ties eventually woke up to these activities and complained to St Petersburg. Vitkevich was recalled but there were others like him who became consuls and dragomans in Russian embassies throughout Asia. They were all care- fully trained by the Russian Department of Foreign Affairs to a method, 'devised by the Emperor himself',[14] to gather as much information as they could, particularly about India, and to act as agent provocateurs among disaffected elements of the Indian population.

Arminius was to write about Vitkevich in his 1885 book *The Coming Struggle for India*, as 'the famous Russian agent, M. Vitkovitch', who was 'a competent rival' to the Scottish explorer Sir Alexander Burnes, the 'Bokhara Burnes' of Great Game notoriety, who had been author of the bestseller *Travels into Bokhara* (1835) and who was killed in Kabul in 1841. In 1837 Vitkevich's meeting with the British officer Lieutenant Henry Rawlinson,[15] near the Persian/Afghan border, had brought the 'shadowy conflict'[16] of the Great Game out into the open. Arminius went on to describe the sad end to Vitkevich's career, after his final mission in Kabul to wean Emir Dost Mohammed away from his alliance with Britain in favour of promises from St Petersburg. Those promises proved too empty 'to satisfy the old grey wolf of Afghanistan' and Vitkevich returned to St Petersburg in disgrace and there committed suicide. It is in this book that Arminius lays out the views that support the notion of his being a convinced British imperialist, with all the detestation of Russia that was typical of Hungarian intellectuals of his time. This Russophobia dated back to Russia's support of Austria during the Hungarian Revolution of 1848–9, which had enabled Austrian suppression of the revolt and paved the way for the behemoth of Austria-Hungary to blunder on from 1867 until the final catastrophe of World War I.

Arminius' opinion of Britain was not, however, caveat free: in following the

---

13 Ibid.
14 Tsar Nicholas I (r. 1825–55).
15 Later Sir Henry, president of the Royal Geographical Society, and well-known to Arminius.
16 Hopkirk, op. cit., 167.

post-Vitkevich trail he would encounter the 'sulky attitude of Dost Moham-med Khan towards England', and go on to note the huge cost in British lives and money of the disastrous First Afghan War (1838–42), which 'imparted the first stain of shame to the English military character in Asia'. This failure Arminius laid squarely at the door of the 'short-sightedness of leading politi-cians, wavering statesmen and irresolute government', and he regretted the waste of 'the personal valour and courage, all the heroic self-immolation, rare circumspection, and ability of single individuals', in the field. Arminius was a cheerleader for Victorian imperialist derring-do but not always for the machine behind it, even when he approved of its ultimate ambitions. He criticised Britain's 'criminal indifference' to Russian activities in Persia and Central Asia, which he believed would put India at risk of the loss of (in his view) far superior British rule. He expressed this forcefully, cataloguing the benefits of British imperialism across all areas of life, from education to agri-culture, and determinedly dismissing all adverse opinion. 'The idea prevailing throughout all Europe that Great Britain is impoverishing India, and getting rich by it', he wrote, 'is preposterous from beginning to end'.

Britain had 'spread the era of a better civilisation', to 'confer upon mankind in the distant East the true blessings, which we are so justly proud of'. What was more:

> ...the mass of the teeming Indian population desire nothing so much as that sort of repose which they enjoy under the strong, mild, and just rule of England, where every man gathers in quiet the fruits of his toil, is not forced to render up his goods against his will, sleeps without fear of violence, has redress for wrongs done to him by his neighbour, performs his religious rites, and follows his caste observances undisturbed, and lifts his eye toward the State as to a Father.

Arminius continued with a question:

> ...can any sober-minded, honest European still doubt as to whom he ought to give preference in the work of civilising Asia? Is it not a shame that the various nations of Europe, influenced by petty rivalries and national vanities, are often blinded to such an extent as to extol Russia at the expense of England?

Indeed, how could any European find merit in 'semi-barbarous and despotic Russia', and thereby 'destroy the *prestige* of the very nation whose banner has always been, and is, the harbinger of a new and better world in the distant regions of the East'?

In the penultimate chapter of the book, Arminius developed his explanation of 'Why ought England to retain India?' He explained why 'every European must feel a lively interest in the maintenance of British rule in India', without which 'the most horrible anarchy will ensue', or the 'barbarous despotism of Russia will inaugurate a new era of Asiatic disorders'. Unexpectedly, he did concede the possibility that Indians might, one day, be 'sufficiently trained in the principles of self-government' and the 'necessary notions of Western culture', to manage 'without the leading strings indispensable for the present and stand on their own feet'. He was blissful in his certainty that, when that happy state was reached, 'the pupil will separate from its master, not with bloodstained hands, but on the most friendly terms'. Meanwhile, Arminius hoped 'the deep sense of duty' of the British nation will 'retain its strength in upholding her beneficial rule over India for many many generations to come'. This is the Anglophile/Russophobe imperialist rampant, with little of the Orientalist's empathy with the East on show, however patronising that also might be seen to be. Arminius had little sympathy of any sort for 'the two chief elements in India, the Brahminic and the Moslem'. The 'Hindoo' was perhaps 'more manageable and docile', and more ready to work for the foreign ruler than 'the old and incorrigible representative of Asiatic fanaticism', the 'Moslem', who, Arminius believed, he knew well from his personal experience, and who was 'inspired by the wildest and most intense hatred of everything that is Christian'.

In his final chapter, Arminius took on his critics, those who described him as a fanatic or a maniac, 'a Hungarian carrying in his breast, in indelible characters, hatred of Russia', who dared to hold political opinions. His defence was that 'he should not be censured for following in his political line the principle of true liberty, and from paying his tribute of admiration to that portion of the European world which he finds to be at the top of our civilisation'. He refuted accusations of membership of the British Conservative Party but admitted to finding its support of imperial policy to his taste, as its 'superior statesmanship' had preserved the '*prestige* of Great Britain all over the globe'. It was, he believed, 'more British, more manly, and more active abroad than the other party' – that other being the Liberal Party which, he held, had actually damaged England's standing. He included for publication several of the letters sent to him in Budapest from 'over-zealous Liberals', which, he assured his readers, he greatly enjoyed.

London, 9th February, 1880

Sir – Being, I presume, a blasted Austrian or Hungarian, I can understand your sympathy with the *manly, energetic and wise* policy of this Government. At the same time, I should advise you to keep your advice to yourself with regard to the British policy in Asia, as although, no doubt, you are very clever, thank God we have in this country men who are, perhaps as far-seeing as you make yourself out to be. Yours obediently…

Or there was this:

3rd April, 1883

(please note. – You cannot truthfully deny anything here stated in your lectures, as you are supported by the Jingonastic [sic] Conservatives.)

Sir, – Did it ever occur to you that the English people (all classes) can best form an opinion on the so-called dispute between England and Russia, without the aid of a foreigner to assist them, as it is a quarter of a century since you travelled in some of these parts?
  There is no war fever in this country by the great bulk of the people except what is kept up by a certain class of press-writers to certain papers who represent the upper class, who are interested with India, and now hold up Russia as a 'bogey'. Why, it is only four year ago [sic] we killed and wounded 5,000 Afghans and attempted to annex a large part of their kingdom. Russia had good excuses then to complain about this debatable land…
  In fact, black as you paint Russia in your lecture, it is white compared with our English annexations and aggression in the various states forming India. Read the conquest of India by the East India Company, and afterwards under the English crown.

By the time he wrote *The Coming Struggle for India*, Arminius was a friend of the prince of Wales, an *habitué* of London society, a member of the Hungarian Academy, and a recognised Central Asia expert. All the same, before we return to the young adventurer, travelling on from Erzurum to Tehran at the start of his most important journey into the badlands of the Middle East, his supposed exploration of their mysteries and of the perils of life as a dervish, we may look ahead to note the 1885 book as a distillation of the opinions and experience he accrued from youth, supporting his ingrained Russophobia and Orientalist view. It is also a staggering piece of imperialistic hubris that seems barely possible today.

5

Persia

Arminius left Hussein Daim Pasha's comfortable house in Erzurum for 'one of the most troublesome étapes of Asiatic travel', across Armenia and what he refers to as the 'Dagar' mountains to the Persian frontier. He took note of poor Armenian houses that were 'underground holes', more like molehills than human dwellings, in which the inhabitants lived with their buffaloes and a good assortment of vermin. On the other hand, after a night of misery 'in company with these evil-smelling animals' and tormented by the smoke and heat from a dung-fuelled fire, he was rewarded by the glorious morning air of the high Armenian plateau, 'that acted like a tonic on my weakened nerves'. The tonic became less efficacious when Arminius began to think of the 'Kurdish robber hordes' who he, and the small caravan of Armenian merchants in which he travelled, would inevitably encounter. They had crossed the Aras River and passed into Kurdistan proper, near the spot where the mysterious sixteenth-century Turkish hero Köroğlu was believed to have lived, when Arminius noticed his companions loading their pistols. It was not until the following day, after a night in the village of 'Eshk-Eliasz', as Arminius records its name, and after the caravan had engaged two guards for the next leg of the journey, that the robbers materialised. The Armenians were quick to act, brandishing their revolvers and rushing to save their baggage but, as Arminius described the event in his *Life and Adventures*, it was his own appearance that had the greatest effect.

He was still wearing his fez with the brass plate, the badge of office of an effendi in service to the Sublime Porte, and the Kurdish outlaws, unafraid of Armenians or Persians, retained considerable respect for the sultan. The thieves stopped in their tracks when they saw him. Arminius told his readers that he 'asked them in a voice of thunder': 'What do you want here?' The leader of the band was an old, one-eyed, grey-bearded patriarch, armed to the teeth with lance, sword, gun, and shield, who assured the 'Bey Effendi' that he and his seven fellows were merely searching for their stray oxen. Arminius drove home his advantage: 'And is it customary to look for oxen, armed as thou art? Shame on thee! Has thy beard turned grey to be soiled by thieving and robbery?' He added a few more threats for good measure and suggested dragging the man to the district governor, whereupon the chastened robbers swiftly left the stage. Arminius was the hero of the hour, rewarded with thanks and gifts of sweetmeats by his fellow travellers. In his earliest account of this experience, he admitted that it was 'the dignity of an Effendi' that had won the day when he had undergone this 'baptism of fire', but, remembering the event later in life, he permitted himself a small homily on the nature of bravery. Heroes, he determined, 'are not born but made, and the most timid home lover can by a gradual process of compulsory self-defence become a very lion of strength and valour'. In his case he had 'in my subsequent travels often been exposed to attacks and surprises of various kinds, until at last I learned to face all dangers boldly and had no more fear of death'.

That evening, in the village where the caravan rested for the night, Arminius and the merchants discovered that their Kurdish guides or guards were well known as 'the most desperate robbers', who had been in league with the marauding bandits. During a 'sumptuous feast' to celebrate the caravan's deliverance, 'there was no end to the tales of robbery' in the neighbourhood. Arminius repeats for his readers the story of a caravan of forty beasts of burden and fifteen men, including an Englishman, who had recently been attacked by a Kurdish robber-chief with twelve men. The Turks and Persians 'took to their heels', leaving their beasts and baggage, but the admirable Englishman, 'who had hitherto coolly stood by and watched the doings of the miscreants', raised his revolver and shot the robber-chief dead. When he was rushed by the rest of the gang of thieves, the Englishman 'did not for an instant lose his presence of mind' but shot one after another dead, shouting that he would kill any who came near. 'The remaining Kurds slunk away', but 'the family of the dead chief instituted a suit for damages' against the English hero, and things might have gone badly for him had the British Consul not interceded on his behalf.

Heroics, his own or those of the stereotypical phlegmatic Englishman, were shortly put out of his mind by Arminius' first experience of Persia. He had forded the Euphrates and left the Ottoman Empire, crossing the Persian border at Diyadin, where his initial excitement was interrupted by the sight of an American missionary family who were returning to Philadelphia after six years in the city of Urmia, in western Azerbaijan.[1] The next surprise came at the village chieftain's house, where he was told he would have to share accommodation with a 'soldier pasha'. He was delighted to find his compatriot and friend from Constantinople, General Kolman, known there as Fejzi Pasha, who was in Diyadin to supervise the building of border barracks. When it left Diyadin, the caravan passed Mount Ararat, where Arminius noted the thriving trade in relics from Noah's Ark. Locals insisted that at least two planks and a couple of masts of the ark were still to be seen in a crystal-clear lake on the top of the mountain. Two years earlier, the British diplomat and Orientalist Edward Eastwick (1814–83), on his way to serve under Charles Alison at the British Legation in Tehran, had encountered the souvenir vendors and been struck by 'the exceeding fitness of the place for the resting of the ark' and the perfect suitability of the region below for 'the culture of the grape of which Noah seems to have set the example'.[2] We will ourselves encounter Eastwick again in this chapter. Meanwhile on the road towards Tabriz, Arminius' party first came across a village wedding and then a stag being pursued by wolves. The stag was promptly shot dead by the caravan's Persian escort, followed by one of the wolves that mistakenly returned for its share of the kill. The deer was immediately and joyously butchered and roasted on a spit.

The Persian countryside was beautiful, but Arminius was disturbed by 'the profound disgust' of the people that greeted his formerly commanding persona as the 'Bey Effendi'. Here in Shiite Persia, 'the Sunnite dog' that he appeared to be was reviled. In *The Story of My Struggles*, Arminius, like plenty of others before and since, wrote of finding 'from my cradle to my old age, in Europe as well as in Asia, fanaticism and narrow-mindedness,

---

1 Urmia was a missionary hotbed. American Presbyterians had been there since 1834, followed by the French militant Roman Catholic Lazarists in 1839 and various English missionary groups thereafter, spreading into other parts of Iran.
2 Edward B. Eastwick, *Journal of a Diplomat's Three Years' Residence in Persia*, Vol. I (London, 1864), 162.

malice, and injustice emanating mostly from the religious people and always on behalf of religion'. His Constantinople accent betrayed his detested 'Sunnitic character' in Turkish-speaking Khoy, the first town over the Persian border, and it was not until he reached Tabriz that he was able to exchange his 'semi-European dress' for the Persian garments that allowed him to go unnoticed in a crowd. He professed himself surprised in particular by the passion roused in the women he encountered against a Sunnite *Osmanli*, or Turk. He was spat upon and had 'pithy oaths' hurled at him – at least, he did in the later descriptions of his journey, although he might have learned to expect such female vehemence from his experiences with women in Constantinople. The two memories may have been conflated into one by the time they appeared in his late memoir, *The Story of My Struggles*.

Impressed by the bazaar in Khoy, with its mix of 'primitive quaintness and the splendour of ancient times', he was astonished by the noise in the narrow streets. The incessant banging of blacksmiths beating their pots and pans competed with the cacophony of the crowd and with two schools where the children, seated on the ground in a half-moon round their deafened teachers, were bellowing their Arabic Quran verses 'like so many infuriated turkeys'. Amid the din, the caravanserai, or guest-house, where the traveller and his companions came to rest was unexpectedly cool, secure, and well-organised, and contrasted favourably with the 'dirty khans' of Turkey. However, the respite was brief before the journey began again. On the evening of 8 June, the travellers set out, pausing in a Sayyid-populated village whose name Arminius gives as 'Hadji Aga'. The Sayyid are the descendants of the Prophet, and the respect they were accorded because of the sanctity of their descent seems to have made Arminius more than a little envious of them, prompting him to record an anecdote concerning a governor of Tabriz, who had condemned a Sayyid thief to death by fire. When local mullahs protested, the governor is supposed to have said, 'If he is a true Seid he will not be touched by the flames', and had the man thrown into the blaze.

Once the travellers reached Tabriz (mythically founded by the energetic Zubaidah, wife of Harun al-Rashid, the legendary Abbasid caliph of *The Thousand and One Nights*), Arminius lost his Armenian travel companions, who had reached their destination in the city. He was both appalled and fascinated by the sheer mayhem around him as he found his way to the caravanserai recommended to him by the emir, where he stayed for two weeks while the hurly-burly tide of unfamiliar Persian life swept up to the door of his cell. He was typically surprised by the fanaticism of the Shiite population and their horror of physical exposure to a European who might make them *nedjiz* ('unclean') should his cloak even brush their feet. This concern about foreign pollution contrasted strangely, Arminius considered, with the washing habits he observed at the basin in the central yard of the caravanserai. Here men were washing their clothes, a baby, and even soaking half-tanned animal skins, while others made their ritual ablutions before prayer in the same water. He was particularly horrified by one individual, 'who must have been very thirsty indeed' and 'eagerly drank of the dark green fluid', but a local, noticing the foreigner's obvious disgust, assured him that Sharia law made it clear that 'a quantity of water, in excess of a hundred and twenty pints, turns blind' – that is, it cannot become unclean.

Edward Eastwick had also experienced 'the temper of the Tabrizis' when dealing with a foreigner and discovered 'no agreeable impression of a Persian city' in regard to cleanliness. Eastwick was informed that running water simply could not be polluted, but advised any future visitor against looking too closely at the women 'washing the filthiest linen in the conduits which convey drinking water into the neighbouring house', in case you 'discover infinitely worse things a little way on'. When he had arrived for the first time at his own house in Tehran and examined his water reservoir, 'The water in it looked more like slime than *aqua fontis*, and the instant I approached it, a lot of obese frogs, who were singing like the chorus in Aristophanes, went down with a splash and a gurgle which set a multitude of efts and other anomalous reptiles in motion in all directions'. Eastwick insisted on the tank being drained and scrubbed but remarked that he had never stopped his servants performing their religious ablutions there, as well as washing every household article in the same water. He concluded that 'the human mind is elastic' and, before he left Persia, his had grown 'reconciled even to these things'.[3]

The great bazaar of Tabriz, today a World Heritage site, was a world in itself, a meeting place for people of all degrees and descriptions. Tabriz was a major trading city; Eastwick wrote of international imports to the value of £1.25 million a year coming into the city via Turkey, in addition to thriving

---

3 Ibid., 182.

exports. Arminius was transfixed by the life he found, by the incidents and characters he encountered, the customs he observed, and the information he gathered in this hive of noise, rumour, and gossip. The sheer proximity and range of existence in the bazaar astonished him: the public letter-writer fighting the racket to catch the whispered words of a veiled patroness; the barber next door flinging the soap from his razor in the direction of the passing pancake-seller, who was carrying his steaming basket through the narrow street. Next door was a miserable soul in the agony of a tooth-pulling operation. There were women loudly arguing from either side of an alley, and a man crying for alms, carrying his severed hand or another limb on a tray, evidence of his punishment for some unknown crime. Arminius absorbed it all as part of his introduction to 'genuine Eastern life': the 'mad carryings on of the Persian traders, craftsmen, beggars, Dervishes, buffoons, singers and jugglers'. Some were particularly eccentric, like the much-admired dervish who had made a vow to speak no other word but the name of Ali, in venera-tion of the son-in-law of the Prophet, the heir to Muhammed in the eyes of Shia Islam. This man, as he shrieked his one-name mantra through the streets, was widely regarded as a saint.

Arminius found the baths (where horse manure was used as heating fuel) filthy in contrast with those of Turkey, and compared their patrons to 'animals driven out to pasture in Europe' as they arrived to the daily trumpet-blast that signalled the filling of the baths with warm water. The smell of henna was everywhere – Persians dyed their hair, beards, palms of hands, and soles of feet. He remarked 'the coat of paint hides the dirt; and a gentleman, or lady, having made use of it can manage to do without washing for several days'. The closeness of communal bathing revolted him too. He watched groups of Persian men scraping and touching each other in a pool and compared their habits adversely with Turkish customs. He was not sur-prised by the hours women took in the baths, considering the habits of their menfolk, but judged the results of their toilettes and the local fashions as less appealing than those of Constantinople. He described 'a kind of beauty mark' tattooed 'onto their cheeks or necks and courtesans even paint daring scenes on their breasts'. In Isfahan, he told his readers, 'an emancipated daughter of Iran had an entire hunting scene engraved on her bosom'.

There were other, more public spectacles to describe. Arminius had met enough Europeans to enjoy moving successfully between European and

Asian society in the city and, through his European contacts, he gained admittance to the investiture of nine-year-old Mozaffar ad-Din, heir apparent to Naser al-Din, the Qajar shah of Persia. Tabriz was the seat of the Persian crown prince during the Qajar dynasty, and Arminius was also there to see the reception of the Italian ambassador Marcello Cerutti as he passed through Tabriz on his way to Tehran. Arminius was disposed to cast a somewhat dismissive eye on Persian pomp and ceremony, but his eavesdropping in the crowd on the latter occasion made it clear to him that the Persians were equally unimpressed by the European display. Arminius commented on the 'sad-looking' Persian soldiers at the investiture, as 'uncomfortable and awkward as possible in the foreign clothes' with their cravats tied every which way; the great wooden platters full of sugar loaves and cakes that occupied one side of the palace garden, 'without which any festive occasion in Persia would be considered incomplete', and the eulogies of a young poet, who not only compared the prince to 'a tender rose' and a 'precious pearl fished out of the sea of the royal family', but also vaunted the received dignity of the 'feeble and pale boy' as 'a powerful hero who, with a single blow of his sword destroys whole armies, at whose glance the mountains tremble, and the flame of whose eyes makes the rivers run dry'. The Italian Embassy, twenty-five strong, were dressed up in full ceremonial uniform, with orders, swords, and plumed helmets in the heat of a June midday. The Persians, who Arminius overheard in the crowd, considered their tight-fitting clothes and short jackets almost indecent, and the European stiff seat on horseback a caricature. This diplomatic parade heralded Arminius' imminent departure for Tehran on roads that were busy enough to be safe for him to travel, even if he was alone, on the 'sorry-looking nag' that was all he could afford.

He also wrote of two incidents while he was in Tabriz that would burnish his linguistic fame. Arminius had noticed another European at the caravanserai, unpacking his bales of merchandise among the crowd, and consulting Arminius' pocket German–Turkish dictionary, published some years earlier in Constantinople. Unable to find the term he needed, the European had flung the book aside with an irritated exclamation, when Arminius addressed him in German: 'the writer of this little dictionary was not exactly a fool', he told the stranger, and went on to point out that he was looking in the wrong place in the dictionary for what he needed. The man, a Swiss businessman named Würth, who was in the city with his colleague Mr Hanhardt, was astounded and annoyed to be addressed by this odd semi-Persian individual, but irritation soon gave way to explanations and apologies, and Arminius was treated to Swiss hospitality for several days. On another occasion, he was sitting in the afternoon heat at the door of his cell busily de-lousing his clothes, when two Englishmen, recognisable by their 'Indian hats', stopped to watch his work. The younger man said to the older, 'Look at the hunting zeal of this fellow!' Arminius wrote of their bewilderment when he looked up and said in English, 'Will you join sir?' When the men asked where he learned English and which country he was from, Arminius chose to play dumb. Locals were already curious about his strangely easy relationships with foreigners. He disappeared into his room but, years later, at a society dinner in London, he recognised one of the men from Tabriz. When Arminius was invited by his hostess to tell the company something of his travels, he asked to be introduced to the man saying, 'I do not know his name but I have seen him'. 'Lord R' denied any former acquaintance until Arminius asked if he did not 'remember the dervish who addressed you in English' in Tabriz? Alder and Dalby speculated that 'Lord R' might have been the future Viceroy of India, Lord Ripon, but there is no record of Ripon travelling in Persia. It is highly unlikely he should have been there in the same year as he became a privy councillor and secretary of state for war in Britain, so the identity of 'Lord R' remains a mystery.

It was the mourning month of Muharram (the first month of the Islamic year, when the deaths of the Prophet's grandsons are mourned by Shia Muslims) when Arminius set out from Tabriz in the company of a group of Sunni Muslims of various nationalities who were engaged in a lucrative deception. Pretending to be Shias, they travelled from village to village offering mourning elegies and publicly commemorating the deaths of the Prophet's grandsons Hasan and Husain, and pocketing the alms they received. These were also the people who acted as paid guards for pilgrims to the Shia pilgrimage site of Karbala and carried the bodies of the dead there or to the even more enormous cemetery at Najaf. Arminius was excited to attend a *tazieh*, a form of religious play on the life of Husain, similar to a Christian passion play or the Hindu *ramlila*, and was impressed by the quality of the acting, especially that of the small child actors. He was less entertained by the impossibility of buying food on the day before Ashura, the tenth and climactic day of Muharram, and felt forced to try his hand at begging. This was not successful but, after a hungry night, he managed to buy some bread and boiled rice the following morning. The weather was now too hot for travelling during the day and travel in the quiet of night made Arminius uneasy, but he was close to Tehran before he had anything real to fear. On this occasion, the putative thieves, who were seen off by our hero brandishing his pistols and threatening to shoot, were not taken very seriously by his companions.

Tehran came into view at last, beneath a bank of early morning fog, and Arminius 'got a glimpse first of roofs covered with green glazed tiles, then of gilded cupolas, and at last the panorama of the whole town'. He had reached 'the gate of the seat of government of the king of kings' and was able to pause to congratulate himself on the satisfactory state of his health. After two months travelling, he was only a little thinner, darker, and more freckled. Now, he had to present himself to Haider Effendi, the Turkish ambassador to Persia, in the role of the slightly eccentric scholar of linguistics described in the letters of recommendation he carried from Constantinople. It was high summer; he had reached Tehran 'in the condition of a boiled fish', and was delighted when he found the entire embassy decamped to silk tents in the cooler mountain air of a village in the foothills of the Alborz Mountains at Shemiran, where the shahs had summer palaces. As a purveyor of letters as well as recent news and gossip from Constantinople, his was a welcome arrival, although the plans he outlined for his onward journey met with horrified amazement. A journey to Bukhara was considered impossibly dangerous and, for the time being, there was no chance of any travel in a north-easterly direction due to the war between Dost Mohammed of Afghanistan and his son-in-law Ahmed Khan, ruler of Herat. The ambassador gave his guest a silk tent of his own, a horse, and a servant, and suggested he enjoy learning about Persia and forget about travelling further for a month or two.

After his first rose-tinted view of the city, Arminius' vision of the glories of the Orient was shaken by closer acquaintance with Tehran. The city walls were built of mud and, as Edward Eastwick had observed, a mud wall 'cannot be a very striking object'. Equally, 'There is nothing very impressive in ... a city of 100,000 inhabitants, living in mud houses.'[4] Eastwick's attention had

---

4 Ibid., 217.

been caught instead by the grandeur of the great wall of the Alborz Mountains to the north-east of the city and by spectacular Mount Damavand. Arminius, fighting his way through the throng in the narrow streets, had no time or inclination to look so high; his attention was all taken up by the dirt and squalor that underlaid even the most illustrious outer show. In the grandest houses, halls and reception areas were richly ornamented and covered with wonderful carpets, but backstage, the rooms where life was really lived were 'most shamefully neglected', and the same applied to personal appearance. 'A person who will spend from fifty to a hundred gold pieces for his outer garments is rarely the owner of more than two or three shirts', and 'soap is looked upon as an article of luxury, being hardly ever used.' The poorer classes used clay. 'Even noble Khans and Ministers possess less underwear than our poorest citizens', Arminius wrote, adding that 'lice are rampant here in the highest circles'. The colour of underwear, he said, was uniformly blue. 'It shows the dirt less.'

He was, as he had been in Constantinople, also offended by the omnipresent pipe-smoking and disgusted by the hospitable custom of passing the pipe from mouth to mouth; and by the habit of eating with the hand from a communal dish in the absence of any cutlery; and by the 'cup of sherbet passed round, in which a dozen men have already steeped their henna-dyed moustaches'. The women in particular smoked like chimneys and 'the unpleasant smell of the breath is noticeable in princess and peasant alike'. Arminius in any case considered Persian women to be 'very far behind those of Constantinople as far as gracefulness and cleanliness is concerned'; complained again of the ubiquitous use of henna by both sexes; and took as dim a view of the enveloping *chador* as any of its critics today. 'You would take them for ambulating mummies rather than attractive women', when they went out dressed 'in a blue sack', with their faces covered with a veil or linen cloth and a thick paste on their hair. 'Imagine', he wrote, 'how a Persian beauty smells during the hot season!' Neither was he impressed by indoor clothing that indecently left the belly bare, and he was embarrassed by female conversation that was blatantly sexual – although he wrote that Persian refinement was confined to elegance in speech, manners, and conversation and he was impressed by the horsemanship of the women. Groups would ride flat-out to picnic by the tomb of a saint or poet, 'plump navy-blue sacks of linen', recognisable as women only by the 'little slippers in the stirrups and the fire in the eyes which penetrates the narrow grille of the veil'. Admirers, presumably attracted by those fiery eyes, galloped up to snatch conversations with their chosen 'fair one who was usually only recognisable by a brooch on her veil'. Arminius, the humble and anonymous observer on his donkey, told his readers, 'I was an eye-witness to such scenes and they always had my fullest attention'.

As Edward Eastwick reported, riding was 'almost the sole amusement in Tehran', and there were foxes and hares enough to turn a 'constitutional canter' into a hunt, with greyhounds taking the place of 'harriers and foxhounds'.[5] Charles Alison had his own pack of greyhounds and his own hawks, and offered a hunt breakfast at the British mission to the dozen or so Europeans who would set out for a day's sport.[6] But this, said Eastwick, was essentially a British occupation. The Russians 'played at cards and walked, the French studied and talked, and the Turks moped and smoked'.[7] According to Arminius only one Frenchman hunted: he 'once stalked a hoopoe, and having slain it with two barrels, sent off his servant at once to get the creature stuffed, as an eternal monument of his prowess'. Like Arminius, Eastwick also noted the importance of the pipe to Persian bureaucratic life, the unwritten rules stalling the discussion of business until after the first pipe has been shared, the inconvenient arrival of a servant with the second just as you reached the most secret part of your conversation, and the constant interruptions for coffee or, as Arminius noted, 'tea of a most undecided character', brought by numerous other servants determined to catch every word of the conversation. Like Arminius, he also noticed filthy streets full of potholes and the generally unhygienic conditions in Tehran that bred cholera, typhus, and dysentery and brought a heavy death toll.

Arminius' familiarity with diplomatic circles in Constantinople facilitated his reception at the European embassies in Tehran. He had a friendly meeting with Charles Alison in the cool of the British mission's garden at Gulhek, and another with Count Arthur de Gobineau, the French imperial envoy, 'under a small tent in a garden like a cauldron'. Gobineau had a

---

5 Ibid., 256.
6 Denis Wright, *The English Amongst the Persians: Imperial Lives in Nineteenth-Century Iran* (London, 2001), 90.
7 Eastwick, op. cit., 256.

passion for ancient Persia and a great interest in Sufism and dervish sects, although he is better known now for his proselytisation of racist views, based on supposed 'scientific racist theory' and his concept of an Aryan master race personified by European aristocracy of Germano-Frankish descent. The common ground between this class-focused French aristocrat and Arminius himself may have been vested in the former's conviction that Russia was the coming power in Asia, in his theories on ethnography, and the low opinions both men shared of modern Persia. Again, Arminius could not resist unfavourable comparisons between Persia and Turkey: 'Iran, the theme of so much poetic enthusiasm, is after all, nothing but a frightful waste; whereas Turkey is really an earthly paradise'. His contempt for Persian education included 'the intensely oriental character of the Government and society', and the lack of 'even the elementary knowledge of the geography and history of Europe', where 'even the heads of the administration very seldom knew French'. The fact that the 'scholars and literati' of Persia were not even particularly interested in Western philosophy and thought was proof enough, Arminius believed, of superior Turkish understanding. Persia was indeed 'at least a hundred years behind Turkey, and would certainly take longer to extract itself from the pool of Asiatic thought', whereas 'the superiority of the Osmanli results from the attention he is paying to the languages of Europe, and his disposition gradually to acquaint himself with the progress that European savants have made in chemistry, physics and history'.

If Arminius' attention was engaged with the sights and sounds of Tehran, including the society afforded by French, Italian, and Austrian officers in the service of the shah, those amusements quickly palled and his feet itched to be on the move again. But he could not start for Central Asia while Herat lay under siege by Dost Mohammed. He wrote 'our European papers seemed to me to exaggerate the whole matter', but soon discovered that no one could travel to or from Herat, not even a Persian. A mysterious outsider, a foreigner however disguised, would have been asking for trouble. Meanwhile, Arminius' attachment to the Turkish Embassy and other diplomatic contacts had facilitated his reception into Persian official society and he had been introduced to the shah. Not surprisingly, he had not thought much of the hypocrisy of the court. On the one hand a courtier might cringe in front of his monarch: 'spare me, I dare not approach nearer to thy person; the glory of thy magnificent splendour dazzles my eyes'; while, on the other, ignore the shah's commands and spread 'the vilest rumours' about him. Now, however, Arminius' introduction into these exalted circles had armed him with a letter of safe conduct from Mirza Said Khan, the minister of foreign affairs. It was questionable how much protection this missive would offer 'the high-born and noble Reshid Effendi' in distant provinces, but it was to prove a useful passport into the society of Isfahan and Shiraz. Arminius maintained that his main goal in travelling to these cities of southern Persia was to continue training for the hardship of his ultimate adventure with 'the dry saddle, dry bread and dry soil', and he did not set off as a high-born Turkish effendi. On 2 September 1862, he left Tehran as the city gates closed for the night, dressed as a Baghdad Sunni dervish in a robe reaching to his heels, with a red girdle round his waist, an interesting-sounding 'water-proof coat' which he describes as a *mashlak*, and a *keffiyeh*, the traditional head-covering.

The caravan set out in midnight silence under a bright moon, with only the hooves of thirty laden mules rhythmically tapping on the hard, burnt ground as a meditative accompaniment to the start of a journey. In this *Canterbury Tales*-esque group of pilgrims were mullahs, merchants, and skilled labourers or craftsmen who Arminius describes as mechanics. He quickly picked a young Sayyid *tazieh* singer from Baghdad as his travel companion of choice. The young man knew others among the group and had the charm and musical skill to become a general favourite, in whose reflected popularity Arminius may well have thought he might bask while, as an Ottoman subject himself, the young singer would have understood the value of acquaintance with the 'effendi' Arminius, if (as we may imagine Arminius deemed politic) that true identity was in fact vouchsafed to a Sayyid, whose community was known for its Shiite beliefs. Arminius did his best to avoid religious discussions, but there was nothing Persians enjoyed more than a good argument and his companions were quite willing to talk with Ghebers (Zoroastrians), Christians, and especially with Sunnis. Luckily his new friend took his side and before long Arminius was able safely to resume his accustomed role as the 'Effendi from Constantinople, the guest of the Turkish Embassy', with a passion to see Isfahan and Shiraz 'the paradise-like'. He only had trouble from one shoemaker, marked by his tall green turban as a descendant of Ali, who persisted in visiting on Arminius the 'sinful usurpations of the three Caliphs' and talked 'with as much animation about the case of succession' from 1,200 years before as if it had happened only yesterday.

His accounts of this Persian journey, regardless of 'the worst imaginable' roads, the indigestible rice and mutton-fat pilaf of Central Asia, and 'all the sufferings' he remembered in his old age, show a revival of the youthful enthusiasm for travel and new experiences and the fascination with unknown places that he had displayed on his first journey east to Constantinople. Somehow that excitement had been lost in his respectable life in the familiar circles of Constantinople society, whereas the discomforts of the first part of his journey to Persia had been so great a contrast to the Bey Effendi's previous comfortable existence that his sense of adventure was beginning to re-emerge. Perhaps this was what Arminius had been looking for with this 'hardship training': a tempering not just of body but of spirit. He was certainly going to need it for the journey ahead; but for now, he was able to relax into the rhythm of travel, abandoning himself 'to the safe gait of my trusty asinine quadruped', watching the stars, and listening to the stories of the Sayyid 'with a soul full of faith'. The caravan halted at dawn for the Azan (the morning call to prayer), then marched on to arrive at a caravanserai before the sun became unbearably oppressive. Men and beasts ate and rested during the heat of the day, then rose to prepare for the night's journey ahead and to eat their evening pilaf. Arminius noticed that the dervish who travelled with them, this time no professional member of a brotherhood but the real mendicant holy man of the type Arminius would imitate, did very well for himself. When 'the savoury steam of the kettle' heralded the evening meal, he would pick up his *kashkul*, 'a vessel made from the shell of a cocoanut', and go from group to group in the encampment shouting the dervish prayer, which to Arminius sounded like, 'Ya Hu! Ya Hakk.'[8] Each person would give the dervish a contribution from his own food, to be indiscriminately mixed in the *kashkul* and eaten 'with a good appetite'. Arminius quoted the 'people of the East' in describing this man, saying 'he carries with him nothing, he does not cook, yet he eats; his kitchen is provided by god'.

The route to Isfahan lay across the Dasht-e Kavir, the Great Salt Desert, to the holy city of Qom and on to Kashan. The desert was legendarily

---

8 The chant was probably 'Hu-hu-hu-hu; ya hayy; hayy-hayy-hayy-hayy; da'im haqq Allah hay' ('You are the guide; you are the truth; no one is the guide but he').

populated by evil spirits, including that of Shemr, the killer of Husain, upon whose loathsome presence the desolation of the region was blamed. It was a frightening place, where shape-shifting columns of sand loomed from the shadowed darkness in the moonlight, and an oppressive silence blanketed the land. The stench of death added to the atmosphere of dread as the travellers came across a mortuary caravan of more than a hundred bodies being carried in coffins, four at a time on pack mules, to be buried in the holy soil of the Iraqi city of Karbala, close to the shrine and resting place of the beloved Husain. Arminius got close enough to the death caravan to see one dead face, which 'was frightful to look at' in the draining light of the moon. The bodies had been on the road ten days with another twenty to go; but others from further afield might take as long as two months to reach their destination. Even the pack animals seemed to try to 'bury their nostrils in their breasts' to escape the smell, while their drivers, as far as possible, kept their own distance. Qom, the city sacred to Fatima, the mother of Hasan and Husain, and the site of her shrine, had its own vast cemetery on the outskirts, nearly three kilometres long and the favourite burial place for devout Persian women.

Qom was also the 'abode of numerous evil-doers' due to its 'privilege of sanctuary' and, Arminius noted, a hive of prostitution. Men were also buried there of course; one was 'reputed to have had 800 legal wives – no wonder that he wished to rest in female company'. (Some might have expected the reverse to be the case.) On the approach to the city, all the bushes were decorated with votive tokens tied to the branches. The scraps of cloth, Arminius was fascinated to find, included 'the costly handiwork of India and Cashmere, the manufactures of England and America, and the humble friezes and coarse linen of the nomadic Turkoman, Arab and Kurdistan tribes'. Occasionally there was a 'magnificent shawl suspended on the branches of a bush' and inviting theft but, Arminius wrote, no pilgrim would dare commit the sacrilege of stealing a pious gift. To mark his own pilgrimage of sorts, he hung a red silk tassel from his *keffiyeh*. He accompanied his fellow travellers into Fatima's tomb, where the value of the votive gifts was magnified with pearls, diamonds, and gold. Arminius believed he was the first foreigner to enter the tomb. He found it splendid, although his Sunni costume was looked at askance, and he was clearly happier visiting the bazaar, famous for its watermelons, and its earthenware made from the holy soil of the city. Here he was spotted as a foreigner by a muslin-dyer who angrily told him: 'We shall get rid of your expensive foreign fabrics and will know all your tricks of trade; and when Persians will be able to do without *ferengistan* manufacture, I know you will come begging to us'.

In Kashan, after a two-day journey from Qom, Arminius headed for the bazaar again, 'the only thing of note'. Much of old Kashan had been destroyed by an earthquake in 1778 but, by the time Arminius reached the city, it had been re-built, and it remains a major tourist destination in Iran today thanks to its magnificent Qajar-era buildings. Perhaps these were all too modern to excite Arminius' interest. Most tourists, wherever in the world, from Budapest to China, would in any case sympathise with his enthusiasm for the bustle and business of life on show and make a beeline for the local market: different, strange, or unique goods for sale, irresistible souvenirs – at least until they reach home – and these days, a wealth of photographic opportunities. Arminius went to the bazaar where the famous brassware of Kashan was made and was interested in the lustre tiles known as *kashi,* which were said to have been invented there and which ornament buildings all over Central Asia. He also heard about a particularly danger-ous variety of scorpion in the town which, unlike the Tabriz fleas, forbore to sting strangers for reasons of hospitality. Arminius wrote that he never saw one of these beasts, but the Science Museum in London holds a group of three brass scorpion-shaped amulets, proof against scorpion sting, that came from the ruins of Kashan after the earthquake. He was more bothered by a different local pest, in the form of strolling players, who pounced on travel-lers and blackmailed money out of them for the sake of peace.

On 13 September, two days after leaving Kashan, Arminius reached Isfahan, a journey through mountain passes and across plains of some 200 kilometres that takes only two or three hours by road today. Isfahan's famed beauty, Arminius wrote, was 'only on the surface'; its streets were as small and dirty as in all the other Persian towns he had seen. When he visited the bazaar, he was disappointed by its near-deserted state, with only a few water-melon sellers in the empty space. He would have known of the adjacent huge space of the Meidani Shah, reputed to be the largest enclosed square in the world, built by Shah Abbas when he moved his capital to Isfahan in the early seventeenth century, thus making the city into one of the biggest and most beautiful in Persia. But more than two centuries later, Isfahan was no longer the crowded cosmopolitan capital it had once been – an important stop on the silk routes; a polyglot melting-pot of commerce and craft, where artisans, merchants, money-changers, and missionaries from Europe and Asia mingled. Now the seat of power had moved, and Arminius saw the double-storied arcades of shops surrounding the Meidan crumbling into the dust. At least he was able to climb to the balcony of the Sheikh Lotfollah Mosque, to see the whole square stretched out in front of him, and to imagine ancient splendour and the square filled with massing crowds. 'Today', he wrote, 'it is a sad and forlorn desert, the silence of the grave brooding over it.'

His letters of recommendation from Tehran carried him into Isfahan society to dine with the Imam Djuma, 'the real pope of the Shi-ite sect' and 'the most influential priest in Persia', of impeccable Sayyid descent. The imam was a rich man who held more power than a king in a city whose inhabitants considered themselves above other Persians and hated the actual king and his royal family. Arminius spent two weeks in Isfahan and 'had an excellent opportunity to see the noteworthy sights and to observe all the classes of society in the town'. He found the merchants and craftspeople to be highly cultivated, poetic, intelligent, well-read, and able to quote 'hundreds of verses of their best poets by heart'. He stayed with his friend the singer, who did very well for himself performing his 'heart-rending lamentations' in the mosques and the bazaar but returned home 'to give way to the merriest and the most rollicking humour'. With him, Arminius met 'people of every kind and rather mixed societies', where, 'although he wore a green turban in token of his descent from the family of the Prophet', the singer 'drank like a trooper'. The Imam Djuma, in his own enormous green turban, attempted to convert Arminius to Shiism and also 'took in quite a lot of intoxicants at night'. The prudish Arminius was shocked by the songs he heard in the imam's house and by 'a veritable orgy' when dancing girls appeared, whose dances seemed to him no more than 'a series of lewd gyrations and gymnastics', in front of an audience that included officials and mullahs.

He left Isfahan with the singer in the same caravan as he had arrived. It had now grown to about 150 animals and sixty passengers, big enough to put heart into Persian travellers who were, Arminius wrote, 'remarkably deficient in that valuable article, the virtue of courage', and who jumped at their own shadows. When the caravan reached the desert plain around Yazd, Arminius saw herds of gazelles as the travellers passed into the province of Fars. He found the constant night marches exhausting, and was impressed by the smaller caravans they met of pilgrims on their way to Karbala, which included young children and women of eighty, making a journey that might take sixty days there and sixty back. As the caravan approached Pasargadae at daybreak, Arminius was excited enough to summon the energy to hurry ahead and scramble up the great marble steps at the tomb of Cyrus the Great and marvel, as the sun rose, at the skills required to move these enormous blocks of stone. He found the names of 'numerous celebrated European travellers' carved into the marble, with other graffiti in Arabic, Persian, and Hebrew – inscriptions that he believed dated from the time of the first captivity of the Jews. He also found the sole Hungarian signature at the site, 'Marothi Istvan, 1839', in a window recess, and carved 'Eljen a Magyar' ('Long live Hungarians') and his own name into the stone.[9]

While Arminius was trying to decipher the graffiti, he was addressed by a local nomad hoping to do service as a guide: 'Hadji, there are no such huge blocks to be seen in Baghdad, are there?' Arminius' disguise, assisted perhaps by the desert dust, had passed muster. His guide, who took him to see the ruins of a building known as 'Solomon's Throne', the massive black marble arch of its gate a little way distant, was easily able to explain how the huge stones had been put into place. 'Art thou not aware that Solomon could freely dispose of the devils and all the spirits of the lower regions?' At a nod the spirits would bring him the largest and most valuable objects from across the world for his miraculous constructions. Solomon's ability to summon all the spirits of the air, whether devils or angels, to do duty as labourers was of course well known from his construction of the Temple in Jerusalem. It was a skill legendarily passed to his descendants such as Emperor Lalibela of Ethiopia (r. 1181–1221), who achieved equally remarkable feats of construction with the assistance of angels in the rock-hewn churches of Lalibela.

When Arminius arrived at Persepolis, those spectacular ruins might have

---

9 It is extraordinary how timeless is the urge to leave one's mark. Even Lord Curzon, that great preserver of historic monuments, quite forgot himself twenty-seven years later when he also carved 'G N Curzon 1889' into a stone niche in the palace of Darius the Great in Susa.

encouraged anyone's belief in angelic builders. Massive blocks of stone, forty to fifty feet long, had been fitted together so perfectly that the joins were barely visible; and he was equally transfixed by the monumental carvings. He stayed three days among the ruins, which kindled 'the fervid imagination of the young traveller' with exquisite carved capitals to the columns and 'reliefs of wonderful beauty'. Here 'a gigantic man struggling with a monster', there a king on a throne, 'the wonderful art exhibited in the shaping of the features and in the various expressions of the human countenance... makes one almost imagine that the cold marble will speak'. When he met a nomadic Turkish tribe nearby, with whom he could speak in their own language, they told him the ruins were infested with devils and djinns who made an infernal noise at night. They also told him of another fabled builder-king, Djemshid, whose powers issued from a magical cup. At the mere touch of the cup to his lips, he could realise all his heart's desire as stones came 'flying from the east and artists from the west'. However, supernatural construction had not deterred local vandalism of the site. The nomads pulled down columns for the sake of 'enough lead for a couple of bullets', gleaned from the crevices where it had been used to hold the column together. Their predecessors in the destruction of Persepolis, they told Arminius, had been Arabs, followed by foreigners from India in search of treasure. Those foreigners went as far back as Alexander's troops who, Plutarch wrote, carried off the treasures of Persepolis on the backs of 20,000 mules and 5,000 camels. Servants of the government of India, passing through Shiraz and visiting Persepolis on their way to Bushire on the Persian Gulf during the first half of the nineteenth century, had not been averse to adding sculptural remnants to their baggage either, as well as their names to the graffiti on the site.[10]

Outside Persepolis, Arminius found a caravan of pilgrims returning from Karbala and was able to join it travelling towards Shiraz. The pilgrims'

---

10 'English who wish to proceed overland to England from the East Indies, come by sea into the Persian Gulf ... land at Bendarabas ... proceed to Shiraz ... and take pleasure in visiting the ruins of Persepolis ... Colonel Johnson had brought with him several coins from Persepolis, where they are dug out of the ground without difficulty; and he also showed us some broken pieces of bas reliefs, having inscriptions on them, which nobody can read ... Besides several coins, Colonel Johnson sent to the Ambassador a piece which had been broken off the wing of a sphinx'. So said Moritz von Kotzebue in 1819. See St John Simpson, 'Making their mark: Foreign travellers at Persepolis', *Achemenet*, Arta 2005.001 (2005), 12.

destination was the village of Zerkum, close to Shiraz, where Arminius was fascinated by the reception they were accorded. Blessed by their visit to the tomb of the beloved martyr Husain, both pilgrims and their asses were bodily carried home in triumph by their relations and were 'freely perspiring from the many embraces' they received. To touch an individual who had made the pilgrimage was itself 'worth nearly half a pilgrimage to Karbala'. Travelling on to Shiraz, Arminius was looking forward to something extraordinary and was thoroughly disappointed when the river Roknabad, of which the poet Hafiz had sung and on whose banks he was buried, was little more than 'an insignificant brook', the surrounding countryside rocky and bare. When he had his first sight of Shiraz itself, however, from the spot where 'the stranger in his admiration involuntarily bursts out into the customary "Allah Ekbar"', he was enchanted. Cypress trees, a silvery ribbon of river, blooming gardens, a wealth of 'proud edifices' shining in the sparkling air under a blue sky, and all bordered by 'a lofty chain of mountains stretching through Kazerum as far as the shore of the Gulf of Persia'.

He found the people of Shiraz to be pleasure-loving and jovial, unchanged since 'Hafiz, the glorifier of wine, sung his odes here', and, from labourer to priest, freely indulging in wine-drinking 'as soon as the dusk of evening sets in' and 'merry-making until midnight, and even later'. He stayed in Shiraz, the final destination of his south Persian tour, for some time, selling his donkey and taking lodgings in a mosque. He enjoyed himself: listening to 'the modulations of the beautiful South Persian dialect', relishing the experiences of his journey and of Persian antiquity that he could treasure, including a drinking party around the tomb of Hafiz in the garden of Mosalla that must have seemed like a dream. A fire was lit and 'our cups went the rounds until dawn', filled with Armenian wine, under a starry sky where each succeeding group of stars was toasted in turn by the company and 'the melancholy songs of Hafiz' were sung to inspire ecstasy. But it was not all so perfect. Arminius was in the guise of a Sunni dervish once again and open to the insults and arguments of the disputatious Shia faithful, although this does not seem much to have dented his pleasure as he made new friends in the city.

When he heard about a Swedish doctor practising in Shiraz, he went to visit him, dressed as a dervish and announcing himself with the usual 'Ya Hu! Ya Hakk!' The doctor had lived in Shiraz for fifteen years and attempted to give him money as the usual way to get rid of a holy beggar, but Arminius turned down the alms and announced 'I am charged by the Sheikh of Baghdad to make a Mussulman of thee'. The doctor, by name Fagergreen, who had heard it all in his many years in Persia, was nevertheless surprised by the commanding tone of this missionary and demanded proof that Arminius had been sent by a leader who so miraculously knew of a *ferenghi* or 'foreign' doctor in Shiraz. When Arminius told him 'One syllable from my master is enough to bestow the knowledge of all the sciences and languages of the world... put me to trial in any language', the doctor was astonished. His astonishment grew when he addressed the dervish in Swedish and Arminius replied with all the Swedish he knew, the opening verses of the national romantic epic, *Frithjof's Saga*, by Esaias Tegnér. When the doctor tried German, the dervish was on much firmer ground, then French, then English, and finally Arminius 'recited a verse from the Quran for the good of his soul'.

Dr Fagergreen began to question him but the dervish swept out, directing the doctor to reflect until 8 o'clock the following morning, 'or thou shall feel the power of my master'. The next day Dr Fagergreen was waiting at Arminius' lodgings first thing in the morning, and although Arminius attempted to continue the pretence, he soon told the doctor who he was. Dr Fagergreen had thought he was a European, but Arminius' fluent Persian had made him doubt his own eyes. Now he was able to ask for news of Tehran and his acquaintances there, and invited Arminius to stay at his house. The dervish explained this unusual situation to his Persian friends by pretending Dr Fagergreen was instructing him in alchemy, which the doctor was understood to practise. Arminius stayed for six weeks, studying not magic but the inhabitants and customs of Shiraz. The delights of the city were not proof against 'extreme excitability' that often resulted in quite random loss of life. Arminius witnessed a 'richly dressed Persian walking superciliously along the narrow side walk of the bazaar', when another somehow got in his way and was mortally stabbed with the 'two-edged curved poniard' that every man carried in his belt and was ready to make use of on the slightest provocation. Arminius suspected public murder was only the tip of the iceberg of other, hidden atrocities, and saw punishments meted out by the authorities that were inventively cruel.

All the same he was happy enough, after three months, to consider spending the winter in Shiraz, but fate intervened in the form of Count

Julien Émilien Rochechouart of the French Embassy in Tehran. Rochech-ouart (1831–79) was travelling with a young Italian naturalist and botanist, the Marquis Giacomo Doria (1840–1913), a member of the Italian mission whose arrival Arminius had witnessed in Tabriz. Doctor Fagergreen, starved of European news, was delighted to be able to entertain more foreigners at his house and Rochechouart invited Arminius to travel with him back to Tehran in a few days' time. Short of money again, Arminius realised the advantages of travelling with this representative of a European power in contrast to the slower and rougher route of the dervish traveller, and made ready to leave. His departure was dramatic. He had gone to take leave of Dr Fagergreen in his room at the top of the house when the whole place was hit by the first shock of an earthquake. Earthquakes are a fairly regular occur-rence in the Fars region and in Shiraz, but the 1825 'great disaster' had killed a quarter of the city's population and, as Arminius wrote, 'the inhabitants of Shiraz know but too well the frightful consequences of this elemental catas-trophe'. Everyone panicked, everything shook and swayed with the second shock that morning, and a roaring noise came from deep underground, while cries of 'Ya Allah! Ya Allah!' could be heard all over the city. Doctor Fagergreen and Arminius collected the doctor's wife and children and the doctor pushed them all outside to find safety while he remained to guard the house from opportunistic looters.

More and stronger shocks came and the cry went up, led by the mullahs in the crowd, that the *ferenghis* were to blame for the disaster. Arminius, fearing for their lives, moved back towards the house where he saw birds flying about and wildly flapping their wings, which he took to be the signal for further shocks to come. Dr Fagergreen came out of his house; the earth shook beneath their feet; and everyone fell to the ground just as a nearby water tank crashed down and gallons of water poured over their heads. The mob was growing, determined to apportion blame and spill foreign blood, and with a shout of 'To arms!', Dr Fagergreen rushed back into the shaking house followed by Arminius, to come out armed with rifles and pistols. At that moment, a neighbouring building fell and, as clouds of dust rose to blanket the city, the mob scattered. After another half an hour with no further shocks, Arminius dared to leave the building. He found Count Rochech-ouart amid a scene of dreadful devastation, with cracked walls and fissures in the street; 'nothing but desolation and misery were to be seen'. Saying a final fond but hurried goodbye to Dr Fagergreen, Arminius and the count set off for the city gates, where a crowd of citizens, who had run out into the countryside for safety, waited fearfully for news of friends and relatives. Arminius rode out past the place where he had first seen the enchanted city of Shiraz and remembered hearing the myth it was doomed to destruction on the Day of Judgement, when the waters of the nearby Derya-i-Nemek (the local name for the famous pink-coloured Maharloo Lake) would once again pour over the city, covering it as it had been covered at the beginning of time. The return journey to Tehran was fast, and Arminius enjoyed talking to the count, who was full of stories of Paris, and watching their Persian escort hunting gazelles with hounds. Persepolis and Isfahan, he saw, had been untouched by the earthquake, and he reached Tehran again on 15 January 1863 for a stock-take of his experiences, new accomplishments, and acquaintances, and to plan his next and most famous journey.

THE DERVISH OF
WINDSOR CASTLE

The Life of Arminius Vambery

Lory Alder and Richard Dalby

Professor Nicholas Kurti
with grateful thanks
for your invaluable help
from
Lory Alder and Richard Dalby

Bachman & Turner

Bachman & Turner Ltd.
London

6

The False Dervish

Looking back at his life in *The Story of My Struggles*, with 'the glow of enthusiasm vanished and the heart and head cooled down almost to freezing-point', Arminius viewed the actions of his younger self in undertaking his Central Asian adventure as 'absolutely unjustifiable and opposed to all common sense'. He admitted that it had been less a matter of careful planning and more of 'a leap in the dark' and a 'rushing forward at random'. He had chosen to ignore his lameness, the distances he would have to cover, the characters of the people and their rulers who he would encounter, the difficulties of maintaining his disguise, the advice of experts based on the experiences of those others who had disappeared, died, or more rarely survived the tyrants and troubles of Central Asia, and the lice, 'which multiply in the most appalling manner'. 'Now I understand for the first time', Arminius wrote, 'why in the Jewish Holy Scriptures the plague of lice is mentioned second after that of the water turned into blood'. All the same, Arminius pointed out, he had 'gone through a hard school in my tender childhood' and he remembered that 'high spirited youth does not easily give way to despair; it has a store of confidence which only disease or age can diminish'.

Readers of Arminius' biographical works sense that, by this stage of his travels, those youthful high spirits and enthusiasm were already diminished by the realities of his experiences. He was still able to congratulate himself on his new ability to brave extremes of climate, to sleep in the saddle, to overcome the handicap of his lameness, and to deal with the metaphorical slings and arrows thrown his way in religious disputes. Now, with the war between Herat and Afghanistan at an end, thoughts of the Hungarian Academy and the travel fund he had been given two years earlier to pay his way through mysterious Tartary added impetus to his plans. If he did not now make that journey, he might, as Count Dessewffy had implored, 'bring his own skull home again', but what chance for reputation in those high halls of academia to which he aspired? Like others before and since, his ambition, and the ultimate purpose of his eastwards journey in the first place, had always been to solve the 'origin question' if not of the Magyar race then of the linguistic roots that were his primary philological interest.

Alder and Dalby, in *The Dervish of Windsor Castle*, note a letter in the archives of the Academy that testifies to a payment of forty-three pieces of gold in January 1863, which Arminius would have received on his return from southern Persia. Unless he now undertook the journey he had originally proposed, there were unlikely to be any further grants. Alder and Dalby wonder if the coins had been accompanied by a message from his Hungarian supporters, requesting news of his plan. If so, such a message might have been answered by the letter, recorded in the Academy's archives,[1] written by Arminius on 20 March 1863. In this, he informed the Academy that he was following his plan of travelling to Bukhara via Herat, but then added a bit of theatricality by tearing it open to add a dramatic *PS* in pencil. This was read to the members of the Academy by the secretary, Ladislaus Szalay, and announced: 'I am reopening this letter. A company of Mahommedan pilgrims from Kashgar returning to Mecca, who I met at the Embassy, *have* incognito of a dervish [sic]. If I succeed in this journey, which in its entirety has never been made by a European before, if I am not betrayed, then...' The letter trailed off and, as Alder and Dalby wrote, no doubt had the intended effect of silencing any criticism from his sponsors for the time being.

Arminius had been back in Tehran for several weeks and had discussed his putative travel plans with various contacts. Most of them remained horrified by any thought of Turkestan, where so many had been taken into slavery by the savage Turkoman tribes, including the shah's French photographer Henri de Couliboeuf de Blocqueville, who had been ransomed in 1861 for 10,000 ducats after fourteen months in captivity. Interestingly, de Bloqueville's book[2] about his time with the Turkomans suffers from few

---

1 *Proceedings of the Hungarian Academy* (1863), I/I, 97.
2 Henri de Couliboeuf de Blocqueville, *Gefangener bei den Turkomanen, 1860–1861*, tr. Renate Pfeifer (repr. Nuremberg, 1980).

of the pre-conceptions of the Oriental 'other' that was judged and found wanting by Arminius. It is the work of a fascinated amateur anthropologist, filled with beautiful illustrations and descriptions of Turkmen society that show genuine interest in and curiosity about his captors' lives and culture. Arminius wrote about meeting de Blocqueville, 'a perfect French gentleman', on his return to Tehran after his Central Asian journey. He portrayed the photographer in captivity, 'loaded with irons on neck and feet' and with 'cutlets of horseflesh the greatest culinary delicacy within reach'. According to Arminius he was 'a ready sympathizer' with the 'magnitude' of the false dervish's sufferings (which may have been a case of the perfect French gentleman having manners to match). Charles Alison appears to have been the person who least discouraged Arminius' adventure. It was his astonishing hope that the Hungarian traveller might discover the fate or even the continuing whereabouts of the British Captain Wyburd, who had disappeared mysteriously in Central Asia more than thirty years earlier in 1835.

Captain Wyburd (actually Lieutenant Wyburd of the Indian Navy and the East India Company) had been sent by the British envoy to the court of Persia on a 'highly important and perilous mission to Khiva'. He had apparently disappeared off the face of the earth before reaching his destination. In 1851 his story was recounted in the House of Commons by Benjamin Disraeli as a question 'which, in his opinion, nearly concerned the national honour'.[3] In 1845 it had been reported that the lieutenant, like several other foreigners and Englishmen, most famously Lieutenant-Colonel Charles Stoddart and his idealistic would-be rescuer Captain Arthur Conolly, had been captured by Nasrullah, the ogre-like emir of Bukhara, and put to death. Stoddart and Conolly's executions haunted Victorian imagination and persuaded one of the strangest travellers of all to go to Central Asia. The Reverend Joseph Wolff, the German-born Jewish convert to Christianity who we first met in the introduction to this book, had gone on his own mission to Bukhara in 1843 to find out what their fates had been. He had escaped a similar death to theirs due only to his extreme eccentricity and bizarre behaviour, and his appearance in full canonical dress, which made the emir laugh. He returned home to report definitively on the fates of Stoddart and Conolly and listed 'Captain' Wyburd among the other victims of the emir.

---

3 Hansard, HC vol. 117, cols. 261–8 (30 May 1851).

Wyburd's sisters had petitioned the government to discover more, and in 1848 Wyburd was discovered to be in fact alive, if it was truly him, and a slave of the khan of Khokan (Kokand). The khan had written to the British agent at Peshawar to enquire whether this 'Wypart' was indeed an Englishmen, as attested by the two Persians with him, who said they had formerly been in Stoddart's service, or 'if Russian, that I may punish him'.[4] Follow-up communications between Peshawar and the khan had yielded no further information and several messengers despatched to Kokand over many months had also disappeared. The Wyburd sisters had petitioned for an English officer, whose expenses they were ready to pay, to be sent to investigate, but this request had been declined, and in any case volunteers were predictably thin on the ground. Now they petitioned the House of Commons as a last resort and, although Mr Disraeli was forced to admit it likely that Lieutenant Wyburd was dead, he trusted that steps might be taken 'from this moment, which might bring about a result which the people of England could not fail to view with satisfaction'. However, it was generally agreed in the House that Kokand was nigh-on unreachable and that 'the geographical and political difficulties were almost insuperable'.[5] Could Charles Alison really have hoped that Arminius might get to the bottom of the mystery of Lieutenant Wyburd, so many years since his disappearance and fifteen since he had last been heard of at all?

If Arminius' accounts are accurate, preparations for his journey into the terrifying unknowns of Central Asia now moved on apace. In *Travels in Central Asia*, he dates his first meeting with the 'company of Mahommedan pilgrims' to 20 March, when he wrote his letter to the Academy. He was clearly fascinated by the ragged mendicants who had walked the desert trails and rough by-ways of his Eastern dreams, and who had made, sometimes more than once, the difficult pilgrimage to Mecca. Haidar Effendi, the Turkish ambassador who was again Arminius' host, had acquired a

---

4 Ibid., col. 263.

5 Hansard, HC vol. 116, cols. 1411–12 (26 May 1851). Much sympathy was expressed to the Wyburd sisters, but today's reader of the Hansard account cannot get beyond the note at the end of this short 1851 Commons debate reading, '*subject dropped*', without thinking it the end of their best efforts to discover anything more about their brother. That is underlined by a short account of Lieutenant Wyburd's fate in *The History of the Indian Navy 1613–1863*, which noted his name as being struck off the Indian Navy list on 2 March 1852, backdated to 16 October 1837.

reputation for his generosity in the caravanserais frequented by dervishes and pilgrims. Now they saw that Arminius, the honoured and unusual guest from Constantinople known as Reshid Effendi, with his gift of tongues and quest for knowledge, might himself be a dervish in disguise, and his reputation also grew commensurately. Arminius became, he told his readers, the first port of call for dervish supplicants at the embassy and the first repository for complaints against the Persians. It was in this role that he met the four hajis on 20 March, who were there to complain of the demand for 'Sunni tribute' that had been made of them at Hamadan on their return from Mecca. This, they well knew, was 'displeasing to the Shah' and forbidden by the Ottoman sultan, the caliph and successor to the Prophet in Sunni eyes. The hajis, Arminius reported, requested no recompense but only asked that steps be taken to save future pilgrims from this unlawful molestation. Arminius the Orientalist expressed himself 'much surprised' by 'words so unselfish proceeding from the mouth of an Oriental'. He took a more careful look at his visitors, discovering in them 'something of nobility', despite their ragged clothes and outward barbarity, and questioned them as to their route onwards from Tehran.

Their spokesman, Haji Bilal, in his huge white turban and with a new green *djibbah*, or coat, over his otherwise ragged dress, had been twice to Mecca and was, he told Arminius, the court imam of the Vang, the Chinese governor, of Aksu in Chinese Tartary (now Xinjiang). He and his three companions were the leaders of a group of twenty-four pilgrims, young and old, from Kokand and Kashgar, with 'amongst us no Bokhariot, no viper of that race'. Arminius remarked on the long-standing enmity between the Bukharan Uzbeks and the Tajiks, such as his new friends, who were essentially Persians. Bukhara's reputation stank of blood and corruption, a journey there was a quest to Mordor, and Arminius admitted it was 'the only city in Central Asia that I really feared'. He also realised that these pilgrims, in whom he had perceived a certain superiority of understanding, might be ideal guides through the dangers ahead. Hajis were indeed 'the best travelling companions one can have in Central Asia, provided one can manage to agree with them'. The haji, he wrote later, 'is well supplied, and it was always surprising to me to see how a man who had only one poor donkey he could call his own, could make a display of a separate tea service, pilou [sic] apparatus and carpet when arrived at the station at which we halted'. He found that hajis were also of 'a merry disposition', and that 'the greatest saint and miracle-worker occasionally indulges in a profane joke'.

However, in his typical fashion, now he had to sell himself to them as simply another pilgrim with a great desire to see Turkestan, 'the only source of Islamite virtue that still remained undefiled', and a wish to 'behold the saints of Khiva, Bokhara, and Samarcand', for which purpose he had travelled in the first place from Roum (Turkey). For his readers he explained this deception, noting loftily 'The Oriental does not understand the thirst for knowledge and does not believe much in its existence. The necessity of my position, therefore, obliged me to resort to a measure of policy, of deception, which I should otherwise have scrupled to adopt'. That statement would certainly have surprised the early Chinese scholars and explorers who were some of the first travellers in the region, but the Effendi's yearning for the great shrines of Central Asia struck the right chord with the hajis. They were surprised, but his determination only confirmed their belief that Arminius really was a dervish. They now felt only the need to point out to one used to comfort the hardships of a journey such as this. Bad roads, 'no house, no bread, not even a drip of water to drink', and every chance of being killed, taken prisoner, or buried in a sandstorm. 'Ponder well, Effendi, the step!'

The false dervish did not, he implied, ponder much before denying any need for 'earthly comforts', let alone 'Frankish articles of attire'. He had then immediately to suffer the embraces of his new friends and companions with 'some feeling of aversion to struggle against'. He did not at all like contact with 'those clothes and bodies impregnated with all kinds of odours', but the deed was done and a route agreed for the party through the lands of the hospitable Yomut Turkoman tribes and the great Karakum Desert to Khiva and Bukhara. This would avoid travelling through country terrorised by the marauding Tekke Turkman tribes, 'who would not hesitate to sell into slavery the Prophet himself', but the desert route meant a passage of forty stopping places 'without a single spring of sweet drinking water', an almost equally frightening prospect. On reflection, Arminius was forced to admit to misgivings about his physical strength and his lame leg, not to mention his fondness for the earthly comforts he had so readily denied. When he announced his plan to his refined diplomatic friends, they thought him mad enough almost to require physical restraint.

Haidar Effendi must not only have been a remarkably broad-minded and sophisticated individual but have also formed a high opinion of his guest. Now, in addition to interviewing Arminius' new travel companions himself and committing to their care Reshid Effendi, 'a servant of the sultan', he also gave them fifteen gold ducats – considerable riches 'for people accustomed to live on bread and water'. Then he took a list of names of all the party and delivered himself of a speech stating his disapproval of the emir of Bukhara. Most importantly and extraordinarily, he further represented Arminius as the Haji Mehemmed Reshid Effendi and armed him with a unique 'get-out-of-jail-free' card of talismanic properties that would later unquestionably save his life. This was the authorised passport of the Sublime Porte, in Arminius' assumed name, bearing the *tugra*, the official signature of the sultan, 'an object of pious veneration to the Turcomans'. It is hard to believe that Arminius had not, in exchange, offered the same intelligence-finding services to Turkey as Charles Alison may have suggested to him for Britain. Arminius discovered that the 'simple children of the Steppes', as he called them, who saw the Turks as their Muslim brothers, would come from far and wide just to view the *tugra* and, after the necessary ablutions, press it to their foreheads. In Khiva and Bukhara, where it was better known, the seal commanded even greater respect.

Before Arminius was to set out on 28 March, he had to make his somewhat hectic final preparations. One component of his luggage that he hoped not to have to use was provided by the Austrian Dr Bimsenstein, physician to the Turkish legation. The doctor, after offering his own opinions as to the un-wisdom of Arminius' endeavour, gave him three strychnine pills to be used as a final release from captivity or torture that was beyond endurance. Meanwhile Haji Bilal seems to have been so constant a visitor to the embassy that Arminius became quite nervous he was being seen as a reliable source of extra funds or of merit within the Sublime Porte. Nevertheless, Arminius took instruction from him on the shaving of his head, and on his baggage and dress for the journey. When he had first visited the hajis in their miserable cells in the caravanserai and found these disfigured 'adventurers' busy de-lousing one another, he had seen them as almost destitute beggars. But as he discovered when their journey began, he had mistaken their Tehran apparel – their best city clothes as it happened – for their travelling clothes. He himself was thoroughly overdressed for the journey in comparison with men now clad in no more than 'a thousand rags fastened round the loins by a cord'. They were all introduced by Haji Bilal who recommended his adopted son, Abdul Khader, aged twenty-five, to Arminius as, to all intents and purposes, his servant, which required Arminius to feed the young man too, thus saving his father that expense. He was then given green tea, which he found disgusting, and repaired to the embassy for a farewell dinner where 'the choicest viands were served, and the choicest wines handed round'. He sat in a velvet armchair as the wine turned his face the same colour as his fez. 'A pious dervish and wine – what a frightful antithesis! Tonight, however, I must transgress, the penance will be a long one...'

Early the next morning he joined his new companions at the caravanserai, devoutly grasping his beard and joining the amens as Haji Bilal beseeched the almighty for blessings on their journey. By the following day he was suffering. The rain had poured down for hours; he was damp, dirty, and hungry, having been too fastidious to plunge into the communal wooden bowl from which the hajis, 'splashing about with their fists', had eaten their supper, and he had hardly slept. The pilgrims lay hugger-mugger together and Arminius was constantly beset by close contact with his companions' extremities. One 'stretched out his foot to scratch me behind the ears'. Worst of all was the 'loud snoring of the Tartars' and the 'moaning of the Persian muleteer, who was sadly affected by the gout'. In daytime, Arminius was fascinated by the enthusiasm and energy of his companions – some, like him, on horses or donkeys, others 'who had journeyed on foot from the remotest Turkestan to Mecca, and back again'. They were a mixed lot, young and old, poor, poorer, and poorest, and included fourteen-year-old Haji Abdur Rahman, whose feet had been badly frostbitten in the snow at Hamadan; Haji Sheikh Sultan Mahmoud, from the family of a renowned saint in Kashgar; Haji Kurban, a well-travelled knife-grinder who had been to Constantinople and Calcutta; a former Chinese soldier from a Muslim regiment; and Haji Abdul Kader the Medjzub ('he who is impelled by the love of God'), who foamed at the mouth after he had shouted the name of God two thousand times. Arminius noted 'Europeans name this state epilepsy'. They sang perpetually, talked of their adventures, their homes, and their lives. Arminius, being seen as a less strictly religious *Roumi*, for all his dervish haji credentials, was not expected to join the general chanting of the Quran or hymn singing, but it was not long before he felt able to join in 'by screaming out as loud as I was able,

'Allah, ya Allah!', thus delighting the younger travellers and embellishing his dervish image in the eyes of all his beholders.

He had by now exchanged his almost respectable Tehran clothes with another 'weak and sickly' pilgrim and looked more the part in a felt jacket, 'innumerable pieces of stuff' as an outer garment, with his feet wrapped in rags, and an enormous turban that 'served as parasol by day and pillow by night'. Arminius listed the details of proper dervish dress when he wrote his *Sittenbilder aus dem Morgenlande* in 1877:

> The Dervish's attire is made up of the *Kulah* (hat) and the *Chirka* (coat). This garment can consist of one piece of cloth but it is considered more pleasing to God if it is cobbled together from a multitude of colourful rags. These rags have to be put on top of each other in a colourful haphazard way, sewn together in big stitches with rough string or thick yarn, and in order to award this *Chirkai-Dervishan* the complete image of a beggar's garment the lower end may neither end in a seam or [be] cut straight but has to hang down in a zigzag line and long shreds. '*El fakru fachri*' (poverty is my pride) said the Prophet. The Prophet is reputed to have owned enormous wealth, and as he led, so his disciples acted and spoke. I was once the guest of a religious leader in Central Asia who despite the fact that he owned several houses and estates wore a *Chirkai-Dervishan* with all sorts of rags and shreds, but only on the inside, the outer layer was made up of fine Atlas [wool] and he turned the coat as he pleased or was necessary.

That slight sneer at the end is, one cannot help but feel, typical.

Clothing was one thing, but Arminius quickly began to realise how hard it was to maintain his disguise beyond that outer shell. The veneer of Eastern polish he had acquired in Constantinople had been mere play-acting compared with his present reality. It was all exhausting. The fatigue of travelling was one thing, the stress of playing a part and being the stranger in the company, trying to fit in and ideally to become invisible, was another. There was the constant fear of the consequences of eventual discovery, of giving himself away by some European habit such as gesticulating with his hands. He strapped them to his body in an effort to lose the habit (a measure he described as a 'ridiculous extreme'), and he was fearful of talking in his sleep in a foreign language. He realised his companions would not understand it, but he could not risk drawing less friendly attention than theirs to his oddities. Indeed, one of the hajis had noticed, he said, that Arminius' snoring differed from the Turkestanis, 'whereupon another interrupted and informed him, "Yes, thus people snore in Constantinople"'. In fact, whether his disguise was ever foolproof is debatable. Arminius seems simply to have got away with his dervish image as much as to have inhabited it (although a good covering of dirt no doubt helped smooth over the cracks). And his strangeness was sometimes an advantage. It added an extra layer of mystery to the expected sorcery of a dervish holy man among the nomadic Turkomans and brought commensurate success in begging. Arminius' linguistic skills were enough that he might be believed to be a Turk – he had after all lived and worked in Istanbul for years. His understanding of Islam and knowledge of the Quran were, so he said, enough that he might be a Muslim; but everywhere he travelled, there were those with keener eyes or senses who were, to a greater or lesser extent, uncertain or undeceived. But at the end of the day, he had the sultan's passport and, if his accounts are to be believed, he was simply lucky. That luck was as important to the story of the false dervish, and as important a hook for the popularity of his tale, as his descriptions of the actual travails and triumphs of his journey.

The party travelled north-east from Tehran, through the Alborz Mountains and towards the southern end of the Caspian Sea, on the route that had also been taken by Arthur Conolly through the province of Mazandaran in April 1830. Arminius described the mountainous province as being in its 'gala attire of spring'. The air smelled of wild rose and hawthorn, blossom-covered fruit trees contrasted with dark forest foliage, and wild flowers covered the grass. Conolly however, in his account, had warned that in the summer the damp forest and terraced mountain paddy fields made it a bad area for malaria, while Arminius' companions complained that this paradise should be possessed by hated and heretical Shias. The area was also full of wildlife. They saw tigers by a water source one evening as they set up camp near Zirab in the Alborz Mountains, and Arminius was bothered by thieving jackals, which were quite unafraid to steal his shoes or his provisions. But there was plenty of food to be found too. Arminius could buy ten pheasants for a penny or two. There were so many in the dense woods that they could be killed with sticks and were cheaper to buy than bread. He and his companions ate 'succulent and finely flavoured' roast pheasant for the next few evenings.

Before they reached the last bastion of Shia Persia at Sari, close to the Caspian coast, they passed close to the shrine of Sheikh Tabarsi. Fourteen years earlier this had been the site of a notorious massacre of hundreds of Bàbis (followers of the religious leader the Bàb and progenitors of the Baha'i faith) by the Persian army. The Bàb himself had been shot at Tabriz in 1850. Arminius was impressed by the gardens of orange and lemon trees nearby, but dismissed the Bàb and his followers as delinquent revolutionaries, 'religious enthusiasts who denied Mohammed and preached socialism' and 'made themselves the terror of the neighbourhood'. From Sari, where they had their fair share of insults from Shia locals, the travellers headed for Karatepe, a village of Afghan settlers, on the shores of the Caspian. Here they hoped for a friendly welcome from their co-religionists, who were regular negotiators between Persians and Turkomans over prisoners, and that this would outweigh proximity to those new 'objects of terror', the 'piratical hordes' of Turkoman marauders and slave traders who hid their boats all along the coast.

As Arminius discovered to his irritation, a stay in the village meant an excess of attention from its inquisitive inhabitants, who had heard from his companions of his standing with the Turkish Embassy in Tehran. As many as were able crowded into his room to observe and pass judgement on this odd creature who had been inexplicably and perhaps divinely inspired, *Mashallah*, to make a *ziaret*, or pilgrimage, to the tombs of the saints of Turkestan. Among them was an Afghan, Mir Mohammed, who had been born in Kandahar and now proposed himself as a new travelling companion and guide since he knew 'the country of Ozbeg and Bokhara'. He was to cause Arminius a good deal of trouble. 'A dervish', was his new companion's general view, 'he is not, for his appearance is anything but that of a dervish; the wretchedness of his dress contrasts too plainly with his features and his complexion'. As Arminius continued to travel eastwards, it is likely that his linguistic abilities also let him down in a part of the world where the many layers and forms of 'dervish' life included multiple local dialects and secret languages. These, the best known of which was Abdoltili, were distinct from the mystical languages of the Sufis and more akin to an unofficial argot.[6] Who knows how quickly Arminius the glossophile would have collected

---

6 Alexandre Papas, *Thus Spake the Dervish: Sufism, Language, and the Religious Margins in Central Asia, 1400–1900*, tr. Caroline Kraabel (Leiden/Boston, 2019).

these new vocabularies as he travelled, but it is likely, as he waited on the shores of the Caspian, that the language he spoke belied his rags as much as his soft hands, pale complexion, and eye colour. He was still and very obviously the cultured effendi from Constantinople, or perhaps something even stranger than that. Either way, he was a tremendous puzzle to the ordinary people he encountered.

When the pilgrims heard that they could travel by boat to Ashuradeh, the sandy, low-lying islands at the tip of the narrow Miankaleh peninsula,[7] they were delighted, but there was a problem. Arminius' peculiarity, and rumoured high status as a possible emissary of the sultan, made him a dangerous passenger for the helpful Afghan boat owner. Since 1836 a Russian naval base had been established on Ashuradeh and the Russians, who provided the Afghans with regular business, might well object to him carrying such a passenger. The conditions on this malarial island for those who served there were miserable, but they did control local piracy with reasonable success. On a bright spring day, however, when Arminius saw the island, he remarked on 'the agreeable impression' it produced. That may have been something to do with the sense of safety engendered by Russian 'war steamers' and 'European modes of existence', although he had no wish to be discovered by the Russians. When the mandatory search of the boat for signs of slave trading was undertaken the following day, 11 April 1863, he was careful to hide his face from the Russian sailors. He wrote that he was afraid the Russians might attempt to dissuade him from his course, and more so, that his European identity might be leaked so that he would become a valuable prize to the Turkomans, as de Blocquevillle had been. As it was, he overheard one Russian remarking, 'see how white this haji is'.

Ashuradeh was the jumping-off point for the short steamer journey to Gomushtepe, 'but three leagues off'. The corresponding Turkoman settlement to Karatepe, Gomushtepe lay at the mouth of the Gorganrud River on the eastern side of the Caspian and is today in Iran. Arminius described it 'in form like a hundred beehives lying close together', for it was an encampment

---

7 Guive Mirfendereski writes in his *A Diplomatic History of the Caspian Sea* (New York, 2001) that the three Ashuradeh islands have been part of the Miankaleh peninsula since the early 1930s. Whenever the waters rose in the Caspian they would reappear as parts of the peninsula itself disappeared, but there has been no re-emergence since the 1930s.

of yurts. Arriving at a similar camp thirty years earlier, the Scottish explorer and diplomat Alexander Burnes (1805–41) had made the same comparison with beehives and wrote 'we might also take the children as the bees, for they were very numerous', and he 'wondered at the collection of so many rising plunderers!'[8] Twenty years later, the Irish journalist Edmund O'Donovan added to the village 'half a dozen rude buildings of brick, for which the materials had been taken from the ancient remains about two miles to the north', remains which Arminius would shortly visit.[9] It was a young Turkoman boatman who ferried the hajis in the end, but not without a request for an extra favour from Arminius. We can only imagine that rumours of his high standing were reaching all he met, even if he had escaped Russian discovery. Yakoub, the boatman, was suffering from unrequited love and required thirty drops of attar of roses from Mecca from the hajis, who were known to carry this perfume from the holy city.[10] He wanted this so that, 'a Jew, an accomplished magician', might 'prepare an efficacious *nushka* (talisman)' to win the heart of his girl. Arminius professed himself astonished that 'this son of the desert' should so trust 'the words of the cunning Israelite', but the hajis were able to produce the blessed attar and 'the joy that he displayed was almost childish'. Two days later, the party embarked in a tender made from a hollowed-out tree trunk. This clumsy vessel, in which they were surprised not to drown, carried them safely from the shore through the shallows to the deeper water where their *keseboy*, a form of lugger about twelve metres long, lay anchored.

Arminius was astonished by his first experience of Turkman hospitality in Gomushtepe and, like de Blocqueville, by the beauty of the Turkman women. They rushed to embrace the hajis and argued amongst themselves for the privilege of housing the ragged pilgrims. At last, Haji Bilal, Arminius, and their closest companions were swept off by Khandjan, the headman, to his own tent near the river on the outskirts of the village, where a shackled

8 Alexander Burnes, *Travels into Bokhara: Being the Account of a Journey from India to Cabool, Tartary and Persia* (Philadelphia, 1835), 170.
9 Edmund O'Donovan, *The Merv Oasis: Travels and Adventures East of the Caspian, 1979–1881*, Vol. 1 (London, 1882), 204.
10 In *Sketches of Central Asia* (1868), Arminius wrote that the hajis 'often transact during their pious pilgrimage, a little commercial business'. Commerce and pilgrimage together were not permitted, but 'no Hadji leaves the holy places without making some purchases. At Mekka he lays in a stock of scents, dates, rosaries and combs, but especially water from the sacred well called ZemZem'.

Persian slave brought them a meal of boiled fish and sour milk. Arminius found cause to complain of the water from a river so well-stocked that it smelt of fish, and so did he after washing in it, but he slept well. Arthur Conolly, when travelling this way, had been, like de Blocqueville, disposed to look on Turkman society and surroundings with a more sympathetic and positive eye. He had found water from the same river 'though not clear, sweet and very drinkable when its mud has been allowed to settle', and noted that 'the Toorkmuns swear by it'.[11] The following morning Haji Bilal told Arminius that he had once again aroused local curiosity and was believed to be working for the sultan on a secret anti-Russian mission to Khiva and Bukhara. In this company, association with the sultan was probably a plus, but the haji recommended Arminius should behave more like the true dervish and less like the effendi. If his 'Roumi' background had allowed some latitude in his knowledge of proper dervish propriety further east, he should now understand and play 'the character to its full extent', know the dervish blessings and be ready to extend his hand for alms as was expected, for 'dervishes exist by such acts of piety'. Arminius seems to have followed Haji Bilal's advice in liberally dishing out blessings and talismans and getting his fair share of supplicants and alms. He was, after all, something different, and who could tell? His blessing might also be something out of the ordinary and convey particular merit.

In the immediate absence of a new caravan for the hajis to join for their onward journey, Arminius set out to learn as much as he could about the place and people in and around Gomushtepe. He managed to get on the friendliest terms with the local mullahs. One, Satlig Akhond, thanked providence for allowing him sight of 'a Musselman from Roum' and announced to a questioner that Arminius' pale complexion was the result of 'the true light of Islam' beaming from his countenance. Kizil Akhond, otherwise known as Mullah Murad, was another new friend. He had studied in the *madrasas* of Bukhara, and Arminius set off in his company to visit the territory of two of the Yomut Turkman tribes in the vicinity. Sightseeing was probably not part of the expected habits of a dervish, but Arminius had established his credentials as a scholar by helping Kizil Akhond translate a

---

11 Arthur Conolly, *Journey to the North of India: Overland from England, through Russia, Persia, and Afghanistan* (London, 1834), 43.

Turkish commentary on the Quran. Since then, the mullah had been his guide, and he now took Arminius to see the remains of the extraordinary wall north-east of Gomushtepe[12] known variously as Alexander's Wall, the Great Wall of Gorghan or of Golestan, and the Red Wall, for the bright red colour of its baked mud bricks.

Arminius described the remains of the wall as appearing more like 'a long line of entrenchments, from the midst of which, at intervals of a thousand paces, rise the ruins of ancient towers', all of similar dimensions. So far as Kizil Akhond was concerned (and he was most surprised by Arminius' interest), it had been built by djinns at Alexander's command. 'Alexander', he assured Arminius, 'was a more pious Musselman than we are, and therefore all subterranean spirits, whether they would or no, owed him allegiance'. So much simpler and more satisfactory to involve djinns and the great general than to unravel the tangles of the actual construction history of this possibly originally Achaemenid structure. It had probably been rebuilt by Khusrao I, the 'Deathless Soul' and Sasanian shahanshah, in good Sassanian bricks in the mid-sixth century CE as a defence against the White Huns from the Central Asian steppe. All this was further confused by the real possibility of Alexander's involvement, as he had a track record of building walls, and then there were the Parthians... The Quran mentions a wall built by 'the horned one' – usually considered to be Alexander because of his customary rams' horn headdress – to keep out the giants Gog and Magog. The possible identities of the giants are legion, but they may have been Scythian tribesmen from around the Black Sea.

Throughout its history, the bricks of the wall had been looked upon as a resource by local tribes and plundered for building works. Arminius, as a suitably learned arbitrator, was called on in Gomushtepe to indicate the proper place for the mihrab of the first mosque to be built in the settlement. Probably his ownership of a compass with which to find the proper orientation of the mosque with Mecca was behind this. Likewise, Alexander Burnes had given the vizier of Bukhara a compass – almost unknown in Central Asia at the time – with which he was able to correct the position of the new Grand Mosque then being built. Arminius noticed that the walls of

---

12 The start of the wall today is near the ancient city once known as Hyrcania/Gorgan and now Gonbad-e-Qavus.

the mosque in Gomushtepe were being built without benefit of foundations and doubted the longevity of the construction, although he supposed that would at least stop the Russians using it as a fort when the 'vast designs of the great Macedonian may be turned to account by the rival ambition of a Romanoff'.

The stated purpose of Kizil Akhond's expedition had been to settle a matter of law. It had taken several days as the travellers had to avoid the marshes near the river, where it flooded regularly, and to circumvent hundreds of wild boars. Arminius realised that it was taking longer than strictly necessary when he saw his companion greeted and given presents in one settlement after another, including those of 'hostile tribes' where Kizil was treated with 'honourable distinction'. Arminius too had his share of largesse, including a 'large felt cap, the ordinary headdress of these nomad tribes'. He was also introduced to the mullah's three different wives and their children, in tents in three different places – another reason for the excursion. His haji companions had not approved of this side-track and had been worried when he was away for so long from Gomushtepe, but greeted his return with good news. The khan of Khiva had been advised to drink buffalo milk for his health, and he had sent his *kervenbashi* or caravan leader to Gomushtepe to buy the beasts. It would now be possible for the hajis to accompany this expert guide and his purchases on their return to Khiva. Arminius was keen to move on and, to his surprise, found his companions had been so horrified by the treatment of the Turkmans' Persian slaves in Gomushtepe that they too could not wait to be gone.

As Arminius wrote, there was 'hardly a Turkoman of the better classes near in whose tent the clanking of the chains of a couple of slaves is not heard'. The village headman, Khandjan, had two, one of whom begged Arminius to write to his parents, 'beseeching them, for the love of god, to sell their house and sheep and ransom him'. More slaves were captured almost daily, chained and abused and, if they were not ransomed, sold on to the slave markets of Khiva and Bokhara. The contrast between the Turkomans' barbaric treatment of these captives, their casual dishonesty, and almost vocational determination to commit blatant robbery, with their enjoyment of life, natural friendliness, and generous hospitality to their guests was remarkable. Arthur Conolly had also noticed the 'frank and kind' manner of the Turkmans when he travelled through their lands on his way to Khiva, and had been inclined to think them 'a much-belied people', and 'totally different from what we had been led to expect'.[13] Arminius, however, was witness to the arrival of a group of slaves, some badly injured, including a teenage girl whose mother had been killed by her captor. The woman had been tied to his stirrups and when she became too exhausted to run beside his horse, he had killed her with his sword. Her daughter, a more valuable commodity, had been carried on his saddle. The rest of the wretched captives, among them two young children with their badly wounded father, had been thrown into a tent. Outside, their captor's family amused themselves 'inspecting the booty he had brought home' and the children 'who were jumping about merrily, were trying on the different garments'. There was absolutely no sense of wrongdoing or shame among the Turkomans at this, so far as Arminius could see. He was also an observer to a case where a 'much revered saint in those parts' had collected 400 ducats as a gift for the holy places of Medina. On the arrival of the mullah, who was the saint's courier, at Gomushtepe, rumours spread as to the riches he carried. While he remained outside the protection of a host he was, by the laws of hospitality, fair game for any local brigand. On the outskirts of the village, he was swiftly divested of the money he carried, stripped of his clothes, and left only with his books and papers, which were of no value to his assailants.

The robbers were easily identified; there was no attempt to cover up the crime and they were brought to a Sharia court sitting *en plein air* in a field. The main culprit freely admitted to the robbery but flatly refused to admit wrongdoing. Arminius wrote that he, as the respected holy man from Roum, had been unable to resist speaking up to point out the wickedness of the accused's actions, but to no avail. The man answered him in some perplexity: 'What wickedness? Is robbery punished in thy country? This is strange indeed! I should have thought the Sultan, the Lord of the Universe, was a man of more sense. If robbery is not permitted amongst you, how do the people live?' Threatened with the punishments of hell under Sharia but no more immediate retribution, the robber was unimpressed and went away to spend his ill-gotten gains on new weapons. The mullah had to return from whence he came, 'having learnt from bitter experience that the Turkomans, although calling themselves orthodox, are the blackest Kafirs on the face of

---

13 Conolly, op. cit., 33.

the earth' – *kafir* being a Muslim term for a non-Muslim. The best recourse of the law, Arminius saw, was not to orthodox religious practice but to superstition. When a horse was stolen from another mullah, who was well-known for the excellence of his horses, by Oraz Djan, 'a young, daring and wild looking Turcoman of about eighteen years old', justice came in a more effective form. He was accused 'before the shade of his departed father or ancestor' by the placing of a broken bow on the deceased's grave. The horse was returned during the night, while Oraz Djan told Arminius that its loss would 'pain him for a long time to come but it is better to lie in the black earth than to have disturbed the repose of one's ancestors'.

After three weeks in Gomushtepe, Khandjan began to assist his guests on their onward journey. He introduced the hajis to one Ilias Beg, from Khiva, who made a yearly visit to Gomushtepe with his camels to carry merchandise back across the desert. Ilias Beg agreed to take extra camels, which the hajis could hire for their own transport. Haji Bilal persuaded Arminius to share a camel rather than show himself to be a man of means by hiring one outright. Poverty was the best security in the Turkoman den of thieves. In a few days they were ready to leave, supplied with flour, water and, at Arminius' insistence, for the sake of his lame leg, a *khedjeve*. This contraption was also known to Conolly, who described it as 'open cribs slung loosely on a camel's sides, like panniers', on each side of which a man might sit and which Haji Bilal would share with Arminius.[14] By now Arminius was increasingly impatient to leave for Etrek,[15] effectively the depot for slaves and goods before the journey across the desert to Khiva, and which was considered to be a cursed place by Persians. There, they would rendezvous with the khan of Khiva's *kervenbashi* and his buffaloes, but there appeared to be no great hurry and Arminius' irritation was not soothed by the fatalism of his companions as the tide of dangerous rumours rose about his identity. 'Thou must perforce remain on Gorghen's banks until the Nasib (fate) has decreed that thou should drink water in another place', Haji Bilal told him. It was unlikely, Arminius considered, that the Russians would do other than

---

14 Conolly, op. cit., 51. The great scholar-explorer Ibn Battuta had used something similar during his travels in Khwarezm in the fourteenth century. He described it as a double litter, the second side occupied by one of his companions.
15 Now Gyzyletrek on the Atrak river in Turkmenistan.

---

laugh at the notion of a Turkish plot against Russia and Persia in which he had a major role, but it might lead to his unveiling as a European, should enquiries be made, and to Turkman captivity as a result.

He had also been introduced by Khandjan to an 'old sinner' of 'sombre repulsive physiognomy', Kulkhan the Pir, or Sufi holy man, who came from Etrek and would be Arminius' host in that 'nest of horror'. The old man was thoroughly unfriendly, and it transpired that he had travelled in Russia and Georgia in his youth and had seen Europeans and European ways of life. Now he was surprised by this so-called Turk who looked so European and not at all, as had been described to him, like the Turks who were known to have originated from a Turkman tribe. Haji Bilal, who had lived in 'Roum', said stoutly that he had never observed any difference between Osmanlis and Europeans, but Kulkhan remained suspicious. In Etrek he grudgingly provided Arminius and his closest companions with a tent and tea, and it was there that Arminius discovered the real source of the rumours about him. Before that, however, there was a final hurdle to overcome ahead of their departure from Gomushtepe, as they awaited the arrival of Kulkhan's son from a successful horse-stealing expedition. When eight young Turkmans arrived on the far side of the river and swam the horses across to where most of the village population waited, Arminius could not help admiring the 'splendid spectacle', 'however much I despised their occupation'. The next morning the caravan set off with the stolen horses, Haji Bilal, and those of his companions who had been able to secure camels. The rest, *Inshallah*, would catch up with them at Etrek. It was a journey of only nineteen kilometres and Arminius was lent one of the horses to ride. Unfortunately, Mir Mohammed, the garrulous opium addict Arminius had met in Karatepe, was now firmly attached to the group, claiming a shared space on Arminius' saddle when the going got rough. They hugely entertained the rest of the caravan when their overloaded horse was frightened by a wild pig and they both fell off.

The laden camels could only cover nine kilometres a day, and they had to spend one night in an encampment of Kulkhan's kin. Arminius was amazed by the demands of hospitality that caused their aged host to greet his guests with delight and to kill his only goat to feed them, giving Arminius the roughly cured skin in which to carry his water. The false dervish again complained about the monotony of Turkman food, mainly aging mutton and camel meat, but the hajis fell on their supper in a manner most gratifying to their hosts. A few years later, Captain Frederick Burnaby, in his famous account of his ride to Khiva, commented on 'the culinary compound' that was 'speedily crackling over the embers of our fire' and was 'not a very appetising spectacle, nor a dish that Baron Brisse would have liked to add to any of his menus'. (Léon Brisse was a famously overweight contemporary gourmet.) But, Burnaby added, after a ride across this country, 'I think I could have eaten my great grandfather if he had been properly roasted for the occasion'.[16] On their arrival in Etrek, the hajis were joined by other travellers who were also awaiting the khan of Khiva's *kervenbashi*.

Once again Arminius was impatient to be on the move. His stock of flour was already running low and, although his 'mendicant excursions' in the settlement were successful, he was depressed by the sight of Persian slaves in chains in almost every yurt. He also came across a Russian sailor from Ashuradeh, who had been waiting and hoping to be ransomed by his government for several years, while the Turkmans demanded ever more exorbitant sums. A shipmate had already died in captivity but, despite his awful situation, this man took much too sharp a look at Arminius for his liking. Arminius found the contrast between the hospitality he received and the Turkmans' treatment of their prisoners both hard to compute and the stuff of his own nightmares if he should ever be unmasked as an unbeliever. In a footnote to his *Travels in Central Asia*, Arminius wrote that he later drew Russian attention to the matter of their countryman being ransomed from the Turkmans. The answer, then as now, was essentially no negotiation – paying ransoms would only encourage the kidnappers. Kulkhan, Arminius saw, treated his Persian slaves particularly roughly. Apart from his role as respected elder of the Karaktchi clan of the Yomut Turkmans, he was honoured as a pious sufi, but Arminius described him as 'one of the best-defined pictures of hypocrisy', and neither liked nor trusted him. As he watched Kulkhan 'directing the close cutting of the moustache' according to the holy ordinance, he saw the man as one of those who 'in the confidence of their own piety, were already dreaming of their sweet reward in Paradise!'

Kulkhan also followed the traditions of hospitality to the letter, taking

---

16 Frederick Burnaby, *A Ride to Khiva: Travels and Adventures in Central Asia* (New York, 1877), 172.

care to guard his guests from the enemy Kem clan, who lived close to Etrek and were notable for their thieving, and escorting the hajis to their meeting with the *kervenbashi* on the other side of the Atrek river. There they were happy to find those of their party who had travelled separately, and Arminius was 'compelled to avow' to himself 'his warm attachment to them all, without distinction'. Mir Mohammed, however, was about to cause Arminius new problems and to reveal himself as the source of many of the suspicions about Arminius' identity. The *kervenbashi*, 'a corpulent and good-natured Turkoman' named Amandurdi, was notably unfriendly when Arminius was introduced by Ilias Beg, and 'the crazy opium eater' was found to be the cause. Haji Bilal revealed that 'this wretched sot of an Afghan' had been telling everyone that Arminius, 'who was able to give him instruction in the Quran and in Arabic, was only a *ferenghi* in disguise'. Bilal was outraged that Mir Mohammed was 'representing a pious Musselman as an unbeliever', but Arminius, either then or later, understood what had happened. Mir Mohammed had been born in Kandahar and was living there when the British took the city in 1840 during the First Afghan War. He had been forced to flee and, ever since, had nurtured an abiding hatred for Europeans and especially the English. He had immediately recognised Arminius as a European and furthermore believed him to be an Englishman. He had, not unreasonably under the circumstances, assumed him to be some sort of secret emissary of probable wealth (which might also, relatively speaking, have been the case). His plan for blackmail under threat of public denunciation had been thwarted by Arminius' close attachment to his haji friends and by his dervish persona, while he had further infuriated the would-be blackmailer by counselling him to give up opium. Mir Mohammed was now taking his revenge.

Amandurdi the *kervenbashi* had, 'like all thoroughbred Orientals', Arminius wrote, been open to the enjoyment of 'anything that looked mysterious'. A good conspiracy theory was a bone to be well chewed, and he had been quite ready to believe Mir Mohammed's story. Arminius described the *kervenbashi* as 'of a kind disposition and very clever'. If so, it is hard not to imagine that he also took a close look at this strange, fair-skinned pilgrim and found good reason to wonder who or what he was. Amandurdi was particularly nervous of leading a *ferenghi* to Khiva, he informed Ilias Beg and Haji Bilal, because he had done so once before. This *ferenghi* envoy had

drawn a map of the entire route, and 'with his diabolical art had not forgotten to delineate any well or any hill on the paper'. There are only a limited
number of Europeans who could have travelled to Khiva in the right period
to have been accompanied by Amandurdi. Was the cartographer a Russian
or an Englishman? Rifling through the lists of known names for a culprit is
irresistible, but there were also many who were barely recorded. Whoever
the traveller had been, the khan had been furious and had executed two
men who had given information to this European. Amandurdi had escaped
with his life 'due to the intercession of influential persons'. Now Ilias and
Bilal had to fight against the man's real fears to save Arminius from being
abandoned on the edge of the desert. The false dervish may or may not have
allayed suspicion by keeping his nose diligently in his Quran and remaining
loftily outside the negotiations.

At last, Amandurdi gave in, on condition that Arminius be searched for
any 'drawings or wooden pens, as the *Ferenghis* generally have', and that he
promised to take no notes respecting the route they would follow, on pain
of being left 'in the midst of the desert'. Arminius, with a show of righteous
indignation against 'the malicious Afghan' who had started all the trouble,
agreed to the terms. He admitted, many years later, to thinking quite seriously about using one of Dr Bimsenstein's strychnine pills to rid himself
of Mohammed the troublemaker once and for all, but murder, for all the
bravado he claimed, was not Arminius' game, even if the impossibility of
making proper notes was a problem that would come back to dent his reputation. Members of the Royal Geographical Society in London were to be
distinctly scathing of the lack of a properly drawn map of Arminius' journey,
but he did what he could to make a record unobserved, using the stump of
a pencil hidden among his rags and relying on memory. However, he was
well aware himself of the opportunities he might have had to map the area
properly, and the value of that record to the British in particular.

It is sometimes difficult to trace his likely route in the present day. Arminius' naming of mountain ranges or other landmarks does not always fit with
what appears to be their most obvious translation or identification; names
and spellings have changed between the 1860s and today; and in some cases
his orthography seems to have been phonetic. Amandurdi's caravan to Khiva
would have followed one of several well-trodden routes, including across the
dreadful wastes of the Karakum desert, choosing whichever, based on local

information, seemed safest at the time and the likelihood of water being available. It would also have been important to take the road most suitable for safe delivery of the valuable but infinitely slow buffaloes to the khan. Amandurdi appears to have gone north and slightly east from Gomushtepe, more or less parallel with but inland from the Caspian shore. The caravan turned more directly east at the confusingly named Balkan Mountains,[17] continuing to the Gaplangyr plateau and the salt Sarygamysh Lake, and on to Khiva past the ruins of the fortress at Sasenem.

Arminius' various accounts of his journey, written from his trawl of memories, often appear bleached of the immediacy, colour, and dimension of daily journal descriptions. His near contemporaries who travelled in Central Asia were able to describe on the spot what they saw, felt, smelled, and tasted and the country, climate, and peoples they were among in the most vivid terms. Their interest, sympathy, sometimes humour or horror still springs from their pages. As W. R. Holmes wrote in 1845, in his *Sketches on the Shores of the Caspian*, 'In Committing the following Sketches to press, the Author claims only one merit, that they were written on the spot of which they profess to give a description and that they are a faithful account of what passed under his observation'.[18] Arminius' tale is drier, less highly coloured, and lacks the leavening or embellishment of such on-the-spot reactions. For all his zest for travel and for knowledge, let alone any other motivation for a journey, Arminius always wanted to be seen as the scholarly chronicler searching for empirical data to support academic theories, and not as a swashbuckling adventurer such as Fred Burnaby – the personification of the Victorian imperialist hero, painting technicolour images of other lands for an avid audience at home.[19] But in its time and place, the dervish adventure

---

17 The name may have been brought to the region in the seventh century by Bulgars, when the area was part of the First Bulgarian Empire. In Bulgarian, the archaic word *balkan* (балкан) was borrowed from Turkic and means 'mountain'. It may have ultimately derived from the Persian *bālkāneh* or *bālākhāna*, meaning 'high, above, or proud house'. The name is still preserved in Central Asia in the Balkan Daglary (Balkan Mountains) and by the Balkan Province of Turkmenistan.

18 William Richard Holmes, *Sketches on the Shores of the Caspian* (repr. New York, 1845), iv. Holmes travelled to the Caspian as a young man after staying with his uncle, who was the British consul in Erzurum. Later he was himself consul for Bosnia and was knighted in 1877.

19 In *Journey to Khiva: A Writer's Search for Central Asia* (London, 1992), Philip Glazebrook quotes the Central Asian pundit Charles Marvin on Burnaby, who, 'thanks to the enterprise of

was a good enough story to give its narrator his own celebrity, and it retains its place in the compendium of travellers' tales of a part of the world that has drawn armchair travellers and putative adventurers since Marco Polo and Ibn Battuta first published their travelogues – and perhaps long before that.

The Khiva-bound caravan started off on the *Chil menzili Turkestan*, those infamous waterless forty stations across the Turkestan desert, which Arminius' haji friends told him were far harder than the forty stations from Damascus to Mecca. There, they said, pilgrims were expected; there were cisterns of water, bread, meat, and shade to be had. In Turkestan there was no such support. The traveller was 'in constant danger of dying from thirst, of being murdered, or of being sold as a slave by the tribes'. There were the lesser inconveniences too: being robbed or 'buried alive under the burning sand-storm'. Even the best preparations might prove useless until there was nothing left 'but to strive to get forward as fast as possible, while invoking the name of Allah'. In *Sketches of Central Asia*, written a few years after *Travels in Central Asia*, Arminius had noted criticism of his earlier descriptions of parts of his journey and proposed 'here to make up for my faults of omission' with additional detail. In fact, *Sketches* does not so much give more detail as present a bird's-eye view of the caravan in the desert into which the lens occasionally zooms. In its new encampment, camels have been loosed to graze on summer thistles and the company of travellers is sitting gratefully at rest, their teacups in their hands. Arminius had by now changed his opinion of green tea. It was 'nothing more than greenish warm water, innocent of sugar, and often decidedly turbid' but 'human art has discovered no food, has invented no nectar, which is so grateful, so refreshing in the desert, as this unpretending drink'. 'I still', he wrote, 'have a vivid recollection of its wonder-working effects'. He had also learned, like Burnaby, the real meaning of hunger after a desert march and remembered, 'an enormous appetite covers a multitude of faults, and hunger is notoriously the best of sauces'.

The desert at night was both more romantic and more dangerous than

---

his publisher, and the advertising skill of the proprietors of a certain pill, has acquired a wider renown as a dashing explorer than any other traveller of modern times'. In fact, says Marvin, by the time Burnaby reached Khiva, 'this vaunted exploit was not a whit more remarkable than the visit of an English tourist to the capital of any Indian feudatory prince'.

during the day. Early in the journey, Arminius had been called upon to use the compass that he, uniquely among his companions, had in his possession, when the caravan swerved off its northerly course and the *kervenbashi* feared they were too close to dangerous marshes. A few nights later the *kervenbashi* fell asleep as the caravan came to the foot of the Little Balkan Mountains, and the camels followed their unreliable noses right into a quaking salt marsh. When Amandurdi realised what had happened, the whole caravan was forced to stop and barely dared breathe on the shaking ground for the three hours until daylight. They were almost overcome by sulphurous fumes before they could find a safe way out. Arminius felt considerable sympathy for the heavily loaded camels, struggling through dry sand that gave way under their feet even when this meant he had to dismount and walk, when he complained of his own suffering with his lame leg. His ability to find the path with his compass improved his standing with the *kervenbashi* no end, and Arminius reported that he now 'loaded me with politeness'. When camp was set up at night, he found the presence of the camels, who lay in a circle around the encampment and alerted it to any outside presence by 'a dull rattle in the throat', a reassuring if smelly presence as they farted their way into the travellers' dreams.

Arminius noticed where wildfires had run out of control in the hot season, and they all saw extraordinary mirages of 'cities, towers and castles, dancing in the air', with 'individual gigantic forms which continually disappeared from one place to reappear in another'. His companions said they were the ghosts of men and cities once existing in that place. The *kervenbashi* said they were always seen in the same places and Arminius believed they related to legends of a lost civilisation in the desert. He did not believe such legends of 'these Asiatic steppes [which] were always, as far back as the memory of man goes, howling wildernesses', and quoted 'a central Asiatic' saying that 'God created Turkestan and its inhabitants in his wrath; for as long as the bitter, saline taste of their springs exist, so long will the hearts of the Turkomans be full of anger and malice'.

The character of the Turkmans was certainly complicated. One of Arminius' companions told the tale of a haji who had dressed himself properly in his poorest rags to go begging and had found himself at nightfall by a lonely tent, where he asked to spend the night. His host was embarrassed and requested, 'deeply blushing', a few *krans* with which to provide his guest some better food than the dried fish that was his only store. Food was found, dinner eaten, the softest carpet offered for the guest to lay his head, and, in the morning, he went on his way with the customary farewell honours. After little more than an hour, the mendicant saw a man running towards him who immediately, 'with violent threats', demanded his purse and all his possessions. To his astonishment the haji recognised his host of the night before, and realising that the man was not joking, handed over his purse, comb, knife, and a little tea – all his worldly goods. His second shock came when the robber opened the purse and handed him back the five krans he had taken for food the night before, saying 'Take my debt of yesterday evening. We are now quits and you can go on your way'. Alexander Burnes' caravan, heading through Turkestan towards the Persian border and Mashhad in 1831–2, had encountered similarly contradictory behaviour, when the travellers stayed 'among thieves to avoid the thieves abroad'. After an enforced ten-day stay in a Turkman village, they were permitted to leave on agreeing that they would pay a local tax on completing the first stage of their journey. However, almost as soon as the caravan started, they were stopped by their Turkman escort and a payment demanded on every camel for escort to the frontier, after which the escort went back to the village themselves.

'The howling wilderness' could also be contrary. Apart from encampments that must be checked to see which of the tribes, friendly or otherwise, might inhabit the anonymous yurts, there were signs of ancient life and of death that was sometimes more recent. There was a pause in the journey while one of the travellers searched among a group of grave mounds for that of his brother. He had died the previous year during a fight with Turkmans intent on the kidnap of a wealthy Persian merchant who had been under his protection in another caravan to Khiva. A day or two later, on 16 May, as the Kopet Dag mountains came into view, the caravan slowed down near a Turkman encampment for the sake of one of the buffaloes, who was in calf and about to give birth. Once it had been established the camp belong to friendly Yomut Turkmans, a rest day was decreed, during which more camels could be acquired from the nomads. Arminius had meanwhile spotted 'a single pillar, which from the distance produced upon the eye the effect of an animated colossal figure', followed by another, a little closer to the mountains. These structures, Arminius discovered (or perhaps he already knew) were known as the ruins of Meshedi Misriyam (now Mashhad-i-Misrian) and had also been mentioned by the unfortunate Arthur Conolly as an area where there was holy ground in which burials might take place. In fact, the ruins had been the major trading city of Misrian, capital of the fertile region of Dekhistan near the Caspian, between the tenth and fourteenth centuries CE. It was on the important caravan route from Hyrcania/Gurgan to Khiva and the Khwarazm region. A little to the north of the city, in the Mashhad/Meskhet cemetery, twenty mausolea had survived into the nine-teenth century, of which five still stand today. There were also much earlier Bronze Age sites in the area but, while the caravan route remained the same when Arminius saw the ruins of the city as it had been when Misrian was an economic centre, the desert had taken over and the ruined city, once protected by a double row of walls, was now the abode of djinns.

Arminius was determined to take a closer look, but the ruins were girded with superstition and it was only with difficulty that he persuaded Ilias and a few others to join him. Arminius was convinced the ruins were Greek due to their construction in bricks identical to those of 'Alexander's Wall'. The sanctity of the area was probably vested in a fable that had reinvented part of the ancient remains as the ruins of the Kaaba, which had first been placed in Turkestan by God because of his misplaced love for the Turkmans. Unfortu-nately for those chosen people, Goklen – a lame devil who was either blue or green – had pulled the Kaaba down and God had picked it up and carried it off to safety in Mecca. This was why the Goklen Turkman tribe, descend-ants of that devil, lived in perpetual hostility with the Yomuts. That night, the buffalo cow delivered her calf, to the delight of the *kervenbashi*, and it was placed for the journey into Haji Bilal's place in the *khedjeve* opposite Arminius. He took a decidedly hard-hearted line when the calf, a very smelly and restive companion, died in the extreme heat on 18 May. There were two more weeks of travel expected before the caravan could reach Khiva, and these would be the most uncomfortable so far. Ahead there were only 'four wells of bitter salt water' and it was unlikely that they would 'encounter a single living human being'. It was early enough in the year that the travellers might hope to find some sitting rainwater, but that would be on the other side of the great Balkan Mountains, more than two days' journey away.

7

Khiva

The route chosen by the *kervenbashi* through the Karakum Desert led across what the local people believed to be the old bed of the legendary river of antiquity, the Oxus, or Amu Darya. (The river was thought to have changed direction from its route near Misrian in protest against its destruction by the wicked Goklen).[1] Arminius, with his compass, was also aware that the caravan's chosen path would bring it close to areas where the feared Tekke Turkmans were believed to camp. He was not encouraged by the issuing of weapons but was careful to note for posterity that, 'as one having most heart', he received a good share of firearms and ammunition. On 22 May the caravan camped at 'Yeti Siri', a place Arminius tells us had been named for the seven wells that were once there. Only three remained, with salty and stinking water, but this was where the *kervenbashi* hoped to find rainwater. A search that evening failed to produce a drop, but the searchers followed human footprints to a cave where they found the Ben Gunn-type figure of a man dressed in skins. For years, he had been hiding in the desert to escape a blood feud after he had murdered his stepfather, who had killed his father. If this excitement took the travellers' minds off the need for water, it was not for long. Arminius had the sense to boil the bad well-water before mixing a little of it

---

1 The truth, unknown to nineteenth-century travellers, was that this dry riverbed had probably never been part of the Oxus but was the relic of another waterway, the Uzboy, a drain for Sarygamysh Lake. Ekaterina Pravilova (tr. Timothy Portice), 'River of Empire: Geopolitics, Irrigation, and the Amu Darya in the Late XIXth Century', *Cahiers d'Asie centrale*, 17/18 (2009). That being said, the Amu Darya (Oxus) has changed direction any number of times over the millennia and those changes, like those of other great rivers, have brought about the births and deaths of cities such as Misrian and whole civilisations that grew along their banks.

with his bread and eating it; but others had drunk it straight and, he wrote (rather smugly), were suffering the consequences. Most of the travellers had also been lubricating the unleavened bread they made each day over camp-fires with personal stores of mutton fat, which Arminius eschewed in case it should increase his thirst. Whether this made him hungrier or healthier than his companions, it must certainly have made him different, but perhaps nobody noticed at this stage. The main concern was always water, as the sun beat down and the deep sand grew unbearably hot under foot.

Arminius was both hopeful and depressed by a sidetrack to a pilgrimage site, 'Kahriman Ata', which the *kervenbashi* felt could not be passed without due reverence. The shrine was probably that of the fourteenth-century sufi Gozli Ata, upon whose triple-length grave, covered with the rams' horns so typical of Central Asian cemeteries, Arminius collapsed with exhaustion. Like other saints of Central Asia whose bodies rest in tombs of astonishing length, Gozli Ata was known to have been a giant and had defended the local wells against the evil spirits who threatened to block them with stones. The thought of wells put new heart into the traveller, but the only water was another icy, brackish pool that smelt too bad to drink. The consequences of drinking bad water might immediately be deadlier than its lack, but Arminius was lucky again. That night there was a heavy rainstorm and, in the morning, there were pools of rainwater from which to fill every possible vessel. The fears of the day before vanished and that evening, Arminius remembered, the caravan camped in what sounds like another mirage: 'amidst small lakes set in frames of verdant meadows'. From here on, the *kervenbashi* told the travellers, they were safe from the Tekke Turkmans and the next day the caravan reached the Gaplangyr plateau, the border of the khanate of Khiva, covered in vegetation and populated by gazelles and huge herds of wild asses. There were also nomad camps where Ilias the *kervenbashi* had friends and was able to procure meat, bread, and *koumiss*, the slightly alcoholic fermented mares' milk that is the beer of the Central Asian nomads.

At the 'Shor Gul' (apparently a salt lake, but one that is difficult to identify today from Arminius' description),[2] there was a stop while the hajis

---

2 Arminius wrote of this lake as being twelve 'English' miles long. It seems most likely that it was either the vastly bigger Sarygamysh salt lake which is about 120 km (75 miles) long, or some smaller nearby body of salt water that has since dried up altogether.

undertook the *ghusl*, the prescribed ablution of the whole body. They then dressed themselves in clean shirts, which Arminius was surprised to see come out of their packs. He possessed no such finery and declined Haji Bilal's offer of a loan in order, he wrote, to maintain the appearance of filthy poverty that was his best disguise. This had been greatly improved by the ritual ablutions in the sand that the Prophet had prescribed for travellers when water was lacking and had, he believed, also been protection against the sun. Now, he told his companions, he would not change his clothes 'until the Khan of Khiva should dress me'. He observed that his friends now 'looked really like gentlemen' as signs of civilisation began to appear on the camel route. There were scatterings of tents and people, an abandoned village of mud huts, and a deserted fort, its high walls visible from far away, where the travellers spent the night. On 30 May they reached an Uzbek village at the end of the desert, where the hajis successfully plied their mendicant business and Arminius noticed 'some articles coming from the beloved west', which delighted him. Four days later, he entered Khiva, the hajis greeted at the gates by happy crowds from all corners of the city, who kissed their hands and feet and even Arminius' filthy rags, 'as if I had been some first-class saint or had just descended from heaven'. He thought at first that Khiva only appeared as beautiful as it did in contrast with the endless emptiness of the desert, but no, he decided, it was better than that: 'the environs of Khiva, with its small *havlis* [town houses], in the form of strongholds shaded by lofty poplars, with its fine meadows and rich fields, seem to me still, after I have visited the most charming countries of Europe, as beautiful as ever'. Even the capital city of the khanate of Khiva, the place we know as Khiva today, made a 'tolerably favourable impression when seen at a distance', with its domes and minarets.

The views of new arrivals into the city of Khiva, throughout its long history as an important trading stop on the silk routes, have naturally been influenced by the circumstances of that arrival. It is doubtful that the Persian or Russian slaves, harried across the desert in shackled lines to their fate in Khiva's slave market, formed any favourable impression of the city's delights. The observations of other foreigners, usually still under some or other compulsion, were also influenced by the seasonal miseries of extreme cold or heat, the fleas, a staple diet of pilaf swimming in fat-tailed sheep's fat, and the level of fear about their reception by the ruling khan, the 'Father of the conqueror of heroes, the father of victory, the King of Khaurism'.[3] When Frederick Burnaby arrived in Khiva in 1876, he was met by the poet-khan, Muhammad Rahim II, who was cultured and charming. By that time Russia had conquered Central Asia, and Khiva was a semi-independent protectorate. Burnaby was 2 metres tall (6 foot 4 inches) and weighed 130 kilos, or 20 stone. His appearance transfixed the people; he must have seemed an almost mythic figure, one of the giants of legend and worth befriending. But other visitors, such as Captain (later General Sir James) Abbott, on an official British mission in 1840, had met earlier khans and had known as he entered the walled capital that this was the lion's den from which he might not emerge. The khans' power was limited by no law other than that of the Quran, and even that was debatable. Khan Allah Quli (r. 1825–42) had informed Abbott that he had executed his last two European visitors, who had claimed to be English but, he was certain, had been Russian spies. Whether the one or the other nationality was more or less likely to mean survival was a moot point. Abbott's mission was to stop the Russian invasion of Khiva by an army that had already set out from Orenburg, on the border with Kazakhstan, to annexe the khanate on the pretext of freeing large numbers of Russian slaves. The tsar would thus also gain that important toehold in Central Asia so determinedly opposed by the British – already fearful of Russian eyes turned towards India. Khiva was a hotbed of rumour, counter-rumour, and an unsurprising misunderstanding of Europe, European politics, geography, and demography. The khanates of Khiva, Kokand, and Bukhara, ruled by men who might be capricious, cruel, and duplicitous, were also at almost permanent loggerheads, a situation confused further by feuds and changing alliances between the nomadic Turkman tribes.

When Abbott reached Khiva in January 1836, Colonel Stoddart was already imprisoned in Bukhara and the life of anyone suspected of enmity or designs on any one of the independent khanates was easily forfeit, especially if they were a foreigner. Abbott did not neglect to take careful note of what he saw, observing 'the appearance of the country is pleasing but it is too flat for beauty'. He ate pheasant and 'the most delicious melons in the world', and wondered 'Was I really at Khiva, that capital so famous and yet so little

---

3 Sir James Abbott, *Narrative of a Journey from Heraut to Khiva, Moscow, and St Petersburgh During the Late Russian Invasion of Khiva* (London, 1843), 106.

known, of which half the existing accounts are fabulous?'[4] He managed to overcome most of the khan's suspicions that the British were only another Russian clan and (as had been suggested to the khan by some of his close advisors) that Abbott was a Russian spy. But he was essentially a prisoner during his time in the capital, confined to one room where he suffered the 'searchingly cold' air of the Khivan winter and where 'if a door was left open, the passage of the wind was detected, as it blew over any liquid, by its sudden conversion to a solid form'.[5] Allah Quli was fascinated by the West and asked wide-ranging questions about everything, from life in Britain, its government, Queen Victoria, the political divisions of Europe, and the pertinent issues of Russian and British policy in Afghanistan and India, to the telegraph, naval warfare, magic, sea monsters, angels, and djinns. Abbott knew his life was subject to the whim of the khan and, like earlier missions, both his own and the planned Russian invasion of 1839–40 led by General Perovsky failed. Later, in the spring of 1840, another British officer, Lieutenant Richmond Shakespear, arrived from India to pick up with Allah Quli where Abbott had left off, and with remarkable success. He found the khan to be 'a good-natured and unaffected person'[6] and somehow persuaded him to part with 416 Russian slaves, who he personally delivered to the commandant of the Russian fort of Alexandrovsk on the Caspian. He went home to Britain to a hero's welcome and a knighthood.

Khan Seid Mohammed, who sat on the Khivan throne when Arminius arrived in the capital, included amongst his previous experience of visitors one Count Ignatiev, who had visited in 1858. Ignatiev, a graduate of the Corps of Pages and godson to the tsar, was an expansionist imperialist and proponent of Pan-Slavism. He had briefly been military attaché at the Russian Embassy in London, where he had taken care to study the details of British military equipment in 'order to clarify all the military and

---

4 Ibid., 70–3. The watermelons of Khwarezm with their green rind and red flesh had been described by Ibn Battuta five hundred years earlier as having 'no equal in any country of the world, East or West, except it may be the melons of Bukhara'. He also noted an international export business in sun-dried melon strips, packed in reed baskets, 'to the remotest parts of India and China'. Tim Mackintosh-Smith (ed.), *The Travels of Ibn Battuta* (London, 2002), 140.
5 Sir James Abbott, op. cit., 77.
6 Richmond Shakespear, 'A Personal Narrative of a Journey from Heraut to Ourenbourg, on the Caspian in 1840', *Blackwood's Edinburgh Magazine*, 51 (June 1842).

political intentions of our enemies in Asia as well as in Europe'.[7] He had been removed from his post after he was caught red-handed, pocketing a newly developed cartridge from a display. Such initiative met with the tsar's approval and Ignatiev had been the choice to lead a mission to Khiva and Bukhara sent out in answer to invitations by their rulers, who had both attended Tsar Alexander II's coronation in 1856. Ignatiev's aim was to discover the possibilities for navigation of the Amu Darya and gain permission for its use by Russian ships, which would open up the region to Russian trade all the way from the Aral Sea to Afghanistan. The additional and undeclared intention of the mission was 'the destruction of the harmful interference of the English, who are trying to penetrate Central Asia and lure it into their sphere of influence',[8] with the intention of ultimately gaining the Russian subordination of the region. The history of Russian involvement in Central Asia, of British attempts to subvert or counteract Russia's efforts, and the constant fervour of Arminius Vambéry's Anglophile/Russophobe stance will be explored later in this book. For now, we may imagine Arminius' delight at reports of Ignatiev's less-than-satisfactory reception in Khiva by Khan Seid Mohammed, the sadistic and fanatical much younger half-brother of Allah Quli. Ignatiev was to write later:

> Our situation in Khiva from the very beginning of our visit was extremely uncomfortable. Under pain of execution it was forbidden for the local inhabitants to visit us or even to speak with us… We were put under guard and kept under arrest. Armed Khivans guarded our living quarters… They were with us day and night inspecting us through the windows or openings in the ceilings.[9]

Moreover, Ignatiev's embassy had to deal with a hostile population who cursed them, played drums and loud music outside their quarters, and made threatening gestures at them. The Russians were convinced they would all be murdered, much like the ill-starred embassy of Alexander

7 Professor John L. Evans (ed. and tr.), *Mission of N.P. Ignat'ev to Khiva and Bukhara in 1858* (Newtonville, MA, 1984), 22.
8 Tsarist documents quoted in Kathleen Hopkirk (ed.), *Central Asia Through Writers' Eyes* (London, 2013), 144.
9 Evans, op. cit., 80.

Bekovich-Cherkassky, sent to Central Asia by Peter the Great in 1717. Ignatiev's negotiations constantly stalled in an atmosphere of misunderstanding
and the total ignorance of the khan and his court of the outside world.
Khan Seid Mohammed also lived in constant fear of plots against his own
life. (He had good reason, after the mysterious deaths of his two immediate predecessors.) Ignatiev was correct in thinking the khan quite capable
of slaughtering possible enemies on the slightest pretext, even though he
understood the danger of conflict with Russia. As the situation became ever
tenser, in an atmosphere already heightened by conflict between the Uzbek
ruling classes and the Turkmen tribes and made yet more perilous by a
famine and a cholera epidemic, Ignatiev realised his embassy was doomed to
failure. The khan declared eternal friendship with the tsar but flatly refused
Russian navigation of the Amu Darya, and the longer the embassy stayed in
Khiva the less likely it seemed they would survive to leave it. Nobody slept
at night and on 28 August 1858, after six weeks in the city, Ignatiev led his
people out of the gates towards Bukhara, writing in a despatch 'I am leaving
with what I arrived with. Let that remain an open and basic pretext for our
activity next year. So our relations with Khiva are as they were before, impossible and humiliating'.[10]

Arminius might have applauded such a diplomatic rout, that so slowed
Russian progress into Central Asia, but the city he entered five years later was
still ruled by Seid Mohammed and the khan's character had not improved.
He also took note of the bad relations between the settled Uzbeks and the
Turkmans, who had an aversion 'to everything in the form either of house
or government'. Despite the nomads living cheek by jowl with the Uzbeks
for centuries, they detested their manners and customs and avoided their
company and, 'although of kindred origin and tongue, an Ozbeg is as much
a stranger in their eyes as a Hottentot is in ours'. As he rode towards the
caravanserai where the hajis were obliged to register their arrival, Arminius
wrote, 'the reader will easily imagine in what a state my spirits were'. He
was all too aware of the character of the khan, who was 'in the habit of
making slaves of all strangers of doubtful character', or worse. At the caravanserai his evil genie, the Afghan Mir Mohammed, gave the false dervish
another bad moment. As the *mehrem*, the khan's chamberlain, questioned

---

10 Ibid., 90.

the *kervenbashi* about his caravan, Mir Mohammed shouted 'we have brought three interesting quadrupeds and a no less interesting biped'. The buffaloes, not seen before in Khiva, must have caused a sensation, but the biped was Arminius, and it did not take long for the whispers of *djansiz*, spy, *urus*, Russian, and *ferenghi* to begin and for the *mehrem* to take an interest. Arminius was rescued by one of the hajis who 'represented me in the most flattering colours to my inquisitor', allowing Arminius to assume an attitude of offended dignity and escape the scene. He also had a card up his sleeve in the name and form of Shukrullah Bey, who had been the Khivan ambassador in Constantinople for ten years and who he felt certain of convincing of his own 'Stambouli' credentials.

Shukrullah Bey had by this time retired to live in the *madrasa* of Mohammed Amin Khan, which had been built in Khiva only a few years earlier.[11] The city of Khiva is nearly 2,500 years old (much older if the myth of its founding by Shem, one of the sons of Noah, is to be believed). It was famed for its crafts, was an important trading point on the silk routes, and has continually risen again after conquest, destruction, or straightforward neglect. From the second half of the eighteenth century, it had also become notorious for the horrors of its slave market and its terrible rulers. Today, much of Khiva (now a restored World Heritage site and largely a museum city) is similar to that which Arminius would have found, then almost newly built under the Qungrat khans and far more heavily populous than the city today. Philip Glazebrook, in his 1992 *Journey to Khiva*, wrote disappointedly of Khiva in its last days as part of the USSR, as lacking 'that unbroken cord of authenticity' that must have been almost too apparent to nineteenth-century visitors, living there in fear of their lives. Instead, it was, and is, a stage-set. There is beauty, but the spirit of the place has disappeared with the dirt that Arminius would so have abhorred, along with the grubby twisting lanes, blank walls, bustling traders, slaves, and whispering spies of earlier days. 'One of the most dangerous cities in the world for a European to enter', until its conquest in 1873, can now only be summoned from old accounts such as those quoted in this chapter.[12]

---

11 Now the Orient Star Hotel.
12 Philip Glazebrook, *Journey to Khiva: A Writer's Search for Central Asia* (repr. New York, 1992), 197.

Arminius did not comment on the strangely truncated but beautifully tiled Kalta Minar that stands beside the Amin Khan *madrasa* in one of the most famous vistas in the city, but he described the *madrasa* itself as 'the finest edifice in Khiva'. Shukrullah Bey, who had been informed of the visit of an effendi, was staggered to find a ragged mendicant in front of him but delighted to hear the authentic 'Stamboul dialect' and quite ready to fall in with Arminius' suggestion that the two had been slightly acquainted in the Ottoman capital. He was also, Arminius wrote, ready to believe that Arminius was a Naqshbandi dervish on a pilgrimage to Bukhara, or at least happy enough for the sake of news of old friends and acquaintances from Constantinople to take his cue. Arminius turned down the old bey's invitation to stay at the *madrasa* but now had his introduction to the khan secured. With the insurance of the sultan's passport, which would command the respect of the ruler, he should have felt more secure as he made his way to the dervish *toshebaz*, the lodgings for holy men, where his travel companions had taken a cell for him. The next day, he was visited by an official from the court bearing a gift and the order to go to the Ark, the royal palace, that evening, as the khan wished to receive a blessing 'from a Dervish born in the Holy Land'. Shukrullah Bey accompanied him, warning Arminius that he himself was in bad odour with the *mehter*, the khan's minister of the interior, who feared the former ambassador might be a rival. Arminius found the *mehter*, surrounded by his officers, in an outer hall of the Ark where crowds waited, like petitioners in a medieval court, for a royal audience. The *mehter* was a Sart (a person of Persian origin who has settled in Central Asia) with a beard to his waist and the ubiquitous enormous shaggy sheepskin Khivan hat. Arminius noticed, to his satisfaction, that the crowds gave way on all sides to the dervish, although the *mehter* was clearly laughing with his companions at this ragged Ottoman envoy. He showed his respect, however, for the office of the sultan by taking Arminius' passport and, before he carried it to the khan, rubbing the *tugra* reverently against his forehead.

Arminius was not impressed by the Ark. Later he wrote of the 'love for ostentation and empty splendour, the glitter of gold and diamonds of oriental life', with regard to the palaces of Constantinople and, so far as he knew, of 'Pekin and Yedo'. In Central Asia, he cautioned his readers, they should not 'expect either to be dazzled or to have their amazement and admiration excited'. He admired the ornamentation on the cannons at the entrance to the Ark, brought thither by Nadir Shah when he invaded Khiva in 1740 and made, Arminius assumed, in Delhi; of the palace buildings however, surrounded by a double wall and 'strangely fortified', he took a dim view. The residence of the khan resembled a poor mud hut, without windows, with no 'particular luxury to be met with inside' apart from several valuable carpets, and with very few rooms and no 'signs of splendour perceptible'. The khan's majesty was signified mainly by his large number of retainers, from the *desturkhandji*, the spreader of the tablecloth, to the *sertarash*, the barber, and not neglecting the *ternaktshi*, the nail cutter, or the *djigadj*, the keeper of the plumes, who walked at the head of the train of servants. The khan wore the same sheepskin hat and heavy boots as all the male population of Khiva, and the same padded silk coats winter and summer, in 'a state of fearful perspiration'. 'On the whole', Arminius considered 'the position of the Prince of Kharezm[13] one little to be envied'. In hindsight, he had some sympathy for a sovereign who had 'to maintain his authority, by inspiring his subjects with the utmost dread', but at the time, when entering the royal presence, Arminius suffered a dose of dread himself. He wrote: 'No European can realise what it is to stand, a disguised Ferenghi, this word of terror to the Oriental, face to face with such a tyrant as the Khan of Khiva and have to bestow upon him the customary benediction'. When he returned to his haji companions and took stock, he admitted his relief that Seid Mohammed, who (he declared, dramatically) 'presents in every feature of his countenance, the real picture of an enervated, imbecile and savage tyrant', had treated him 'in a manner so unexceptionable'.

He had entered the open-air hall of public audience, where the khan sat on a dais above the crowd, preceded by Shukrullah Bey, who introduced him as an acquaintance of all the most important pashas in Constantinople. After the proper prayers and greetings, punctuated with beard stroking, Seid Mohammed questioned Arminius about his journey, his view of the desert, the Turkmans and Khiva, and about his plans. Arminius perjured himself successfully in answering that the perils and pains he had survived had been richly rewarded by the sight of his majesty's beautiful presence. Attempting to speak Uzbek instead of Ottoman Turkish, he thanked Allah that he

---

13 Khwarazm is an oasis region of Central Asia watered by the Amu Darya, of which Khiva was an important part. It is now partly in Turkmenistan and partly Uzbekistan.

had been 'allowed to partake this high happiness and discern in this special favour of Kismet, a good prognostic for my journey to come', and assured the khan that he needed nothing when the holy breath imparted by the head of his dervish order could 'support me four of five days without any nourishment'. The khan's instruction that he should be given twenty ducats and a good stout ass was refused in the case of the money, for it was a sin, Arminius chided the khan, for a dervish to keep money. However the dervish at the same time found enough nerve, under these promising circumstances, to point out that holy writ prescribed a white ass for pilgrimages and to request that such a one should be guaranteed.

News of his favourable reception spread quickly, and the dervish found himself in demand, forced to accept endless invitations and requests for blessings or for that sustaining holy breath. This was particularly efficacious in the case of women who came to his door suffering from heat and over-work in their high headdresses, 'muffled in large gowns' and with heavy boots on their feet. Arminius did not neglect to point out their beauty as compared with Persian women, whatever he thought of their clothes. Invitations always involved eating, and he was horrified to be forced to eat from huge dishes of rice swimming in fat before sunrise and the morning prayer, and then again and again throughout the day. His haji companions managed to stuff themselves cheerfully with vast quantities of food and wash it down with 'from fifteen to twenty large soup plates full of green tea'. At least he found that it was considered quite respectable in the summer only to wear a simple long shirt to walk about the city, if it was spotlessly white. His dervish services were presumably proving profitable. He was also beset by questions about religion and about the sultan, who was imagined 'as a Musselman, whose turban is at least 50 ells in length, whose beard extends below his breast and his robe to his toes'. Arminius did not think the truth of the matter, that Sultan Abdulaziz wore his head and beard shaved and had his clothes made by a Parisian tailor, was likely to meet with much favour or comprehension. Worse still, 'how much Chateau Lafitte and Margot [sic] garnished the sovereign's table in the reign of Abdul Medjid!' Meantime the gardens of the mosques, he found, were a delightful place to loiter in the summer heat and he also met Haji Ismael, who had spent twenty-five years in Constantinople and who maintained a memory of Arminius' father, a mullah in the Topkhane district (at least, so he said). Haji Ismael had a reputation as a magician and chemist, and had survived prescribing an unsuccessful medicine to the khan for his impotence. He had merely been sacked, but had sensibly declined the khan's later efforts to reinstate him after his female successor, who had prescribed 500 doses of a medicine which had 'a directly contrary effect', had lost her head. The buffalo milk was the most recently suggested remedy.

Arminius and his companions were so successful in Khiva with their 'Hadji business' that Arminius was to proclaim 'the Khivan Ozbeg, although but rough-hewn', the 'finest character of Central Asia'; but trouble was brewing. The *mehter's* scheming against Shukrullah Bey had dragged Arminius back to the notice of the khan, with insinuations that he was a sham dervish. Arminius survived a calligraphic test of his authenticity by appealing to the vanity of the ruler with an immaculate aphorism, but was given a demonstration of the fate of those who broke the khan's law or were his prisoners of war. He saw a group in a courtyard, divided into young men who would be sold as slaves, and old, who were to be punished by execution or mutilation. Eight old men were bound hand and foot and laid on the ground where their eyes were gouged out by the executioner, who wiped his knife clean on each beard in turn. Arminius believed this mass retribution was unusual. The prisoners, from the Tchaudor tribe, were being punished for a shocking attack on a rich caravan the winter before, when the robbers had left their victims to die in the frozen desert. Only eight out of sixty in the caravan had survived. Generally, the khan was more interested in punishing crimes against religion, for which there was a daily toll of ingenious punishment – for example, in this stone-free place, the instrument for the standard stoning of women accused of adultery was hard balls of mud. When Arminius was taken to the treasury to collect the stipend for his stay (ordered by the khan and apparently acceptable to the dervish), he encountered a new form of barbarity. The treasurer was engaged in arranging *khilats*, robes of honour given by the khan to his meritorious subjects. They were ornamented in bright embroidery, the level of ornamentation varying according to different levels of merit. The following day, Arminius was witness to their specific values as symbols of service to the khan when a horde of dusty horsemen arrived in the main square with strings of prisoners. A sack, tied to each saddle, turned out to be full of severed heads. The riders, 'taking hold of the two sides of the one end, spilled their contents on the ground as one does with potatoes'. The heads were then carefully counted by the treasurer and a receipt issued with which the rider could claim the correct *khilat* for four, twenty, or forty heads.

Arminius claimed to have passed, 'in my incognito as a Dervish, the most agreeable days of my whole journey', in Khiva. Regardless of the risk he was, in retrospect at least, oddly approving of many of the 'customs of the country', which seemed to suit his puritanical views. Here, although members of the royal family 'frequently transgress' with 'spirituous drinks', the khan himself did not. There was a level of restraint in 'the national character of the Tartar' that was 'chiefly marked by seriousness and firmness', and although music was popular and the Khivans excelled at singing, 'to dance, jump, or show high spirits' was, in the eyes of the locals, 'only worthy of women or children'. He also, rather surprisingly, approved of the royal harem, 'where comparatively little time is lavished upon the embellishments of the toilet'. On the contrary, he noted, the women had 'very little leisure for idleness'. They were kept hard at work, as tradition demanded, making clothes for their khan and 'carpets or other stuffs for the use of the prince', thus maintaining 'many remnants of simple refinement'. During the summer, the royal family moved to castles whose names Arminius gives as Rafenek and Tashhauz, built by Khan Allah Quli in the Persian style and 'distinguished by possessing some window-panes'. As the crowded city heated up, Arminius too decided to escape, on an exploration of more of the khanate before the caravan set out for Bukhara. He accompanied a young mullah who had joined the caravan in order to reach Samarkand and who wished to visit his home at Kungrat in the north of the khanate, where his parents had recently died. The village (now a stopping-off point for travellers to the salt desert landscapes of the devastated Aral Sea) was about eighty kilometres south of the water and was even then 'of far more miserable appearance than those in the south'. That did not stop it being a centre for nomad trading and a market for dried fish from the Aral Sea. The journey would give Arminius an opportunity to see more of the Khivan khanate and to travel by boat on the waters of the mighty Amu Darya.

Although Arminius could not know it when he arrived in Khiva in 1863, the khanate was already in a decline that would culminate in its invasion by Russia in 1873. In 1863 however, Khiva remained relatively well organised in terms of daily life. Even in 1819 the Russian general Nikolai Muravyov-Karsky, who had undertaken a three-year exploration of Turkestan, had written, 'In Germany itself I have never seen such careful tending of the fields as in Khiva'.[14] There was good irrigation, although this was a further source of strife as water was diverted to settlements away from the Turkmen nomads; and the wide diversity of crops included those excellent melons later to be eaten by Fred Burnaby. The finest mulberry trees in the region grew a few kilometres outside the city of Khiva near the Amu Darya, and there was a flourishing silk business. Out in the countryside, where Arminius now travelled, he found 'numberless herds of cattle' and 'abundance of game in the forest', with 'numerous wild beasts'. There was fishing and shooting too, in season, on the Aral Sea. Much of the region was well populated – Arminius noted 'the chain of havlis is scarcely interrupted', and there were successful towns all along the banks of the Amu Darya. He saw the ruins of ancient fortresses and civilisations that might have been Parthian or those of Nestorian Armenians, as well as tombs claimed as Muslim shrines with as complicated an origin story as 'Alexander's Wall'.

Arminius was finally able, unseen, to take a few notes on the Amu Darya, the river that was believed to promise so much as a strategic route for trade and/or invasion. He well knew of the Scottish explorer Alexander Burnes' assertions on the navigability of the river from thirty years before, and of the Russian admiral and explorer Alexei Butakov's journey to map the river from the Aral Sea up to Kungrat in 1858.[15] For himself, he observed portentously that:

> the Oxus is the typical representative of the country it traverses – wild and unruly in its course, like the temperament of the Central Asiatics. Its shallows are as little marked as the good and bad qualities in the Turkoman; daily it makes for itself new channels similar to the nomad, whose restless spirit, wearied of staying long in one spot, is ever craving for novelty and change.

---

14 Quoted in UNESCO's *History of Civilizations of Central Asia, Vol. V: Development in Contrast: From the sixteenth to the mid-nineteenth century* (Paris, 2003), 71.
15 This led to further exploratory journeys upriver and, in 1862, to the first steamships being launched on the Aral Sea.

He found the river remarkable if not 'navigable throughout its entire length', as Burnes had thought. In its upper waters, so far as he could tell, it was able only to bear the rafts that he saw carrying fuel and timber to the treeless plains. 'The greatest traffic', he reported, 'is undoubtedly on that part of the river which flows in the Khanate of Khiva', where it provided the favourite and cheapest means of transport both up- and downstream. He could not see that the river had 'the capability of becoming the powerful artery for traffic and communication in Central Asia, which politicians, when speaking of the future of Turkestan, confidently expect', and he could not see that it could ever be of the 'same importance as the Yaxartes,[16] whose waters at this very moment are ploughed by Russian steamers'. He must have been delighted to be able to report so negatively for Russian ambitions. He was quite certain what the alternative would have been if the river had supported shipping throughout its length. With steamers on the Oxus, the Russians would not only have 'been able to keep the Khanate of Khiva in check, to garrison the fortresses of Kungrat, Kiptshak and Hesaresp', but they would have been enabled to introduce 'with the greatest ease a strong corps d'armée by Karakul into Bokhara, and thus into the very heart of Central Asia'.

Arminius observed that the main problem with the river (apart from the waterfall known as Kazankitken,[17] where boats had to be towed close to the shore, and dangerous cliffs, between which the river ran furiously in a narrow channel, and the unpredictable currents and the continual deviation in the flow from its original channel) was the preponderance of rapidly changing sandbanks and the changes in the riverbed in the different seasons of the year. In the end, he was disposed to agree with the diplomat and Orientalist Sir Henry Rawlinson, 'who founded his assertion on a very valuable Persian manuscript, that in former times the Sea of Aral had no existence whatever'. Sir Henry shared this belief with plenty of others, including those hopeful earlier Russian explorers. In 1867 Admiral Alexei Butakov, the 'father' of Aral Sea navigation, was presented with the Royal Geographical Society's Founders Medal by the president and great geologist and archaeologist Sir

---

16 Jaxartes or Syr Darya.
17 The spot 'where the cauldrons went to the bottom' – a vessel loaded with them was supposed to have sunk here.

Roderick Murchison. In his address to the society on that occasion, Sir Roderick made clear what he thought of Sir Henry's tale. He noted that few European travellers had seen the Aral Sea in the past and Butakov could be considered to have made 'what might almost be called the geographical discovery of the Aral Sea', although, he pointed out, 'this great mass of salt water had been known to Arabian geographers for several centuries under the name of the Sea of Khwarezm'. He mentioned the 'enterprising Hungarian Vambèry [sic]' as one of very few 'stray travellers' who had 'explained to the civilized world' the real state of the Central Asian region.[18]

The mysteries of the Oxus and Jaxartes certainly deserved explanation. In Sir Henry's time, there was a belief that the Oxus and Jaxartes had originally and conveniently flowed into the Caspian Sea. According to the legend, the rivers had then changed direction around 500 CE to flow into and form the Aral Sea, and later, for 200 years between about 1300 and 1500, reversed their route back into the Caspian. Early Russian ambitions had focused on the idea of once again redirecting the Amu Darya in that direction.[19]

When Admiral Butakov had first brought his 15-metre schooner, the *Konstantin*, to the Aral Sea in 1848, it had been the world's fourth biggest inland body of water at 67,000 square kilometres, a giant fishy larder where, it was said, fishermen only had to beat the water with a stick to take a catch. Before the 1960s it supplied 50,000 tons of fish a year, but in the 1980s all commercial fishing ceased. The USSR had diverted the waters of the rivers that fed the sea to feed instead the thirsty cotton beds of Soviet design and development and improve the lot of the Soviet masses. Most of the water was wasted, vanishing into the Kazakh and Uzbek sands from unlined canals. The rivers were also contaminated by pesticides and poisoned the land they had once fed so successfully. By 2004, the Aral was reduced to 17,000 square kilometres in two separate bodies of water and had become

---

18 Sir Roderick Murchison, 'Address to the Royal Geographical Society', *Proceedings of the Royal Geographical Society of London*, 11/5 (1866–7), 185–229, 202–3.

19 Sir Roderick found himself unable to regard the Persian manuscript on which Sir Henry based his support of this idea as 'of sufficient value to override the conclusions to which I have arrived on many independent grounds'. He believed, unsurprisingly since this continued to happen, that the Oxus had changed direction many times in history, but he did not believe that the Aral Sea had ever not existed. It was the case, however, that, in that long-lost history, 'there were no geographers to record the fact' of its existence (ibid., 205).

---

too salty for almost all species of fish. The birds had also disappeared. If the Aral Sea had only mythically not existed in the far and distant past, in the twentieth century, at the hands of humankind, the myth became true. It has been one of the greatest-ever environmental catastrophes.

Arminius and the young mullah returned from Kungrat to Khiva by road via Kunya-Urgench, the old capital of the Persian Khwarezm empire. They were lucky to fall in with another group of travellers who offered the loan of two of their good horses to these hajis 'out of pious benevolence', and they reached Kunya-Urgench on the fourth day. The city had been built at the crossing of two important caravan routes, from the south to the Volga in the north-west, and from the west into China. It was one of the most important cities on the silk routes and known to the Islamic world as 'the heart of Islam', but it had a tragic history. In 1221 it had been destroyed by Genghis Khan and the population massacred. It revived but, 150 years later, after its ruler had rebelled against him, Timur razed it to the ground and ordered barley sown on the site so it would disappear for all time into the earth. A change of direction away from the city of the ever-wayward Amu Darya, on whose banks Urgench had been founded, was the *coup de grace* to its greatness, and the capital of Khwarezm moved to Khiva.

The area has long since been re-inhabited and a new town built; but the old remains as a graveyard, over which tower the eleventh- to fourteenth-century remnants of glorious survivors of tyrannical conquest. Arminius was underwhelmed by these ruins, 'however much its former splendour is extolled in words and writing', and considered it could only have been a centre of 'no higher than Tartar civilisation'. He mentioned the 'mosque' (actually the mausoleum) of Turabek Khanum, wife of Qutlugh Timur who ruled Khwarazm between 1321 and 1336 on behalf of the Golden Horde, and those of the thirteenth-century sufi Najm ad-din al Kubra and of the sixteenth-century Sultan Ali. The former, he noted, had recently been restored by 'the liberality' of 'the builder Khan, Muhammad Amin'. He completely ignored the most dominant feature of the site, the remaining sixty towering metres of the Kutlug-Timur minaret, one of the tallest and most ancient minarets in Central Asia, which dates from 1011 CE. Today Kunya-Urgench is one of the main ornaments of Turkmenistan, barely metres from the Uzbek border and an easy drive from Khiva. Although it is hardly on the international tourist track, it is a busy site for domestic pilgrimage and its excavation, preservation, and restoration continue under UNESCO auspices. The now-glorious azure tiles on the conical domes of the Sultan Tekesh and Il Arslan mausoleums may have been hidden by dust and tombs more ruinous than today when Arminius saw them, with only the bulk of the Turabek Khanum mausoleum standing out above the mass and the minaret, with its spectacular decorative brickwork, a tapering finger pointing at the sky.

From here, Arminius and the mullah continued on the safest but longer of the two routes back to Khiva. It avoided potentially hostile Turkmans but was an obstacle course of ditches and irrigation canals. When they returned, Arminius found the hajis keen to depart for Bukhara and went to bid farewell to Shukrullah Bey, who made every effort to dissuade him from this next dangerous journey. Shukrullah Bey, Arminius suspected, must have seen through his disguise (the bey had, after all, not only lived in cosmopolitan Constantinople but had also been to St Petersburg several times and had met Englishmen in Herat). For a *ferenghi*, Bukhara was an even more dangerous proposition than Khiva, and the whims of its emirs even more unpredictable. The present emir, Muzaffar al-Din, was the son and successor of the dreaded Nasrullah who had executed Stoddart and Conolly, and Arminius did not have the comic potential of the Reverend Joseph Wolff to get himself out of trouble.

Arminius visited the khan to give his farewell dervish blessing before his departure, but when the khan requested he return to Khiva so that a Khivan envoy might accompany him to Constantinople, Arminius replied only that 'kismet', or fate, would decide. One visit to the Khivan lion's den was enough, and he had yet to survive Bukhara. At least, by the generosity of the Khivans, all the hajis were well equipped for the journey. They set out with donkeys to ride, bags of stores, luxuries like white flour cakes, rice, butter, and sugar, and with pure white turbans on their heads, a veritable team of Nasreddins.[20] Arminius also had a share in a camel to carry his baggage, to which he had added various manuscripts that he purchased in Khiva. He also had a new friend who, ultimately, would return with Arminius to Hungary.

---

20 The thirteenth-century Sufi wise man is a comic hero in thousands of Central Asian stories. His statue stands in the centre of Bukhara.

The mullah, Ishak, who Arminius had met at Khiva and who had accompanied him to Kungrat, now became his constant travelling companion. Referred to by Arminius as 'my Tartar', the young man behaved essentially as his servant and 'invariably shrank from placing himself in a position of equality', but instead, 'accommodated himself ungrudgingly to his master'. Ishak was astounded by the false dervish's transformation in due course from zealous holy man to *ferenghi* but, after he had travelled with Arminius to Hungary, he accommodated himself to this new and entirely alien way of life. Arminius was to write that Ishak 'rarely feels any longing for his native home' and 'loves our Western civilisation', where 'the various differences of religion and nationality are scarcely ever felt' and 'thousands of people come in daily contact with each other, without quarrels, fighting, or bloodshed ensuing'. (Ishak learned to speak Hungarian very quickly, but perhaps he did not read the newspapers.) Arminius convinced himself that Ishak's mind was occupied by the benefits of the Christianity responsible for European 'civilisation and refinement of life', and 'that the great struggle with himself has begun'. Ishak lived in Hungary with a friend of Arminius' for a year after Arminius went to London and, by the time he returned, the mullah had literally put on Hungarian clothes and was at ease in his adopted country. That did not stop his desire for travel, his whole journey having begun as a quest to reach Mecca, and this may have remained his ultimate goal whatever Arminius thought. He worked for Arminius running errands and, Arminius stated, became assistant librarian at the Academy, although there is no record of this appointment. He seems to have been something of an Eliza Doolittle for Arminius' philological studies, and even though he set out once for Vienna and then again towards the East and Constantinople, he came back. He was known to Rustem, Arminius' son, who was born in 1872, and to his famous first pupil at Pest University, Ignaz Goldziher, but eventually he disappears from the record. Intriguingly, after Arminius' death, a book entitled *Memoirs of a Tartar* was published. Written in the 1880s, it is considered to be fiction, but it is the account of a 'Tartar' who had returned to Central Asia after a long stay in Europe and includes opinions well known to have been held by Arminius himself – a more detailed and sophisticated account of the views he assumed on Ishak's behalf. One might guess that by then Arminius' 'Tartar' had become merely a literary device.

But then again... Alder and Dalby discovered a Muslim grave at the edge of the Calvinist cemetery at Velence, between Budapest and Lake Balaton. Its tombstone, surmounted by a crescent and a star, bears the following inscription:

Here rests
Mollah Sadik
Turkish Asian
Monk
Born 1836
Died 22 May 1892
Blessings and Peace
To his ashes[21]

According to their investigations, it was believed that Ishak had married a woman from Velence, and they wondered: 'Are Ishak and Sadik one and the same? Ishak might have been his Islamic name and Sadik a family name. Or were there two Mollahs roaming this part of the Hungarian countryside at the same time?' A more recent memorial album of Arminius' life, published by the Slovak Cultural Ministry in 2016, confirmed Ishak's death near Velence and that he had suffered from emphysema from the 1870s. So perhaps this is indeed Arminius' companion's final resting place.

---

21 The Hungarian original reads 'Itt Nyugszik, Molla Szadik, Asia Torok, Szersetes, Sz.1836, Megh22 majus1892, Aldas es beke, Hamvaira'.

8

Bukhara

The caravan left for Bukhara on a Monday afternoon, seen off, Arminius reported, by crowds whose 'feeling of devotion forced tears from their eyes'. The travellers stayed the first night not far from the city in a *kalenterkhane*, one of the hostels for dervishes that were a feature of the caravan routes. The following day Arminius ate mulberries 'as thick and large as my thumb' from the trees they passed and, in the *kalenterkhane* at Khanka, found two half-naked dervishes who offered him a share of their opium and were most surprised when he declined. He took tea instead and watched as the opium eaters fell asleep, one with an expression of pleasure on his face, the other, 'the agonies of terrible fear'. From Khanka, the party reached the Oxus, its yellow waters swollen by the spring melt from the mountains that appeared in the distance 'like a cloud suspended perpendicularly from heaven'. The 'water grits under the teeth, just as if you had taken a bite of a sandcake', and Arminius doubted local lore that suggested there was no water in the world comparable for 'sweetness and good flavour'. He had to admit his error once the sand in the water had settled, writing that he had never found any water 'so precious as that of the Oxus'. To cross on the ferry required a local passport paid for in Khiva, and the hajis had only one between them, but Arminius, no doubt with the assistance of Shukrullah Bey, had one of his own that gave free passage on all forms of transport and through all frontiers for 'the Hadji Mollah Abdur Reshid Effendi'. Getting across the river was still a performance, however, as the boat ran aground on sandbanks and the hajis had to load and unload themselves and sometimes carry their pack animals bodily to and from the vessel.

The caravan made slow progress on land as well as water, allowing

Arminius to wander off the route to visit a local nomad market. There he found more dervishes, with 'frames reduced to mere skeletons' due to their use of *bhang* (a form of cannabis). Arminius blamed the habit on the Quranic ban on 'wine and spirituous liquors' that he so deplored under other circumstances, and saw that the dervishes had a decent trade in the drug with Uzbeks, who gave contributions in exchange for a pipe of their 'darling poison'. He also saw Kirghiz women on their horses in the market, selling *koumiss* straight from skin containers into the mouths of their customers. Testing his language skills, Arminius asked one woman about her wandering life. 'We cannot be so indolent', she answered, 'as you mollahs, and spend the entire day in one place. Man must move about, the sun, the moon, the stars, the water, animals, birds, fish, all are moving; only the dead and the earth lie motionless'. Today he would find the however-many-greats granddaughters of the *koumiss* vendors pouring the same drink from plastic flagons into paper cups. They might no longer ride to market on the horses they herd and travel with in the verdant summer months, but they are still on the move and still busy, as they field a small child, gossip to a neighbour, bellow against the surrounding racket into the mobile telephone permanently in one hand, and get on with knitting a winter jersey. Arminius wrote that he could not drink *koumiss*, it was too acidic, but it is a taste that can be quickly acquired by the demands of good manners.

As their caravan trailed along the banks of the river, the pilgrims met some merchants returning from Bukhara to Khiva, who assured them of the safety of the road. The very next day they came across two naked sailors who had been robbed of everything, including their boat, by a group of Tekke Turkmans 150 strong. The *kervenbashi* insisted on an immediate change of course that would take the caravan away from any danger on the river, and instead follow a desert route to Bukhara. As the first station on this road, which they were taking in the high heat of summer, was known as *Adam-kirilgan*, or man-destroyer, the choice was frying pan or fire. The *kervenbashi* calculated the new route at six days, during which time the travellers would be on 'firm and even ground' and for three days of which water should be findable. Once among the desert sands, they should only be unable to find water for one day and a half.[1] Arminius realised on the first day that their

---

1 When Ibn Battuta travelled from Khwarezm to Bukhara in the fourteenth century, the

supply of Oxus water was evaporating far more quickly in the heat than this calculation had allowed. They were marching for five or six hours a day, for fear of being overtaken by the so-called *tebbad*, the scorching fever-wind carrying suffocating quantities of sand, which lands like flakes of fire on any exposed skin and buries everything in its path. Then two of the camels died at a station called *Shortukuk*, where the eponymous salt-fountain that might have watered the animals had been choked with sand by the wind. The travellers could think of nothing but water, and Arminius described the horrors of thirst, its effects on the characters of his companions and, graphically, the death of one of them. He saw 'the father hide his store of water from the son, and brother from brother', and concluded that when each drop meant life and 'men feel the torture of thirst, there is not, as in the other dangers of life, any spirit of self-sacrifice, or any feeling of generosity'. When one of three brothers died in his presence, Arminius noted: 'His tongue was quite black, the roof of his mouth of a greyish white', and he wondered 'whether, in these extreme sufferings, water would have been of service', adding, 'but who was there to give it to him?'

At last, the caravan came in sight of mountains, but their animals were too exhausted to reach them before they had spent another day in the sand. Somehow Arminius had preserved 'about six glasses of water in my leathern bottle', which he was eking out drop by drop until he found his tongue had begun to turn black also, when he drank half his store in one go. On the fifth day, although the mountains drew slowly closer, he was struggling. Then the *tebbad* came and covered everything 'with a crust of sand two fingers thick'. But the dreadful wind seems not to have affected the caravan as badly as anticipated, and Arminius saw none of the symptoms of fever and vomiting it was believed to bring. By that evening, the travellers had reached wells, which provided water for the animals but proved unfit for humans, and the next day Arminius thought his end was nigh: 'I was completely broken down; I felt my power of resistance had deserted me and had no hopes of ever surviving the night'. He described the 'dreadful internal fire' and 'the torture of thirst unallayed', but after falling asleep on his donkey as it

journey took eighteen days in the sands, including six without any source of water. He seemed to consider this quite run of the mill, but then he was travelling in winter, without the scorching summer's heat.

somehow continued to carry him, he woke up to find himself on the ground in a mud hut, being fed tepid milk mixed with salt and water by men who he recognised as Persians.

They were shepherds, out with large flocks of sheep sixty kilometres or so from Bukhara, and Arminius was astonished that these Shia Muslims,[2] who were in fact captives themselves, should be prepared to share the little that they had with a group of Sunni mullahs. There was also a small boy 'of great intelligence', who had been captured with his father and now awaited ransom with 'hardly anything but a few little rags to cover his weak little body', to whom Arminius gave 'one of my own articles of attire'. The Persians gave the travellers a little extra water and, after getting lost overnight searching for a shrine on the edge of the desert, they found themselves on the banks of a freshwater lake. That night they were in the *kervenbashi*'s home village, close to Bukhara, where they were visited next day by officials of the emir who were essentially immigration, customs, and excise. All their possessions were listed, and the travellers questioned and described in writing. Arminius was impatient. 'What a ridiculous proceeding – a long string of questions respecting Khiva, a land of kindred language, origin and religion with Bokhara, their frontiers having been for centuries and centuries coterminous...'

The leading official, Rahmet Bey, the emir's vizier, had immediately recognised Arminius as a foreigner and thought him a likely source of rich pickings, but Arminius decided to play the holy fool. He took his donkey up the courtyard steps and into the room where the official sat and introduced it by name. He then showed the disappointed man the rags of clothes and old books in his bag, leaving Haji Salih, who was influential in Bukhara, to explain the who and why of this strange Turkish dervish and his unusual pilgrimage. That afternoon, the hajis rode through the same gardens and orchards described five hundred years earlier by Ibn Battuta and watered by the Zeravshan river. They forded the river close to the old ruined stone bridge a league and a half from Bukhara, just as 'its clumsy towers, crowned, almost without exception, by nests of storks', came into view.[3] With its 350

---

2 It was strictly prohibited by Sharia law that Muslims should be sold as slaves, but this did not stop the trade in Shia Persians who were not only deemed heretic by Sunni Muslims but, in the fanatical khanates, declared *kafirs* – 'unbelievers' – and therefore fair game.

3 Storks were always part of Bukhara, birds of good omen who returned to nest every year on the towers and domes of the city. Eugene Schuyler saw an enormous nest on top of the Kalyan

mosques[4] and over 100 *madrasas*, '*Bokhara es Sharif*' – 'Bukhara the noble' – was the holiest city in Central Asia and probably the most dangerous for a foreigner. Arminius was determined not to be impressed, but he was one of a very select few visitors. Even by the time the writer and soldier Fitzroy Maclean arrived at the moonlit city walls in 1938, after a longer walk than he had anticipated from the nearest railway station at Kagan, he was able to remark that few Europeans at all had seen Bukhara. Those who had described the city were mostly well-known names: from Marco Polo in the thirteenth century and Anthony Jenkinson, the first explorer of Russia, in the sixteenth, to Russian envoys such as Florio Beneveni, who was in Bukhara on behalf of Peter the Great in the early eighteenth century. Alexander Burnes was here, in the vanguard of the British and Russian explorers and adventurers of the nineteenth century; there was the bizarre Reverend Wolff in his full canonicals and shovel hat; Eugene Schuyler, the first American to travel in Central Asia in the 1870s (who was to go on to be one of Arminius' first and most trenchant critics), was here too;[5] and then there was Count K. K. Pahlen, member of the Tsarist senate, in 1908.

There were others of course: nameless and numberless Russian slaves and equally nameless Russian soldiers and their famous or infamous commanders; and spies of any number of nationalities, on British and Russian payrolls, masquerading as merchants, pilgrims, or just part of the flotsam and jetsam drifting between East and West, but Bukhara was, for much of its history, a mysterious place. To the West, along with Samarkand, it was a fabled and fantastic symbol of the East, epitomising the alien romance of Asia. Alexander Burnes, when he saw Bukhara, more accurately described the city as a cosmopolitan hive of trade, populated by a 'moving mass of human beings'. 'From morn to night the crowd assembled raises a humming

---

Minar. In the 1970s they left the city and have never returned. Fake nests now memorialise their departure.

4 Also said to number 365 – one for every day of the year.

5 Schuyler is an interesting contrast to Arminius in many ways, and we will encounter him again. He had the advantage of a comfortable, if by no means grand, New York background, and an excellent education. By the time Schuyler was travelling through Central Asia, a decade after Arminius, Russian presence in the region was an established fact, and Schuyler did not have any need to pretend to be anything other than what he was. He was also a very considerable linguist and, although his view of Russian presence in Central Asia was not uncritical, overall, he considered it beneficial.

noise', and 'it is with difficulty that a passage can be forced through the streets'. Almost anything could be bought there: 'the jewellery and cutlery of Europe, the tea of China, the sugar of India, the spices of Manilla', and there were both Turkish and Persian books for sale at the bookstalls. In fact,

A stranger has only to seat himself on a bench of the Registan, to know the Uzbeks and the people of Bokhara. He may here converse with the natives of Persian, Turkey, Russia, Tartary, China, India and Cabool. He will meet with Toorkmuns, Calmuks and Cossacks from the surrounding deserts, as well as the natives of more favoured lands.[6]

There was also a large and prosperous Jewish community, engaged in all the business of the city – owners of camel trains, bankers and merchants, and cloth dyers. 'They knew all the secret dyes which glowed in the Bukhara rugs', and 'the hands of half the city's Jews were stained to the knuckles with dye'.[7] Burnes had found them 'remarkably handsome', the features of the unveiled Jewish women 'set off by ringlets of beautiful hair hanging over their cheeks and necks'. To Fitzroy Maclean, more than a century later, Bukhara appeared 'still a completely eastern walled city of enclosed mud-built houses, each looking inwards on its own courtyard' and, he wrote 'while in Tashkent, East and West lie side by side and often intermingle... Bokhara has remained, and, I think, cannot but remain, so long as it survives at all, wholly Eastern'.[8] Perhaps the essence of the city had somehow solidified at its heart, defying an ever-changing present. It became even more veiled from foreign eyes under the implacable Soviet rule that Maclean had sought to sidestep when he travelled into Central Asia than it had been under the extreme rule of its emirs.

Arminius knew he had 'fallen into the chief nest of Islamite fanaticism'; the place where, the proverb had it, the light which in other parts of the world 'descends upon the earth from above... in Bokhara... rises from below'.[9] Haji Salih took him to stay at the dervish *tekke* where there were

---

6 Alexander Burnes, *Travels into Bokhara*, ed. Kathleen Hopkirk (London, 2012), 185.
7 Colin Thubron, *The Lost Heart of Asia* (London, 2004), 99.
8 Fitzroy Maclean, *To the Back of Beyond* (London, 1974), 86.
9 Quoted in Alder and Dalby, op. cit., 144.

forty-eight cells round a courtyard planted with trees, and where the leader, or *khalifa,* was the grandson of its founding saint, as well as being court imam to the emir. Haji Salih was a disciple of the saint and introduced 'Hadji Reshid' as a good Mussulman and a learned mullah to this 'man of gentle demeanour and agreeable exterior, whom his snow-white turban and summer dress of fine silk well became'. The *khalifa* regretted that the emir was away from the city and so he could not present Arminius to him. This news may have come as a relief and gave Arminius a chance for sightseeing, although the vizier, Rahmet Bey, continued to be suspicious and sent spies to try to catch him out in some mistake of religious knowledge, language, or action. When his agents provocateurs failed, Rahmet Bey invited Arminius to his house, where he had assembled a gathering of the *ulema* (Muslim scholars and theologians), some of whom had spent time in Constantinople and who engaged Arminius in learned conversation. He managed to turn the discussion, earnestly inquiring of these holy men as to their beliefs, traditions, and interpretation of the Quran, and 'praising loudly the Bokhariot Mollahs'. He passed the test, but the vizier had another card up his sleeve in the form of a little man claiming to be an Arab from Damascus but who, Arminius was quite certain, from his appearance and his poor Arabic, was another European.

The man was thoroughly embarrassed as he told Arminius that he had been on a pilgrimage to Khotan in China, and Arminius was 'strongly disposed to think that he was playing a part similar to my own'. Another spy? Probably, but who this amateurish-sounding individual was working for is a mystery. The British and Russian spies were likely to have been excellent linguists, with credible cover stories, so the mystery man may have been some poor tool of the viziers, hoping that Arminius would not draw attention to his lack of skills. Alternatively, the intention may have been to recruit this latest foreigner to the emir's pervasive espionage service. If Arminius heard his odd visitor's full story, he kept it to himself, and writing of Rahmet Bey much later in his life, he described the suspicious vizier in quite a different light: 'The only pleasant memory left to me of those days is the kindness I received from Rahmet Bi', who 'quieted the suspicions of the Governor of Kerki on my account and helped me safely over the border'. Even so, Arminius took due credit for Rahmet Bey's friendliness, writing; 'the poetic muse had a hand in Rahmet Bi's friendliness. He sometimes wrote Persian verses and was delighted when he could read them to me and gain my approbation'.

Rahmet Bey's own view of the Turkish haji was later related by a Russian diplomat, a Herr von Lankenau, who was in Bukhara in 1869 and enquired about a 'very pious haji' with a lame leg. Rahmet Bey told him: 'Although many pilgrims go to Bokhara and Samarcand every year, I can guess which one you mean. He was a very learned Hadji, much more so than all the other wise men in Bukhara'. He assured the diplomat he had seen through Arminius' disguise, 'but I knew too that he was not dangerous and I did not want to ruin such a learned man. It was the Mollahs' own fault that they did not guess whom they had with them'. That story, when it reached him, might well have been responsible for Arminius' later opinion of the vizier, but enough of an understanding was reached between the two men at the time for Arminius to request a letter of safe conduct from Rahmet Bey before he left Bukhara. He only reported the conversation between von Lankenau and Rahmet Bey in his final memoir, *The Story of My Struggles*, in 1904, when he denied that anyone had ever really detected his European identity, 'on account of my fortunate talent for languages'. Had they done so, he wrote, 'I should certainly not now be in a position to write my memoirs'. And as ever, his international reputation, built on the drama and dangers of his dervish journey, would have been sadly reduced by any hint of knowing indulgence of his true identity from those he had encountered. The sultan's *tugra* was Arminius' best insurance and the key to opening official doors in Central Asia. Tsar or queen-empress were distant threats, while the papers of those unbelievers were passports to damnation, but with the *tugra* and Rahmet Bey's letter in his pocket, Arminius was as safe as was possible for anyone inside Bukharan territory:

> Be it known, that the holder of this letter, the high-born Hadji Abdur-reshid, from Turkey, has come hither with the intention of making a pilgrimage to the graves of the saints in noble Bokhara and in paradisiacal Samarcand. After accomplishing his pilgrimage to the graves of the saints, and having paid homage to his Highness the Emir, he returns to his home. He is in possession of a writing from his Highness the Sovereign of all true believers and the Imam of all Moslems (the Sultan); it is therefore seemly that the said Hadji should not be inconvenienced by any one, neither

on the journey nor at any station, but that every one as he is able should honour and respect him.

Nonetheless, in Arminius' colourful opinion, Bukhara was 'a most perilous place, not only for all Europeans, but for every stranger, because the Government has carried the system of espionage to just as high a pitch of perfection as the population has attained pre-eminence in every kind of profligacy and wickedness'. Had Arminius but realised, there was more to the emir's xenophobia than straightforward religious fanaticism and fear of Russian or British interference. Hidden treasure was at stake. The Russians had been aware of the existence of gold in the region since Florio Beneveni had sent his valet, Nikolai Minera, to explore the mines around the Syr Darya river during his time in Bukhara from 1721 to 1725. Secrecy about the mines had been enforced by the emirs with the usual brutality. Workers who were retired from the workings had their tongues and eyes put out, and anyone suspected of knowing the location of the mines was instantly executed. It has even been suggested that Stoddart and Conolly may by some means have discovered their existence, making their executions a necessity in the eyes of Emir Nasrullah. (It is equally likely that court whispers or Nasrullah's own paranoia manufactured this final nail in their coffins.)

Whoever did or did not know it, fear secured the secret, and the emirs' hidden mines had disappeared into legend when Bukhara fell finally to Soviet Russia. They were not re-discovered until the 1960s. In 1908 Count Pahlen had thought the 'emir's yearly income and the volume of his amassed and hoarded wealth', which 'ensured a total of fantastic proportions', was based on 'a system of taxation equivalent to a series of financial and trade operations'.[10] It was essentially extortion at every level, and neither the count nor any others suspected the emir's golden nest-egg, hidden in the background. Arminius wrote 'my readers will not feel surprised that we should have but a scanty knowledge of the mineral riches in the three Khanats [sic]'. He was inclined to 'the opinion of Burnes, that Central Asia possesses either no precious metals or extremely few, and that the gold dust in the Zerefshan is not the property of the country but washed down by the small rivers that rise in the Hindukhush'.

---

10 Count Von Pahlen, *Mission to Turkestan: Being the Memoirs of Count K K Pahlen, 1908–1909*, tr. N. J. Couris (Oxford, 1964), 74.

The day after his arrival, Arminius and Haji Salih set off with four of their travelling companions to visit the bazaar and see the city. Arminius thought 'the wretchedness of the streets and houses' and the foot-thick dust everywhere gave 'an ignoble idea' of the 'noble Bukhara', but he allowed himself to be astonished by the bazaar, where 'the strange and diversified intermixture of races, dresses and customs' presented 'a very striking spectacle to the eye of the stranger'. Like Burnes, he noted 'the noble, pre-eminently handsome features' of the Jewish population; the men, he felt 'might sit to any of our artists for a model of manly beauty'. They, and the Indian Hindus (of whom he was predictably less admiring), were required to distinguish themselves by wearing 'a Polish cap' so that 'the salutation Selam Aleikum may not be thrown away' on them. Of the unkempt Afghans he saw, he remarked that they looked 'like persons who rush to safety from their beds into the streets, when their houses are on fire'. He also saw goods from Europe, especially from Russia, being sold. There was nothing of much intrinsic value but, Arminius wrote for his British audience, he remembered his heart beating faster when he saw the words 'Manchester' or 'Birmingham', as if he had 'met a countryman'. When the American Eugene Schuyler arrived in Bukhara in 1873, he found American revolvers in the bazaar, as well as French and German goods.[11]

Arminius was much taken by the fine cottons of Bukhara. The local *aladja* was striped blue and white, and there were naturally multiple different silks, but best of all was the leather. The boots 'for male and female wear, are tolerably well made; the former have high heels about the size of a nail's head'. Bukhara had a fashionable veneer to maintain: 'a dandy takes especial care to have his turban folded according to the idea in force at the moment', and pedestrians in their heels put on the '*reftari khiraman* (the waddling or trotting step) which Oriental poets find so graceful, comparing it to the swaying movement of the cypress when agitated by the zephyrs'. In a rare flash of genuine and relatable humour, Arminius thought it 'like the gait of a fatted goose floundering on his way home', but pointed out 'our stiff, rapid pace is just as displeasing to an Oriental eye, and it would not be very polite to mention the comparison they make use of with respect to us'. Men rode in 'thigh-length boots with dandily pointed toes', and Arminius was fascinated by the importance vested

---

11 Eugene Schuyler, *Turkistan: Notes of a Journey in Russian Turkistan, Khokand, Bukhara, and Kuldja*, Vol. II (London, 1876), 94.

in the *sound* of a new robe, the '*tchakh-tchukh* or rustling tone' of a *tchapan*, displayed by its seller putting it on to parade 'up and down a few paces to ascertain whether it gave out the orthodox tone'. Schuyler would describe Bukhara as 'a metropolis', with 'every day seeming like a bazaar day'.[12] Arminius himself wrote that to the Kirghiz, Kiptchak, and Kalmuks, 'making excursions hither from the desert', and to the wild Tartar, 'Bokhara is his Paris or his London'.

Alexander Burnes wrote of the people of Bukhara that they 'delight to appear before their king in a mottled garment of silk, called *"udrus"*, made of the brightest colours and which would be intolerable to any but an Uzbek'.[13] But under the glossy, brightly coloured urban exterior, life was darker, poorer, and more fearful. The notorious Emir Nasrullah had died in 1860 and had been succeeded by his son, Emir Muzaffar al-Din, who Arminius saw in Samarkand. The emir was then 'in the forty-second year of his age, of middle stature, somewhat corpulent' and with 'a very pleasing countenance'. His finer points, including 'the gentleness and affability of his manners' in his youth, did not stop him however from being a tyrant, a fanatic, and the 'declared enemy of every innovation'. No one was allowed to rise far in the emir's kingdom, and conspicuous consumption was forbidden beyond the external glitter that was a cover for the poverty and wretchedness shared by both high and low estates. This extended into the royal harem, where the women made their own clothes, and the royal kitchen, where the menu was the same 'native food, pilaff, and greasy, fried or stewed, mutton',[14] complained of by every traveller and eaten by everyone (although Emir Nasrullah had so many levels of food tasters that his must have arrived cold and congealed on the royal plate). No wonder fine food was not a feature of this royal court.

The emir's spies were everywhere, seeking out religious or political infraction, and the people dared not speak his name without adding, 'God grant him to live 120 years'. They must devoutly have hoped he would not. The city in truth was in a state of decay, outer show and inner rot,[15] and the

---

12 Ibid., 88.

13 Udrus is actually a silk or silk and cotton fabric dyed by the ikat or double ikat method. Kathleen Hopkirk has pointed out that, by the later nineteenth century, violently coloured chemical dyes were being used which would have appalled Burnes even more than the relatively quiet natural colours he observed. Burnes, *Travels into Bokhara*, ed. K. Hopkirk, 185.

14 Schuyler, op. cit., 86.

15 Even the outer show was crumbling; the twenty-first century city owes its glory to Russian

populace lived in constant fear under the shadow of the grim royal palace, the infamous Ark. While Arminius was in Bukhara, three Italians, crafts-men and merchants, languished in the frightful vermin-filled pit where Conolly and Stoddart had been held. In the centre of the town, the principal mosques were towered over by the Kalyan Minar, with its glorious brickwork that is one of the wonders of Bukhara, its design so clearly fitted to its dual roles as guide to prayer and guide to safe harbour, a lighthouse to travellers in the sand sea beyond the city walls. And yet, ever since the Middle Ages (and as late as 1920), it also had a more gruesome role as a place of execution. Prisoners sewn into sacks were thrown from the top to their deaths.

Death, disease, and fear were constant companions in this city of dreams, where Arminius was constantly asked, 'Now then, what do you say to Bokhara the noble?' Cannabis use was endemic, and life was a circle of dirt, filthy water, dysentery, typhoid, and cholera. So much, Arminius thought, for a city 'whither flock thousands of scholars to learn the principles of a reli-gion that consecrated the principle that cleanliness is derived from religion'. He found the summer heat intolerable and craved the cold water he dared not drink for fear of 'the filaria medinensis', the guinea worm, 'with which every tenth person here is infected'. This horrible parasite enters the body as a larvae carried by tiny water fleas, ingested with contaminated water. Months later the adult worm, up to 120cm long, emerges from some part of the body, often the feet. Arminius wrote that people in Bukhara thought as little of this affliction as a European of a cold, but the 'itching sensation' as the worm began to emerge could lead to severe pain and dreadful infections. Treatment, for the brave, was to have the worm instantly cut out. More usually it was gradually drawn out under careful pressure over several days, winding it round a stick until the whole worm was removed. 'The barbers in Bokhara', Arminius wrote, 'perform the operation with considerable skill'. They had plenty of practice. Joseph Wolff, he added, had carried 'one of these long memorials of his journey' all the way back to England, where it had been 'extracted in Eastern fashion by the late Sir Benjamin Brodie', the first president of the General Medical Council. Sir Benjamin had only once in his life travelled even as far as France, so he must have been fascinated by this ori-ental export, if unlikely to have had any previous experience of its removal.

---

and independent Uzbek restoration from the 1960s onwards.

On arrival in the city, Arminius had dressed 'in a costume such as they wore in Bokhara', with a 'gigantic turban' and a 'large Koran suspended from my neck' and was so tanned 'that my own good mother would not have recognised me'. On his first day, exhausted by sightseeing, he sat in a tea shop, in the shade of the mulberry trees that surrounded the polluted water of the Divan-begi pool,[16] and watched a procession of fifteen Naqshbandi dervishes. They were probably staying in the nearby Khanakha of Divan-begi and were 'a sight not to be easily forgotten – the mad jumping about of these dervishes, in their wild fanaticism, with tall caps on their heads and their long flowing hair, waving their sticks and bellowing forth in chorus a hymn'. Arminius the dervish now believed he should strive to be taken for a holy leader, far removed from these extraordinary mendicants, but even so there was no escape from the curiosity and distrust he encountered. He was different and why was he there? He was delighted when he overheard endorsement of his disguise: 'What extreme piety, to come all the way from Constantinople to Bokhara alone in order to visit our Baha-ed-din,' even if that was followed by 'but these people have nothing else to do, their whole life is prayer, piety and pilgrimage'. Perhaps there were just too many holy men in Bukhara. If Arminius was happy that his disguise passed muster among them, the populace nonetheless showed them no material respect. Mean or thrifty hands stayed firmly in pockets, and there was little scope for lucrative holy begging or the expected payment for dervish blessings and incantations. Peeved, he compared people 'who boast that they are refreshing themselves at the very fountain of the pure faith' unfavourably with the Turks. Bukhariots considered the Osmanlis, even the sultan himself, inferior if not corrupt in their religious practices, and Arminius 'could not but internally felicitate the Turks on retaining, in spite of their being under the influence of a corrupt Islamism, many good qualities and fine traits of character'. He considered the Bukhariots to 'delight in nothing but the blackest mendacity, in hypocrisy and in impositions', and their religious practice to be no more than the 'external appearance' of piety insisted on by the authorities.

Arminius also disapproved of the fact that 'in this city where the

---

16 The city was full of these artificial reservoirs, fed by underground canals and water sources for the city, which were infested with guinea worm and other parasites and responsible for much of the disease in the city. Most were filled in under Soviet rule.

civilisation has retained with the greatest fidelity its antique stamp of Oriental Islamism', women 'ever the martyrs of Eastern legislation, come in for the worst share'. Turkey had modernised considerably, and the veil, he declared, was 'rather treated as part of the toilette than as the ensign of slavery'. In Persia he had described the women as 'tolerably well muffled up', but that was nothing compared to Bukhara, where women were so covered by their horsehair veils, dark blue robes, and heavy boots that they might be mistaken, said Arminius, 'for clothes wandering about' – always supposing, he added, they left their houses at all. He had never seen a man in company with 'his other half, or third, or fourth, as the case may be'. After George Curzon returned from his Central Asian exploration in 1888, he wrote that he had frequently been asked what the women of Bukhara had been like and that he was quite unable to say, due to their heavy veils and 'big blue cotton dressing gowns', but he too commented upon the beauty of the unveiled Jewish women.[17] And then there was the trade in slaves. When Arminius was in Bukhara, an able-bodied man was selling for the equivalent at the time of £2 or £3 sterling but, when the Persians had been defeated near Merv in 1788–9 and 10,000 prisoners were taken, a man could be bought for a tenth of that price. Much later, when Arminius wrote his *Life and Adventures* in 1883, he admitted humankind's indebtedness to Russia for stopping this terrible human trade in its territories; but when Eugene Schuyler reached Bukhara in 1873, the Russian ban on slavery then in place did not stop him from hearing of a caravan of sixty slaves arriving at the city and being able to visit a slave market and buy a young boy in order to set him free.

Bukhara did have its compensations. It might be 'the most shameless sink of iniquity that I know in the East', but it had 'something of the metropolitan character' that could not help but appeal to a man 'who had been wandering for a considerable time through the deserts of Central Asia'. There was 'good hot bread', tea, fruit, and cooked food, and he had two new shirts made. There were bookshops where he found treasures 'which would be of incalculable value to our Oriental historians and philologists', which he regretted he could not buy for reasons both financial and as being prejudicial to his disguise. Schuyler noticed that 'books were unwillingly

---

17 George Curzon, *Russia in Central Asia in 1889 and the Anglo-Russian Question* (London, 1889), 175.

sold to an "infidel"' and was sure that many of the best were hidden from him, but this should not have affected Arminius in his dervish disguise. Had Arminius advanced his study of language beyond those few books he could safely carry? He had encountered people from all the countries and races of Central Asia at the crossroads of Central Asian life, but he had hardly been in a position for careful philological study. Schuyler heard of ancient books in 'languages unknown to the learned men of Bukhara' in the emir's library and wondered if they might have come from the famous library of Brussa (Bursa), looted by Timur and supposed to have ended up in Samarkand.[18] That would have whetted Arminius' appetite and might have helped his linguistic endeavours but, instead, he found himself being lectured by a Chinese tea-seller expounding on the sixteen different varieties sold in his shop. He was also, with his tourist hat on, able to 'recommend as a dainty' the steamed dumplings, or *manti*, that he ate at the house of a Chinese Tartar who invited the hajis to dine. He commented, 'It seems singular that the Chinese should employ steam in the preparation of their meats'.

As part of his image, and, as he had proclaimed pilgrimage to be one of the main purposes of his journey, Arminius visited the shrine of Bahauddin, the fourteenth-century founder of the Naqshbandi order, 'distant two leagues from Bokhara'. This was part of the weekly routine for most of the population of Bukhara at the time. In the case of the pilgrim dervish, it was expected that he should go twice during his. Transport to the shrine, in the form of 300 fleet-footed asses, was laid on from the centre of the city; these beasts, by reputation, moved 'with indescribable speed' towards the tomb but 'evince the greatest indisposition to quit it', due to their devotion to the saint. If pilgrimage to this shrine was an essential ingredient of Arminius' cover for his journey, by the time he wrote about it, he seems to have considered the recalcitrant asses of greater interest to his readers and gave scant attention to 'the renowned Bahauddin Naqshband, founder of the order bearing the same name', even if he was, according to Arminius, 'the chief fountain of all those extravagances of religion which distinguish Eastern from Western Islamism'. Bahauddin was the national saint of Turkestan, and his tomb has remained an important site of pilgrimage, even clandestinely during the seventy years of the Soviet era, as a visiting Colin Thubron was to attest. It had first been shut

---

18 Schuyler, op. cit., 97.

down, then turned successively into a Museum of Atheism under Stalin, a silk factory, and a fertiliser store, but its symbolic power could not be destroyed. Just as it had been a centre of rebellion against Sovietisation in 1917, so it was to the shrine that protesters marched from Bukhara in 1987 as the Soviet system took its last gasps. Schuyler, in 1873, 'found an immense bazaar going on there and the streets were thronged with a crowd of people of every class and condition'. He did not immediately take seriously a mullah who walked beside him in the crowd with a large stone in his hand, muttering, 'just let me hit him, and he will drop dead at once and there will be one Kafir the less'.[19] Schuyler's companions realised the man was serious and, taking away his stone, drove the mullah into a field and gave him a good beating.

The tomb itself, like so many Sufi sites in Central Asia where Islam, local animism, and (sometimes) residual memories of Zoroastrian beliefs have come to some unspoken accommodation over the centuries, was covered with 'the usual rams' horns and rags'. Arminius had noted also 'a broom that served a long time to sweep out the sanctuary in Mecca'. Pilgrimage to the shrine of Bahauddin had become a sort of substitute in Central Asia for the Haj, with a threefold pilgrimage there being the equivalent of one to Mecca itself. The most important point of the pilgrimage, in a further echo of Mecca, was a black stone embedded in a wall near the tomb, which was known as the *sianghi murad* and which Arminius called 'the stone of desire'. It had been 'tolerably ground away and made smooth by the numerous foreheads of pious pilgrims that have been rubbed upon it' after circumambulating the saint's tomb. It was supposed, Schuyler would write, to 'cure and to prevent all maladies of the head' and was a part of the black stone of the Kaaba given to Bahauddin by Abraham.[20] Today, at the grandly restored, spotless, and ornamented shrine where Schuyler's 'immense bazaar' is still recognisable, the Uzbek government campaign against superstition in religious practice has long since removed any sign of rams' horns from the tomb, and the black stone has been coated with whitewash. But there is still an ancient mulberry-tree trunk nearby. It grew from Bahauddin's staff and, if you crawl underneath it, will grant your wish.

19 Ibid., 113.
20 Ibid., 114.

9

The Turning Point

The sparsity of holy charity in Bukhara had reduced the finances of Arminius and his companions to such a level that they were forced to sell their pack animals and hire two carts for transport toward Samarkand. Arminius shared his hideously uncomfortable vehicle with Haji Salih; they were bounced about 'like balls on a billiard table' until he felt quite seasick. But there were compensations. He had heard about the cultivation of the countryside between Bukhara and Samarkand, as the road ran through the Zeravshan river valley and, on the second day, there were villages, bazaars, and inns all along the road, and stalls with huge Russian samovars, 'ever on the boil', dispensing tea. Arminius would remember the mellow sense of relative safety and well-being on this journey, regardless of the dreadful cart, hauled by a poor maltreated horse. He also had time to think warmly about the travelling companions from whom his way would shortly part: 'My friends seemed to endear themselves to me more and more the nearer the moment of our separation approached', and he reflected, with some trepidation, on his looming, more solitary, journey from Samarkand back to Europe. This road was marked by milestones, attributed by Arminius to Timur, which reminded him of the historic importance of the routes he traversed, stretching all the way to China, and of the comings and goings of the ancient civilisations they crossed. The present emir's religious fervour was embodied in prayer platforms built along the road as alfresco mosques, 'so', Arminius reflected, 'each age has its own peculiar objects in view!' The locals, he discovered, had a view of their ruler that would have gladdened that tyrant's heart and considered that, after his successful incursions into neighbouring and rivalrous Kokand, their lord and master was well on the way to ruling China. After that he would undoubtedly take possession of Iran, Afghanistan, and 'Frenghistan' ('these they considered as adjoining countries'), and continue all the way to 'Roum'. 'The whole world, in fact, is, according to them, to be divided between the Sultan and the Emir', wrote Arminius.

As the travellers grew close to Samarkand, he saw 'the domes and minarets, with their various colours, all bathed in the beams of the morning sun', and could not help but find the view 'very pleasing'. Even in Marco Polo's day, Samarkand had already been 'a very large and splendid city', and now the great *madrasas* of the Registan (the central square at the heart of the city) and the dome of the Gur-e-Amir, Timur's mausoleum, stood out in the distance from the mulberry trees in the surrounding gardens. Curzon called the city 'the Macaranda of the Macedonians, the Samokien of the Buddhist pilgrim Hiouen Tsang, the Sumar Margo of Sir John Mandeville, the favourite and also the final resting place of Timur, the capital, with 150,000 inhabitants, of Sultan Babur, the combined Athens and Delphi of the remote East',[1] but, once he had entered Samarkand, Arminius was disappointed. The carts rolled heavily through the Bukhara gate and into the city through a vast, spreading cemetery, and the dream metropolis at the centre of the world became a real place of dirt and ruins, markets and people. On closer acquaintance, Arminius grudgingly acknowledged 'the ancient capital of Central Asia, from its site and the luxuriant vegetation in the midst of which it stands, as the most beautiful in Turkestan', but his bubble had been sadly pricked and he set about his sightseeing with his usual highly critical eye.

The travellers had halted at the caravanserai near the bazaar, where hajis were given free quarters, but their arrival had not gone unnoticed. They were invited to dine that day at the house of the official in charge of the emir's Samarkand palace, and Arminius was invited to lodge in the palace itself. The emir was due to arrive in the city, where he spent the summer months, after his victory in Kokand, and the hajis decided to delay their onward journey until such time as Arminius had been presented to him and had found other companions with whom he could begin his return journey. Arminius, meanwhile, was clearly distracted by the thought of losing his friends, by the prospect of his next journey, and of an audience with another unpredictable

---

1 Curzon, op. cit., 210–11.

ruler. His descriptions of the sights of Samarkand, seen during the eight days before the emir arrived, smack of the whistle-stop tour of today's hurrying traveller and the reiteration of guidebook descriptions. Arminius was also handicapped by the dangers of being seen to write notes, and told his readers he would 'only particularise the more remarkable' places he saw. He may have filled his time exploring 'several hundred places of pilgrimage', but his Samarkand comes across more as a place to be ticked off the list than one of spectacular wonders. In his 'character as a Hadji', Arminius set out first in search of saints, but as all the history of Samarkand 'is intimately blended with some holy legend', he felt it 'a very agreeable duty to see everything'. The tombs of the Shah-i-Zinda necropolis, the 'Living King' complex, ruthlessly restored in the twenty-first century, would have been dustier and less cared-for in Arminius' day: scarred by time and travails, the dazzling turquoise tiles sometimes slipped or fallen, and the 'forty tolerably broad marble steps' ascending to the mausoleums, the haunt of maimed and blind beggars. There were caretakers, nevertheless, who conducted Arminius and the hajis from tomb to tomb, or, as they thought, room to room, for the complex had been misleadingly identified as Timur's summer palace. It was built round the tomb of Qutham ibn Abbas, the 'Living King' – cousin to the Prophet and Samarkand's patron saint, who converted the Sogdian civilisation of the region to Islam in the seventh century. Legend held that he had been decapitated by the local Nestorian Christians; neatly catching his own head, he jumped into a deep well and lives on. He is expected to return one day as the defender of Islam. He may also have been swallowed by the friendly rock where he stood before he was decapitated, but his expected appearance to defeat the Russian invaders, a few years after Arminius' visit, failed to happen and, as the American traveller Eugene Schuyler would report in 1873, 'his fame has of late somewhat fallen off'.[2]

In the decoration of the Gur-e-Amir, the tomb of the savage and all-conquering Timur, Arminius found 'evidence of taste truly artistic'. He saw the great slab of jade covering Timur's tomb and was led by the superintendent of the building, rather unwillingly, to visit the actual grave in the vault below. He was also shown the Quran on the grave, said to have been

2 Schuyler, op. cit., Vol. I, 247.

written by Osman (Uthman), the Prophet's secretary and third caliph.[3] It
had reputedly been part of the loot from the library at Bursa, but Arminius
did not believe it. In fact, he did not believe in the existence of the famous
library at all. It was indeed an extraordinary idea, that the barbaric Timur
might have taken the time to arrange the transport by mule, over some
6,500 kilometres, of a treasury of Armenian Greek manuscripts which no
Tartar could have read or, probably, cared to try to read. Of the Registan
and the great *madrasas* forming the centre of Samarkand, Arminius had
little to say; they were 'likely soon to become perfect ruins'. Only the Bibi
Khanym Mosque, ruined since the Persian Nader Shah invaded in 1740,
met with his favour. Carriages for hire were stored in its massive crumbling
interior, but Arminius found 'its pavement completely covered with mosaic
made of earth, the composition and colouring of which are of incomparable
beauty and so firmly cemented that it occasioned me indescribable trouble
to cut away the calyx of a flower; and even of this I could only remove in a
perfect state the innermost part'. (He was only doing what everyone else was
doing.) 'Although', he wrote, 'the work of destruction is eagerly proceeded
with, many a century must the people of Samarkand continue to tear away
and cut down before this work of annihilation is complete'. Bibi Khanym
stands now, still shedding shards of azure tiles, as restoration work, begun
under Soviet rule in the 1970s, continues to recreate its original grandeur
and reverse the process of destruction. 'So much', wrote Arminius, 'for the
ancient and historical city of Samarkand'.

Samarkand was particularly busy when he was there because the emir's
troops had poured into the city at the end of their campaign against the
khanate of Kokand. At least it had an easier climate in the summer than
Bukhara, Arminius thought, but he remarked that the water, recommended
to him as 'ambrosia', was detestable, even compared with Bukhara's broth of
disease and pollution. In discussion with Haji Bilal and Haji Salih, he had
finally made his mind up about his route home. The former had been keen to

3 Eugene Schuyler wrote of this Quran that it was 'a most beautiful manuscript, written
entirely in Cufic characters upon parchment'. He told the story that it had been written by
Osman himself but carried eventually to Samarkand by Khodja Akhrar, the fifteenth-century
Naqshbandi leader. After Russia took Samarkand, the imams of his mosque sold it for 125
roubles, and it was removed to the Imperial Public Library in St Petersburg, now the National
Library of Russia.

take Arminius with him to Akhsu in Armenia and, from there, send him on via Tibet and Kashmir, or via Beijing, to Mecca, but Haji Salih had objected. He thought Arminius should come back to see Kokand when the region was at peace, then go on to Kashgar in China and on further. But for now, he should go back to Tehran via Herat and return from there to Roum. The distances were otherwise too great and Arminius too reduced in circumstances to survive in lands of 'black unbelievers' where no charity would be forthcoming. 'A journey', Arminius thought, that 'Marco Polo himself would not have ventured, is really grand', but 'moderation whispered in my ear'. It would 'be a pity if I sacrificed the experience which I had acquired, however trifling, in a hazardous and uncertain enterprise'. He was only thirty-one and may have envisaged returning at some time to continue his journey eastwards. Possibly he had simply had enough of travelling, quite apart from thinking that his credit might altogether be running out with the Academy if he did not report to them soon on his experiences. (His philological findings, if they existed specifically, are not explored in his accounts of his travels.)

A major theme in Arminius' writings is always that of religion, in particular fanaticism, 'the chief cause of hypocrisy and impiety' in every faith; and according to him, the further east one moved – and he included even 'the inhabitants of India, Thibet and China' in this judgement – the worse this became. It seems he had truly seen enough of the East for now. It had not been the Orient of his youthful imaginings. Haji Bilal accused him, jokingly, of cowardice, as he turned his face once more to the West, 'and the European reader may agree with him', but he began to prepare seriously for his departure. Then the emir arrived: a public holiday was declared in Samarkand and 'kettles of monstrous size' were set up in the Registan to cook huge pilafs to feed the population of the city. Each contained 'a sack of rice, three sheep chopped to pieces, a large pan of sheep's fat (enough to make, with us, five pounds of candles)' and 'a small sack of carrots', all of which was boiled together. Tea was also served, and 'the eating and drinking proceeded bravely'. The following day, Arminius and the hajis presented themselves at a public audience with the emir and were alarmed when an official informed them that his majesty wished to see Haji Reshid alone. Arminius' fears grew as he waited in an anteroom, when a court official stroked the back of his neck, remarking, Arminius hoped as a joke, 'Unfortunately, I have left my knife at home today'. On entering the emir's presence, Arminius recited a sura and a prayer 'for the welfare of the Sovereign', and took, without permission, the rightful seat of a holy man, 'quite close to his royal person'. The emir was well informed as to Arminius' pilgrimage but asked, as he well might, 'and hast thou no other object in coming from such distant lands?' Arminius' claim, with his lame leg, to be a *Djihangeshte*, a world pilgrim, for whom it had always been 'the warmest wish of my heart to behold noble Bokhara and enchanting Samarkand', astonished his questioner. When he remarked on the infirmity, the false dervish hastened to point out that the emir's illustrious ancestor, the 'conqueror of the world', Timur-i-Leng, Timur the Lame, had been similarly afflicted. Pleased with this answer, Arminius reported, the emir questioned him about his impressions of Bukhara and Samarkand, and Arminius 'incessantly strove to ornament' his answers with verses from the Quran and the flowery Persian of diplomacy. This, Arminius wrote, 'produced a good effect upon him, for he is himself a Mollah and tolerably well acquainted with Arabic'. A servant was shortly sent for, a whispered command given, and Arminius told to follow the man. Terrified again of 'that dreadful death which was ever present to my mind', Arminius was taken 'through a number of yards and halls', until they reached a darkened room where he was told to wait. Expecting the worst, he was relieved when his guide reappeared, carrying a parcel which contained 'a highly ornamental suit of clothing' and some money to support him during his journey.

Arminius hurried back to his friends. He wrote later that he had heard that the vizier Rahmet Bey had sent a report to the emir that had made the ruler suspicious. But given what we know, from the account of the Russian diplomat Herr von Lankenau, of Rahmet Bey's tolerant attitude toward Arminius, that is perhaps another instance of him gilding the truth for the sake of a better story. The American Eugene Schuyler also met Emir Muzaffar al-Din, ruler of Samarkand, when he was travelling towards Bukhara from Qarshi and the emir was encamped some distance from the large 'station' of Karaul with his army. Schuyler had heard that the emir's subjects loathed him and 'believe him to be gifted with the evil eye'. He was reputed to have inherited his father's cruelty without his strength of character, and Schuyler thought he looked 'flabby and unhealthy', with uncontrollably shaking hands, which Schuyler put down to overuse of aphrodisiacs.[4] If the emir and

---

4 Schuyler, op. cit., Vol. II, 84.

the khan of Khiva were indeed regular users of the aphrodisiac 'Spanish fly', prepared from the local *Lytta vesicatoria* beetles, poisoning themselves in this way cannot have improved their tempers and might well have exacerbated their unpredictable behaviour. Arminius and the hajis may well have been right to be nervous of the emir's attentions, but the sultan's *tugra* was never to be ignored, even if the emir's frightened people insisted on their ruler's equal standing with the Ottoman sovereign. At the same time, like Rahmet Bey, the emir may have been genuinely curious about this extraordinary visitor rather than viewing him as a threat. Whatever the real level of danger, Arminius felt able to congratulate himself 'on the flexibility of my tongue', which had got him out of another potentially tricky situation. From his account, the hajis were still nervous on his behalf and recommended he should immediately leave Samarkand for the far side of the Amu Darya. There, he might await a suitable caravan for Herat 'amongst the hospitable Ersari Turkomen'.

The final parting from his friends was now at hand. In retrospect at least, Arminius was overcome with emotion. 'My pen is too feeble to convey any adequate idea of the distressing scene that took place between us; on both sides we were really equally moved'. He had been travelling with the hajis for six months and they had been his comrades in all the dangers, disasters, and successes of the journey. They had looked after and looked out for their strange foreign companion and, Arminius knew, 'Separation was, in our case, equivalent to death'. There was no chance of them meeting again and he longed, he wrote, to 'communicate the secret of my disguise to these, my best friends in the world', but he thought how dreadfully Haji Salih would have felt the deception and 'determined to spare him this sorrow'; 'he must, I thought, be left in the fond delusion'. What did the hajis know, in the end, of their unusual companion? If Haji Bilal and Haji Salih ever returned to Tehran, did they have questions for the Turkish ambassador, or did they put their meeting and journey with Arminius down to kismet and leave it at that? It is easy to believe that the travellers had become true friends, even if it was not in Arminius' nature to express emotion and friendship, or to describe such a parting without his pen spluttering into sentimentality. He 'wept like a child, when tearing himself from their embraces', and they 'were all bathed in tears'. He 'turned round many times to look back. At last, they disappeared, and I found I was only gazing upon the domes of Samarkand, illuminated by the faint light of the rising moon'. His later readers in Victorian London must have loved it.

It is only fair to remind ourselves here that Arminius, on his dervish journey, was young, adventurous, and for all his linguistic sleight of tongue and enquiring mind, knew little of Central Asia beyond the knowledge he had picked up during his years in Constantinople. He had not studied the history, knew little of the people or the geography of the region and, if he knew of the most famous English travellers there, did not know – or completely ignored – earlier writers of other nationalities, especially the Russians, who had already written in depth about these territories adjacent to their homeland. Nominally on a mission for the Hungarian Academy, he was as much following his own nose, his own dreams and inclinations when he set off into Turkestan. He probably fitted the bill for Charles Alison and/or others in the diplomatic world, for whom he might keep his sharp eyes and ears open for snippets of information, but if there was some other secret or official purpose to his meetings with the rulers of Central Asia, he never committed it to paper. The anomalies and self-aggrandisement in his accounts of his travels are a part of the contradictions of the man himself. He had a ready tongue, enough chutzpah to pull off a disguise, a reasonable knowledge of Islam, and those same actorly abilities to call on that he had first begun to polish as a Jewish altar boy in the Christian Piarist college at St Georghen years before. If, later in life, the scholar's clothes would fit Arminius more justly, the false dervish was not a scholar, he was simply a storyteller – like other travel writers before and since. It is a pity that his determination to present himself as an academic so often detracted from this. He might embellish the truth on one side of the page but, on the other, revert to pompous moralising and portentous but not always well-checked facts – flaws that were to be anatomised by Schuyler in his scathing review of Arminius' *History of Bukhara from the Earliest Period Down to the Present,*[5]

---

5 There is a postscript to this. According to Arminius, he received a letter from Schuyler in 1886 which he quoted in *The Story of My Struggles*, in which Schuyler asked to meet him if he was willing 'to overlook some hasty criticisms of mine when I was in Central Asia'. Arminius wrote that he gave Schuyler 'a warm reception' and had 'corresponded with him ever since'. Schuyler, one can only imagine, was fascinated to meet the false dervish in person whatever he thought about his stories.

which Schuyler included in his account of his own travels, published in 1876.[6]

In the first place, Schuyler took extreme issue with Arminius' claim to be the first 'to traverse regions where I have had scarcely any, or absolutely no, predecessors', and provided a considerable list of those predecessors. As a result of this false claim, 'the very small particle of what is really new in his book is lost in the mass of what is old and well-known, which in most cases too, he has misunderstood and has erroneously studied… It seems, in short,' Schuyler concluded, 'that Mr Vambéry, in beginning his work, had not the slightest acquaintance with the history of Central Asia; and in the simplicity of his soul regarded his own gradual emancipation from complete ignorance on this subject as discoveries which would astonish and delight the learned world'. His book, Schuyler considered, was not, therefore, 'a conscientious and learned work, the result of many years' study, but a very light and superficial compilation, put together somehow or other in a few months, and with very frequent errors and omissions of the most unpardonable character'. But none of that would matter had the book not been received by 'unlearned persons in the West and Russia', at its author's own estimation, 'as a monumental work, and in this quality been lauded to the skies'. Schuyler proceeded to pick apart the preface, introduction, and nineteen chapters of the *History* in excoriating terms, pointing out a plethora of mistakes – geographical, historical, dynastic, anthropological, linguistic, and economic. Schuyler is critical even of Arminius' linguistic abilities. He was minimally prepared to mark the credit column in Arminius' favour with regard to his 'endeavour to correct the orthography of peculiarly Turkish names, which has been corrupted by the ignorance of the Turkish dialects' by Arab and Persian historians, but could not help but condemn Arminius for writing the names 'most frequently, not as they are pronounced by the natives, but as they are pronounced in Constantinople only'. Finally, Schuyler took care to point out that it was not only he who held these views of Arminius' *History*. Professor Alfred von Gutschmid, a German Orientalist and expert on Eastern languages, 'does not find words enough to brand the manner in which the author set about the work, for which he was not at all fitted by his education, the want of conscientiousness which he has displayed in his

---

6 'Appendix II' in Schuyler, op. cit., Vol. I, 360–89.

labour and the vaingloriousness with which he has proclaimed the unusual qualities of his history'.

*

Of his new travelling companions, Arminius had little to say. They were 'far from being to me like those friends from whom I had just parted', but he was still well served by young Mullah Ishak (who would find his life taking a most unexpected turn from now on). The road was easy enough, passing through desert which 'may be styled a moderate-sized field, with deep wells, and populated by shepherds and their flocks'. Arminius thought it bore resemblance to the grasslands of the Hungarian puszta. The roads were safe, due to strict enforcement by the emir, but Arminius came across another instance of unlawful enslavement. A young woman in another caravan travelling to Qarshi had been sold by her husband to an old Tajik, and begged the haji Arminius, 'tell me where it is written that a Mussulman can sell his wife who has borne him children?' Arminius agreed it was a sin, but the old man just laughed, 'for he had, probably, already an understanding with the Kazi Kelan [the judge] of Qarshi'. It took the caravan three nights to reach that city, where Arminius had an introduction from the hajis to a certain Ishan Hassan. He advised Arminius to buy an ass, as they were cheap in Qarshi, as were the knives, needles, thread, glass beads, handkerchiefs, and Indian carnelians that were traded in the city. With these accoutrements, Arminius might barter for bread and melons with the nomads on his route, padding his income further with the usual blessings and amulets and all the panoply of efficacious beliefs of those times.

Qarshi, it seems, was a cheerful place, where the fashionable strolled beside the river in the afternoons and the tea stalls with their giant samovars made a busy trade. It was also a centre for the grain trade in the region: for the pink salt, mined nearby and fashionable today as 'Himalayan' rock salt; for tobacco; and for raw opium. When the travellers set out again, for the town of Kerki on the Amu Darya river and the frontier with Persia, Arminius' saddlebags were filled not only with the manuscripts he had bought in Bukhara but also with his new pedlar's wares. The journey was only twenty kilometres, but the caravan spent two nights camping along the way in domed *sardaba* – the traditional water cisterns of ancient Iran. At one, they found a large encampment of Uzbek nomads whose cattle and children were splashing about in the water 'and spoiling its flavour a little'. At Kerki the river was nearly twice as wide as the Danube where it passed through Budapest, with a fort on either side and a ferry that took three hours to make the crossing as it was swept downstream by the current. Arminius was congratulating himself on getting a free ride as a haji when the hajis were stopped by the *deryabeghi*, who superintended the ferry, and accused of being runaway slaves escaping to their Persian homeland. Arminius' companions were quickly released as their language and features proclaimed their non-Persian origins, but he was altogether more of a puzzle. Losing his temper, he handed over his passport and demanded, in several languages, to see the governor of the fortress. The governor was a Persian from Tabriz and a former slave himself, who told Arminius he had been in Constantinople on several occasions and recognised him easily as a foreigner. Nothing, he said, would happen to Arminius, but every freed slave was required to pay a border tax of two ducats and they all tried to avoid it by disguising themselves, often as hajis.

Arminius soon discovered it was not only slaves who tried to avoid the levy. The *kervenbashis* also colluded in the deception. They charged freed slaves a large fee for their protection in a caravan, but that made them responsible for any taxes. When Mullah Zeman, the *kervenbashi* of the Herat-bound caravan, who Arminius had already met in Samarkand, arrived more than a week later, his caravan included forty emancipated Persians, and Arminius witnessed the habitual argument over the number liable for tax. It was usual for a *kervenbashi* to get as many genuine hajis as possible together for a caravan, so that former slaves might be hidden amongst them, but everybody involved knew the game too well. It took a whole day for customs officials to check 'the bales of goods, the men, horses, camels and asses' and, when the caravan set out, it was accompanied by an official to make sure no one else joined who had by-passed the border post. The governor returned Arminius' passport with a few coins, five *tenghe* – a useful amount, Arminius found, when his caravan reached the khanate of Andkhoy (now Afghanistan). There, one *tenghe* bought fifty melons. 'These melons', however, were 'far from being so good as those I had seen on the banks of the Oxus'. They were still probably the best thing about Andkhoy, which was notorious for its dreadful climate and water. A Persian verse said of the place 'vaunt it not for it is a real hell'.

While waiting for Mullah Zeman, Arminius and Ishak had been exploring the country, travelling among the local Turkmen tribes as far as Mazar-i-Sharif in what is now Afghanistan. Their guide here was Khalfa Niyaz, an important *ishan*, or leader of Sufi lineage among the Ersari Turkmen, who had a *tekke* where a number of students were taught. He also had permission from Mecca to recite sacred poems: 'In doing so he used to place before him a cup with water into which he spat at the end of each poem'. This bizarre practice allowed the sanctity of his text to enter the water, which was then sold 'to the best bidder as a wonder-working medicine.' 'There is only one quality of the Turkmens', Arminius wrote, 'that they have retained uncorrupted, hospitality'. He appears to have been quite uninterested in Mazar-i-Sharif, which competes with Najaf in Iraq to be the site of the real tomb of Ali, the cousin and son-in-law of the Prophet. He summoned some enthusiasm for the famous Gull-i-Surkh roses that 'grow upon the pretended tomb of Ali, and have the sweetest smell and the finest colour of any I ever saw', and was slightly more interested by the nearby ruins of ancient Balkh, which showed its original size. Beyond that, 'only a few heaps of earth are pointed to as the site of the ancient Bactra, and of the modern ruins there is nothing remarkable'. This supposed 'Mother of Cities', it was true, was by now nothing more than an Afghan village of barely '2000 souls', as it was described by Alexander Burnes.[7] The place was rightly notorious, as Arminius painfully discovered, for its scorpions. After he had enjoyed an evening with a group of Turkmen nomads, who had brought favourite poems for him to read ('it was delightful to have them sitting around me in the stilly night within view of the Oxus rolling onwards' and 'listening to me with rapt attention'), he fell asleep around midnight close to a wall. A little later, he was woken by appalling pain in his right foot. He had been stung by a scorpion. Suffering agonies that 'darted from the tips of my toes to the top of my head, rushing up and down like a stream of fire', Arminius was convinced he would die and beat his head on the ground. The Turkmen instantly applied a tourniquet and sucked the poison from the wound. They had seen it all before and now simply tied the patient to a tree until he calmed down and fell asleep. The pain had abated by the time he woke.

It seems surprising, when writing with his later London audience in mind,

---

7 Burnes, op. cit., 80.

that Arminius did not claim to have emulated Burnes in hunting out the graves of the Englishman William Moorcroft and his companions, to add a little colour to his account of the ruins of Balkh. Arminius had certainly heard of Moorcroft and had earlier followed the Moorcroft trail at Andkhoy, where an old Uzbek claimed to remember the *Hekim Bashi*. These unfortunate earlier travellers in the region had died mysteriously, reputedly of poisoning, near Balkh in 1825, as they returned from Bukhara towards India. Moorcroft, a former employee of the East India Company, had been one of the first to warn of the dangers of Russian influence in Central Asia. He had qualified as a veterinary surgeon in France, and the old Uzbek assured Arminius that he had been a 'clever magician and a good physician'. As to his death, the old man is supposed to have informed Arminius that Moorcroft had died of a fever in his uncle's house.

When Mullah Zeman's caravan finally set out from Kerki, Ishak and Arminius, on his 'heavily-laden ass', were joining a party of 50–100 people, 400 camels, and 190 asses, plus a few horses. Among his fellow travellers were many tragic stories from the emancipated slaves: an old man who had reduced himself to beggary to pay the ransom for his son; another whose whole family had been captured, and who had been searching for his wife and six children. Only four children had survived, and he had been able to ransom only the younger two. There was a young man who had ransomed his mother; and a father and son who had already gained their freedom once, only to be captured again for a further two years. There were, Arminius wrote, at that time, more than 15,000 mounted Tekke Turkmen, whose livelihood was kidnapping. The present caravan however was too large to be at risk and had arrived safely at Andkhoy where 'it swelled to double its former size'. From there, they faced a long march to avoid coming too close to the village of Khairabad, on the road to Maymana, with its rapacious Afghan population. Two days later, the travellers arrived at Maymana itself, centre of the small independent Uzbek khanate of the same name, where the *kervenbashi* presented the hajis with two sheep in acknowledgement of the efficacy of their prayers in preserving his caravan. Arminius had claimed for himself the role of senior haji and was responsible now for sharing out the roast meat as they celebrated with hymns and a ritual prayer or *zikr*, where 'we shouted out to the full extent of our voices two thousand times, Ya hoo! Ya hakk!'

In Maymana, Arminius was again nervous of being unmasked. Mullah

Khalmurad, who had inspired him in Constantinople with his tales of his own Central Asian travels and had given him lessons in Chagatai, was reputed to be in the town. The mullah, 'a very cunning fellow', Arminius wrote, had realised, 'on the Bosphorus', that Reshid Effendi was not the real thing. He had offered to be Arminius' guide to Bukhara, on the grounds that he had undertaken the same service for that eccentric clergyman, Joseph Wolff, but Arminius had foiled his intentions by suggesting Mecca as his real destination. Arminius was sure, 'in spite of the kindness with which I had loaded him', that Khalmurad would denounce him if they met, and it does seem perfectly possible that the mullah might not have considered Arminius' deception a kindness at all. As insurance, Arminius took care to ingratiate himself with the well-respected Ishan Eyub, leader of a *tekke* in Maymana, eventually asking the *ishan* about Khalmurad. He was relieved to hear that the mullah had died in Mecca. Ishan Eyub introduced him to the mullah's young son, who was now in his care. Arminius presented the child with 'a whole string of glass beads' and said three *fatihas*, the prayer that is the first *surah*, or chapter, of the Quran, for the salvation of Khalmurad's soul, an act that no doubt reflected in part his own feelings of relieved gratitude. Later, back in Tehran, he was told by the Turkish *chargé d'affaires* that a mullah of exactly Khalmurad's description had been at the embassy a month earlier and had spoken of his former pupil. So the two men might have crossed paths on their separate journeys, and Arminius had been lucky again.

Of Maymana, the town at the centre of this small khanate, there was little good to tell. It was 'extremely filthy and ill built and consists of 1,500 mud huts, and a bazaar built of brick, that seems about to fall'. The khanate was, however, strategically important: 'he who would wish to take Bokhara must destroy Maymene, or be sure of its friendly feeling'. Arminius was unconvinced of its ability to resist such an invader, based on what he could see of the town's meagre defences. The citadel was on a hill overlooked by 'still higher hills, whence a battery could in a few hours reduce it to ashes'. He thought Maymana's reputation was based more on the bravery and 'resolute warlike character' of the khanate's inhabitants than the walls and ditches of its fortifications. It was another important trading post, with an export business in raisins, aniseed, and pistachio nuts to Persia and Baghdad, and regular horse-markets where the finest horses were sold for a quarter of the price they would fetch in Persia. There were the usual issues over local tolls and taxes to be paid by the caravan, and Arminius became involved in the release of a group of Russian exiles, who had been arrested by a relative of the khan on suspicion of being runaway slaves. As it turned out, they were criminals, more properly rebels, of Turkish origin, from the Caucasus, who had been sentenced to exile and hard labour in Siberia by the Russians. They had escaped into what is now the vast Kazakh Steppe, eating grass and roots to survive, until they reached a nomad encampment. From there, on a journey of over 3,000 kilometres, they had travelled to Bukhara where, astonishingly, the emir had given them money for travel expenses. They had been threatened before with capture as runaways, but it was only on reaching Maymana that this threat had been realised. Arminius was petitioned by the *kervenbashi* and other members of his caravan to vouch for the fugitives' true status as they attempted to return home to the Governorate of Yelisavetpol (a region now divided between Azerbaijan and Armenia). Once again, the reader cannot help but wonder why Arminius, who succeeded in having the captives released, would have included such a dull, truncated version of their remarkable escape story in his account, even if it did provide another instance in which he could be cast as the hero of the hour. One would relish more of the captives' own quite extraordinary account but, on that, Arminius is unforthcoming.

Nonetheless, we learn that the 'whole karavan was rejoiced', when the escapees joined it, and the journey towards Herat continued, interrupted only with the usual quarrels as more taxes and tolls were demanded at every local frontier. At the Maymana border, the *yuzbashi* who oversaw the border area had the effrontery to extract 'whip money', usually only given to an armed escort, from every passer-by. Arminius was sorry to see the last Uzbek nomads at this point – 'open-hearted, honest people', who 'left in my mind the most pleasing recollections of any natives of Central Asia'. There were less friendly Turkmen tribes on the route the caravan now took, through a fertile valley of north-west Afghanistan towards the Murgab River, but the caravan was large and the khan of Bala Murgab sent out an armed escort of Jamshidi tribesmen to accompany it. When the escort departed, at the mountain pass leading to the river, whip money was exacted once again, with the freed slaves forced to pay double. The following day, as the caravan forded the river in the early morning, Arminius' ass slipped and fell on the stony riverbed. Arminius was soaked through. He had placed his knapsack with his manuscripts on the back of a camel, so they survived, but he was thoroughly put out by his wetting. His funds were also alarmingly low and, while the caravan rested for four days by the river, he took once again to his dervish trade and to selling his remaining pedlar's stock to the local population. This did not go well. The 'beautiful light green' waters of the Murgab flowed through a poverty-stricken region where people lived under shelters of tattered rags, and bread was of far greater importance than blessings or beads. Arminius hoped to explore the ruins rumoured to exist nearby (probably those of Marw al-Rudh, a city founded by the Sasanians in the fifth century CE). This proved impossible, but then Arminius had not entirely believed the rumours of towers and pillars 'dating from the time of the Parsees', on the partisan grounds that they had not been researched by the English, 'who had adequate knowledge of Herat and its environs'.

It was a four-day journey with horses from Bala Murgab to Herat, but double that with camels, and for Arminius it dragged. A journey which, he pointed out when he reached Herat, might be accomplished from Bukhara in twenty or twenty-five days, had taken six weeks. Along the Murgab, the caravan passed the ruins of a castle of the Timurid Sultan Husayn Bayqara (r. 1469–1506), during whose benign reign, Arminius wrote, 'the whole of the neighbourhood was in a flourishing state', with 'many pleasure-houses' built along the river. From the Murgab, the caravan then took three hours to cross what is now known as the Zarmast Pass in the Paropamisus Mountains. Late that night, it reached the town of Qala-e-Naw, riven by rivalry and quarrels between local and traditionally persecuted Hazaras and the Heratis. Arminius was disposed to side with the Heratis, who were ruled by the British ally Sher Ali Khan, the emir of Afghanistan, and who had recently succeeded his remarkable father Dost Mohammed Khan. Baba Khan, the Hazara chief in Qala-e-Naw, did not endear himself to Arminius in any case when he arrived in person to demand customs duty from the caravan. When a message of complaint was despatched by the *kervenbashi* to the governor of Herat, 'instead of duties, a famous sum was exacted for whip money', which even the hajis could not escape, and Arminius was forced to pay two francs for his ass. The merchants in the caravan swelled local coffers further by buying quantities of pistachio nuts and *berek*, the cloth woven by the Hazara women from camel wool and used to make the traditional Turkman coats called *chekmen*. Four days later, after a cold and hazardous mountain journey, the caravan arrived at Karukh, only a few kilometres from Herat. The caravan's home city had been taken by Dost Mohammed after a ten-month siege (his final act in unifying Afghanistan), shortly before his death. After an absence of six months, the Heratis among the party were desperate to see how their homes had fared, but they were hampered once again by 'the officer of the customs'.

Arminius had hoped, in Afghanistan, to find 'a land already half organised, where, through long contact with Western influence, at least something of order and civilisation had been introduced', and to dispense finally with his dervish 'disguise and sufferings'. He once again declared himself 'cruelly deceived'. Afghan petty officialdom proved itself, if anything, more brutal and rapacious than anything he had previously encountered. At Karukh, everything in the caravan was minutely examined and listed, and the travellers were forced to strip to 'shirt, drawers, and upper garment', with every item of clothing declared liable to duty. The hajis were taxed heavily, including their asses, and those who could not pay were forced to sell their animals on the spot. The governor of the town, Bator Khan, arrived to levy his personal whip money wearing a European-style military tunic, which cheered Arminius no end. His reaction, however, was noted by Bator Khan, who then questioned the *kervenbashi* about the foreign-looking haji. Attempting to draw in Arminius, who he suspected of travelling on a secret mission, he treated him with considerable affability and finally made as if to shake hands. The false dervish saw the trap coming and quickly raised his own hands to give the traditional blessing. Bator Khan went away laughing, curious but unconcerned once he had paid his dues. Arminius, meanwhile, was puzzling over the governor's title of *mejir*. He had also discovered *kornels* and *djornels* among Afghan officers, and it only dawned on him after some time that these were majors, colonels, and generals, the ranks possibly quite randomly applied. In Herat he also noticed that the favourite garment for Afghan men was 'the red English coat', and that 'weapons are borne by all'. Military rank, to add to an arsenal of pistols, sword, dagger, rifle, and shield, even for trips to the bazaar, was undoubtedly in fashion with the 'wild, martial-looking Afghan'.

When Captain Hippisley Cunliffe Marsh of the 18th Bengal Cavalry saw Herat, a decade after Arminius, he wrote of the broad, well-watered valley where the city was situated, 'which, if the country were quiet, would be one large sheet of cultivation. As the land is fertile and the climate good, a few years would turn all this desert into a garden'.[8] Arminius too remarked on the 'character of loveliness and of fertility' of the countryside surrounding Herat, regretting the 'political importance' that had made it 'an apple of discord to adjoining nations'. Colonel G. B. Malleson entitled his book on the region *The Granary and Garden of Central Asia*.[9] Poor Herat, sitting in what the classical historian Herodotus described as the 'bread-basket of Asia', sheltered by the Paropamisus Mountains and watered by the Hari River, was situated at a confluence of the great trading routes between East and West; and the glorious city of a Timurid golden age under Shah Rukh Mirza (1377–1447) was and is a bone that has been fought over throughout its history.[10] For the Russians, Colonel Paul Venukoff wrote: 'If the English were to establish a political and commercial preponderance at Herat, we should hardly be able to hold our own in northern Khorassan and Merv'.[11] In the nineteenth century it became the 'Gate to India', as described by the 'hero of Herat', Eldred Pottinger, who had joined the Afghans defending the city against the Russian-supported Persians in 1837.[12] Now Malleson wrote: 'The possession of Herat by Russia, means the possession of the one line by which India can be invaded. The possession of Herat by England means the annihilation of all the Russian hopes of an invasion of India'.[13] In 1885 the British would destroy the great Timurid Gawhar Shad Musalla complex of Herat to give themselves a clear line of fire against the Russians, who never came, and the battles for the city continued in the twentieth and on into the twenty-first century.

Arminius found the place in ruins after the most recent siege of Herat,

---

8 H. C. Marsh, *A Ride Through Islam* (London, 1877), 148.

9 Colonel G. B. Malleson, *Herat: The Granary and Garden of Central Asia* (London, 1880). Malleson was a writer and historian, as well as a military man, and as much of a Russophobe as Arminius.

10 Shah Rukh Mirza was the son of Timur and a great patron of the arts, most particularly in Herat.

11 Quoted in Charles Marvin, *Reconnoitring Central Asia: Pioneering Adventures in the Region lying between Russia and India* (London, 1886), 54.

12 Pottinger (1811–43) was an Anglo-Indian army officer and diplomat who became a Victorian hero for his role in helping the Afghans defend the besieged city successfully against a Persian army that included Russian officers. He was another Russophobe and player of the Great Game, the goal of which was to keep Russia out of India.

13 Malleson, op. cit., 87.

when the Afghans under Dost Mohammed took the city on 27 May 1863, but wrote: 'it is astonishing to us how rapidly the wounds inflicted seem to have scarred over', although 'entire quarters of the town remain solitary and abandoned'. The 'diversified throngs' he found in Herat included Afghan soldiers wearing shakos as well as their English uniforms, 'a covering for the head contrary to the prescriptions of the Koran', and he felt he had 'fallen upon a land where Islamite fanaticism had lost its formidable character'. He supposed he might at last safely give up his disguise. He saw that many of the soldiers had also shaved off their moustaches and wore whiskers, 'an appendage regarded as a deadly sin in Islam', and wondered if he might even meet British officers in the city. His financial situation was now dire, and he had been forced to sell his ass for a mere twenty-six krans, of which most had gone in tax on the sale and in paying small debts to his fellow travellers. It was cold now, and he was short of food and sleeping in an open ruin, but he was cheered by the thought that Persia was only ten days away. The problem was how to get there. A caravan to Mashhad would not start out until it had more passengers, and the Tekke Turkmen were cheerfully plundering close to the city, which was still in a state of flux after its Afghan conquest and where the newly appointed governor, Dost Mohammed's grandson Yakub Khan, was only sixteen years old. Then Arminius heard of a Persian envoy who was returning to Tehran and begged to be allowed to accompany him. The Persian was quite uninterested and only asked Arminius if he had brought any horses with him from Bukhara. Arminius thought the man was suspicious of his disguise, which was probably true, given that many of Arminius' former haji companions abandoned him at this point and were welcomed into the envoy's train. Only faithful Mullah Ishak remained and begged every day for food, which he also prepared and 'even refused respectfully to share with me out of the same plate'.

Finally, Arminius went to see Yakub Khan. He found the young prince in the damaged Charbagh Palace, where public audiences were held in a large hall overlooking the ground where Afghan troops drilled. Arminius noticed that they were commanded by an officer who gave the orders, 'Right shoulder forward! Left shoulder forward!' with a genuine English accent. He was impressed enough by the troops to describe their 'very military bearing, far better than the Ottoman army'. Indeed, 'these might have been European troops if most of them had not had on their bare feet the pointed Kabuli shoe'. At the entrance to the hall, the assembled crowd made way for the haji Arminius with Ishak in attendance, both clad in enormous turbans and typically tattered dervish dress. Yakub Khan was sitting in a chair by the window where he could watch his troops outside, wearing a high-collared military uniform and with his vizier on his right. His other courtiers and officers bordered the room and, after the usual dervish blessing, Arminius strode up to the prince, pushed the vizier, 'a corpulent Afghan' who was rumoured to be both stupid and corrupt, out of his way, and sat down next to Yakub Khan. There was some laughter in the room at this treatment of the vizier, but Arminius ignored it and raised his hands to 'repeat the usual prayer required by the law', saying in Arabic, according to his own translation: 'God our Lord, let us take a blessed place, for of a verity Thou are the best quartermaster'. As he spoke the prince looked him full in the face and, as all around stroked their beards in the customary fashion, reacted in complete amazement: '*Walla au billa, Inghilizi hasti*', meaning, 'By God, I swear you are an Englishman', and burst out laughing. Clapping his hands, the young man continued examining Arminius' face carefully, saying 'Hadji, tell me, you are an Englishman in disguise are you not?'

Arminius must have felt quite confident of his abilities in facing down this mere boy, although, he wrote, he regretted it, but he 'had cause to dread the wild fanaticism of the Afghans'. He might also have had cause to dread payback from the discomfited vizier, and he replied, 'Have done, Sire! He who takes, even in sport, the believer for an unbeliever, is himself an unbeliever'. Yakub Khan was embarrassed, saying that he had never seen a haji from Bukhara who looked like Arminius. The sultan's passport was duly produced, and Arminius explained that he was 'not a Bokhariot, but a Stambouli', who had met Yakub Khan's cousin in Constantinople in 1860 and been present at his reception by the sultan. Yakub Khan gave Arminius some money and requested he visit again during his stay in Herat. He did not speak of his suspicions again, although his initial reaction had some consequences for Arminius during his time in Herat. Years later, during Yakub Khan's long exile in India after his abdication of the Afghan throne in 1879, he was questioned by Colonel Robert Warburton[14] about the by then

---

14 Sir Robert had a remarkable life. He was born in Afghanistan to an Afghan mother, Shah Jahan Begum, a niece of the emir, Dost Mohammed, and Lt. Col. Robert Warburton of the

well-known story of his meeting with Arminius. Yakub Khan remembered it well. He had known Arminius was a foreigner and presumed he was English, before the false dervish had sat down beside him in his audience hall. He told Warburton:

> I was seated in an upper chamber, watching a parade of my troops, and the band was playing on the open ground in front of my window. I noticed a man beating time to the music of the band with his foot. I knew at once that he must be a European, as Asiatics are not in the habit of doing this. Later on, when this man came into my darbar, I charged him with being a Feringhi, which he denied. However, I did not press the matter, being afraid that if suspicions had been aroused against him, his life might not have been safe.[15]

Warburton commented:

> Strange it must seem to have associated hourly for months throughout his dangerous travels in Khiva and Bokhara with his darwesh companions, to have shared in all their meals, and joined in all their prayers, and yet to have defied all detection; and then to have been discovered by one keen-eyed observer for beating time with his foot to the music of an improvised European band playing on the glacis of the fortress of Herat.[16]

The story of the audience with Yakub Khan flew around Herat and, Arminius complained, 'everyone wanted to detect in me the Englishman'.

Royal Artillery. He spent much of his career on the North West Frontier, spoke Persian and Pashto, and was hugely influential with the Afghan tribes, from whom he raised the Khyber Rifles.

15 In his *Travels in Central Asia*, Arminius claimed to have written to Yakub Khan before he left Mashhad for Tehran, and 'congratulated him on his perspicacity', while also admonishing him 'when any person was obliged by local circumstances to travel incognito through his country, not to seek publicly and rudely to tear off his mask'. One rather hopes this arrogant letter was a fabrication or that it never arrived. Arminius was castigated for writing it by his critics on the grounds of endangering the lives of other Europeans travelling in disguise. Hippisley Cunliffe Marsh's experience with Yakub Khan suggests this was at least unlikely in his domain.

16 Sir Robert Warburton, *Eighteen Years on the Khyber* (London, 1900), 89–90.

One old man in particular, with a reputation as an astrologer and astronomer, tried to persuade Arminius to take a letter from him to the Russian ambassador in Tehran. Arminius could not convince him that he had nothing to do with the Russians. Others, he wrote, thought him another Pottinger, a hero arrived to save Herat, a scenario that must have been a later invention for his English readers. Pottinger's heroism in the defence of Herat had been magnificently blown up and framed by the British imperial propaganda machine but was unlikely to have held much purchase in Afghan and Persian imaginations. Meanwhile, Arminius waited for a caravan in the siege-scarred city, listening to terrible tales of 'the covetousness of the filthy grasping Afghan', personified by the vizier, who had enriched himself to the extent of affording 'two houses with vineyards' in Kabul. This man's administrative capabilities were non-existent, and his constant answer to any question or complaint was reputed to be '*Her tchi pish bud*', or 'Everything as before'. The city, cowed by war and the Afghan forces, was easily governed by fear, but Arminius considered that the native Herati would take up arms were they to be led and 'long most for the intervention of the English, whose feelings of humanity and justice have led the inhabitants to forget the great differences in religion and nationality'. He was writing for his English audience again.

Shortly before his departure from Herat, Arminius visited the Musalla and the tombs of the patron saint of Herat, the eleventh-century holy man Khwaja Abdullah Ansari, and of Dost Mohammed. Whatever Arminius' opinion of the Afghans in general, he was prepared to admire Dost Mohammed as 'the founder of the Afghan nation'. The saint (at whose feet the emir had asked to be buried), Arminius managed to mistake for an earlier Abdullah Ansari, who had been a contemporary of the Prophet's. He regretted that the Musalla had 'suffered shamefully during the last two sieges' and that the Polish and Alsatian officers present during the campaigns by the Persians to take back Herat 'could not interfere to prevent such acts of vandalism', although the destruction wrought on the Musalla then was as nothing compared to that of the British forces two decades later, during the Panjdeh incident of 1885, which would be described by Sir Olaf Caroe[17] as 'a

---

17 Sir Olaf Kirkpatrick Kruuse Caroe KCSI, KCIE (1892–1981) has been described as the 'quintessential master of the Great Game' and the 'foremost strategic thinker of British India' in the years before Indian independence.

blot on our escutcheon'. ('Who', Caroe wrote, 'would blow up St Paul's or the Abbey under threat of war?')[18]

On 15 November 1863 Arminius set out again, in a caravan of 2,000 people, for the journey of some 370 kilometres to Mashhad. Half the caravan were poverty-stricken Hazara from Kabul, on a pilgrimage to the Shia shrine of Imam Reza. Arminius and Ishak were also now penniless, and had to beg for whatever they could get to eat in the villages where they camped. Arminius began to hint to an indigo merchant, who gave him a seat on one of his mules, that he was not the destitute beggar he appeared and would, once in Mashhad, have funds at his disposal. As he began to dispense, day by day, with the disguise and manners of the dervish, so he also appeared to lay aside any remaining sympathy or enthusiasm for the peoples and places of the East. He was travel-weary and could find little good in his experiences. The Afghans among his fellow travellers, who had previously proclaimed themselves *ghazi*, warriors of Islam, also now turned their coats, announcing themselves to be English subjects and requesting introductions to the English agent in Mashhad. 'The Oriental', wrote the false dervish, with unconscious irony, 'is born and dies in a mask; candour will never exist in the East'. In Kohsan, at the border between Herat and Persia, the travellers were forced to wait two days while the final Afghan duties were paid, and the last alarm of the journey was raised when a great cloud of dust was sighted approaching the village, and the cry of 'The Turkmen! The Turkmen!' went up. As the cloud and the sound of pounding hooves came closer, it was seen to be a vast herd of wild asses, which turned at the last minute and disappeared again into the desert.

There were still a few days' travel through the no-man's land between Afghanistan and Persia, emptied of people, herds, and settlements by marauding Turkmen raiders. On this final leg of his journey, Arminius drained the bitter dregs of his adventure, enduring the icy wind blowing from the north-east, which made him certain he would freeze to death. The 'hard-hearted Afghans' refused to lend him a spare horse blanket, and he

---

18 Olaf Caroe, 'The Gauhar Shad Musalla (mosque) in Herat', *Asian Affairs*, 4/3 (1973), 295–8. When Herat was threatened by the Russians, the British and Afghans destroyed much of what remained of the Musalla to stop the attacking Russians using the buildings for cover. In fact, the destruction turned out to have been completely unnecessary.

watched as they wrapped themselves in their fur cloaks and jeered 'Dance, hadji, and thou wilt get warm'. (Ishak's sufferings are not mentioned.) Arminius finally cast off his despondency at first sight of 'the very cupola, under which the mortal remains of Imam Riza repose, blazing with its resplendent light far into the outlying country'. It seemed to him, he wrote, 'a beacon which was to guide me to a harbour of safety', and he was able almost to 'imagine myself one of the pilgrims who hail with emotions of unutterable thankfulness and pious joy the sight of the holy place, after having wearily wandered over the immense distances from their several homes'. Nature too 'seemed to have put on her holiday garb', as the caravan approached the city on a fine autumn morning, where it 'lay there like a rich and glittering gem'. Arminius 'fairly rioted in the consciousness of being able now to turn my back upon the black and ugly experiences of the past and looked forward to the attractive vistas of a bright future'. His caravan reached one of the city's caravanserais through streets 'crowded with a dense mass of humanity, rolling in an endless stream along the thoroughfares' and the noise and bustle of life which 'was quite agreeable to me after the experience of the dull and stolid constraint so characteristic of the cities of Turkestan'. In the caravanserai, Arminius washed, probably his first proper wash aside from his fall into the waters of the Murgab, since he had left Tehran, and did his best to tidy himself up before setting out to find the house of Colonel Dolmage, an English officer in the Persian service and an acquaintance from Tehran.

Stopped at the front door by a servant, who slammed it in his face, Arminius rapped on the door again and walked straight past the man as he protested at the ragged haji's impertinence. Arminius told the man to inform his master that 'a stranger from Bokhara wished to see him', and then waited in a room furnished in European style, with the *Levant Herald* lying on a table, which he picked up and began to read. Colonel Dolmage walked into the room and stared at this extraordinary ragged stranger who finally spoke, saying 'What, Colonel, do you not recognise me?' The colonel had apparently heard something of Arminius' journey and, seeing his present condition, 'tears of manly compassion rose to the young officer's eyes'. He asked, 'For God's sake, what have you been doing?' Dolmage's invitation to Arminius to stay at his house was accepted, and he also introduced Arminius to the governor of Khorasan, Naser-al-Din Shah Qajar's uncle, Sultan

Murad Mirza, 'whose English predilections are so well known'.[19] Hippisley Cunliffe Marsh described Murad Mirza as 'one of the most accomplished men of his time', and Arminius observed the 'praises rightly bestowed' on the prince-governor by Russian and British diplomats. He was in no mood to find fault now he was comfortable and safe, and reported his reception 'with particular kindness and affability' by the prince on several occasions. Under his administration, Arminius wrote approvingly, Khorasan 'has not suffered more from the incursions of the Turkmens', and 'the roads begin everywhere to assume an appearance of bustle and animation'. Marsh however was shocked that the sultan was responsible for the fate of three Turkmen, caught 'red-handed in a raid on some village in the neighbour-hood'. He came across their bodies, crucified with tent pegs on the wall at the end of a lane, and remarked 'So much for the civilisation of Persia'.[20]

It is hard to imagine that Arminius would not have been as shocked as Marsh by the Turkmen's crucifixion, in spite of his view of the robber tribes and approval of Murad Mirza's sobriquet, 'the kingdom's naked sword'. However, he took great pleasure in relating to Murad Mirza, in this Shia stronghold and holy city, 'how the bigoted and suspicious Emir of Bokhara, who styles himself, to the disgust of all the Shiites, "Prince of the true believers", had suffered himself to be blessed by me'. For want of any other form of dress, although Arminius had 'said adieu to all disguise as a Dervish', he continued to wear his dervish clothes.[21] As a result, he was able to gain entrance to the shrine of Imam Reza. There, he was shown around by 'several loitering Seids', who thought he was a Bukhariot, for his facility with 'the dialect of Central Asia', and refused to believe the Stambouli story. He congratulated himself on going where previous *ferenghi* – Conolly, Fraser, Burnes, Tchanikoff, Eastwick – had been unable to pass, and where

19 Dolmage had an adventurous life in Mashhad. Interested readers will find more about him in Edward Eastwick's *Journal of a Diplomat's Three Years' Residence in Persia*, Vol. II (London, 1864).
20 Marsh, op. cit., 104–5.
21 It was in Mashhad by chance that Marsh had changed his European clothes for the 'native dress' in which he continued his journey to India. Marsh's new clothes were those of an upper-class Persian, and he received important advice on the cut of his *shalwars*, 'large enough to have taken a baby in on each side' (ibid., 101), from the English *vakeel*, or representative, in Mashhad. But unlike Arminius in his haji tatters, he was advised not to attempt access as a 'Sunnite pilgrim' to the shrine of Imam Reza.

Marsh himself would also fail; even if, Arminius wrote, 'the months of compulsory pilgrimage' had 'strangely palled my appetite' for Islamic holy sites. He admired, nonetheless, the incredible wealth of the offerings at the shrine: 'precious ornaments of every imaginable shape', including a plumed crest of diamonds, a shield and sabre studded with rubies and emeralds, and 'carpet stuffs with diamond and precious stones woven into them'. He was also impressed by the devout pilgrims of all kinds and classes:

> None are too high or too low for the performance of acts of pious tenderness; the sons of Khans, the Mirzas and the poor peasants mingle freely together; and it is a touching and sublime spectacle indeed, to see these sons of Asia, both rude and refined, pressing forwards to kiss, with unfeigned humility, the silver trellis, the padlock hanging from the door of the grating and the hallowed ground itself.

By the time Arminius reached the refectory of Imam Reza, where pilgrims were given food, he had changed his tune, and although he went 'splashing about with my fist in the plate' of 'rancid fat and damaged rice', he 'thought it best to save my appetite for a more favourable occasion'. Writing of the experience, he then attacked the 'avarice and greediness' of the Persians, which encouraged their devotion to Imam Reza, not because of his sanctity but because of 'the vast and fabulous wealth of which he is supposed to be the owner'. His descriptions of the holy places of Mashhad, admiring or not, were written in Arminius' later memoirs when perhaps he thought his account of his experiences in the city needed more added colour. For example, he included a story, first documented by Joseph Wolff, accounting for the 'precarious condition' of the Jews in Mashhad, following the massacre and forced conversion of Jews in the city in 1839. The real catalyst for the massacre and forced conversion is unknown, but according to the tale, a Persian doctor advised a Jewish woman 'to plunge her hands into the entrails of a newly slaughtered dog' to cure a skin disease. The woman had undertaken this most unlikely cure during Eid-al-Adha, and had been seen and accused of mocking the Muslim festival, when goats were slaughtered to remember the sacrifice of Abraham. The blood of a dog would be equally impure to Jew or Muslim, and the story is plainly of the nature of a blood libel. Whatever the cause, Mashhad's Jews now believed it necessary to pretend to Islam to survive. According to Arminius, when he caught sight of a former fellow traveller from his journey from Bukhara, who he knew to be Jewish, and greeted the man by calling, 'Yehudi, Yehudi', the man begged him to stop, saying 'here I must play the Moslem'. Arminius' final pilgrimage in Mashhad, according to his later account, was to the tomb of Ferdowsi, author of the great epic poem the *Shahnameh*. The omission of any mention of this visit in his earliest book on his travels might indeed have been pointed out as an astonishing gap in the explorations of an Orientalist scholar. The tomb stands at Tus, north of Mashhad, and Arminius used Ferdowsi's famous 'high-mindedness' to take another swipe at contemporary Persians: 'What an abyss is there between the modern Persians and their great poet!'

10

Going Home – From Mashhad to Tehran

Arminius remained in Mashhad with Colonel Dolmage over Christmas 1863. From there, he wrote to Baron Eötvös, the patron and champion back in Budapest through whom he had acquired his original passport, describing the sufferings and dangers of his journey. Besides promoting Colonel Dolmage to a general, he also claimed great success in his philological researches.[1]

Your Excellency,

You will be able to appreciate my feelings when you will have heard the details of the dangers I was exposed [to] during my journey…

Today I arrived in good health on Persian soil and am staying in the house of the British General Dolmage where for the first time I can hear European sounds again and use European writing. I travelled with twenty-eight hadjis to Turkmenia where I stayed three months and from there I travelled across the terrible Hyrcanian desert (twenty-two days, three stinking wells); We arrived in Khiva, the ruler of which received me well… I was able to study the Karakalpak, Ychaudor and Khirgiz dialects. Despite all advice to the contrary I covered ground, travelling from Khiva to Bokhara (on which neither Conolly nor Muravieff had ever set foot

---

1 'Improving' the ranks of his hosts was a persistent habit. The 'Muravieff' he refers to in this letter was Count Nikolay Nikolayevich Muravyov-Amursky (1809–81) – diplomat, statesman, and general, who was responsible for much of the Russian expansion into Central Asia and the Amur river basin.

before). In Bokhara the Emir in residence and the Emir's chief officer were suspicious of me, but could do me no harm since the Sultan's letter and my linguistic ability enabled [me] to thwart his plans. From here I went on to Samarkand...

The letter continued with descriptions of the journey and its attached hardships, and then:

So much about my journey; as far as the results are concerned only the future can tell. But I can tell you Excellency now already that my efforts were crowned with unexpected success.

I was able to decide the Finno-Turkish problem without the shadow of a doubt on the strength of my own experience and on the evidence of my manuscripts.

My unexpected good fortune enables me to throw a spark of light into the darkness in which the origin of my nation is shrouded; this spark does not yet shine but the future will set it aflame and posterity will not forget the obscure limping Jew.

I succeeded because I was able to explore central Asia in depth... If my work can be published in Europe I hope that my efforts will not have been in vain.

Your Excellency, my noble benefactor, the star from the West beckons already... but I would be grateful if the Academy would send me another fifty pieces of gold.[2]

He left, with Ishak, for Shahrud, almost equidistant between Mashhad and Tehran, on 26 December. They were both riding good horses provided by the governor, with all the other necessities for a thirty-day winter journey, so that Arminius could now travel like a rich man with his servant. He commented that 'his heart burned with delight' as he rode out of the gates of Mashhad and 'advanced, nearer to the West, that I loved so well'. In the caravanserai at Shahrud, he came across an English merchant, a Mr Longfield from Birmingham, there to buy wool and cotton, and shocked the man by greeting him with a 'How do you do?' After he explained who he was,

---

2 The English translations of this letter are given in Alder and Dalby, op. cit., 178–9.

Arminius and Longfield embraced, to the astonishment of Ishak. Longfield was delighted to discover an English speaker, and Arminius 'spent a famous day with him and a well-informed Russian who acted there as agent for the mercantile house of Kawkaz'.[3] From him, Arminius heard of a Russian factory in Shahrud and wrote:

> From the Gulf of Kamchatka down to Constantinople, throughout all Asia, the influence which the Russians wield is enormous, and there is none other so threatening as that to the rival interests of Great Britain. Inch by Inch they gain upon the ground occupied by the British lion, nor is the time far distant when there must ensue a close and bitter contest.

Poor Mr Longfield – his activities required him to carry large amounts of money and Arminius heard later that he had been robbed and murdered a few months after their meeting.

It took ten more days to reach Tehran, during which time Arminius 'played the Iranian' and the winter weather closed in with a biting north wind and several feet of snow, which had frozen like walls against the sides of the road by the time they arrived at the caravanserai in the village of Ahuan. Arminius described himself as just beginning to relax and warm up, while his 'pilar and roast fowl' were prepared, probably by faithful Ishak, when a cavalcade rode into the courtyard. It was, he wrote, a 'princess of the royal blood', arriving with her escort, and other guests were being thrown out of their rooms to make space for these more important travellers. This was Arminius' final opportunity to employ the heroics and quick wits that had saved him throughout his Central Asian adventure. The escort, told by the landlord of the caravanserai that the occupier of the best room, who refused to come out, was a haji and a Sunni heretic, banged on the door with the butts of their guns and threatened to 'grind thy bones to meal'. 'My tartar', Arminius reports, was terrified, but Arminius 'seized gun and sword' and handed his pistols to Ishak with instructions to use them as soon as he was told. It was of course Arminius' tongue that saved the day. He believed the men had seen his 'martial preparations' from a window and they 'began to parley'. This allowed him full rein and, as he told it, 'the

---

3 Probably the Kavkaz-Merkuz company.

elegance of the Persian which I employed in talking with them, rather staggered them', so that they began wondering aloud if this haji was after all the lowly Central Asian pilgrim they had imagined. Arminius then dramatically announced himself: 'I am neither Bokhariot nor Persian. I have the honour to be a European and my name is Vambéry Sahib'. This had a most desirable effect, such that 'terms of abuse were followed by expressions of politeness', and all parties were soon getting on famously. The two Persian officers who Arminius permitted to share his room soon fell asleep, 'snoring like horses', after over-indulging in *arrack*, and Arminius set about explaining matters to the amazed Ishak. The younger man, it seems, had seen and heard quite enough that was extraordinary by now to accept this situation without much difficulty.

The following day, they rode on across the 'cheerful plain of Damgan' to the city 'supposed to be the ancient Hecatompylae'.[4] Arminius began finding fault again when he could see no signs of Hecatompylos, the old city of many gates, among the 'miserable caravanserais' and few lowly dwellings of Damghan. 'Of course', he wrote, 'one must make large deductions from all assertions made by either Greeks or Persians, who rival each other in the noble art of bragging and exaggerating'. (As Alder and Dalby remarked, that noble art was one in which Arminius was a master.) But by the time he published *Sketches of Central Asia* in 1868, to add more detail to the *Travels*, his first account of his journey, he had decided on a higher opinion of the Persians and their civilisation. 'Europeans have borrowed much from these wonderful people', he was to write then, and 'Iran from time immemorial was the seat of civilisation'. He then followed his own lead through a maze of prejudices and convictions to describe the differences between West and East Iranians, including their physiognomies and 'moral properties', in terms of course wholly unacceptable to the modern reader. It is perhaps comforting to recall that many of Arminius' views were questioned even in his own time for their reliance on brief personal experience and cod science, unsupported by scholarly investigation or prior study.

He was of course expressing views that had, in part at least, been formed by and were shared by many other European and British travellers. Henry

---

4 The remains of the ancient Parthian capital of Hecatompylos are now generally believed to be at Šahr e-Qumis, between Damghan and Semnan.

Pottinger, who travelled in Persia disguised as a Muslim merchant in 1810, described the country as 'the very fountain-head of every species of tyranny, cruelty, meanness, injustice, extortion and infamy'.[5] As late as 1898 Joseph Rabino, an agent of the Imperial Bank, complained of the 'astounding ignorance of Persia in England';[6] Lord Curzon's *Persia and the Persian Question,* which Rabino at least considered a fairer estimation, was also often thoroughly offensive. Curzon objected to the 'Accomplished manners and more than Parisian polish' of educated Persians, that covered, 'a truly superb faculty for lying and almost scientific imposture'.[7] In return, Persia's views of her British visitors were just as scathing. They were, for a start, 'too apt to behave as they did in India'[8] and were anyway unclean infidels. It took the soldier and diplomat Percy Sykes to describe the Persians as 'the finest and most gifted race in Western Asia',[9] and by then, time had moved on and it was the twentieth century.

At his next stop, Semnan, Arminius was disappointed not to find the teacakes for which the place was said to be famous. He managed to find only a few mouldering specimens and was told both that they were so popular that they were all exported, and that 'hard times have caused even the quality of the tea-cakes to deteriorate'. These excuses gave rise to further mutterings about the Persian character and 'unblushing fraud' but, with some 230 kilometres to go, Tehran was drawing closer. Then, on 20 January 1864, Arminius hastened towards the Turkish Embassy that he had last seen ten months before, and where he was greeted and given rooms by Haidar Effendi's successor, Ismael Effendi. He remained there for two months, until he was so restored 'that I felt capable of commencing a similar tour'. 'The Persian capital', he wrote, 'appeared to me, when I saw it again, as the very abode of civilisation and culture, affording to one's heart's content all the pleasures and refinements of European life'. Typically, there was a 'but': 'Of course, a traveller from the West, on coming to the city for the first time,

---

5 Sir Henry Pottinger, *Travels in Beloochistan and Sinde* (London, 1816), 212.
6 Quoted in Firuz Kazemzadeh, *Russia and Britain in Persia: Imperial Ambitions in Qajar Iran* (London, 2013), 316.
7 Quoted in Denis Wright, *The English Amongst the Persians: Imperial Lives in Nineteenth-Century Iran* (London, 2001), 155.
8 Ibid.
9 Percy Sykes, *Ten Thousand Miles in Persia or Eight Years in Iran* (London, 1902), 457.

is bitterly disappointed in seeing the squalid mud hovels and the narrow, crooked streets'. When a man had 'completely adapted himself to the Tartar mode of life', Arminius informs us grandly, it was no wonder that 'he turns half a Tartar himself'. He supported this by remarking on the 'good-natured sallies' of European friends, who 'went so far as to insist upon my having been transformed into a Tartar', to the extent that his eyes, they jested, had 'assumed the oblique shape peculiar to that race'. 'This good-natured chaff afforded me great amusement', he says. Today, we can only wince. This whole passage in his writings sounds unwittingly like an episode of *Blackadder*. That ordinary, 'close-fitting European dress' now seemed uncomfortable to him does sound perfectly reasonable, however.

'The surprise and astonishment of the Persian public at the capital was general', Arminius wrote, when it heard of the false dervish's 'perilous adventure'. Indeed, in his absence, the rumour-mill had been grinding stories of various terrible fates he was supposed to have suffered, torture and execution on the orders of the emir of Bukhara amongst them. The shah heard the tales and expressed a desire to meet the unexpectedly living Arminius, and he was formally presented to Naser al-Din by Ismael Effendi. The shah asked about other Central Asian rulers and about the state of Herat and 'expressed astonishment at the journey I had made', while 'the courtiers present were 'dumbfounded with the easy coolness' he displayed when faced by their supposedly terrifying sovereign. The shah presented him, 'as a mark of special favour', with the Order of the Lion and Sun,[10] fourth class, 'consisting of a plain piece of silver', and a Persian shawl. Arminius was also received at the British Embassy by Charles Alison, where the conversation no doubt also included descriptions of the Central Asian rulers and the state of their domains. Arminius did not expand on the details beyond noting Alison's and his two secretaries' joy 'at his successful journey and happy return'. This feeling, he wrote later, had been general among the embassies, who 'did not fail to acquaint their respective governments with my remarkable adventures'. He was 'quite astonished at the ado made about my performance; nor could I very well comprehend the extraordinary importance attached to my dervish trick, which presented itself to my

---

10 The order had been founded by Fat'h Ali Shah in 1808 especially for foreign officials but was later extended to Persians.

imagination, apart from the real dangers, rather in the ludicrous light of a comedy brought to a prosperous end'. Although this was the long view of his adventure, there can be little doubt that the false dervish was pretty pleased with himself (as well he may have been) with a story of adventure that had so caught public imagination, and which would do much to carpet the passage of the rest of his life.

Arminius made a point, in the *Travels*, of thanking the English diplomats for the recommendations that were to lead to 'so much unmerited support' when he arrived in England. As well he might. Charles Alison's letters introduced him to: the prime minister Lord Palmerston; the Turkophile linguist and diplomat Lord Strangford; Sir Henry Rawlinson; and Sir Justin Sheil, the former envoy to Persia. Arminius had written to Alison to report on his travels or, more specifically, on Bukhara, in a letter dated 1 February 1864. Alison passed on a brief resumé of this letter to Lord Russell, the foreign secretary, only two days later and thus, it seems, the foundations of Arminius' fame when he arrived in London were laid. He might have discovered very little that was new or of immediate use with regard to the fates of those taken prisoner by the emir, going right back to the unfortunate Wyburd and to Conolly and Stoddart, but he had proved his credentials well enough to be assured of acceptance in Britain as a celebrated linguist and explorer and, more importantly, in the long run, as a useful expert and informant on Central Asia, as well as on Persia and Turkey.

As background to the supposed fates of these famous captives, in his letter to Alison, Arminius wrote:

It was the middle of July when I arrived in Bokhara. Two days after my arrival I heard that two Italians, who came from Orenbourg with the purpose to buy a great quantity of silk, had been taken prisoner by the first Vezir of the Emir, himself being at the same time in the campaign of Khokand. Several false rumours spread out by the treacherous government reported that the Feringhee had brought fifteen cases of tea, moistened with diamond water, to poison the inhabitants of the very sainted town. Another told that they made night day and day night – yet a third related that they were English spies and that the Russian government gave the counsel of their arresting.

Rahmet Bi, the mentioned Vezir, wrote to the Emir for further orders and he received the resposal [sic] to confiscate the 8,000 Tillas they brought with them and to arrest at the same time the 4 Nogai Mussulmen [Russian subjects] who accompanied them.

The Italian merchants were fortunate. Arminius wrote that he had heard from 'Rahmet Bi' himself that they had been well-treated and fed, and he believed that they would not be killed 'if Russian intrigues don't change the situation of the Tartarian Prince'. But alas for Captain Wyburd: 'I could not discover any trace nor hear a single word of the unhappy Captain Wyburd whose unknown fate Your Excellency deigned to call to my attention before my starting to Central Asia'.[11]

He had heard of 'several Russian captives' and 'an unfortunate German watchmaker' who had fallen foul of the emir, and there had also been a mysterious 'young Englishman, about twenty-four years old, who came from Baghdad, via Herat to Bokhara'. He had finally been murdered in Kokand, and a Kokandian had told Arminius that 'the young feringhee was of a beautiful exterior and a very clever man'. He had been killed because he had wished to go from Kokand to Kashgar, in southern Xianjing, China, 'which intention gave suspicion that he will make guns for the Governor of Chinese Tartary', with which Kokand was, at the time, at war. Perhaps this was Wyburd, re-emerging briefly at last.

Finally, and almost inevitably, since their deaths had become part of the whole Central Asian landscape so far as the British were concerned, Arminius revisited the fates of Conolly and Stoddart. He had nothing to add to the Reverend Joseph Wolff's account, only reporting that 'the papers and effects of these two martyrs' were said to be held in the Samarkand archives, but he did not know if this was true.

In response to all this, Alison wrote to Russell:

During the year 1862 I made the acquaintance of an Orientalist of some distinction, Mr Vambéry, who was then making preparations for a journey to Bokhara, Khiva, Khokand and Samarkand in the disguise of a mendicant. Among other things, Mr Vambéry took an interest in the fates of those Europeans who have preceded him in this perilous enterprise and

---

11 Alder and Dalby, op. cit., 198.

---

which formed the subject of our conversation before his departure, that of Lieut. Wyburd was not unknown to him and Your Lordship will observe from the inclosed copy of a letter addressed to me by Mr Vambéry since his return that he has no information to impart on that painful subject.[12]

The evidence must by now have been enough to make concrete the final acceptance of Wyburd's death, and Arminius' name had become as well-known as he might have hoped in British circles and throughout the diplomatic community in Tehran. It was broadcast outwards from there, and his sensational story soon found purchase with the international press. He sent an account of his travels to the Hungarian Academy, and he was also courted by the Russians. The Russian minister plenipotentiary, Nikolay Girs (1820–95), encouraged Arminius to think of a glittering career in St Petersburg, but Arminius could never overcome his dislike of Russia and Russian autocracy and turned him down. The Russians, unsurprisingly, are not acknowledged in the *Travels*, but the French *chargé d'affaires*, Count Rochechouart, certainly is and would provide Arminius with letters of recommendation to the 'principal statesmen' of France. Arminius finished his description of his Tehran triumph with an odd little anecdote about a Mr Szanto, a Hungarian tailor who had left home years before to avoid conscription. Szanto had followed the emigré's path to Constantinople and then continued to Tehran, mostly on foot. He had been about to travel on to Peking in 1848 when he heard news of the uprising in Hungary and attempted to return to fight for his country's independence, but had only got as far as Constantinople when he heard the Revolution had failed. Once more, the poor wanderer had gone East, via Tabriz to Tehran. Now, Arminius wrote, the tailor spoke an extraordinary tongue, a mixture of all the languages he had picked up on his travels, but 'his generous heart' had warmed to the story of his adventurous compatriot, for whom he decreed he would make a pair of pantaloons. Arminius showed no grace whatsoever in refusing this gift and the garment was given to Ishak instead, who found it 'ridiculous'. Szanto, however, according to his chronicler, 'was beside himself with delight and pride at having been the first tailor who had put a Tartar into a pair of European trousers'.

---

12 Ibid., 197.

Conventionally clad once again as a member of European society in Tehran, Arminius was asked for blessings by some Turkmen. These men had either met or heard tell of the Turkish dervish when they were in the Turkmen settlement of Gomushtepe (see pages 98–105) and were now travelling on business in Tehran. 'They assured me that my fatihas had worked wonders, and that the people in Gomushtepe were often wishing to have me there back again', wrote the false dervish.[13] It was 'the last occasion on which I performed spiritual functions of the kind', but his imagination 'caught fire at the idea of my religious fame' as he pictured what he 'might achieve among these untutored Children of the Desert'. He pictured himself as one of those oriental heroes who 'shroud themselves in a mysterious magical obscurity and crowds follow blindly their lead'. Luckily (we may well think) time was pressing and, on 28 March 1864, Arminius and Ishak left Tehran for Trebizond.

---

13 Alder and Dalby, op. cit., 204.

11

The Dervish in London

One has to gasp at Arminius' attitude. As Alder and Dalby remark, he had travelled nearly five thousand kilometres in dervish disguise, through Turkestan, Afghanistan, and Persia, yet failed completely to grasp what the word 'dervish' encompassed. For him the figure of the dervish was 'the very personification of Eastern life', yet it was also a symbol, for Arminius himself, of all that he found most objectionable in his personal characterisation of that life as 'idleness, fanaticism and slovenliness'. Arminius had played out the rituals, prayers, and conjuring of his dervish role, just as he played other roles throughout his life; but to him, Sufi mysticism remained wholly inaccessible and, to his limited comprehension, a dervish was only 'a cross between a beggar and a madman – at best a humbug'.[1] Perhaps this is the place to point out the psychological truism that if you play a role you despise, you are also despising yourself.

The journey to Trebizond was an easy one and one that Arminius thoroughly enjoyed – describing it as going in the right direction, away from 'the haunts of savage barbarism and of unimaginable dangers' and back to 'civilised lands and my own beloved country'. When the travellers finally arrived in Constantinople, Arminius 'saw in the Turks a totally civilised nation, who are in great advance over their brethren in faith and in nationality who dwell in the interior of Asia', and he found the city 'many times more enchanting than before'. He took himself off to see the long-serving

---

1 Alder and Dalby, op. cit., 191. Years later, Arminius would give a sycophantic-sounding talk to a group of Hungarian clerics at Sopron on the subject 'A dervish is only half a man – A Hungarian clergyman is a whole man (for he fulfils a social function)'.

Austrian ambassador, Anton von Prokesch-Osten, who had been in the Sublime Porte since 1855. Prokesch-Osten was a friend of Arthur de Gobineau, shared his interest in Sufism and dervishes, if not his opinions on race, and must have been fascinated by Arminius' account of his travels. The old ambassador, Arminius wrote, barely recognised his 'emaciated and weather-worn visitor'. He advised Arminius that he should go straight to London with his story, since 'England is the only country full of interest for the geography and ethnography of inner Asia', and that the false dervish should 'style accordingly' the account of his travels. Prokesch-Osten told him to 'keep yourself strictly to the narrative of your adventures; be short and concise in the description; and particularly abstain from writing a book mixed with far-fetched argumentations or with philological and historical notes'.[2] Arminius also called on the grand vizier, Mehmed Emin Ali Pasha, who had known and lent manuscripts to Reshid Effendi in the past. The vizier, who alternated his post with that of foreign secretary, through five incarnations of the former and seven of the latter, was a great statesman whose acquaintance would certainly have been worth banking for future use.[3]

That then was it. The journey was over, and Arminius left the grand vizier to board the steamer for Constantia and thence to Budapest. There was but one more task before the ship weighed anchor: Mullah Ishak had to be left behind, to follow his own path of pilgrimage to Mecca. Arminius once again took up his 'feeble pen' to describe an 'unspeakably painful moment' in his life. Ishak, he assured his readers, had 'become like a brother', one to whom he now handed over most of his cash and all his Eastern wardrobe and equipment, plus advice for his behaviour on his pilgrimage and his return thereafter to Khiva. Ishak, however, 'burst into a torrent of tears' and announced his intention of renouncing the 'beguiling object' of the holy places and, instead, remaining with Arminius, crying: 'I am ready to part with my home but I cannot separate from you'. Arminius delivered himself of a homily on the subject of foreign places, people, and customs, and the

---

2 It's ironic that Arminius might have achieved the greater respect he so desired in academic circles if he had indeed engaged more deeply with the 'far-fetched argumentation' in the areas that had been the catalyst for his journey in the first place.

3 Unfortunately, this deft and urbane statesman, who had begun his career in public office at the age of fourteen, died in 1871, aged only fifty-six.

scant likelihood of Ishak ever again returning to his 'paternal seat in Khiva', but Ishak once again burst out: 'Believer or unbeliever, I care not which, wherever you go I go with you. Good men cannot go to bad places. I have implicit faith in your friendship and I trust in God that he will take care of us both'. With that the ship's bell rang, both men boarded the steamer, and away they went towards the Danube.

During the river journey, Arminius again met with acclaim and interest, but there was a good deal less excitement when he reached Budapest. Baron Eötvös greeted him on his arrival and, although history doesn't relate what the baron made of Ishak (or vice versa), Eötvös was frank about the difficulties Arminius was going to face in the Budapest academic milieu. Arminius quickly realised that, although there might be newspaper articles and invitations, he was not to get the sort of 'rousing welcome' accorded to the great English explorers, and that his fellow academicians were unimpressed by the tale of his adventures. Arminius had no track record as a serious scholar, yet his travels had been funded by the Hungarian Academy as a serious research project. Now, he appeared at one of the regular Monday meetings of the Academy with an improbable adventure story and wearing a fez, which was considered highly unsuitable, while the manuscripts he carried might or might not throw light on philological investigations into the roots of the Hungarian language. Arminius had been 'not a little proud of the manner in which I had travelled'; now he was once again the poor Jewish misfit whose friends began advising him to return to the official career he had begun in Constantinople. There his talents were appreciated, and he had useful contacts. Others spoke of a professorship in Oriental languages at Pest University but, although that idea had some purchase in his mind, for the moment Arminius wanted more lucrative prizes. In fact he had almost certainly decided to go on to London even before he left Tehran, bearing the sheaf of letters of introduction that were to be a far better passport to success than his Turkic manuscripts had proved to be in Budapest.

Arminius had written in February from Tehran to Jozsef Budenz,[4] librarian of the Academy, telling him of his intention to pass on the intelligence he had gleaned in Central Asia 'to the English cabinet', and to Edward,

4 Budenz was a specialist and later professor of Altaic languages at the University of Budapest and became a full member of the Academy in 1871.

prince of Wales, who was, he had heard, very interested in the region.[5] The problem now for Arminius, as so often, was funds. The Hungarian Academy did not think him much of an investment and it took his old supporter, Baron Eötvös, to lend him 'a few hundred florins' from the Library Fund. The loan came with conditions that humiliated Arminius yet further: he was required to leave his manuscripts in the safekeeping of Count Emil Dessewffy, president of the Academy. He felt (and told Count Dessewffy that he felt) treated as if he were a 'vagabond without any sense of honour' and, giving full vent to his injured pride, 'I who have been slaving and suffering for the good of the Academy as few have done before me... I, the fanatical enthusiast, have to give a guarantee for a paltry few florins'. If he did speak to Dessewffy in those words, his reputation at the Academy would only have been further damaged. The fact that the manuscripts could be said by rights to have belonged to the Academy seems to have escaped Arminius altogether. To his later readers, he appealed 'was it strange that I begin to think that all this humiliation and mistrust, all this cruel misapprehension, and this wilful ignoring of all my trouble and labour was due to my obscure origin and the ill-fated star of my Jewish descent?' He comforted himself that 'true Magyar explorers of Christian faith would have fared no better in the intellectual morass of the Hungary of those days', and here he may have been right. It was probably questions of education and class as much as his Jewishness that stood in Arminius' way, even if he did not help himself.

The 'modest viaticum' that he had found so offensive was enough to get him to London. He was on the move again, a bare four weeks after arriving in Budapest, and this time he travelled alone. He could not afford to take Ishak, which was a blow to his sense of theatre as well as a loss of companionship: Ishak 'would have made a capital figure at Burlington House before the Royal Geographical Society'. Arminius packed up his notes, all those letters of recommendation, and the few manuscripts he had held back from the Academy, and set off directly to London in the latter days of May. By the time he arrived, his spirits had risen. He had seen notices about himself in the daily papers as he passed through Vienna, at Cologne he was interviewed by the *Kölnische Zeitung*, and on the train from Dover to Victoria Station, he regaled his fellow passengers with his story. One of them, a Mr Smith,

---

5 Quoted in Mandler, op. cit., 54.

took him to the Hotel Victoria[6] when they reached London and paid for his room. Later, Arminius wrote, this mysterious individual found private lodgings for him, paid the first month's rent, and disappeared into the London smog, never to be seen again.

Arminius hastened to present his letters of introduction and found he was in the right place at last. Victorian London loved an explorer and was keenly aware of the dangers of Central Asia, where a handful of brave *Christian* heroes had diced with death, parleyed with terrifying tyrants and, like Conolly and Stoddart, generally come to ghastly if noble ends. But Arminius had outdone them all. Untrammelled by considerations of soldierly duty and proper form, he had travelled as the poorest of the poor and was therefore able to paint a broader picture of those mysterious places. And he was an actor at heart, and a storyteller with all the right opinions regarding British imperial superiority. The pomposity of his prose must belie his live performances: in delightfully imperfect English, larded with inventive Persian and Turkish quotes, and spiced with a sprinkling of other languages whose names alone were completely unknown to the general public, he would have been the personification of the exotic explorer and Orientalist. As we know too, from photographs of Arminius in London, he was happy to pose and perhaps even to perform in 'eastern' or 'dervish' costume.

He described his 'hearty welcome' from those grand beings to whom he had introductions and his surprise that more ordinary mortals should also show 'sincere appreciation of my labours'. But then, he wrote, 'how could it be otherwise' in England? With its 'widespread colonies' and 'gigantic universal trade' and interest in the 'remotest corners of the earth', 'England', he wrote, is 'the only land of great universal ideas'. 'Britishers' did not care about 'the origin and antecedents of their heroes' and 'gladly forget the title of "foreigner"' if said foreigner 'happens to have enriched their knowledge of lands and peoples'. This rosy picture nevertheless had its thorns. Arminius believed he was seen, with his sunburned face, as a 'disguised Asiatic', beyond the pale even of all that 'Britisher' liberality. His command of Persian and Turkish which, he wrote, 'I spoke without the slightest accent', only added to his slightly *too* exotic image. All such suspicions, however, were laid to rest

---

6 Very possibly the two-year-old Grosvenor Hotel at Victoria, near where the Dover train arrived.

when the former Hungarian freedom fighter, General György Kmety, aka Ismail Pasha, who had helped Arminius in Constantinople, came forward to vouch for him and to promote his cause. His first visit to Sir Henry Rawlinson – that same Henry Rawlinson, veteran of the Great Game, who had met Vitkevitch all those years before – went well; in fact, the conversation, held mainly in Persian, was something of a catechism. Sir Henry was a Persian expert with wide experience in Central Asia and had been a Russophobic proponent of a forward-looking policy in Afghanistan. He wanted details of the capture of Herat, of affairs in Bukhara and Kokand, and particularly of the movements of Russian military detachments in the region. Arminius was impressed by 'the comfort and luxury surrounding an English literary man of distinction' in Rawlinson's house at 16 Belgrave Square, but Sir Henry was also a practical soldier with years spent in the field. We do not know what he made of Arminius, but the Russophobic dervish certainly had the potential to be useful. In contrast, with Sir Henry Layard, under-secretary for foreign affairs (and better known as the excavator of Nineveh), and Sir Roderick Murchison, then president of the Royal Geographical Society, Arminius was to find himself at odds. There was no shortage of people who shared Arminius' views on Russian ambitions, but Layard was not one of them. He told Arminius cheerfully that 'the Russians are a nice people; their Emperor is an enlightened, noble prince, and the Russian plans in Asia cannot mean mischief against the interests of Great Britain'. Arminius also noted wryly 'the pair of magnificent malachite vases' in Sir Roderick's house, a gift from the tsar to a man who was 'much liked at the Court on the Neva'. Murchison nonetheless treated Arminius as a traveller of importance, and he received a valuable invitation to lecture at the Royal Geographical Society.

His meeting with Percy Smythe, 8th Viscount Strangford, was also somewhat tricky. Strangford was only a few years older than Arminius (dying in 1869 aged only forty-three), was president of the Asiatic Society, and was an extraordinary linguist who had also lived in Constantinople for a number of years. He spoke perfect Turkish, among many other languages, and Arminius observed he 'would have been taken by everybody for a downright Effendi, had it not been for the peculiarly Celtic shape of his head'. He also knew Hungarian and 'even the language of the gypsies'. Strangford was also, unlike his guest, extremely learned and well-read. Arminius, who had been certain of his unique skills in 'Eastern-Turkish' in London and in the whole of Europe, was astonished to hear Strangford recite the Chagataic poems of Navai.[7] These poems, he commented, 'had hitherto escaped my attention' – as had, the reader suspects, their fifteenth-century Sufi author. Strangford was able to translate the poems for Arminius and, possibly projecting his own feelings onto this remarkable scholar, Arminius assured his readers that 'envy and jealousy had no place in the noble heart of Lord Strangford'. In his memoirs, years after Strangford's early death, Arminius was to make the astonishing claim that Lady Strangford had told him 'this veritable mine of Oriental knowledge' had died 'holding in his hand the volume of my Chagataic Grammar which I had dedicated to him'. For now, however, Strangford 'took a fancy' to Arminius and 'gave himself all possible pains to introduce me everywhere, and to level the ground before me'. This process was eased by an additional meeting with the diplomat Sir Justin Sheil and, perhaps more importantly, his wife. Lady Sheil (the writer Mary Leonora Woulfe) took the 'ci-devant dervish' in hand to educate him on 'the complicated laws and social tone of the West End' and helped turn him into the lion of the London season. 'No easy task, if you consider that the said dervish, although a European by birth, had never before been west of his own country, and that his education and his continual studies were not made to facilitate such a change in his life'.

Lady Sheil was herself well travelled. She had been married in 1847, while her husband was on leave from his post as British envoy to Persia. Her life with him in Tehran produced the first three of the pregnancies that eventually resulted in ten children and, on her return to London, her memoir, *Glimpses of Life and Manners in Persia* (published by John Murray). It is a mixture of her own experiences and of information garnered from her husband, from visitors to the embassy, and others who she met in Persia. If she gave a copy to Arminius, it might have jogged his memory of his own experiences. Mary wrote about 'various kinds of derveeshes [sic] and their ceremonies' and had also encountered 'the most dreadful and unendurable smell' emitted by a caravan carrying corpses to Karbala while riding outside Tehran.[8] She also wrote at some length on the Turkmen, their slave dealing,

---

7 Ali-Shir Nava'i (1441–1501), also known as Nizām-al-Din ʿAli-Shir Herawī.
8 Lady Mary Sheil, *Glimpses of Life and Manners in Persia* (London, 1856), 192–7.

and the lives of slaves in Persia at the time. She was disposed to find their treatment 'perhaps as favourable as that institution will admit of' and concluded that slaves in Persia 'are not treated with contempt as in America' and were 'frequently restored to freedom'.[9] Mary had also learned Persian, in order to better communicate with the people she met in Tehran and especially the women of the royal harem. Arminius must have begun to wonder if the language was not, in fact, some kind of *sine qua non* of London intellectual society.

On 27 June 1864 he gave his lecture at the Royal Geographical Society in Burlington House. *The Times* reported next day on the heavily accented English in which he spoke for over half an hour, but Arminius believed he had made himself understood. The account of his travels, written for the purpose, had been delivered in advance of Arminius' speech by Clements Markham, the explorer and honorary secretary of the Royal Geographical Society, so the audience did not have to strain too hard to understand him. Markham had noted Arminius' original motive for his journey, 'to study the affinity between his native tongue and the languages of Tartary', but Arminius' sense of the dramatic encouraged him to add new theatrical flourishes to his account for this appreciative audience, which then made their way into his published accounts. Comprehensible or not, he played his part to the hilt, although he did not appear in the fez that had been found so offensive in Budapest. He described the khan of Khiva dramatically as 'a sick tyrant with very frightful features' and a mass murderer, although the emir of Bukhara was 'a man of good disposition' who had only committed 'many tyrannical and barbarous acts' for political expediency.[10] In the dinner given beforehand, at Willis's rooms,[11] where the dervish traveller's health was proposed by Sir Roderick Murchison, Arminius ended a short speech of thanks with a Muslim blessing delivered (so he typically records) with 'all the eccentricity of the Arabic guttural accent' and 'all the

---

9 Ibid., 244.

10 Later, and presumably after he had been to the opera, Arminius was to describe the emir and his durbar, in their colourful silks, as 'more like the chorus of women in the opera *Nebuchadnezzar* than a troop of Tartar warriors' – pantomime villains to be laughed at by superior Western sensibility.

11 Previously the famous Almack's Assembly Rooms, conveniently placed in King Street, St James's, a short distance from Burlington House, Piccadilly.

queerness of genuine Moslem gesticulation'. His lecture he likewise ended with a 'blessing with the genuine Arabic text', which supposedly nearly brought the house down. Strangford was heard to say 'Well done, dervish', and Arminius believed he had arrived.

He must have been even more delighted when Sir Henry Rawlinson, in his own speech, praised him for his Arabic scholarship and for his exploration of a region of great political importance. Sir Henry began by saying that twenty-five years earlier, there had been great alarm at Russian influence in Central Asia but times had changed since the Afghan War. Now, he said, he took a moderate view of Russian advances that had, in some places, brought the borders of the Russian and British Empires as little as a thousand kilometres apart. He did not think that the present 'supineness' of British public opinion was any more justified than its previous fear, but he did not wish to 'infer hostility to England on the part of the Russian government as it extended its frontier towards India'.[12] No European, he believed, had travelled before through the *terra incognita* from the Caspian to Khiva, and Arminius could also claim to be the first European to have lived in Samarkand since the Castilian ambassador, Ruy González de Clavijo, had an audience there with Timur in the early fifteenth century. Rawlinson, who may have been in the same post-prandial good humour as Arminius, and who was wearing the same 'jolly and radiant after dinner face' Arminius also ascribed to Murchison that evening, was full of superlatives. Vambéry, he said, had done something 'exceedingly remarkable', and he doubted if there was one European in a thousand who could have survived his apprenticeship in Constantinople. But not everyone was so impressed. One member questioned whether Arminius' travels had not in fact covered the same ground as those of Joseph Wolff? Lord Strangford assured him that Wolff had never been to Khiva and agreed with Rawlinson that no foreigner had visited Samarkand for centuries.

The questions then moved on to the subject of commerce, the Russian hold on the Central Asian cotton industry, and the Russian goods Arminius

---

12 Report in *The Sun* (29 June 1864). By the 1870s, Sir Henry was a member of the Council of India and had become a fully paid-up member of the 'forward school' with regard to stopping Russia's advance towards India. He published *England and Russia in the East* in 1875 which would influence the government at home and Lord Lytton, the Viceroy, in India.

had seen in the markets of Khiva, Bukhara, and Samarkand. Murchison and Rawlinson, however, were in accord that evening in their conviction that 'the advance of the Russians could be in no way detrimental to our great Indian Empire'. Arminius observed that the favourite argument among men such as these and Strangford was: 'There is room enough in Asia for England as well as for Russia; there is no reason for jealousy and no fear of a future collision'. Another member remarked that it would be easier 'to send an army from the banks of the Thames to the banks of the Indus than for the Russians to send an army from their frontier to Peshawar', and noted that there was Russian interest in Bukhara 'long before we had an empire in the East'. This son of the empire then reverted to the contemporary concept of the 'standard of civilisation': that the civilised states, Russian and British, were, by their advances, bringing 'savage nations under a regular system of government'.[13] Although the papers expressed similar sentiments regarding Russia and advocated 'strict neutrality', an attitude that Arminius put down to 'apathy, ignorance, and self-deceit', he was also aware of others 'who were in favour of activity and watchfulness' and who he soon came to know better.

As well as noting his accent, *The Times* reported on the extent of his travels, 'through districts that had not been visited since the days of Marco Polo', and announced that 'The Explorer' intended to make another journey, this time from Samarkand to China. Arminius saw how other explorers were feted in London and believed he understood what it was that led to their celebration in Britain as compared to the lack of interest he had received in his native land. He came to the conclusion (or rather, had come to the conclusion by the time he wrote his memoirs) that explorers such as John Hanning Speke, his rival Richard Burton, and even David Livingstone, to name but the best remembered of their number, were not 'admired, distinguished and rewarded for their great learning but rather for their manly character, their personal courage and spirit of enterprise'. In addition, these were the men who had discovered

> where the best and the cheapest raw materials are to be had, and where the industrial products of the Mother Country can be sold most

---

13 Details of the Burlington House meeting on 27 June are taken from Alder and Dalby, op. cit., 221–5.

advantageously. He clears the way for the missionary and the trader, and in their wake, for the red coat... so now it is expected that the explorer's zeal and love of adventure will help to expand the country's political and commercial spheres of interest.

The famous explorers were the scouts and the vanguard of empire and, Arminius would write, 'The English saying, "Trade follows the flag", can hardly be called correct, for first of all comes the explorer, then the missionary, then the merchant, and lastly comes the flag'.

Looking back, he realised that his own travels were of lesser value, at least to a nation of shopkeepers. He was not laying a path for conquest, by whatever means or for whatever commercial purpose. He had set out in an entirely different tradition, that of the simple pursuit of knowledge, albeit knowledge that might have political connotations. Unfortunately for him, he did not have the credentials he needed to be valued in that sphere in Hungary in advance of his journey, and his travels, so far as Hungarian academia was concerned, did not do much to change this. But in London, he was flavour of the month during the 1864 social season, and he continued to promote his 'expert' image there throughout the rest of his life, with continuing support from the great and the good. To the British, he decided, the intelligence he had gathered of Central Asian rulers and, of course, Russian movements and influence, had been of political importance and his 'dervish incognito' had provided popular success – as had, he took care to stress, the linguistic skills 'and Asiatic idioms' on which his claims to serious scholarship were founded. For all his efforts for the British Empire and his impressive list of acquaintance, Arminius remained a curiosity in England, the foreign explorer, or at this time just 'The Explorer', who would have been assumed to have equal or greater stature in his own country. He was shrewd and realistic enough to see that the tidal wave of invitations to every possible event and from people he had never heard of that now washed up on the doorstep of his lodgings in Great Portland Street, or at the Athenaeum Club where he had an entrée, were based on fashion, the need to be part of the latest craze. He also saw that there was 'a strong dose of snobbishness, in which England excels', that required less notable society to ape 'the great, the wealthy and the highly cultured' by inviting him to events that might have nothing to do with Central Asia.

In truth, Arminius found the mores of London society difficult to comprehend and had to endure 'the burdens of my reputation with patience', even while admitting that he viewed his English fame with 'a good amount of satisfaction'. It is hard to believe, after travelling the Central Asian roads in his company, that he really looked back on his travels with the nostalgia he describes in his later memoirs. Perhaps by then he had forgotten his documented miseries. However, his empathy with David Livingstone, who, he reported, once told him 'how happy was my life in Africa; how beautiful is the freedom amidst naked barbarism as compared with the tyrannical etiquette of our refined society!', did not last long. He put such thoughts down to 'momentary depression'. All the same, he did not fit well enough in London to be comfortable, however he was lionised. He decided that he was best suited to 'the medium stage of culture' and the 'golden middle way' of life in Hungary, regardless of his treatment at home. The gentlemen of the Hungarian Academy would not have been pleased with such middling approbation from an autodidactic nobody, which placed their national culture between the 'highest and the lowest stage of civilisation', 'the noisy, restless centre of Western activity' and the barbaric East. Arminius was constantly torn, as he later remembered, between admiration and scorn for the life of the wealthy in Britain, as well as the hustling pandemonium of London. For the time being, however, he had other concerns. After his public relations triumph, publishers lined up to commission a book of the dervish's travels. Lord Strangford had already introduced him to the best known of them all: John Murray, publisher of Livingstone and Darwin, Layard and Mary Sheil, the *Journal of the Royal Geographical Society*, and creator of *Murray's Handbooks for Travellers*.

Arminius was forced to sit down and somehow make a book from the 'meagre notes written on small paper scraps with lead pencil' that had been hidden in his clothes and were now barely legible. For the rest he relied on memory and the storyteller's art. He complained bitterly of the lack of the manuscripts held by Count Dessewffy which would, he announced, have provided him with further background for his account, but *Travels in Central Asia*, written and revised in three months, was nonetheless an instant success and its author was described by the *Literary Examiner* as a 'true Magyar'.[14]

---

14 *The Examiner* (17 December 1864).

All the same, Arminius's reaction to literary success was mixed. He became part of the 'literary forum of the élite', the circle that frequented John Murray's house in Albemarle Street off Piccadilly, and became a favourite of the Murrays' sons for the stories he could tell,[15] while the 'highly instructive and very amiable Mrs Murray' (as he described her in his first letter to her husband after his return to Budapest in December 1864) added her own efforts to improving the social graces of the dervish. Charles Dickens told him 'that Murray's house is not built of brick but of human brains', but the bouncy tone of Arminius' letters to Murray after his first visit to England were offset by the fact that he had not enjoyed the writing process and that, while John Murray 'behaved towards me in a satisfactory way', so far as payment for his book was concerned, his mood flattened when he found his 'material situation not very much changed'.

His £500 advance from Murray did, briefly, make him feel very rich, but he spent at least half of it while he was in London, turning himself into a 'distinguished foreigner', and he was horribly disappointed that no more money was forthcoming. A letter to John Murray in June 1865 makes it quite clear that he thought the publisher was making a profit at his expense. It is close to insulting, even as it protests that Mr Murray 'must not feel yourself offended'. Arminius was convinced of the absolute uniqueness of his travels and the extent of public fascination with himself and his adventures, especially given the whole scenario of the Great Game being played out across Central Asia. That conviction stayed with him throughout his life, but the curiosity of others was inevitably finite. John Murray's son Hallam later looked into the accounts to discover that Arminius had received *all* the profits for the *Travels*, not just the half that had been agreed; and Arminius was later obliged to write to Hallam's brother, John Murray IV, in 1905, apologising for impugning their father's memory with the complaints made about those profits in his final memoir, *The Story of My Struggles*, which had been published by Fisher Unwin in London the year before. In the letter of apology, while protesting any intention 'of offending the memory of your father', he could not resist harking back to 'the greatest privations' of his life and dervish journey, followed by the great success of a book that had,

---

15 Sir Walter Scott quoted in George Paston, *At John Murray's: Records of a Literary Circle 1842–1892* (London, 1932), 210.

nevertheless, in terms of ultimate profits, caused 'this greatest disappointment in my life'.

Arminius was always concerned about money. He had fought to survive a hardscrabble life from birth, and was invariably disposed to think that he was not getting his proper dues. In London he was also exposed to 'the wealth, the comfort and the luxury' on display in the houses he visited. At the duke of Argyll's house near Richmond, Arminius turned down the services of the liveried footman who, to his astonishment, had come to help him undress. He 'turned down the brocaded coverlet and lay down on the undulating bed' and thought of the comparison this made with his lodgings in Three Drums Street in Pest, where he had shared a bed top-to-tail with the thin tailor's apprentice. He was amazed, too, to find himself part of a society where, 'notwithstanding the strictly aristocratic etiquette', he might find himself standing, in his hat, in the reading room of the Athenaeum, reading *The Times* opposite the elderly prime minister, Lord Palmerston. Later, when he met the prince of Wales, the future Edward VII, then aged twenty-three, at the late-night Cosmopolitan Club, he was quite staggered by 'the apparent indifference shown to the Queen's son'. The 'future ruler of Albion', who Arminius approached 'with the utmost reverence and awe', was affability itself, and the dervish reported that he 'plucked up courage' to sit down and talk to him for half an hour. This was the beginning of a lasting friendship that would see Arminius as a royal guest at both Sandringham and Windsor.

Lord Palmerston had seen the memorandum about Central Asia that Charles Alison had requested Arminius write during his last stay in Tehran, and Arminius had been introduced to the prime minister at a dinner party at Murchison's house. When he visited the old statesman at home in Piccadilly, Palmerston remarked, 'You must have gone through nice adventures on your way to Bokhara and Samarkand!' (His opening gambit with Livingstone was also reputed to have been, 'You had a nice walk across Africa!') Perhaps explorers were a strange breed to Palmerston, but he was fascinated by Arminius' account of his journey in disguise, if less keen to engage on the subject of Russian advances in Central Asia. Palmerston had taken a clearsighted view of Russian ambitions in Turkestan over many years but, in 1864, although Russia was pushing determinedly forward in Asia, he was fully engaged with issues of war and alliance closer to home. Austria and

Prussia, with Russian collusion, were tussling with Denmark over the disputed territory of Schleswig-Holstein, and the prime minister was fighting against parliamentary opposition to his pacific policy towards the German nations. Possibly too, while he wished to hear what Arminius could tell him, he had no reason to trust this strange foreign traveller's opinions on British foreign policy.

The European powers were jostling for position in that busy summer, while the Russians quietly moved to conquer the cities of Turkistan, Aulie-Ata (Taraz), and Shymkent,[16] preparatory to taking Tashkent the following year. In November 1864 Prince Alexander Gorchakov, the great Russian foreign minister, wrote a memorandum that was supposed to justify Russian policy in Central Asia and allay British concerns. It was in keeping with the philosophy of the gentlemen of the Royal Geographical Society that all civilised countries were forced to secure their borders with 'half-savage' populations by subduing them. It was also mendacious. An earlier memorandum to the tsar from the war minister Dmitry Milyutin had stated in July 1863 that 'In case of a European War we ought, particularly to value the occupation of that region, which would bring us to the Northern border of India… By ruling Kokand we can constantly threaten England's East-Asian possession'.[17] Leaving aside the question of the still-distant prize of India, Central Asia was clearly proxy for disagreements between Russia and Britain in less hidden parts of the world. In particular the Russians sought leverage against the London Straits Convention of 1841, which had denied their navy its route to the Mediterranean through the Dardanelles and which was deeply resented in St Petersburg.

In one version of his memoirs, Arminius reports a conversation with Lord Clarendon in the autumn of 1864, after the 'Russians' capture of Tashkent',[18] when he reported that 'the public opinion of England seemed to have been roused suddenly from its stupor'. Clarendon, who had been foreign secretary from 1853 to 1858 and took the post again in November 1865, had admitted, Arminius wrote, that his short but grandiose final chapter of *Travels* had been correct. In this, Arminius had forecast doom in Central Asia, brought

---

16 All in Kazakhstan, close to the Uzbekistan border.

17 Quoted in Seymour Becker, *Russia's Protectorates in Central Asia* (Abingdon, 2004), 13.

18 The Russians did not take Tashkent until May 1865, although they were close at hand and took Shymkent in Kokand in October 1864, so there may be an error of names in the original publication. Or, it may be a typical Vambéryism.

on by British apathy. The timing he gives of his conversation with Clarendon however is most unlikely, as Russia did not capture Tashkent until June
1865 (although an attempt had been made in 1864). It seems possible, nevertheless, that Clarendon, at some time during Arminius' stay in London,
had held to the party line that so frustrated the Hungarian hawk, by stating
that 'Russia's policy in Central Asia is framed in the same way as ours in
India'. Russia, Clarendon said, was 'doing services to civilisation and we do
not much care if she takes Bokhara'. Newspaper reviews of the *Travels* had
sung the same tune, the *Literary Examiner* for example dismissing the final
chapter on 'Russian aggression' by stating, 'we have long since ceased to have
any apprehension on this subject and are now satisfied that our former fears
were but a costly and dangerous illusion'.[19]

As David Mandler has noted, other British newspapers over the next forty
years used Arminius' articles on the geopolitics of Central Asia and Russia
to keep the Great Game in the mind of the public, characterising Arminius as either 'a clear-headed Cassandra or as an alarmist'.[20] In his memoirs,
published in 1883, long after Russia had taken a grip on the khanates of
Turkestan, Arminius comforted himself over the 'deplorable blunders and
short-sightedness of the British statesmen' and the generally relaxed attitude
in London towards the politics of that far-away region. The 'leading men in
Eastern matters', the Strangfords, Layards, Rawlinsons, and their colleagues,
he believed, were 'thoroughly up on these questions'. Behind or before
them stood the thin red line. With the 'dogged perseverance, patriotism
and undaunted courage' of the British officer and even the private soldier,
the 'crushing superiority of Englishmen' would last. None of that stopped
Arminius from beating the anti-Russian drum for the rest of his life. He felt
obliged to keep Britain up to the mark he had assigned it when he entered
London society as a thirty-two-year-old linguist, traveller, storyteller, actor,
and exotic curiosity. And he always hated Russia.

The acquaintanceship he later described of his time in London was
remarkable, figures whose ghosts have drifted through the lives of generations of British schoolchildren as the great heroes of the Victorian age. Of
the statesmen, Lord Palmerston attracted Arminius most as a 'downright

---

19 *The Examiner* (17 December 1864).
20 Mandler, op. cit., 60.

Britisher, with a French polish and German thoroughness', not to mention the 'jocular remarks' that were part of his conversation. There was William Spottiswoode the mathematician, who had also travelled in Russia and Hungary; Lord Stanley of Alderley, who converted to Islam in 1859 and became the first Muslim member of the House of Lords; William Wilberforce's son, the Bishop of Oxford and anti-evolutionist Samuel Wilberforce; Lord Lytton, later Viceroy of India; the poets Algernon Swinburne and Matthew Arnold; Charles Dickens, who in 1865 wrote an article on 'The Hungarian Dervish' in his magazine *All the Year Round* that must have gladdened the dervish's heart; and Mary Mohl, friend of Madame Recamier and wife of the German Orientalist Julius von Mohl. Then there were the explorers: Burton, who he met at the house of the poet, politician, and literary patron Lord Houghton; William Gifford Palgrave (1826–88), soldier, Jesuit priest, missionary, and explorer of Arabia; James Augustus Grant (1827–92), Scottish soldier and explorer of Eastern Africa, who searched for the source of the Nile with Speke; John Kirk (1832–1922), a physician, explorer, and diplomat, who travelled with Livingstone; and John McDouall Stuart (1815–66), the Scottish explorer of Australia; as well as David Livingstone himself. Livingstone, Arminius remarked, had told him: 'What a pity you did not make Africa the scene of your activity'.

The tale Arminius told of his meeting with Burton is typical in its improbability; and there is no doubt that stories of those days in London were embroidered by the time they reached his memoirs. This particular anecdote is coloured by the kind of self-aggrandisement Arminius could never resist. When he first met Burton, he was supposed, at Lord Houghton's behest, to have played a trick, hiding behind a door to recite the Al-Fatihah in Arabic as the explorer arrived. Burton, Arminius related, instantly cried, 'That is Vambéry!'

Meanwhile, he was concerned with the translation of his book into French and German, which might help improve his financial situation. He requested an advance of twenty guineas from John Murray, on the grounds that he was forced to move house, as the bad light in his lodgings was harming his eyesight, and asked the publisher to add to the book one of the photographs taken in Tehran of himself dressed as a very clean dervish. Might this have been prompted by the following? When Arminius met the diarist Sir William Hardman at the house of Robert Cook, John Murray's business partner, Hardman was, Arminius wrote, 'very curious to see him, for reports say he got so inured to dirty habits during his Dervish life, that he has abandoned the use of soap and water for years'.

By this time Arminius had become 'wearied by the endless series of dinner parties in London' and wanted to escape the merry-go-round of 'splendid, but to me already tiresome, English hospitality'. He took himself off to Paris 'to have a look about in French society'. He was armed with the letter of introduction, provided by Count Rochechouart in Tehran, to the French foreign minister, Count Drouyn de Lhuys, plus others from his English friends to a number of 'literary men of distinction', and one from Count von Rechberg, the Austrian foreign minister, to the Austrian ambassador to France, Prince von Metternich. Parisian society, Arminius found, was curious about his dervish travels for the sheer theatre of his disguise, but it did not invest explorers with the status of great men and was not much interested in Central Asia. All the same, he thought *Voyage d'un faux derviche* 'had a pretty good sale' with its author looked upon as 'some modern Robinson Crusoe'. He comforted himself that the French were impressed by his linguistic abilities and related an evening spent among 'representatives of ten different nationalities', all of whom he conversed with fluently in their mother tongues. After that, he was 'regarded by many as a real miracle'. Napoleon III had read his *Travels* in English, and he was taken by Prince von Metternich for a personal audience with the emperor at the Tuileries. Arminius did not think much of this 'thick-set man, with his flabby features' and 'whitish-grey eyes'. Perhaps his grand life in London had made him blasé about an upstart emperor, one who Tsar Nicholas of Russia had refused to call 'mon cher frère' but only 'mon bon ami'. Napoleon III congratulated Arminius on surviving a journey for which he did not look strong enough. This reference to his lameness must have rankled, but the emperor also engaged him on the question of a Parthian ancestry for the Turkmen, a level of ethnographic enquiry that the false dervish was unlikely to have encountered in royal circles in London. Sadly, there is no record of his answer, but Arminius did allow his interlocutor to be 'tolerably versed in the writings of Arrian'[21] and of the writers of antiquity in general, even if 'his knowledge of the modern geography of Asia was sadly deficient'. The

---

21 The historian Arrian of Nicomedia composed the *Anabasis of Alexander*, still one of the best accounts of the campaigns of Alexander the Great, in the second century AD.

emperor asked more questions, about Persia and Herat, but Arminius still refused to be impressed. After another meeting with Napoleon at Princess Mathilde Bonaparte's salon, Arminius wrote, 'I could not discern a trace of that greatness of which for years I had heard so much'.

He was happier to meet the old statesman François Guizot, who he admired; the philosopher Jules Barthélemy-Saint-Hilaire; and the Orientalist and Hindi scholar Garcin de Tassy; but 'generally speaking, France left me cold'. And France, perhaps, was not that interested in the intensely Anglophile and Russophobic opinions of the dervish. Arminius reported press rumours that he had been 'entrusted by Lord Palmerston with a secret mission to the Tartars', or another to gain French support for Britain against Russia. He also, he recorded, inspired the character of the hero in a romantic novel, who gained a throne when a Tartar princess fell in love with him. Arminius thought its author was a Polish prince, but maddeningly gives us no further details than that. His own book was published by Hachette and serialised in *Le tour du monde*, for which he would receive no additional fee. The false dervish, always ready to see a slight or a swindle, had had quite enough, and he complained to John Murray about publishers in France and in Germany, his next stop as he made his way back to Hungary. He gave a lecture in Leipzig, but decided the Germans 'have as much notion about Central Asia as the Khan of Khiva has about Germany'.

12

The Prophet in His Own Land

The traveller who arrived in Budapest in late October 1864 would look back in later life on the attention he received on this return to his own country. 'Small nations in the early stages of their cultural development', Arminius would write, grandly, 'often follow the lead of greater, mightier, and more advanced lands in their distribution of blame or praise', and Hungary was then nothing more than 'an Austrian province'.

At this point he was essentially unemployed, but he knew exactly what he wanted: 'the Chair of Oriental Languages at the University of Pesth as a fit reward for my extraordinary struggles in life'. This was an ambition that might be described as an extraordinary *folie de grandeur*, but Arminius acted with equally extraordinary audacity to achieve it. He went to Vienna to enlist Emperor Franz Joseph to his cause. Bypassing the usual channels of employment and advancement in academic Hungary meant treading on a lot of toes, and Arminius did not now add to his small store of friends in that world. He was also expediently baptised into the Calvinist church at the end of December – not to curry favour with a Christian monarch well known for his pro-Jewish stance and policies, but to improve his standing, he hoped, in other, less liberal quarters.

In Vienna, before he could stand in front of the emperor, he had first to be humiliated by 'the mediaeval spirit which ruled the highest circles of Austrian society' and which did its aristocratic and bureaucratic best to put this lame Jewish nobody in his place. His new religious credentials held no more sway in this milieu than his travellers' tales. He fulminated against this treatment of a celebrated explorer, who had shaken hands with other 'royal personages of the West', but he was received kindly by the emperor himself.

The right of an ordinary citizen to have a private audience with his sovereign had been decreed by Franz Joseph[1] when he came to the throne, and a theoretically modernising emperor now offered his subjects the same privilege of meeting face-to-face as existed in the Central Asian durbars where Arminius had bearded ogres. Franz Joseph, according to his petitioner, barely heard his request before granting it, adding, Arminius told his readers, 'Your sufferings deserve a remuneration, and I shall look into your case'. The emperor did pause to wonder how many students Arminius would find when there were few, even in Vienna, who studied Oriental languages. Arminius replied, 'If I can get no one to listen to me, I can learn myself', at which the emperor 'smiled and graciously dismissed me'.

Royal favour was one thing, but Arminius had to fight his corner in a far more judgemental and prejudiced court. The rector of the Catholic Pest University (who later became a bishop) greeted him, Arminius reported, with the words 'Do you suppose we are not fully informed as to the treacherousness of your character? We are well aware that your knowledge of Oriental languages is but very faulty and that your fitness to fill the chair is very doubtful'. Arminius, stung, denounced the Catholic Church as a 'hotbed of intolerance and blind prejudice'. After all he had accomplished 'in the service of my people', he wrote aggrievedly, he was only to be tolerated, at best, because the emperor had decreed his appointment. Moreover, that appointment was only as a 'lector', earning 1,000 florins a year, 'a remuneration equal to that of any respectable nurse in England'. But his bitterness at his treatment in Hungarian academic circles was a little ridiculous. He might have been feasted and feted in London, supported by the press and lionised by upper-class society that made him the fashion, but he knew full well that Hungary would be different. Riding roughshod over the rigid statutes of the academic society he aspired to join could only increase his unpopularity and encourage unfavourable rumours about his qualifications to join that society. In this period, anti-Semitism in Hungary was also far more overt than anything he had experienced in Britain, where he had

---

1 A key scene in Joseph Roth's novel about the end of the Austro-Hungarian Empire, *The Radetzky March*, has Baron Trotta personally petitioning the emperor, whose life he had saved at the Battle of Solferino, to have the incorrect legendary version of the event removed from school textbooks.

successfully presented himself as a 'true Magyar'. That did not stop him later happily telling a completely fictitious story of a meeting with Prime Minister Benjamin Disraeli:

> 'Pray, Mr Vambéry, what is your nationality?' the Prime Minister asked.
> 'Hungarian,' replied Arminius.
> 'And what is your religion, Mr Vambéry?'
> 'Protestant.'
> 'Indeed! And was your nationality always Hungarian and your religion always Protestant?'
> 'No, Mr Disraeli, I was born a Jew.'
> 'Ah,' said Disraeli, delightedly, 'I knew it, no one but a man of our race could have had the dauntless perseverance to go through all you have gone through and successfully overcome so many difficulties.'[2]

In Hungary, the story was told that when Baron Eötvös had asked Arminius, for the requirements of an official document, 'What is your religion?' Arminius had replied furiously, 'I protest!' 'All right', the Baron said, 'then I shall enter you as a Protestant'.[3]

In fact, it hardly mattered if Arminius had become a baptised Protestant. The sincerity of his affiliation to any faith or religious belief would always be questioned, with or without a baptism certificate. In Britain those questions might add to his curiosity value but not in Hungary, and he did not help himself by persisting in publicly hedging his bets. Rumour had it that he had converted to Islam for his dervish role or during his years living in Constantinople, like so many others. The rumours of his true religious affiliation pursued him into old age, with the story of a caller discovering him sitting with his prayer shawl on his knees and with phylacteries on his arms. He claimed most often to be a free-thinker or non-conformist. Such catch-all terms implied that he would always attempt, chameleon-like, to fit his religious and, if he could, his racial habit, to his changing environment; but at home in Budapest and in the inflexible world of Hungarian academia,

2 Recorded by Esmé Howard, Lord Howard of Penrith, in his *Theatre of Life: Life Seen from the Stalls* (London, 1936), 162–3.
3 Alder and Dalby, op. cit., 250.

such changes of guise could never overcome the requirement for hard facts and solid credentials. Rumour and doubt were his enemies' best weapons. Arminius' formal qualifications were non-existent, his religion in question, and his claims as to his travels could never be properly proved. What, his critics might ask, did they amount to? He was no Burton or Livingstone. Even in Britain, Arminius' travellers' tales had been queried and, at this stage in his life, it would have been easy for a critic to pick holes in his self-taught scholarship. Arminius himself claimed that his life experiences made up for any lack of formal education, but now in his early thirties, with his linguistic skills and his dervish journey his only credentials, that boast would have struck some as laughable.

The contentious (or in his eyes, lowly) appointment to the University of Pest provided Arminius with a level of respectability. It would become the backdrop to the rest of his professional life and domestic existence in Budapest, and give him credentials abroad as Professor Vambéry, the famous Orientalist, rubber-stamping his dervish backstory with the imprimatur of academia he so craved – quite regardless of the opinion of the learned circles he had so rudely and uniquely breached in Budapest. Later explorers of Central Asia, such as Arminius' compatriot Aurel Stein and the Swedish explorer Sven Hedin, who made their own longer and more extensive journeys in Central Asia, became famous in their lifetimes because they supported their research with careful documentation and with tangible discoveries. Arminius' journey may have been bold, but its stated philological purpose was dissipated in the dervish adventure story, and it produced no real academic results.

This is no doubt why the dervish was forgotten by British history and Hungarian academia for much of the twentieth century. It is only recently that Arminius has been rediscovered, with the exhibition of his life and travels held in Budapest late in 2019. David Mandler's scholarly study *Arminius Vambéry and the British Empire* (2016) carefully explored his role and importance in that sphere and concluded that his sometimes Western and sometimes Eastern 'performative subjectivity' made 'him a repository of both the Eastern Other and the Western Brother' as well as 'a representative of Hungarian-ness despite his Jewish origins'.[4] Until these recent

---

4 Mandler, op. cit., 157.

spotlights were shone on his life, ever since his death in 1913, Arminius has turned up only occasionally as an actor in British imperial history. The sharp-eyed and curious might decipher a dusty label with his name in a museum display in Central Asia, or be intrigued by the mention of a 'Professor Vambéry' in Bram Stoker's *Dracula*. In 1979, he was comprehensively memorialised as *The Dervish of Windsor Castle*, but that excellent book has long since disappeared into the dustier reaches of second-hand bookshops. The copy I have is signed by Lory Alder and Richard Dalby and makes me wonder how many of the single edition were printed at the time.

In a different age, the slings and arrows thrown at Arminius at home, in particular by his most famous pupil, Ignaz Goldziher, would have reverberated further afield, but then was not now. For the rest of his life, outside his own country, Arminius played a part, exactly as he had on his dervish journey. Just as then, he found the supporters he needed with a mixture of bombast, bravado, opportunism, and determination, plus a quick mind and memory, a polyglot raconteur's tongue and, as time passed, a more genuine scholarship. There were also other traits in Arminius' character, opinions in opposition to the standard beliefs of his times and to the society to which he aspired, that were born of his own experience and innate inclination. These included his Russophobia, his promotion of the British Empire, and his determination that it should both lead the world and be defended. At the same time, he held views that make him a more sympathetic character today than the somewhat pompous, self-congratulatory peevish *kvetch* who emerges from his autobiographies. The real Arminius remains contradictory – the face behind the mask, the costume, and the assumed character always elusive.

David Mandler noted 'Vambéry's projection of a likeable persona in his narrative' that draws the reader in to feel 'a sense of familiarity and solidarity with the author'.[5] That persona as 'the little Jew boy and the hungry student' is the one Arminius describes in the *Struggles* – a heroic and appealing figure, who had the determination to succeed against all the odds. The self-made man he became, playing multiple parts, might still be applauded for his *chutzpah* and remarkable success, but the story of the brave boy's life is spoiled by the adult's constant dissatisfaction with his lot and his craving

---

5 Ibid., 93.

for more and bigger and better prizes. On the plus side, Mandler quotes the newspaper report of Arminius' objection to 'the assumed inferiority of the negro' in a paper given by Dr John Crawfurd[6] at a meeting of the Ethnological Society of London in April 1865, during Arminius' second visit to Britain.[7] The term ethnology had only been coined late in the eighteenth century, and race – or, more precisely, the races of humankind – was no better mapped than the source of the Nile had been before Speke, or better understood than electricity before Edison. Even so, the opinions of Dr Crawfurd (who was a friend of Sir Roderick Murchison and who opposed slavery and believed in universal suffrage) were wildly complicated and contradictory, with a theory based on the polygenist notion that the different races came from multiple origins made by God and not from a single source.

Arminius understood racism from personal experience. He had been an underdog for most of his life, on grounds of both race and class, and racist theories were never to be entertained by him. He complained of the 'narrow mindedness and ridiculous prejudice of the Christian West against its fellow countrymen of a different creed', the fact that 'people questioned the genuineness of my Hungarianism' as a Jew, and of Western class prejudice which, he maintained, was less oppressive, 'in spite of the anarchy, barbarism and tyranny prevailing', in the East. Even so, his own Orientalism, in the Edward Said sense of the term, is manifest in his inability to see equal merit in an 'eastern other'.[8] However great his claims might be to understand the Central Asian world and, indeed, to be a repository of its knowledge, however much the Jewish scholar might be the round peg in the

---

6 Dr Crawfurd was much in evidence in the papers of the Ethnological Society, airing his polygenist views in the early days of ethnology as a study. This writer declares an interest in Crawfurd for his birth on the small Inner Hebridean island of Islay where her own family has roots and from which beginnings Crawfurd made a long career worth a trip to Wikipedia for a resumé of its breadth. His racism and polygenist theories were often laughed at even in his lifetime and his opinions were seen as contrary.

7 *The Physical and Intellectual Characteristics of the African or Occidental Negro* and Arminius' response are taken from a report in the *Cheshire Observer and Chester, Birkenhead, Crewe and North Wales Times*, on 15 April 1865, quoted in Mandler, op. cit., 61 ff.

8 Edward Said's famous book *Orientalism* (1978) explores the way Western 'Orientalists' have come to represent the Middle East, with no particular distinction between countries and peoples, and how those representations constructed and perpetuated a racist and romanticised view of the peoples of the Middle East as 'the other': inferior, exotic, and subservient.

round hole of Orientalist study, Arminius was too busy creating his public image to admit empathy with the peoples of Asia, or to allow them to be his equals. If this conflicted with his otherwise more sympathetic view of racial others with whom he more easily identified, so be it. Like Dr Crawfurd and others in those days of exploration and discovery, he was contrary and contradictory. Or it may be that the ability to enumerate his real beliefs eluded him as well.

Occasionally, among the tangled thickets of his written opinions, the dichotomous nature of his views emerges. In his final memoir, *The Story of My Struggles*, the last chapter (entitled 'The Struggles End, and Yet no End') appears to set out to square the circle on religion, nationality, class, and society. The reader can glimpse the sceptical twentieth-century man, who had observed and experienced, understood and abhorred the continuing prejudices of his time: 'The fact that Asia in our days is given up as a prey to the rapacity of Europe is not the fault of Islam or Buddhism or Brahminism. The principles of these religions support more than Christianity does the laws of humanity and freedom, the regulations of state and society', he writes. Then there is: 'If there be anything likely to weaken or shake one's patriotism, it is the narrow mindedness and ridiculous prejudice of the Christian west against its countrymen of a different creed'. But no religion shines for long. 'The ethical standard of faith' might be higher in Asia than in Europe but, east or west, religious belief to Arminius was all 'outward show, miracles and mysteries':

The spirit of the twentieth century, cries, 'Let there be light'. The intellectual acquisitions of our century can no longer away with the religion of obscure antiquity; knowledge, enlightenment, and free inquiry have made little Europe mistress of the world, and I cannot see what advantage there can be in wilfully denying this fact, and why, in the education of the young, we do not discard the stupefying system of religious doctrine and cultivate the clear light of intellectual culture.

Arminius also wrote as a son of the age of revolution. He decried 'the conduct of the uneducated born aristocrats' and noted that accomplishment 'in literature, art, science, and intellectual advancement generally is for the greater part the work of people not favoured by birth'. Indeed, 'privileges of birth are nonsense', and 'if pedigreed nobility is really so essential to the well-being of a state, how can we account for the lamentable decay of Persia, where there has always been such a strongly pronounced aristocracy?' He went on to remark that such views made it 'only natural that I could never quite fit into the frame of Hungarian society' as 'the self-made man'. At the same time, he is the 'autobiographer' who tried to create for himself the position he felt entitled to within that society. He complained of those who 'chase after orders and decorations', but never saw the similarity with his own ambitions in accepting 'such distinctions' when they were conferred. Instead, he wrote that 'a public refusal of them seemed to me making a useless parade of democracy', as well as being straightforwardly rude.

At the end of his life, Arminius was still relying on the tried and trusted roots of his fame, placing himself among 'the learned' through an exaggerated catalogue of the hazards of his travels sixty years before, and of his hard work and intellectual prowess in all the years since. He portrays himself as an ascetic, eschewing social occasions, the theatre, and the 'mostly frivolous' evenings of 'scholars and writers' where 'spirituous drinks', which 'I have always abominated', played 'an important part'. Instead, he 'made it a rule to go to bed at nine o'clock' and 'kept the question of utility in the foreground', by recalling with satisfaction the change in his fortunes from youth to old age. Above all, he gave thanks to the lucky star that had saved him from 'the executioner's axe' and from dying of thirst 'on my journey through the Steppes', and without which 'all my perseverance, patience, ambition, linguistic talent, and intellectual activity would have been fruitless'. That intellectual activity, he pointed out, in one final burst of self-contradiction was not on the 'stereotyped paths of Orientalism':

> How can one expect that a man who as Dervish, without a farthing in his pocket, has cut his way through the whole of the Islam world... how can one expect such a man to bury himself in theoretical ideas, and to give himself up to idealistic speculations? A bookworm I could never be!

Typically, right at the end of *The Story of My Struggles,* is the appendix in which Arminius records Eugene Schuyler's apology for his criticism of Arminius' *Travels.* As Alder and Dalby point out, he was 'the kind of man who provoked strong passions: his contemporaries either adored or detested him'. Even in his marriage, he felt he had not gained the contentment that should have been his.

Arminius had spoken to his friend and fellow Orientalist Aron Szilady of his intention to find a 'pretty rich maiden', and in 1868 he married Kornelia Rechnitz-Aranyi amid, he wrote, a chorus of 'pity for that poor girl', who would undoubtedly immediately be abandoned in favour of 'adventures in the interior of Asia'. People were, Arminius said, 'grossly mistaken'. Although his journey remained central to his reputation, he was more than content to enlarge upon its drama from the comfort of the marital home. Poor Kornelia, however, had little in the way of acknowledgement from her husband: he barely mentions her beyond the brief note of their marriage. Perhaps he felt an image of happy domesticity did not suit that of the lonely adventurer. 'A home – a "sweet home" – in the English sense of the word, has never fallen to my lot, even on ever so modest a scale… my wife, a homely, kind-hearted, and excellent woman, was ill for many years and if it had not been for the beautiful boy with whom she presented me, I should never have known what domestic happiness was', he wrote. The 'beautiful boy', Rustem, was born on 29 February 1872, and he too remembered that his mother was always ailing and understood little of his father's work. 'She had no interest in it, and only saw to it that there was no dust on the polished furniture and that there was a tasty meal on the table.'[9]

The Zionist leader Max Nordau includes a pen-portrait of Kornelia in the appreciation he wrote for a posthumous edition of *The Life and Adventures of Arminius Vambéry*, published in 1914. Max Nordau could not have known Kornelia as well as her son did, but his description of her was warm and rings true to her appearance in those few photographs of her that exist. Nordau describes her as having been 'in her youth strikingly beautiful, a fact that was convincingly suggested by her appearance even in her mature years'. She was also 'possessed of profound and extensive culture and imbued with artistic interest, imparted to her by her parental home', but she 'never tried to outshine her husband'. He goes on to describe a weakness for the Budapest poppy-seed pastries, *Beugel,* that were discovered by Kornelia,

---

9 Rustem Vambéry quoted in Alder and Dalby, op. cit., 260, from conversations with Robert Vambéry, Rustem's son.

who then always served 'this glorious piece', evidently 'created and tenderly cared for by her own hands', when he came to dine at the Vambéry apartment. Kornelia seems to have had almost no existence outside the domestic sphere, but she was recorded as accompanying her husband to Constantinople shortly after her marriage, and on another of his visits to Britain. Who knows what her chronic illness may have been – some sort of undiagnosed depression, that took her to her bed, out of the way of her bullying husband, and where she could, in turn, make demands of the servants? She would certainly not have been unique for her time in escaping from the difficulties of her married life to her bed and to invalidism. Rustem remembered her continually ringing her bell and remarked, 'petty-mindedness was mixed with broad-mindedness in mother in an extraordinary way'.[10]

Life in the Vambéry household sounds far from entertaining for his much younger wife, bearing in mind the shortage of frivolity, theatres, and other social occasions. Another guest remembered Kornelia as 'a modest and retiring figure',[11] sitting in an armchair in the hall of the apartment under a bare bulb (an example of Arminius' meanness). Nordau speaks of Arminius' 'hypnotising brilliancy' and the 'fascination of his living word', but this more attractive side of his character is hard to discover in his surviving papers. Alder and Dalby, from their conversations with Rustem's son, Robert Vambéry, detected 'a domineering and autocratic husband and father, seeking to impose his will by force and never seeing any standpoint but his own'. This was a man whose 'petty tyrannies would even extend into the nursery', where he would force Rustem to eat food he disliked until he was sick. It may be only in the undocumented ephemera of friends' remembrance, long lost now, that the searcher would find any light in the gloomy picture of Arminius' home life. Only the slightest echoes remain from the recorded memories of friends such as the novelist and dramatist Mór Jókai (1825–1904), who considered Arminius' lectures as original and powerful and among his favourite reads, and Kalman Mikszáth (1847–1910), another important novelist and satirist, and a long-term friend. There must have been moments of laughter, such as when Rustem, who was an insomniac, fed meatballs spiked with sleeping pills to his neighbour's barking dog, but

---

10 Alder and Dalby, op. cit., 260.
11 See ibid., 468.

in general the Arminius home was one of silence and study and dominated by Arminius himself. Arminius was an early riser and an early-to-bedder. The Vambérys slept in separate rooms, and Arminius maintained he was engaged for most of the day 'exclusively in serious study' with 'graver study' in the evening and a period in the afternoon engaged in 'politics and journalism, with the help of a secretary'. In due course, that involved dictating 'leading articles or other matters in different languages at the same time', although Arminius found this too stressful to continue when he 'approached the fifties' and was beset by 'headaches and congestion'. Somehow or another, teaching was fitted into this routine as well.

What more do we know of the wife who had to accommodate herself to this? She had been born in 1850, and she and Arminius were married for forty-five years. In 1882, Arminius wrote to William White, later British ambassador to Turkey, 'A misfortune has befallen me in my family, namely the serious illness of my wife, who I am doomed to see to fade away in a lingering death, for she has an incurable disease where medical skill is of no avail, it is a great calamity but I must submit to the trial of fate!' Richard Dalby, who owned this letter, remarked of Arminius, 'it appears he was more concerned with the effects of his wife's illness on his home comforts than on the patient herself'.[12] As the years slipped by and there was more money available, Kornelia visited spas as well as doctors, but whatever her 'incurable disease', her husband did not see her fade away. She outlived him, dying in 1914. She was remembered by her grandson, Robert, as an eccentric. He told a story of her astonishing the waiters in the grand dining room of the Sacher Hotel in Vienna by breaking a raw egg into her soup.

Kornelia's own family were decidedly unusual. Her stepfather, Professor Lajos Aranyi, whose family came from Transylvania, was a well-known anti-Semite who believed that the best way to deal with the Jews was to 'dilute their blood, till it finally disappears, by intermarriage'.[13] History does not relate what the professor thought of his son-in-law. His wife, Johanna Joachim, was herself Jewish and the sister of the famous nineteenth-century violinist Joseph Joachim, a friend of Robert and Clara Schumann and of Brahms. Joseph and Johanna's family included as their great-nieces the

---

12 Ibid., 468–9.
13 Ibid., 260.

Aranyi sisters, more celebrated violinists, this time of the early twentieth century, who collaborated with several of the great composers of the time, including Elgar. They settled in Britain and were said to have re-discovered Schumann's forgotten violin concerto after receiving a message from the composer during a séance. In 1891 another Joachim cousin of Kornelia's, Gertrude, married Rollo, the son of the foreign secretary and later prime minister Lord John Russell. That must have appealed to Arminius.

Professor Aranyi is considered the father of pathology in Hungary, and was the first person there to undertake autopsies. He financed the first post-mortem laboratory at the University of Pest and was reputed to have carried out thousands of post-mortems and gathered 3,500 anatomical specimens. The professor and Johanna had four children together, and when their third child, Zoltan, died tragically of diphtheria at the age of six in 1862, the professor, who had become an expert in the art of embalming as well as his other mortuary skills, decided to embalm and preserve this child's body and record the process. When preservation was complete, Zoltan's body, dressed in velvet clothes, took up permanent residence in a chair in his father's study next to his desk, where Arminius and Kornelia saw it when they visited.[14] One wonders if Arminius shared the tale with Bram Stoker, in which case it must have added a bizarre contemporary element to his own accounts of ancient Hungarian folktales from the dark Carpathian forests of Transylvania.

*

The association with the Aranyi family was still in the future when Arminius returned to London early in 1865 to consolidate his fame with further public appearances, add to his acquaintances, and keep an eye out for better opportunities than those provided by a poorly paid university appointment. As Franz Joseph had anticipated, when 'Professor' Vambéry[15] began work at the university, students for courses in Turkish, Arabic, and Persian were

---

14 After the professor's death in 1887, the mummy remained in the house until it was given to the National Museum of Budapest in 1925, where it was displayed surrounded by toys. It came to rest at last in the Semmelweis Museum of Medical History in Budapest, but only after its trousers had been stolen by Russian soldiers during World War II.
15 He was not appointed professor officially until 1867.

distinctly thin on the ground. He spent much of 1865 travelling between Budapest and London, with a stay in the village of Koritnitza in the Carpathians in July.[16] He was back in Britain in September, before returning to his unproductive grindstone at the university, writing to John Murray on 30 July about the chances of finding work as a dragoman 'in the distant east' through British contacts. It seems highly unlikely, were Arminius even qualified for an embassy job, that such a self-effacing role would have satisfied him. A university post (albeit naturally he wanted the grandest) must always have been the best option.

He was, as he said himself, not a true adventurer. Not, at least, in the sense of a Burton, a Stein, or a Livingstone, once his youthful enthusiasm for the new and unknown had been knocked out of him on his Central Asian journey. But he was certainly an adventurer through life; the thread of one always led back to the other, and his original 'adventure' remained his calling card. He clearly believed that the aura of something extraordinary about him excused his unorthodox university appointment and the equally unorthodox means of its acquisition. That it was so frowned on by genuine academics was, quite regardless of bigotry, understandable in view of Arminius' behaviour and lack of any qualifications for his post. Ironically, a combination of this self-belief and, presumably, the fruits of all those years of study, led to him being seen as the grand old man of Hungarian Orientalism, taken at his own estimation in western Europe and the USA Sir Ronald Storrs – linguist, oriental secretary in Cairo, military governor of Jerusalem in 1917, and friend and colleague of T. E. Lawrence – believed Arminius to be the greatest Orientalist in the world. Alder and Dalby also quote Major E. C. Johnson, author of *On the Track of the Crescent* where he definitively describes Arminius as 'the discoverer of the Asiatic birthplace of the Hungarian people and language', which would, as they wrote, 'have incensed his critics in Budapest'.[17] But finally, Arminius' reputation began to take root in Hungary. There was no doubt he worked for it. His lectures, most notably in Britain as a champion of the empire, were extensively covered in the press. His international correspondence was enormous – books, articles, and

16 Now Liptovska Osada, a village in northern Slovakia.
17 See Major E. C. Johnson, *On the Track of the Crescent: Erratic Notes from The Piraeus to Pesth* (London, 1885), quoted in Alder and Dalby, op. cit., 246.

published letters, quite apart from private communications, flowed from his apartment in an endless stream, 'with people of various rank and degree in Turkey, Persia, Central Asia, India, China, Japan, America and Australia'. He felt he had contributed his 'mite to the enlightenment and improvement of my fellow-creatures', and it was a 'joyful discovery that my books were being read all over Europe, America, and Australia'. Reviews of his publications, however mixed, added to his celebrity. Today, Arminius Vambéry, with his earliest pupil Ignaz Goldziher and his more widely known protégé Aurel Stein, are seen as the three most famous Hungarian Orientalists. But while Aurel Stein, who took British citizenship in 1904, received all the decorations and recognition Arminius could have craved, Goldziher, nearer at hand, became his teacher's greatest critic.

Either the natural inclination to secrecy of a man who had invented himself, or simply the continuing hostility and suspicion he encountered at the Royal University of Pest,[18] led to Arminius teaching from his home. He gave lectures in other forums but not at the university. He only took on one or two students at a time, and his teaching methods were unusual. One new student reported being told, 'Go home, buy yourself a Turkish grammar, and come back in six months' time when you have learnt it'.[19] Perhaps he believed his students should emulate his own autodidactic learning experience. He was impatient with them and often gave the impression of not wanting them at all, but he was proud of their successes when they reflected well on him. His greatest triumph was the young Ignaz Goldziher, a prodigy who became a renowned scholar of Islam and is credited as the founder of Islamology. Aged five, Goldziher remembered, he had 'the serious study of the original text of the Bible behind me';[20] aged eight he began intense study of the Talmud; and at twelve he was reading medieval Jewish philosophy in the original Hebrew. When he was thirteen, he pressured his father into gaining permission for him to give his bar mitzvah speech from the pulpit of the synagogue in their hometown, Székesfehérvár. By the time the family moved to Budapest two years later, Ignaz had a library of 600

18 Now Eötvös Loránd Tudományegyetem, or Eötvös Loránd University (ELTE), renamed in honour of the physicist son of Arminius' patron.
19 Alder and Dalby, op. cit., 254
20 Raphael Patai, *Ignaz Goldziher and His Oriental Diary: A Translation and Psychological Portrait* (Detroit, 1987), 15.

books. He began at the university studying classical languages, philosophy, and German literature and, with Arminius, he added Turcology. He was a brilliant scholar, supported in his education as his teacher had been by Baron Eötvös, and by Professor Môr Ballagi (1815–91) – Jewish intellectual, Protestant theologian, and Hungarian linguist. Ignaz wrote of his love and gratitude for Arminius, from whom 'I acquired my sincere love for Oriental studies' but, by 1881, he was describing his teacher as the 'arch-liar' and ten years later as 'the great swindle-Dervish', who was 'characterised by dirty greed', 'mocked the faith of his fathers' day by day', and 'countered all assertions of idealism' with the 'meanest and most obscene expressions'.[21]

The real reasons for the rift between Arminius and 'the great Goldziher' have been the subject of argument among interested academics during the intervening years.[22] It is not difficult, reading much of Arminius' autobiographical work, to be in sympathy with Goldziher's views, but his detestation of his former teacher and long-term supporter may have been aggravated by the difficulties of his own life and character. In spite of being drawn strongly to Islam during his own youthful travels and studies in Damascus and Cairo, Goldziher was a devout Jew. His career suffered from the endemic anti-Semitism so familiar to Arminius, and he also had a bitter relationship with the wealthy and hierarchical Jewish establishment of Budapest. He was a complicated man who was prey to breakdowns in his mental and physical health, and fostered simmering resentments against those he believed had wronged him. Arminius was not the only friend or supporter he fell out with, but Goldziher's scholarship far outstripped that of his teacher. He may have seen Arminius as a traitor and an apostate for his Christian conversion, and did undoubtedly see him as an ill-informed belittler of Islam and the scholarship of Islam that Goldziher himself revered.

Goldziher was far from being the only person who thought 'the Dervish' a fraud, but he was the one who took the deceptions most personally. His decrying of Arminius was based on his own serious scholarship but had been exacerbated by the way in which his own early success had been claimed as the triumphs of his teacher. Arminius' claims to his own great understanding

---

21 Ibid., 17.
22 See Raphael Patai, *Ignaz Goldziher and his Oriental Diary: A Translation and Psychological Portrait* (Detroit, 1987); quoted in Mandler, op. cit., 109–53.

of the Quran were easily refuted, and his invention of Quranic maxims to suit his own beliefs and prejudices must have maddened a genuine scholar. It was also clear to Goldziher that Arminius, with his lack of Quranic learning, could not possibly have got away with his disguise as a dervish, when he did not even understand a matter as basic as the specificity of the *fatiha*, the blessing asked of the dervish on his travels, repeated many times a day by the observant Muslim in the five prescribed daily prayers.[23]

Other mistakes made by Arminius regarding the Quran or Islamic history would also have been obvious to Goldziher. Facts given correctly in one of his books might be transformed in another to something entirely fictitious. His *History of Bokhara*, for example, was panned by Eugene Schuyler among myriad other critics, and Arminius himself admitted that he 'had not studied the subject sufficiently'. He held that his knowledge was based on the unique experience of his travels, but in the case of Bukhara and Samarkand, he was not in either city for long enough to do more than scratch the surface of the life around him. Goldziher was also appalled by the sheer vanity of his teacher: the boasting, the bombast, the vainglory and fabrication, that seem so obvious to the contemporary reader of Arminius' works. Arminius claimed to have had experiences far beyond the reality of his life and travels. He had been to Mecca he said, had been commissioned to translate the Bible into 'Tatar', and travelled to Tibet in the footsteps of Marco Polo. His 'reality' became ever more fabulous as his stories were told and re-told, and the dervish made the most of the doors they opened to him, including into the University of Pest.

Nordau, in his eulogistic introduction to *The Life and Adventures* (the same in which he described the amiable and beautiful Mrs Vambéry), wrote of his first meeting with Arminius in 1875, at dinner at the Vambéry apartment, where Goldziher was also present. Nordau described Arminius as 'extremely prepossessing', with an 'exceptionally individual' head and 'deep-lying eyes' that were, as a rule, 'kind and rather waggish'. They were no less than 'lordly eyes', the eyes of a man who was 'one of the elect few... a born leader of men'. 'In his eyes', Nordau wrote, 'I read his nature, his evolution and his history'. His voice, speaking German, 'without any Hungarian or Austrian accent',

---

23 Lawrence I. Conrad, 'The Dervish's Disciple: On the Personality and Intellectual Milieu of the Young Ignaz Goldziher', *Journal of the Royal Asiatic Society*, 1990/2, 225–66.

was 'harmonious, strong and purposely mellowed', and his conversation 'sprightly and pointed'. And so on, to the extent that the reader might well believe those hypnotic eyes still held Nordau under their spell. Beyond the hagiography, however, Nordau spoke nothing but the truth when he spoke of 'the Eastern fairy-tale teller' and 'the Scheherazade translated into the masculine'. Arminius' books 'do not convey the fascination of his living word, when, full of temperament, dazzling with colour, it evoked rapid, quick and magnificent memory-pictures' and 'bubbled forth, ever fuller and richer'. Nordau remembered quite forgetting the time until Goldziher, less dazzled by the show, kicked him – gently, he said – under the table. Nordau's memories may have been coloured exaggeratedly in memoriam, but there is little doubt of the spell of Arminius' story-telling ability. His 1869 lecture to the Mechanics Institution in Aberdeen was reported in the *Aberdeen Press and Journal:* 'the lecturer proved himself to be possessed of a fund of humorous anecdote'. The traveller's story was losing nothing with the passing years.

Arminius' final pupil, Gyula Germanus (1884–1979), lived long enough to be interviewed by Alder and Dalby for *The Dervish of Windsor Castle*. Germanus' was a truly adventurous spirit. Another Jewish Hungarian, he converted first to Calvinism and then to Islam; studied in Constantinople; campaigned with the Young Turks; was condemned to death by the sultan and snatched from the gallows at the last minute; was invited to India by the polymath Rabindranath Tagore and lived there for some years; nearly died again in the Arabian desert; was one of the first Europeans to undertake the Haj; and was certainly the first to photograph Mecca after concealing a camera about his person. All that is no more than the bare bones of his life. His true levels of scholarship were, like Arminius' and probably with reason, questioned in Hungary, but there was no doubt of his vast practical experience and the extent of his travels. He became a member of three Arab academies, even though he was never elected to the Hungarian Academy, and he remembered Arminius' taking solitary daily constitutionals on the Danube embankment where, with his furled umbrella and wearing a bowler hat (at a time when top hats were *de rigueur* in Hungary), Arminius 'accosted workmen lingering on the pavement' to tell them the 'incredible, fantastic, stories of his life'.[24]

---

24 Alder and Dalby, op. cit., 478.

Germanus told Alder and Dalby of his Turkish and Persian studies with Arminius (his 'adored master') starting in 1903, and of his own subsequent journey to study in Constantinople. Arminius, he said, by then in his seventies, was thoroughly irritated by students asking to learn with him, saying crossly, 'You can remain a decent citizen without knowing a single Turkish word'. Germanus told him that he had learned Turkish himself, and some Arabic, but wished to learn Persian. The old teacher handed him a 'thick Turkish book' and thundered 'Read!' It was a section 'from a report of a hospital in Constantinople' and, to Germanus' surprise, his reading and translation passed muster. He was sent off with a copy of the thirteenth-century Persian poet Saadi's great epic *Golestan*, from which, Arminius told him, he would 'get a perfect knowledge of Persian'. Germanus remarked that he had first 'to learn English in order to use the Persian–English dictionary!'[25] If Germanus was a big enough man in old age to rise above doubts about the character and scholarship of his first Orientalist teacher, he was in a minority. Open warfare broke out around Arminius, most notoriously in Hungarian academia, as the debate continued on the origins of the Hungarian language.

Arminius' hobby-horse quest had resolved nothing in this almost impossible argument. Peace has never fully been declared in the Ugric–Turkic war, right up to the present day. In the nineteenth century, as described earlier, questions on the origin of language were often far more to do with political determination and national identity than comparative linguistics. In 1870 Arminius, perhaps to shore up his own academic credentials, threw a stone with his publication of an article entitled 'Magyar és török-tatár nyelvekbeli szóegyezések' ('Hungarian and Turco-Tatar Word Cognates'), published in *The Linguistic Magazine of the Academy*. He acknowledged the 'Finnish' elements in Hungarian but claimed a far stronger relationship with Turco-Tatar. The argument could, therefore, go either way; to a disinterested onlooker with only the slightest knowledge of a handful of modern languages, spiced with a sprinkling of vocabulary from the ancients, the game, if not a serious study of language, appears an easy one to play but never to win. Unfortunately, this was not the dilettante dabble, the fascination of a brilliant amateur for knowledge or an academic argument for its own

---

25 Ibid., 493.

sake that has so often ignited higher scholarship. Arminius was not playing games, and neither were his opponents in the language wars, and his contribution lost him old friendships as well as exacerbating enmities.

Of particular note among those now ranged against him was his old friend Josef Budenz; Paul Hunfalvy, who was a generation older and had taught Budenz; Bernat Munkacsi, a student both of Budenz and Arminius; Josef Szinnyei, university librarian and expert on Hungarian genealogy; and Ferdinánd Barna, linguist, translator, librarian of the Hungarian Academy, and an expert on Finno-Ugric languages who had translated the *Kalevala*, a collection of Finnish legends. Arminius was far from the only polyglot in Hungary in his lifetime whose linguistic ambitions outstripped his skills. Budenz himself (who reputedly dismissed Barna's translation as the 'Barnevala') was German by birth and had arrived in Budapest, aged twenty-two, after taking a degree in Oriental studies and classical languages at the University of Göttingen. His spectacularly fast rise to become a full member of the Hungarian Academy by 1868 and to gain the Chair of the Department of Comparative Altaic Linguistics at the University of Pest aged thirty-six was, regardless of his real brilliance, almost certainly due to the politics of language at the time. Despite his appointment as a full professor to study the Hungarian language, he only began to learn the language at the age of twenty-three. He did not like Hungary or Hungarians, never wholly mastered their tongue, and considered his research into it 'useless matters'.[26] Arminius meanwhile considered Budenz's theories 'altogether too fantastic and too airy for my practical notions'. He championed his own position into old age, noting the national and political issues involved in the question. With regard to Hungarian ethnogenesis, he chose by then to point out that the 'prosaic derivation from a confused ethnical group', 'patched and pieced together from the most diverse elements', like every 'single nation in Europe', was far more likely than any romantic legend of origin sought by 'Magyar patriots'.

Nonetheless, whether informed scholar or wayward charlatan, and for all his self-cultivated aura of singularity, Arminius, in the role of teacher, was for some an inspirational figure, and set several talented men successfully on their chosen path.

---

26 Lászlo Marácz, 'The "Ugric-Turkic War" and the Origin of the Hungarian Language', *International Review of Turkish Studies*, 2/4 (2012), 8–23.

Late in his own life, Germanus wrote of Arminius' part in the language war: 'He may have made mistakes concerning some details, yet his scholarly insights into ancient Hungarian ethnogenesis, today, long after his death, have been proven – although often without admitting to it – by those working with different and more perfect tools'.[27] Ethnogenesis was, as we have seen, the bigger picture and one that Arminius denied trying to answer, but it was always the elephant in the room of the language wars. Paul Hunfalvy indeed had pronounced, 'one should consider the origins of nations as being the same as those of their language'.[28] In his final book, published posthumously in 1914,[29] Arminius returned to the puzzle of Hungarian ethnogenesis, the holy grail of the youthful adventurer. He concluded by opening the question to seekers in the future, pondering where, if records of ancient Hungarian history barely exist and are unreliable, Hungarians could search for their origins? His 'answer was unequivocal: from linguistics, especially from the Magyar tongue's Turkic legacy'.[30] Others on his side in the language war included his student Josef Thury, who became a teacher, historian of ancient Hungary, member of the Academy, and translator of Chagatai. Among his other students, Sandor Kegl and Ignác Kúnos were also students of and close to Goldziher in the tight network of Hungarian academia. Kunos was a linguist, Turcologist, and folklorist, and Kegl, who came from a wealthy Catholic family and whose views were esteemed by Goldziher, became an important Persian scholar while managing his extensive family estates.

Arminius left another inheritance, as well as his students. The Swede Sven Hedin, who explored Central Asia, the silk roads, India, and Tibet, and who discovered the source of the Brahmaputra, read the *Travels* in Swedish in

---

27 Quoted in Mandler, op. cit., 24.

28 1986 article by Professor Istvan Vásáry. Ibid., 25. Hunfalvy (1810–91) was one of the most famous Hungarian linguists engaged in the question of the origins of the Hungarian language and people, was founder of the first journal on the subject, and promoter of the Finno-Ugric theory of the origins of the people and language of Hungary, as opposed to Arminius' belief in their Turkish connections'.

29 This final work was entitled *A Magyarsag Bolcsojenel, A Magyar-torok rokonsag kezdete es fejlodese* (Budapest, 1914) – very roughly 'An investigation into the beginning and development of the Magyar–Turk relationship'.

30 Nándor Dreisziger, 'Ármin Vámbéry (1832–1913) as a Historian of Early Hungarian Settlement in the Carpathian Basin,' *Hungarian Cultural Studies*, 6 (2013).

his childhood and, aged twenty-one, visited Arminius in Budapest in 1886 on his return from his first journey to Persia. The two men became friends, with Arminius contributing a foreword to Hedin's 1887 book *Genom Persien, Mesopotamien och Kaukasien* ('Through Persia, Mesopotamia and the Caucasus'). Hedin was a regular visitor to Budapest and speaker at the Hungarian Geographical Society on his lecture tours.[31] In a photograph of 1903, Arminius is shown with Hedin and the other famous Hungarian Orientalists of the day, their names now largely forgotten outside their own country. Arminius quite clearly holds centre stage. Aurel Stein, the greatest Hungarian-born figure of oriental exploration, is missing from the photograph because he was working for the British as Inspector of Schools in the Punjab.

Both in the country of his birth and in his adopted country, Britain, Stein is claimed and acclaimed for his discoveries. Sir Edward Denison Ross, who catalogued the Stein collection for the British Museum, described him as 'the pride of two nations and the wonder of all'.[32] Stein himself was less satisfied with the museum. He was most concerned about the cramped storage for the artefacts he had collected on his second expedition into Central Asia between 1906 and 1908, and the difficulties of cataloguing them properly in a badly lit basement. Exhausted after his travels, he wrote a somewhat desperate-sounding letter, full of crossings out, begging for Arminius' intercession with the king on his behalf for the proper preservation of the collection. Arminius' reply in English is a formally emollient promise to do what he can to help, in contrast to an earlier letter written to Stein in Hungarian. In it he addresses the younger man in Hungarian idiom literally as 'my highly respected lad', hopes he will come to Budapest, and congratulates him warmly on the 'peerless success' of his epoch-making discoveries.[33] In 1897 Arminius told Stein that he intended to propose the creation of a customised new chair in Indo-Iranian philology for him at the university.

31 Hedin made many lecture tours to support his travels and his family. After his Tibetan expedition in 1908–9, he arrived at the Viceregal Lodge in Simla in his disreputable travel clothes with six Tibetan servants. When he gave a lecture after a dinner, he 'got so carried away', wrote the Vicereine Mary Minto, that he 'thought he was once again in the unexplored regions of Tibet. He went on speaking for 2 and a half hours instead of for an hour and a half'. See Anabel Loyd, *Vicereine: The Indian Journal of Mary Minto* (Delhi, 2016), 207.
32 Edward Denison Ross, *Both Ends of the Candle* (London, 1943), 106.
33 Cat. Stein LHAS 2 53, Hungarian Academy of Sciences. It's worth noting that Arminius and Goldziher were both friends of Stein's uncle, Ignaz.

In early 1898, he wrote to tell him the faculty had voted in his favour. By the time the appointment was confirmed, however, Stein was again on his way to Central Asia, at the start of his greatest adventure.

Arminius received his formal appointment as professor at the university in 1867 and at last became a full member of the Hungarian Academy in 1876. He would remain, if well known, always the outsider at home, until the full range of his connections abroad, especially with royalty, were revealed in Budapest much later in his life. Until that time, his journeys outside Hungary, especially his regular trips to Britain, his status in that country, his view of the British Empire, of Russia and Persia, and his involvement in Anglo–Turkish relations, were apart and different to his life in Budapest, although they were bridged by his literary and journalistic output. His credentials abroad as Professor Vambéry relied not only on the lasting effects of his fame in London after 1864 but also on the perception in Britain of his standing as an important academic and the greatest Orientalist authority in Hungary, if not Europe. He was generally believed to be the greatest living expert on Central Asia since Marco Polo – a claim which might have been laughable to any number of others, especially the Russian geographers and explorers who walked those paths before Hedin and Stein – but all the same, Arminius was well informed on the region and its affairs. This might not have been so much from his personal experience but from contacts and correspondence that criss-crossed the old trade routes through Asia back to Europe. He read every newspaper and whatever messages and despatches came his way and, if his skills in Persian and Turkish were not so rare in London, he is believed also to have read Russian. This was unusual: Russia was becoming less Francophone in the second half of the nineteenth century, but French remained the universal language of the halls of diplomacy. In the field, multilingual British and Russian officers, meeting by chance or design at the edges of their empires in Central Asia, may have communicated in several tongues, but Russian was low on that list. Arminius, the established and much-published Russophobe, who trailed his forebodings through the corridors of British imperial diplomacy and via the British press into the consciousness of the British public, would have said *know your enemy.*

NETTERVILLE BRIGGS,   PHOTO., LEAMINGTON.

10ᵗʰ March. 1869.   *A. Vámbéry*

13

The Russian Menace

On his arrival in London in 1864, Arminius' warnings about Russia had fallen on ears that were deaf, disinterested, distracted, or just doubtful of the messenger. By the last months of that year, advance notices for the publication of the *Travels* and for Arminius' lecture at the Athenaeum had appeared in British newspapers from the *Kentish Chronicle* to the *Dublin Evening Mail.* In December, the *Literary Examiner* gave a review of 'Mr Vambéry's curious, interesting and instructive volume', with extensive quotations. It reported his warning of imminent danger to India from 'Russian aggression eastwards' but dismissed earlier British fears of Russian advances in Turkestan as 'costly and dangerous illusions'. Russia, the review continued, was 'only pursuing the very same policy which we ourselves have for a hundred years in India'. The Russians were 'in juxtaposition to a people ruder than themselves' and 'must fight and beat their neighbours, or be harassed, plundered and invaded'. Such action was further justified, since 'Russian rule may be rough, but it cannot fail to be a great improvement on Turkoman rule, according to the account given by Mr Vambéry'.[1] The first report of his travels in *The Times*, in February 1865, noted 'Mr Vambéry thinks that England is too indifferent to the progress of Russian designs in Central Asia', and went on to state the paper's own position: that a 'rivalry between Russia and England' was 'affirmed to be an absurdity' and a question 'long ago worn out and out of fashion'.

The tribes of Turkestan are wild, rude and barbarous, and it is a matter upon which we congratulate ourselves, if Russia takes upon herself the

---

1 *The Literary Examiner* (17 December 1864).

onerous and meritorious task of civilisation in those regions. Such is the state of public opinion which Mr Vambéry ascribes to us, and we can only hope, for our part, that it may long endure as a proof of our own moderation and good sense.[2]

The Treaty of Turkmenchay in 1828, ending the Russo-Persian war of 1826–8, had brought Russian imperial influence to the borders of Afghanistan and only a step away, or so it seemed, from India. The first move in what was to become the 'Great Game' was made by Sir George de Lacy Evans, who had fought at Waterloo and was to go on to command the 2nd Division at the Battle of Alma in the Crimea in 1854. He published *On the Designs of Russia* as early as 1828, as Russia began her steady advance into Central Asia. In the fourth and final volume of his splendid *History of Central Asia*, Christopher Baumer contextualises the century of rivalry between Britain and Russia that was 'fought out in proxy battles', going right back to the 1807 Treaty of Tilsit between Russia and France. The Great Game, also called a 'Tournament of Shadows' by the Russian foreign minister Count Nesselrode (1780–1862), took place primarily in Afghanistan, as well as in Crimea, Persia, Xinjiang, and Tibet, but was always directed from afar, as Russian ambitions moved ever southwards in search of territory, influence, and trading ports.[3] Arminius' involvement was as a type of self-appointed manager, who saw himself as being licensed by his limited reconnaissance of the field of play to push his own team into the right position as he saw it. Today we might describe him as a pundit.[4]

Right from the beginning, battle lines were drawn in this debate as on the ground. The economist Thomas Tooke (1774–1858), who had been born in Russia, spoke Russian, and worked in St Petersburg, had hastened to refute Sir George with *A Few Words on Our Relations with Russia, Including Some Remarks on a Publication by Colonel de Lacy Evans Entitled 'Designs of*

---

2 *The Times* (14 February 1865).
3 See Christopher Baumer, *The History of Central Asia: The Age of Decline and Revival*, Vol. 4 (London, 2018).
4 The true pundits, needless to say, the real shadows on the ground, whose anonymity has cloaked their importance, were a different breed. They were the Indian surveyors who painstakingly and secretly mapped the wild outer regions of British India for the *Survey of India*, gathering intelligence wherever they travelled.

Russia', by a Non-Alarmist. He believed in a Russian expansionist policy but considered Russia incapable of seriously challenging Britain or of wishing to do so. As a good and thrifty economist, he warned of the 'peculiar evil of a war against Russia', which would severely damage British finances and trade, and refused to entertain any possibility of Russia attempting an invasion of India, on grounds of the lack both of desire and of the technical ability to do so. In addition, he pointed out, the development of an enlightened liberal elite in St Petersburg suggested that Russia was now a place to do business rather than battle. Sir George then countered with *On the Practicability of an Invasion of India* (1829),[5] and so the argument continued, in actions and in words. Adventurous young men, Indian, British, and Russian, played out their hard game in the mountains and deserts of Central Asia, and the politicians and newspapers of the empires waxed hot and cold in their national capitals until Germany became a greater threat than any other and the Anglo-Russian entente of 1907 brought this chapter of Central Asian adventures to an end.

The game, however, was far from lost or won when Arminius arrived in London, even if England had relaxed into a half-time complacency. This attitude was bolstered by the policy of 'masterly inactivity' towards Afghanistan favoured by the statesman and civil servant Lord John Lawrence, who at the time of Arminius' arrival was viceroy and governor-general of India.[6] He had been warned. As home secretary in 1853, Lord Palmerston had presciently declared that:

> The policy and practice of the Russian Government has always been to push forward its encroachments as fast and far as the apathy or want of firmness of other Governments would allow it to go, but always to stop and retire when it met with determined resistance, and then to wait for

---

5 If the argument between Evans, the dyed-in-the-wool traditionalist and jingoistic serving soldier, and Tooke, the international free trade economist, seems an obvious clash, that would be too simplistic a view. The dispute was based on different understandings of the hazards implicit in changing balances of power between empires and the means of their resolution. Evans later became a Liberal MP who fought for reform of the army, in particular, for the abolition of commission by purchase.

6 Lawrence's attitude might be summed up in his own words: 'that we will leave the Afghans to settle their own quarrels, and that we are willing to be on terms of amity and goodwill with the nation and with their rulers *de facto*'.

the next favourable opportunity to make another spring on the intended victim. In furtherance of this policy, the Russian Government has always had two strings on its bow, moderate language and disinterested professions at St Petersburg and at London; active aggression by its agents on the scene of operation.[7]

Now Palmerston was prime minister, but there were other problems to be faced and the alarums and excursions of Central Asia had always been a long way from London, even if not for those who had lately walked in the diplomatic enclaves of Constantinople and Tehran, seen the Russian ships on the Caspian, and were convinced Russophobes. Russian foreign minister Prince Gorchakov's memorandum of 1864 was only one of many meretricious communications with London regarding Russian intentions towards Tashkent, Bukhara, Khiva, and the ancient city of Merv on the Silk Road, each of which was to find itself annexed in turn. The historian Christopher Baumer regards the serial promises from St Petersburg to have been cover not only for conquests in Turkestan but for a series of Russian plans to invade India in 1854, 1855, 1869, 1877, and 1878.

Throughout the late 1860s, as the Central Asian khanates began to fall, Arminius' was a voice upraised in the general wilderness of unconcern about Russia's territorial ambitions. In 1864 and 1865, there were a few others who sounded cautionary notes in the columns of the press as Russia pushed into Turkestan, but it was not until the 1870s and 1880s that the alarms rang louder. Arminius was busy, as we have seen, with his establishment, both domestic and professional, in Budapest, his visits to Britain being largely taken up with the lectures that kept his name in the spotlight and sold his books. But he had written to *The Times* as early as June 1865, as 'A Traveller from Central Asia', to point out the divisions between the khanates that would cause one and then the next to topple into the arms of a strong ally, and cautioned 'the Russian outposts in Central Asia have got so far now, they are unable to stop'. He was right. Russia had no intention of stopping and growing incentives to go on. Thomas Tooke was dead by the time Russia

---

7 Christopher Baumer, op. cit., 297. Baumer writes, 'In the view of the present author, the Russian annexation of Crimea in the spring of 2014 and the outbreak of fighting in Eastern Ukraine show that Palmerston's assessment is still valid today'.

freed her serfs in 1861, but the economist would have understood that new impetus for territorial expansion. At the same time, the American Civil War almost stopped American cotton exports, and Russia needed a new source of cotton over which it had control.[8] Arminius the Hungarian philologist would have understood that Russians also had a romantic sense of an Asian heritage stretching back to their conquest by the Mongols of the Golden Horde, and the belief that 'all these peoples of various races feel themselves drawn to us, and are ours, by blood, by tradition, and by ideas'.[9]

The Times, however, remained unconcerned. An article a few months later was careless of Russian advances in Central Asia: 'She is not advancing half as rapidly as the British in the Punjab, all this Russian danger is a phantom of our own creation.'

A review in *The Times* of October 1866 of *The Russians in Central Asia*, written by the young Kazakh scholar and ethnographer Shoqan Walikhanov (1835–65), maintains this tone.[10] It deserves almost to be printed in full as an example of contemporary indifference and assumed superiority to the unknown other. The reader will get some sense of it from its description of a 'whole country, which, without exaggeration, is nothing but one vast waste… This Sahara along the banks of the rivers' where 'nothing intervenes to break the monotony of the scene, save here and there badly cultivated rice fields and plantations of cotton', left 'by the lazy and improvident population to the care of Allah', and where 'constructed above the numerous remains of ancient cities, long since mouldering beneath the soil, stand the miserable hovels of a wild and barbarous race, demoralised by Islamism and reduced almost to idiocy by the political and religious despotism of their native rulers'.

Russia, the reviewer decides, is going to waste herself by taking on 'the obligation' and the cost of doing 'all that many generations of native sovereigns have left undone'. Slight chance then of any Russian threat to India

---

8 Cotton became the destructive legacy left to Central Asia long after the demise of the British and Russian empires and the latter's Soviet successor. Cotton production on a vast scale is the major factor in the loss of the Aral Sea and to a future of water shortages and ecological and economic damage in Central Asia.

9 Jennifer Siegel, *Endgame: Britain, Russia and the Final Struggle for Central Asia* (London, 2002), 3.

10 Shoqan Shyngysuly Walikhanov, *The Russians in Central Asia* (London, 1865), 49.

and, if that were not enough, an expedition would have to rely on a supply chain stretching all the way from the Russian base on the Ural River at Orenburg. It would be forced to travel across 'the dreary steppes' where calamity of one sort or another was inevitable, and overcome the insurmountable 'precipices and glaciers' of the Hindu Kush before it could 'measure swords with the British Army'. Indeed, the reviewer remarks, 'the best cure for a geographical panic is a map, and a good one accompanies this work... An interval of 500 miles which separates the new Russian military line from the frontier of Cashmere, does not to ears attuned to express trains sound a very formidable obstacle to invasion, but a glance on the map at the kind of country which makes up those few hundreds of miles is very reassuring'.

A small article, reprinted across several papers in August 1867, noticed Russia's 'conquests on the plateau of Central Asia' as part of the inflation of Pan-Slavic ambitions, and fully realised the impact of events in one faraway place on those nearer home. It suggested they were both proxy for the battle for supremacy in Europe and intended as a 'strategic diversion, whenever England might ally herself with the European Powers to protect the Black Sea and Turkey against Russian occupation'. 'Every one of her mysterious operations gives token of a design to deluge Europe with her multitudinous hordes and to drown in her Pansclavonic [sic] supremacy'. It requires, however, 'a certain effort to look off to distant countries' when 'the political atmosphere of Europe is so portentously clouded', even if 'with our present means of communication, no part of the world is really distant' and nothing can happen anywhere without it 'reacting directly or indirectly upon the social and political struggle for existence in Europe'.[11] Neither politicians nor the public in Britain were really prepared to part the European clouds and look for trouble further afield at this stage. The anonymous article was probably prompted by the appointment in July of the Russian General Konstantin Petrovich von Kaufmann (1818–82) as the first governor-general of Turkestan, with licence and the ability to conquer. He had taken Samarkand by the following summer.

So began the subjugation of Bukhara and the click of the khanate dominoes, falling one by one. With Bukhara subdued, the Russians were at the borders of Khiva. In 1869, the port and fortress of Krasnovodsk

---

11 *Northern Standard* (17 August 1867).

(now Türkmenbaşy) was established on the eastern shore of the Caspian as a staging-post for troops and supplies from Russia, and negotiations began between Russia and London to define the borders of Afghanistan. This led to the Anglo-Russian agreement of January 1873, where Russia agreed to Afghanistan being outside her sphere of influence as the effective buffer zone between Russian imperial ambitions and British imperial defences. In the summer of that year, the Khiva khanate fell, and Russia was almost in position to threaten Herat and, regardless of the agreement, to make forward plans to open the door into Afghanistan and perhaps to surmount the mountain barriers to India. In 1876, the khanate of Kokand was annexed by Russia. By the summer of 1878, Russian diplomats were busy at Kabul, attempting to seduce the amir Sher Ali Khan into opening his front door *to* them and his back door into India *for* them. By then the 'forward school', the hawks of British opinion concerning Central Asia, had more influence on government at home and in India, and British sabres were rattling as a prelude to the second Anglo-Afghan War. But the Russian advance continued.

Arminius wrote to *The Times* under his own name in November 1868 regarding the importance of a British diplomatic presence in Central Asia. The letter, speaking of the visit of an envoy from Kokand to Moscow, must have been so far outside the interest of most readers in London as to sink without trace, but Moscow noticed. A report taken from the *Moscow Gazette* on Gladstone's statement to parliament in the spring of 1869,[12] regarding British attempts to contain Russia in Central Asia, notes the advice of Arminius. This 'implacable enemy of Russia' advised the British to send consuls to Central Asian cities, 'perhaps to intrigue with the natives and to arm them against us?' It suggested that if this was the background to ambiguous and 'evasive' statements of friendship made by the prime minister in parliament, Russia should take it as a 'timely warning'. The article first took a defensive tone as prelude to a distinct threat. It stated:

Only a matter of extreme necessity has forced us to extend our Asiatic frontier further south. We believe we have a right to expect some reward for the sacrifices made on that occasion and if our hopes are fulfilled, shall

---

12 Reprinted in several British regional papers, including *The Homeward Mail* (3 May 1869).

not only retain possession of the vast markets of Turkistan, but through it gain access to Chinese Tartary.

The writer acknowledged it 'is but natural the English should try to throw impediments in our way in that direction' and recommended them to 'let alone' and not interfere with Russian interests. Or else, it concluded, 'in the event of an Eastern war Turkistan will be a formidable basis of operations for us against the English'.

British reprints of this article are appended with another from the St Petersburg newspaper *Golos*. The language here is significantly harsher:

The commercial war being waged between England and Russia, on the northern frontiers of Afghanistan, is not at all unlikely to give way some day to a combat with more sanguinary weapons than weights and measures. In this case, the rifles presented to the Ameer by the Earl of Mayo would stand him in good stead, though, for the matter of that, the Ameer, after taking pounds sterling, is quite as likely as not to try roubles for a change.

Lord Mayo (viceroy of India 1869–72) had given two batteries of artillery and several thousand rifles to Amir Sher Ali as a token of British friendship and support, and tacitly as added insurance against Russian ambitions. Arminius, nursing his Russophobia in Budapest and reading more of the same, more regularly, and first-hand in Russian, must have seethed. How many other letters and articles from him landed on British editors' desks in those years of relative calm, and were swept into wastepaper baskets as other concerns took precedence in their columns? He was quite aware that it was only 'when the Central Asian question became acute' that his 'pen was in actual request' and was aggrieved to have 'had to force myself upon the public'. In *Sketches of Central Asia*, in 1868, he railed against 'the sanguine views of the English optimists with regard to the strength of their fancied bulwarks'. He was correct in doubting English defences, but his arguments become much too complicated as he adds one dislike to another to create a chain of alliances that might carry Britain's 'sly and powerful adversary', the 'Muscovite neighbour', all the way to Calcutta via the contradictory links of his own mutable prejudices. A taste of the whole will suffice: the Muscovite could hardly 'forbear from profiting by the happy occasion which plays into her hands the Mohammedan population of India, more than thirty million strong', who 'are filled with unspeakable hatred of the British rule' so that they 'often murder a British officer walking about the bazaar'. Then there were the Armenians, 'scattered through Persia and India', and 'more catholic than the Papist, more Russian, more orthodox than the Tsar himself'. Every one of them in Asia 'is to be regarded as a secret agent of Muscovite policy'. In any case, 'the Russians are Asiatics' ('scrape a Russian and you will lay bare a Tartar', Arminius trumpeted, nastily) and Tsar Nicholas, the same who had refused to call the French emperor *mon frère*, 'in presence of the Tartar princes of Central Asia' behaves 'not as Emperor of all the Russias but as a Khan on the Neva'. And so on, and so on, as 'the gigantic empire of the House of Romanoff' used 'discord, bribery and corruption', not to mention 'lavish draughts of vodki' and other presents, to support Russian ascendancy and threaten India. And India could only suffer now from 'Russianizing', when 'even the worst enemies of Great Britain will be unable to deny that the caste-system of the Hindoos and their many inhuman customs have suffered a mighty blow from English influence' and are now 'advancing with wonderful strides on the path of our civilisation'. To such an extent, in fact, Arminius believed, that 'we shall be obliged to own that England's subject races stand, not only above their yoke-fellows in Russia but even above many of the Russians themselves'. Russia might seem European and 'imbued with the spirit of our civilisation', but 'lift the outer covering' of a Russian and find, beneath his 'remarkably dirty exterior', a drunk, 'his religion bordering on fetishism', servile and ignorant, with 'coarse, unpolished manners'. What then can the cultivated Muslims of Central Asia learn from Russia? The urbane Russian foreign minister, Prince Gorchakov, and his successful general, von Kaufmann, at that moment busy rolling out the khanates one by one, could only have laughed.

Arminius continued to be appalled by the lack of knowledge, let alone the lack of concern, about events in Central Asia through the last years of the 1860s and into the early 1870s. When he was not bombarding British editors and politicians with letters, he was writing papers for publications including *Unsere Zeit* in Germany.[13] His pieces pursued the Russians across

---

13 See Arminius Vambéry, *Central Asia and the Anglo-Russian Frontier Question: A series of political papers*, tr. by F. E. Bunnett (London, 1874).

Central Asia, reiterating his Russophobia with a repetition of the abuse he had employed in *Sketches* and his conviction that Russia intended to take India. It pointed out the fulfilment of many of his earlier prophecies on their advance, after 'the majority of the British Press and the official papers in India attacked my political views in rather strong terms and the *Pall Mall Gazette*[14] even honoured me with the title of chief alarmist'. Now, he remarked, only a year later, 'their views have taken a strange turn'. Returning to his own experiences in Samarkand and Bukhara, he marvelled that those distant places 'will now be visited by Russian soldiers and soon no doubt by Russian Popes' – the latter, one suspects, the more offensive prospect so far as he was concerned. He also complained of the policy of 'masterly inactivity' of Lord Lawrence. Russian ambitions now encompassed the trade routes into China, and sepoy deserters from the Indian army were either helping to build fortifications in Afghanistan or had joined the Afghan army, ready to fight the British. Arminius was certain there could be no 'lasting relation of friendship' between Russia and Britain' and 'Mr Gladstone & Co. should remember the worth of Russian promises'. The *Sketches*, Arminius wrote, 'found a good sale'. The *Athenaeum* was doubtful of its author's syntax but felt 'bound to own that he is a correct exponent of the Russian policy in Central Asia'. The reviewer wondered what 'peculiar reason' had made it an 'understood thing, that no heed should be taken of the advice' which Arminius had 'voluntarily given England on the subject of Russian advances'. The answer, it believed, was in the 'several errors in the account of his travels', but there was neither now 'the time or the space to attempt any further explanation of the reason why M. Vambéry has not established himself as an authority among us', and 'nor need we be apologists so long as the book which we are now noticing is read with the attention it deserves'.

Those 'errors' had haunted Arminius since his poorly researched *History of Bokhara* had been published in 1873 and been attacked so determinedly by Eugene Schuyler. The book had been turned down by John Murray and seems to have been written on the rash assumption that no one knew as much

---

14 The *Pall Mall Gazette* was a highly influential evening paper founded in 1865. Initially founded as 'Conservative' but relatively impartial, it became a Liberal mouthpiece, and, under the editorship of W. T. Stead, from 1880, it became known for investigative journalism and as the initiator of modern newspaper campaigns for moral causes of national importance. It is referred to in several contemporaneous works of fiction, including Bram Stoker's *Dracula*.

about the subject as Arminius did. Even so, he refused to allow any other 'the knowledge of the Oriental and Russian languages' or the 'prolonged and intimate acquaintance with the theme' that gave him an advantage over his 'literary competitors'. The *Athenaeum* began its review of the *History* gratifyingly enough, saying 'Nobody knows more about this wild region than Professor Vambéry'. *The Times* called the book 'instructive' and Arminius 'a true scholar', who had 'spent years travelling in Turkestan and Persia', and whose 'book possesses the real merit of knowledge and experience', but, apart from those kind if questionable statements, the book's principal crime is that it is *boring*. From the point of view of a reader today, of histories of Central Asia and of contemporary tales of the Great Game, there are so many that not only inform but add all the colour and excitement that so thrilled readers in Arminius' time and still do so today, quite regardless of our different understanding of such exploits. Arminius' original *Travels* might have lacked the ironic humour inherent in much of the literature of nineteenth-century exploration, but it was still a good story. Once he began writing as the scholar and authority, however, most of his writing became pompous, portentous, and redolent of self-importance, as over-furnished with extraneous furbelows as a bourgeois Victorian drawing room. And the musical box in the corner played the same tune *ad infinitum*, even after the British marching band had joined in and, later still, gone home.

Worst of all, for the *Athenaeum*, *The History of Bokhara* confirmed the very opposite of its author's intentions: that 'whatever may be the effect of Russian neighbourliness on our India Empire, it is for the best interests of mankind that Russia should continue her onward advance' and bring the benefits of civilisation to the barbarians. Schuyler himself doubted in public that Arminius had been to Central Asia at all, a refrain taken up by Vambéry decriers all the way to Russia. Oddly enough, whilst many of Schuyler's criticisms were entirely reasonable and there is a great deal easily questioned in Arminius' accounts of his journey, the dervish was entirely in the right over one small fact that became more or less a standing joke. It concerns, of all things, Arminius' description of 'fatty-tailed sheep'. Schuyler wrote that it was a well-known fact that sheep in Central Asia had no tails at all, and that this was certain proof that the false dervish had lifted his zoological details from the fancies of Herodotus. Arminius fought back: serious authorities agreed with his 'ethnographical, historical and philological' conclusions, and a differing view was largely a question of changing times. In 1863 no European had been safe in Samarkand and 'now, look, only a few weeks ago, a Miss Mittelstedt had given a concert to Russians and Tadjiks'. Arminius did admit to 'meddling in philological matters without first consulting the appropriate works', but he had to wait for the Irish journalist Edmond O'Donovan to publish his own extremely entertaining account of Turkestan in 1882 for vindication on the sheep,[15] whose physiology could not be a question of interpretation. O'Donovan had been, to say the least, unimpressed by Turkmen cuisine. 'Turcomans [seem] to have a predilection for meat the odour of which is rather higher than that which would be pleasant to European nostrils', but the sheep, he wrote, 'are of the big-tailed variety, and all the fat of their bodies seems to concentrate itself in the tail, which cannot, on the average, weigh less than twelve pounds'. The tail was 'considered an extra-luxurious dish'.[16] Other questions might remain but, over the sheep, Schuyler was obliged to offer an olive branch.

Arminius had an opinion on everything in what he considered his sphere of influence, and he shared them with a lengthy list of European and American publications. His name even appears in newspaper reports from Calcutta, where he did not hesitate to criticise the actions of the government of India, criticisms sometimes disputed by more proximate commentators. If his advice was not always welcomed and his badgering a thorn in the side of the London Liberal (and liberal) establishment, he was at least no longer alone in his concerns, especially among those for whom Asia was a geopolitical reality rather than a concept. Among them was Edward Eastwick, last seen in Tehran, enquiring in a letter to *The Times* in June 1871 about the veracity of a claim from Arminius that Yakub Khan had taken Herat. This was an event of considerable importance to the situation in Afghanistan, had been denied by the under-secretary of foreign affairs,[17] and was then proved true. After his years in Persia, Eastwick had been private secretary to Lord Cranborne (later Lord Salisbury and Conservative prime minister) when

---

15 Edmond O'Donovan, *The Merv Oasis: Travels and Adventures East of the Caspian during the Years 1879–80–81* (London, 1882). O'Donovan was special correspondent for the *Daily News*, had been in the Foreign Legion, and observed the slaughter of the Turkmans at Geok Tepe by General Skobelev in 1881. He was killed in 1883 in Sudan at the Battle of El Obeid.
16 Ibid., 339–40.
17 Lord Enfield, later 3rd earl of Strafford.

Cranborne was secretary of state for India; had written several of John Murray's *Handbooks* on Indian destinations; and had become an MP himself in 1868. In 1871, he called the attention of the House of Commons to 'the state of affairs in Central Asia' and the Russian policy of 'absorption of native territories' that required 'the utmost vigilance'. In answer, Gladstone explained that Russia had made an undertaking not to interfere with Afghanistan while Britain used her 'moral influence to ensure the good behaviour of Afghanistan', and Russian progress in the region should be regarded, the prime minister said, as 'advancing the cause of civilisation'.[18] Worthy justification for a continuing policy of 'masterly inactivity'.

The election victory of Disraeli's Conservatives over Gladstone's Liberals in early 1874 was a tipping point in policy towards Russia. Disraeli's beliefs about empire have been a matter for ongoing debate[19] but, led by him, the Conservatives were the party of empire and the proponents, with Queen Victoria, of the great beneficent imperial enterprise. His government promoted a forward policy in Central Asia that reversed the determined inactivity of the previous regime and took a hawkish view of Russian approaches towards Afghanistan and India (Russian aggression by now had also been amply demonstrated by the Russo-Turkish war of 1877–8). Russian expansion through the Dardanelles threatened the British route to India, and Russian troops had reached the walls of Constantinople. Jingoism prevailed. The Great Game warmed up again, and a renewed interest in events in Central Asia, in Russian ambitions, and in the individuals involved on all sides is easy to see in any trawl through the newspaper archives, with experts going into print in books that brought Central Asia and Afghanistan back into the spotlight. These, now, were not only the gung-ho Victorian heroes such as Hippisley Cunliffe Marsh in 1873 or the intelligence officer Frederick Burnaby in 1876, but increasingly more sober commentators, including Sir Henry Rawlinson in 1875 and Demetrius Charles Boulger, founder of the *Asiatic Quarterly Review*. In his 1879 work *England and Russia in Central Asia*, Boulger pointed to 1863 as the turning point in Central Asian strategy and in the rivalry between Russia and Britain, when the concept of 'a

18 As reported in the *Bolton Evening News* (23 April 1871).
19 See C. C. Eldridge, *England's Mission: The Imperial Idea in the Age of Gladstone and Disraeli, 1868–1881*, particularly Chapter 7: 'Disraeli's Imperial Ideas' (London, 1973).

boundless prospect of conquest' had been opened up to the Russian people after the emancipation of the serfs. Since then, Russia had used the excuse of 'the depredations of her semi-barbarous neighbours' to advance into the khanates while giving assurances to Britain, 'in accordance with the necessities of European politics', on the inviolability of Afghanistan and thus the preservation of a 'neutral outerwork' to India of 500 kilometres as its narrowest point.[20] Experience of Russian actions and broken promises over the past fifteen years should by now make it 'impossible to feign ignorance' of Russian ambitions towards India. No faith whatsoever should be vested in Russian guarantees, that 'are no guarantees, and sully the paper on which they are written'.[21]

Rawlinson meanwhile carefully laid out the history and relationships between Persia, Russia, and Britain in Asia and concluded, with regard to the present situation, 'I counsel nothing rash or premature' as long as Russia 'held aloof from Merv, we should hold aloof from Herat'.[22] The city of Merv was an important trade hub of the Silk Road and had been the eastern capital of the Seljuk Sultanate (1037–94 CE). At its height during the twelfth century, the city was famed for its learning and culture and was one of the largest and most cosmopolitan in the world, with an estimated population of half a million. It fell to the Mongols in 1221 when much of the population was executed, and it never regained its former glory. It was finally razed to the ground in 1788–9 by the emir of Bukhara. Today the remains stand as great sandy mounds outside the modern Turkmen city of Mary. The entire province was bloodlessly annexed by Russia in 1884. The terrible slaughter of the Turkmen tribes by General Skobelev's army at Geok Tepe in 1881,[23] and the deaf ear turned to applications for assistance from Merv to Persia and to Britain, had helped to open more doors to the Russian advance and, with

---

20 Demetrius Charles Kavanagh de Boulger, *England and Russia in Central Asia*, Vol. II (London, 1879), 345–8.

21 Ibid., 366–8.

22 Sir Henry Rawlinson, *England and Russia in the East: A Series of Papers on the Political and Geographical Condition of Central Asia* (London, 1875), 365.

23 Fierce resistance against Russian encroachment into Turkestan by the Tekke Turkmens was finally overcome when General Mikhail Dmitriyevich Skobelev captured the Tekke stronghold of Geok Tepe after a twenty-three-day siege and massacred thousands of Turkmen soldiers and civilians both in and outside the fort. Skobelev (1843–82) was a hero of the Russo-Turkish war and the conqueror of Turkestan, known to the Turkmans as 'Bloody Eyes'.

the taking of Merv, the line of march was clear to Herat through the Heri-Rud valley. The mountain gateway to India through Afghanistan might then be opened to Russia by force or by diplomatic guile. And where Russian troops led, their railway followed. It had reached Merv by 1886. Soon troops would be carried from the Caspian right to the border with Afghanistan, lines of supply opened up… and there was a Liberal government once again at Westminster.

Prime Minister Gladstone, described by Arminius as 'the zealous advocate of an Anglo-Russian alliance in church and politics', who 'particularly disliked my political energy', was the liberal dove as Conservative hawks and Russophobes foretold disaster. When the khanate of Khiva fell to the Russians in 1873, Gladstone had written to his close friend, the talented Russian journalist and propagandist Madame Olga Novikov, regretting the possible effect on the balance of power in Europe but remarking 'I should tell you first that about Khiva I do not care two straws. Further, I believe it just possible that there may be a bona fide pressure for its annexation to Russia'. Disraeli nicknamed Novikov 'the MP for Russia',[24] and the Liberal and friend of Gladstone's Sir Charles Dilke called her a 'horrid beast'. Known by her pen name of 'OK', she was a highly skilled proponent of the spin-doctor's art many years before the coining of that term and was rumoured to have had an affair with Gladstone. She described Arminius as 'one of the greatest Russian haters in the world' and, he wrote, 'did her utmost to discredit me in England'. In 1885, however, Arminius and his Russophobic views were a perfect fit with popular opinion, and Britain, again led by Gladstone, was at the brink of war.

After the annexation of Merv, the British government protested to St Petersburg and received the answer that Russian actions had been at the request of the Turcomans, who desired the benefits of civilisation. But on this occasion the 'civilisation' trope was not enough, so Russia proposed the joint delineation of a permanent frontier between Afghanistan and Russian Central Asia – a line, measured out on the ground, to divide empire indelibly from empire, Turkman from Turkman, and leave Afghanistan isolated but far

---

24 *MP for Russia* became the title of her book of *Reminiscences and Correspondence*, edited by W. T. Stead and published in London in 1909. Her articles were widely published, including in the *Pall Mall Gazette*.

from inviolate, between Scylla and Charybdis. The Joint Afghan Boundary Commission, headed by General Peter Lumsden (1829–1918), was supposed to start work in October 1884, but the British arrived late and the Russians procrastinated. Winter came on with continued military activity in the disputed regions as Russia tried to push the border as far south as possible before the frontier was agreed. British imperial attention was also deflected towards Sudan, where General Gordon was besieged in Khartoum, but in January 1885 reports of Gordon's dramatic death, seen almost as a martyrdom, unleashed patriotic fervour in Britain; meanwhile in April, the news of what became known as the 'Panjdeh incident' where Russian troops captured an Afghan border fort, added extra impetus to public outrage. The floodgates of outrage opened, and 1885 became a bumper year for 'Great Game' literature,[25] with publications including Arminius' *The Coming Struggle for India*.

Charles Marvin, the best-known British writer on Central Asian affairs at the time, was a brilliant young journalist who had worked with his father in Russia in his youth, spoke Russian, and had excellent contacts among the Russian military. Dalby and Alder describe him as 'none too scrupulous a journalist, catering to the sensation-loving section of the public'.[26] He was certainly a populist writer, and he had been arrested in 1878, when he worked in the Foreign Office, for leaking a secret Anglo-Russian treaty to the *Globe*. Marvin had learned the entire document by heart and escaped prosecution when it was discovered that there was no law to cover such a crime. He was in some respects a surprising admirer of Arminius. He described the *Travels* as 'undoubtedly one of the finest books of the kind we have in the English language' and the only one to get 'the full aroma of the East' and realise 'what Central Asia really is'.[27] Marvin was a Russophile, or, he said himself, 'I suppose, both a Russophile and a Russophobe' – one who loved Russia but, in his identity as 'a citizen of the English Empire' rather than 'merely a Liberal or Conservative Englishman of Lesser England only', was a 'vigilant and anxious observer of the Russian advance towards India'.[28] He became Arminius' new champion.

---

25 See P. Hopkirk, *The Great Game*, for more details.
26 Alder and Dalby, op. cit., 295–6.
27 Charles Thomas Marvin, *Merv: The Queen of the World* (London, 1881), 19.
28 Charles Thomas Marvin, *The Russians at the Gates of Herat* (New York, 1885), i.

Marvin's first book on Central Asia had been commended by no other than General Mikhail Skobelev (he of Geok Tepe). In 1881 Marvin came to popular attention in Britain with *Merv: The Queen of the World*, which he dedicated to Arminius. The book described the explorations of 'the Central Asian pioneers', British and Russian, and built a picture of the history, culture, and situation in Turkestan. In his re-telling of Arminius' dervish journey, Marvin deplored British attitudes to a man who had 'unswervingly adhered to the line' he had taken up in support of the British Empire. It had 'most decidedly not enriched him' and had lost him all his friends in Russia and many in Hungary. Had he instead taken the tsar's shilling, he would have been 'deluged with those favours which the Czar's statesmen know so well how to confer upon powerful writers who assist them'.[29] Marvin joined with Arminius in denigrating successive British governments of both hues for a foreign policy that 'oscillates between puerility and poltroonery'.[30] He also praised Russia for her efforts in the exploration and civilisation of Turkestan, remarking on the poor effort of the Royal Geographical Society as compared with the Russian Imperial Geographical Society, suggesting that the Royal Geographical Society might 'devote some of its funds to the translation into English of some of the numerous valuable Russian maps' of the region.[31] He was right; the Russians knew Turkestan. General Skobelev himself had spent most of a decade there before he destroyed Geok Tepe, and had reconnoitred the region disguised as a Turkman before the taking of Khiva in 1873.

In 1885, 'the annus mirabilis for all who addressed themselves to the Russian menace',[32] Marvin managed three books on the subject. These included *The Railway Race to Herat: An Account of the Russian Railway to Herat and India*, in collaboration with Arminius, on one of the foremost concerns of all those with an eye on Russian access to India, and *The Russians at the Gates of Herat*, which was written and published in a week. Peter Hopkirk, author of *The Great Game* (1990), described most of the publications that now appeared on this subject as 'little more than polemics'[33]

29 Marvin, *Merv*, 19–20.
30 Ibid., 380.
31 Ibid., 29, n.
32 P. Hopkirk, op. cit., 419.
33 Ibid., 421.

and written by men who (Arminius aside) had not set foot in the regions they discussed, and Arminius himself had not seen Asia for twenty years and knew nothing of arms, armies, and tactics. Most of the titles on the publishing bandwagon showed little variation on a theme easily identifiable in any language: *Les Russes et les Anglais dans L'Asie Centrale*, *The Cossack at the Gate of India*, *Der Russische Feldzug Nach Chiwa*, *Afghanistan and the Anglo-Russian Dispute*, *L'Afghanistan: les Russes aux portes de l'Inde*. The last, by the French–Belgian journalist Paul Adolphe van Cleemputte, observed that events in Central Asia could not be separated from the balance of power nearer home and from Russian territorial ambitions dating back to Peter the Great. He believed France might do what she could to preserve peace but war was almost inevitable, and then she must retain strict neutrality. From the USA, Brigadier Theophilus F. Rodenbough, retired from the US cavalry, carefully totted up the troops and guns that might stand on either side of the Afghan border and wrote:

> As these lines are written the civilized nations of the world await with bated breath the next scene upon the Afghan stage. Seldom when two gladiators, armed and stripped, enter the arena does a doubt exist as to their purpose. Yet such an exceptional uncertainty attends the presence of England and Russia on the border of Afghanistan.[34]

The only person to write with real authority and knowledge about the Russian threat to India was Major-General Sir Charles MacGregor, the head of the new Intelligence Unit of the Indian Army. His book *The Defence of India*, initially intended as a highly confidential report to the governments of India and Britain, ended with his assertion 'that there can never be a real settlement of the Russo-Indian question *till Russia is driven out of the Caucasus and Turkistan*' (his italics).[35] The book was seen in London as extremely inflammatory; peace was to be kept with Russia; printing in India was stopped and copies of the book called in. But MacGregor was about to

---

34 Theophilus F. Rodenbough, *Afghanistan and the Anglo-Russian Dispute* (New York, 1885), 124.
35 Sir Charles MacGregor, *The Defence of India: A Strategical Study* (Shimla, 1884), 241.

be vindicated. His less expert hawkish allies were busy driving his message home in London even as officers of the Russian Imperial Army boasted openly in St Petersburg of their coming conquest of India.

There could be little remaining uncertainty about Russian purpose once Russian troops moved on from Merv towards the Afghan border in February 1885. The boundary commission was stalled by winter inaction and Russian intent, and Russia now laid claim to the Afghan oasis of Panjdeh (where it had already seized a fort) between Merv and Herat. In spite of new assurances to London and appeals for peace from Queen Victoria to Tsar Alexander during March, Panjdeh fell on 30 March. Afghan casualties, according to the Russians (the only eyewitnesses), were high: 800 as opposed to 40 Russians, and war appeared inevitable. That it never happened was largely down to Abdur Rahman Khan of Afghanistan (r. 1880–1901), who Rudyard Kipling might have described, like his ship-wrecked mariner, as a 'man of infinite resource and sagacity'.

The Coming Struggle for India, written in twenty days, was not published until August 1885, but Arminius was in Britain from the end of April that year, enjoying a sort of triumphal tour that was heralded by newspapers across the country. It took in Sheffield, Brighton, Newcastle upon Tyne, Edinburgh, Glasgow, and London. Arminius had written grandiosely to *The Times* on 17 April to announce his visit: 'You may imagine how excited I am at seeing that my twenty years labour have not been thrown away entirely, that the great nation which I have loved since my youth has shown herself worthy of my attention'. And, he added, he had already received 'a number of congratulatory letters' from all over Britain. He arrived like the conquering hero, not hesitating to hark back to his dervish fame in his lectures, observing that travelling did not 'present any particular difficulty to the former mendicant dervish, considering the essential difference existing between a ride on camel back... and a seat in the sleeping-car running directly from Vienna to Calais'. On his arrival in London, he had been met from the train by a footman and swept off by carriage to an apartment in Sackville Street. It belonged to Russell Shaw, who had made his fortune in Argentinian railways and had travelled in Turkey, Persia, and Asia. Mr Shaw also provided his staff and cigars, and only appeared himself to welcome his guest, make sure he had everything he desired, and again to bid him goodbye three weeks later. Arminius regretted never seeing him again: Russell Shaw died in 1887 after a journey round the world,[36] and Arminius described him as possessing 'unquestionably a true type of English amiability'. In gratitude he dedicated *The Coming Struggle for India* to Shaw in a letter reproduced as its frontispiece: 'In other countries an author would have hardly ventured to dedicate to his friend of Liberal persuasion a book containing a strong criticism of the Liberal party. But in England fair play is fully admitted in political opinions, even if they come from a foreigner'.

Arminius' journey, the length and breadth of Britain, sounds by his own account and from the reports in provincial newspapers like a royal progress. At railway stations, lunch-baskets and flowers were delivered to his compartment bearing notes 'From an admirer' or 'From a grateful Englishman'. He stayed in the grandest houses 'and thus I got an insight into the prevailing ideas and notions of the British people which increased my admiration and enthusiasm for this remarkable nation'. In London he was deluged with 'something like twenty invitations for various meals and parties', in only one day. Luckily, a private secretary presented himself and his services 'gratis, from purely patriotic motives', to assist in the triage of such excess. At a lunch in Portland Place, he reported meeting with Hasan Fehmi Pasha, the Ottoman ambassador, who he 'astonished' with 'the genuine Stambouli accent', as well as addressing him in French. It seems probable that the ambassador was being diplomatic, as it was hardly likely that Arminius' fame had not gone before him. Nevertheless, the meeting led to another at Claridge's with Howard Vincent, MP for Sheffield, whose diverse earlier career culminated in his joining the Conservative Party after a world tour had persuaded him of the benefits of imperialism and the importance of stopping immigration. Arminius travelled in his company to his lecture in Sheffield, where he wrote of being met by a large crowd and 'an outburst of hurrahing'.

On 27 April *The Sheffield Daily Telegraph* welcomed Arminius with a verse that begins 'From the "blue Danube" to the silver Thames / Fares forth that wearer of the sandal shoon, / Who toiled beneath Bokhara's burning noon,' and ends 'Alone, who – keen beyond the common ken – / Read the dark workings of the Russian hand, / Well winds her welcome from all

---

36 Russell Shaw's biography can be found here: https://www.icevirtuallibrary.com/doi/pdf/10.1680/imotp.1887.21049, accessed online 29 Sept. 2023.

Englishmen.'[37] Arminius wrote that he found it all exhausting, although he repeatedly mentions the 'modest honorarium' he received for each lecture. But there were riches in the receipt of such extraordinary plaudits too, and in being proved right at last. He gave himself a puff: 'many of my views have thus in course of time been justified by events', and he believed himself to be acknowledged in Britain as 'the Asiatic politician and the staunch friend of the realm'. More direct admiration, exemplified by the enthusiasm of his reception wherever he went on his tour, also shored up his energy. He was 'received everywhere in England with open arms and made much of by all classes of society'. He regretted that the working classes were 'sadly lacking in information about the Colonies and India', although they were 'truly enthusiastic for the Imperial standing' of their country; and Arminius used his lectures to 'draw the attention of the public to their commercial and political interests in the Orient and urged them to exercise their civilising influence over Asia'. In Newcastle, he describes speaking to a crammed hall where 'one could have walked over the heads', and where he asked his audience if they would now allow 'the most precious pearl of the British crown to fall into the enemy's hands?' The frantic, 'No! No! from all parts of the house', almost reduced him to tears, and he was astonished by the passion of these 'people of the foggy north'. In the south, at Brighton, a well-dressed, elderly woman had taken his hands to say 'in a choking voice: Oh, my dear, precious England, you had indeed done it good service', and 'God in heaven will reward you'.

On 6 May he gave a lecture under the auspices of the 'Constitutional Union'[38] entitled 'England and Russia in Afghanistan, who shall be mistress?' at Willis's Rooms in London. The event was chaired by Edward Stanhope and the audience included: Colonel George Malleson, Indian army officer and historian; Lord Napier of Magdala; Field Marshal Lord Strathnairn; Viscount Cranbrook; Lord George Hamilton; and Sir James Fergusson, former governor of Bombay. The Conservative faces of Empire were out in force that evening, and a resolution was proposed by Lord George Hamilton (shortly to become first lord of the admiralty in Lord

---

37 By James Dow – perhaps a follower of his contemporary, the notorious poetaster William McGonagall.
38 Probably the Constitutional Club, a Conservative gentlemen's club founded in 1883.

Salisbury's first government), 'That this meeting deeply regrets the apparent intention of Her Majesty's Government to abandon the position taken up by the Prime Minister in his speech on the 27th of April, which obtained the unanimous vote of the House of Commons'.[39] That vote had agreed an £11 million credit, divided between Sudan and Afghanistan, for war expenses, but a new agreement with Russia had been announced on 4 May. It neutralised Panjdeh, pending further negotiations between Russia, Britain, and Afghanistan to agree borders. *The Times* reported 'it would not be correct to say that the announcement elicited any show of enthusiasm even among the Radical supporters of the Government'. The people had girded their loins for war and were not easily to be diverted. Arminius rallied his bellicose admirers with a stirring speech against Russia and her further advance into Afghanistan. 'If we gave in at Pendjeh it would be Herat next, it would be Kandahar and then the Bolan Pass', and the frontiers of India. 'War with Russia', he cried, to loud cheers within Willis's Rooms, 'is unavoidable – the sooner it comes the better for this country!'

With a general election looming, the Conservatives were also campaigning. On 6 May there was another meeting going on up the road in the North Paddington constituency where Mr Lionel Cohen, the Conservative candidate, was being supported by Lord Randolph Churchill. Churchill slammed Gladstone, accusing him of putting party before country and telling his audience, 'You are being deluded and betrayed into as great a surrender of national and Imperial interests as was ever negotiated by a British ministry'. If the anti-war 'Nonconformists' who supported the Liberals 'realized the beneficent nature of the great civilizing work we are carrying on in India they would heartily support any Government which would oppose Russian aggression'. More to the point, Churchill told his audience, was 'the positive national advantage' of keeping India, and the 'positive material value in pounds, shillings and pence'. India was 'an inestimable and inexhaustible source of national wealth'. The government's latest action was a surrender to Russia, the most 'fruitful and formidable threat to your Indian Empire'. A resolution was moved:

That this meeting desires to express its entire want of confidence in

---

39 Reported in *The Times*.

the present Ministry, whose legislative incapacity, scandalous malad-ministration, and feeble and vacillating foreign policy has aggravated domestic distress and involved the country in most formidable foreign complications, and looks forward to the approaching elections with the hope that they will place in power a strong and capable Conservative Administration.[40]

Arminius could hardly have asked for more.

Gladstone, beleaguered on many fronts, and unpopular for his failure to relieve Gordon at Khartoum, lost the budget vote on 8 June 1885 and Lord Salisbury became prime minister of a short-lived minority government. Lord Randolph became secretary of state for India, but the Central Asian situation had cooled to diplomatic wrangling by the time Arminius set down his view of the situation later that summer. The Joint Afghan Boundary Commission gained space to begin work and eventually to bargain its way to a settlement in 1887 that allowed Russia to retain Panjdeh in exchange for concessions elsewhere. Arminius had been introduced to Lord Randolph in London in the spring of 1885, but if he and the noble lord sang from the same hymn sheet at this moment of high tension in Central Asia, it is doubtful that Arminius held much sway in the corridors of power. His rabble-rousing on his pet subject did not amount to real influence, and the recent revival by Hungarian academia of Arminius Vámbéry as one of its greatest and most influential Orientalists has led to a number of appreciatory papers that add a slightly deceptive gloss to his role in Britain. Much of this has to do with lan-guage and nuance. A 2020 paper[41] analyses replies to Arminius from three important British Conservative politicians,[42] including Randolph Churchill. The author notes that Arminius 'corresponded with several politicians on a daily basis', and was a 'particularly popular advisor among British Con-servatives in this period'. The paper uses one letter each from Randolph Churchill, Lord Curzon, and Arthur Balfour, written between 1885 and 1905,

---

40 All reported in *The Times*.

41 Sárközy Miklós, 'Arminius Vámbéry and British Conservatives: Some Further Notes on Their Correspondence', *The Arabist: Budapest Studies in Arabic*, 41 (2020), 187–206.

42 The letters, now in the University of Maryland Libraries, Washington DC, were part of the estate of Arminius' grandson, Robert. They may have been preserved by the family, when much else was lost or sold, due to their well-known authors.

as evidence of Arminius' valued influence on British policy in the Middle East and his prestige in British political circles.

The alternative view is that the brief messages from the pre-eminent Conservative politicians of their times are not indicative of any such influential position. They are instead perfect examples of the polite dismissal employed by men, and particularly politicians of the class of Churchill, Curzon, and Balfour, before electronic communication reduced the process to even barer bones. Arminius held some eminence in learning and experience, he could tell a good tale, had been accepted in society as a celebrity, and became a friend of royalty. Regardless, however, of the merits or otherwise of his opinions, there were other experts who could be relied on for a broader, better informed, and more objective view of the interdependence of geopolitical balances in Asia and in Europe.

It does not take a cynical eye to read the check to Arminius' outpourings in letters from men who might have greeted him in London society as 'my dear Vambéry', and then made strenuous attempts to avoid further conversation. The 1885 letter from Randolph Churchill for example, shortly before he became secretary of state for India, regrets that he will be unable to attend a lecture given by Arminius on *England's Future in Asia*. Does that really hint 'at the cordial relationship between them'? It is simply a straightforward expression of polite regret, as convention would demand. That it was preserved by Arminius' descendants adds no special lustre beyond that of the famous sender. In the case of Curzon, he and Arminius may well have exchanged a great many letters; Curzon knew Arminius in London and was happy to meet him in Constantinople on his exploration of Persia in 1892. As Esmé Howard remarked later in a report from Budapest, where he befriended Arminius during his tenure as British consul general, 'Vambéry has written on so many subjects which have always interested Curzon'.[43] Nevertheless, as Miklós's paper itself admits, 'Vambéry's influence on Curzon cannot be assessed with certainty', and it is a spectacular stretch to engineer, from possible further correspondence that may not ever have existed, that 'Vambéry's proposal for creating this buffer zone was probably the main impetus behind Curzon's establishment of the North-West Frontier Province in 1901'. While Curzon's later support for Hungary at the Versailles Peace

---

43 Alder and Dalby, op. cit., 457.

Conference of 1919 may have involved a liking for Hungary and Hungarians in general or in particular, it was certainly more focused on the balance of power and economic considerations than on his friendship with Vambéry, who had been dead since before the war. Curzon's letter of March 1898 to Arminius thanks him for 'your very kind complimentary remarks about my Indian frontier speech', copies of which he enclosed, and is pleased to 'have the encouragement and approval of so great an authority and so illustrious a pioneer'.

By the time Balfour wrote to Arminius in 1905, Miklós observes that the old Orientalist's 'political influence had, to some extent, lost its former prominence'. He was still deluging British politicians and the Foreign Office with his prophecies of doom (and he was also, as we shall see, dunning them for payment for his services as an informant on Turkey and Asia), but times and tides in Europe and Central Asia had moved on. The world-weary tone that rings so true from Balfour's pen might be read not as an expression of pessimism about the future of Russia in Central Asia to a valued expert on the subject but, more plausibly, as a relatively impatient snub to any further pursuit of a stagnant subject by an old crank.

Professor Vambéry,

I am greatly obliged to you for your letter of the 17th. In it you point to a real danger. But it is one I could hardly properly deal with in a speech, the danger, I mean, of Afghan misgovernment in Afghan Turkestan, and the opening this will give to the growth of Russian influence in that region. There is I fear no way of dealing with this. We cannot civilise Afghan methods, and we cannot prevent Russia deriving some advantage from them. It is one of the weaknesses of the position, which has to be recognised, but which, so far as I can see, cannot be remedied.

Arminius published his 1885 letter from Lord Lytton in full in *My Struggles,* as an example of his worth as an advisor on Central Asia. He had written to Lytton about the British withdrawal from Kandahar and the Afghan frontier territories they had occupied since the end of the second Anglo-Afghan War, during Lytton's disastrous viceroyalty. Lytton thanked Arminius 'for your interesting and valuable letter', continuing:

I little thought when I had the honour of making your acquaintance many years ago… that I should live to need and receive your valued aid in endeavouring to save England's Empire in the East from the only form of death against which not even the gods themselves can guard their favourites – death by suicide. I fear, however that its present guardians, who have Moses and the prophets, are not likely to be converted – even by one of the dead.

Arminius of course took all this at face value, to point out the rarity of such a missive to a 'mere journalist' from the pen of great statesman anywhere in 'Non-English Europe'. He went on, predictably, to another of his attacks on 'the mediaeval prejudices still prevalent in Austria' as opposed to 'enlightened' England, where Disraeli could play such a major part in the 'actions and operations of Albion, so infinitely greater, mightier and more impressive' even than Rome; and on Russia and 'the government of the Czar, that frightful instrument of tyranny, that pool of all imaginable slander and abuse, that disgrace to humanity'.

It is difficult to believe that Lytton's letter was written in all seriousness. How seriously the Russians took Arminius is harder to tell. Press reports of the reception his lectures received may have concerned them, by his own efforts his name appeared regularly in Russian newspapers, and Madame Novikov busily undermined and spread rumours about him. Nevertheless, if he could congratulate himself, late in life, that his 'literary activity was a thorn in the eyes of the cunning Muscovites', his real status in Russia, metaphorically speaking, was probably about the same as that of the barking dog fed sleeping pills by his son. When he had first arrived in London, Arminius' celebrity opened doors that he had not imagined possible. Thereafter his good contacts across East and West and linguistic skills should have made him a valuable purveyor of information across continents, but his focus was always too polarised and prejudiced. That polarisation meant he was never more than an irritant, quite often to his allies as well as his enemies, a self-appointed and self-publicising agent provocateur. It is hard to believe for example that sophisticated Russian ambassadors to London, such as Baron de Staal – admittedly a peaceably inclined envoy – thought him a serious danger. Arminius wrote of their 'attempts to turn me aside from the path I pursued and to discredit me… But their trouble was all in vain, for the bitter hostility of a despotic Government and their venomous darts must remain without effect against the expressed approval of a free nation and the approbation of the whole Liberal West'. When creating his historical image in his old age, Arminius entertained no doubts of his own importance.

The Coming Struggle for India was published simultaneously in English, Gujarati, French, and German and was an instant popular success, although *The Times* review, on 26 August 1885, was interested but not excited. 'If it does not add to our information, it at least supplies some very interesting speculation', it reads, and 'the general reader will find it a very pleasant means of gaining some idea how the empires of England and Russia have grown in Asia, and why their respective interests have clashed on the borders of Afghanistan'. The reviewer thought 'Professor Vambéry may count upon a wider circulation and greater attention for his recent volume than some of its many predecessors have received' but refused to share his 'apprehensions' that an agreed Afghan border and the combined determination of the governments of India and of Afghanistan would not be enough to curtail Russian ambitions.

Arminius wrote that the book 'caused a great sensation, far beyond its intrinsic worth. It was also a lucrative speculation'. The *London Evening Standard* began its review, of 14 August 1885, with 'The least interesting chapter in this interesting book is the last, which the author devotes to himself. Why should he, a Hungarian savant, plunge into the troubled stream of English politics... to preach a stronger doctrine on the subject of the Russian advance than commends itself to the judgement even of the most jealous of home-born patriots?' It then proceeded to answer its own question, generally favourably, towards 'the sympathetic scholar', who is able to add 'that pleasant flavour of personal experience' to 'the authority of a prophet whose forecasts have to a very large extent been fulfilled'. Broadly, the press agreed; the *Liverpool Mercury* of 17 August echoed other reviewers in its belief that 'although we think the author has much exaggerated the dangers to England from Russian aggression in the directions of India, his volume possesses a distinctive value in showing the British public the value of our great Indian possession'.

The *Athenaeum* demurred. 'Herr Vambéry's views are well-known' it said, and none of his suggestions 'would strike an ordinary person as very original'. He was looked upon 'by a good many as a partisan solely inspired by hatred of Russia and not by the "strictly humanitarian views" and love of England which he puts forward'. It was hardly surprising such an opinion prevailed when he applied 'such terms as "imbecility" and "criminal indifference" to the leading statesmen of one of the great parties of the country', 'the more especially if he is a foreigner occupying a chair at a distant university and therefore not under provocation'. The 'How dare he!' echoes down the years. *The Coming Struggle for India* attacked almost everyone: Russia, the peoples of Central Asia, Germany, France, Afghanistan, and India's Muslims – 'of the two chief elements in India', the 'Brahminic' was 'much more amenable to civilising influence than the Mohammedan'. Most of all, the book attacked the Liberals. From this broth of the damned, it only exempted a sort of mythical England and an equally mythical British public, the 'solid rock of Anglo-Saxon character', that lacked only the right leadership.

The success of Arminius' tour had gone to his head. In old age he remembered 'the widespread popularity of my writings', those who 'could not help expressing their appreciation of them, and the 'Press of England' that 'had at last ruefully to admit that I was right, that I had rendered the State great service, and that I had contributed many a brick to the building up of the wall of defence around the Indian Empire'. Indeed, the former commander-in-chief of India, Field Marshal Sir Donald Stewart, had told him 'my writings had often stimulated the sinking courage of the officers in India and stirred them up to endure to the end'. The 'frequent letters of appreciation' he received from India were another fillip to his self-regard, and allowed him to condescendingly dismiss letters such as those quoted earlier that had described him as a 'jingonastic Conservative' as well as a 'blasted Austrian or Hungarian'.

Arminius was in his pomp after his British lecture tour. *The Coming Struggle* greatly revived his popular image and as a prophet he felt vindicated. He would live to see Russia consume much of Central Asia. Soviet Russia would finish the job and invade Afghanistan before another century had passed, but that was the future. Now, Arminius hurled his contribution to the fashionable literature of 1885 into the smelter of jingoistic propaganda with a vehemence that can have surprised neither his admirers nor his detractors. Today his book is almost unreadable. Like its fellow polemics that year, it must be seen in the context of its time, but there is something about the tone taken by the author, so self-satisfied and superior, so damning of any alternative viewpoint, that its original context does little to improve it. That is quite apart from statements about religion and race and all the tropes about the merits of British rule in India, in contrast to the 'horrid crimes', the 'rioting and disturbance', the 'kidnapping, forgery, adultery, and perjury', and comments about the '*Thag*' and '*Dacoity*', that are bound to make a contemporary reader shudder. Arminius had never been and would never go to India, but he could still write:

> If the high terms in which I speak of England's doings in India should be taken for an outburst of unconditional admiration, I will only point to the fact that it is the ex-dervish, the ex-effendi, and the traveller amongst Eastern people as one of themselves, who speaks in these lines; it is the student of Eastern character, for years and years, who got the conviction that it is easier to take a laden camel through a needle's eye, than to penetrate the obstinately conservative mind of an Oriental with anything like reform, innovation and new ideas. If I now add that Hindostan is the cradle and the fountainhead of all those qualities which constitute the true and unadulterated mode of Eastern thinking, with all its queer notions of life, of politics, and religion, my gentle reader will easily perceive the utter astonishment I feel on seeing the success English civilisers have obtained hitherto in that very hot-bed of Asiaticism in India.

In other words, this was a man who saw India and Central Asia as almost interchangeable. If Russia succeeded in advancing into India, 'the mass of the teeming Indian population' living lives of 'that sort of repose which they enjoy under the strong, mild and just rule of England', might instead expect 'a miserable existence under the horrid abuses, tyranny, and disorder of utterly corrupt Russian officials, and the dawn of a better era still hidden in the far future'. He ended by hoping to 'draw the attention of Europe in general, to the excessive increase of the power of barbarous and despotic Russia'. But, he wrote, 'in looking around amongst the European nations to discover the one fittest to form an effective barrier against this ruthless aggression', Germany 'still wants a good deal of time before she matures into such a manhood as to come forward as the real defender of liberty', while France, that 'large room full of *enfants gâtés*',[44] offered little security 'owing to

---

44 Literally 'spoilt children'.

the fickle minds and puerile freaks of her citizens'. He concluded it was only Britain that could 'furnish the necessary material for effective bulwarks', therefore, the British must be animated 'to maintain their position in Asia, which is inseparably connected with their power in Europe'. Should that animation be inspired by his book, Arminius ended, 'I shall deem myself abundantly rewarded'.

In brief, *The Coming Struggle* embodies all the reasons why statesmen such as Curzon, Churchill, and Balfour, however imperially disposed, would have avoided being buttonholed by its author.

It is unexpected, therefore, as David Mandler points out, the same man might be capable of a less laudatory view of the civilising influence of the West on the East. In an appendix to his last autobiographical work, *The Story of My Struggles,* headed 'My Relations with the Mohammedan World', we find this:

> ...the more intimately I became acquainted with the conditions of the various countries of Europe the more clearly I seemed to see the causes of the decline in the East. Our exalted professions of righteousness and justice after all did not amount to much. Christianity seemed as fanati-cal as Islam itself, and before very long I came to the conclusion that our high-sounding efforts at civilisation in the East were but a cloak for mate-rial aggression and a pretext for conquest and gain.

This apparent Damascene conversion had little to do with questions of empire. It reflected only his negative view of the tyrannies of Christianity in comparison with a more positive opinion of the leaders of the Indian Muslim community, shared at the time by a number of British politicians and administrators in India and in London. The same views colour his 1889 letter to Nawab Abdul Latif, the moderniser, educator, and founder of the Mohammedan Literary Society in Calcutta. It is egregiously patronising, congratulating the Nawab on 'rendering good service both to your people and your faith by encouraging your fellow-believers to follow in the path of Western culture and education', and 'in showing your co-religionists the superiority of Western culture as seen in the English administration'. He admits:

I am not an Englishman, and I do not ignore the shortcomings and mistakes of English rule in India, but I have seen much of the world both in Europe and Asia, and studied the matter carefully, and I can assure you that England is far in advance of the rest of Europe in point of justice, liberality and fair-dealing with all entrusted to her care.

Hastening to his own interests, Arminius wrote of his continuing hope of seeing India, 'under the patronage of your Society', and 'delivering some lectures in the Persian tongue to the Mohammedans of India', to 'try to contribute a few small stones to the noble building raised by your admirable efforts'. The letter, he assured readers of the *Struggles*, was 'much commented upon and regarded both by Englishmen and Mohammedans as of great importance'. Supposedly the letter produced an invitation to visit, but neither the patronage of the Mohammedan Literary Society nor funding, for which he had applied to the Foreign Office, was forthcoming. Arthur Godley, the permanent under-secretary for India, wrote to Sir Philip Currie, assistant permanent under-secretary of state for foreign affairs (and later ambassador to the Ottoman Empire) regarding a question from the chancellor of the Duchy of Lancaster, Lord Cross, as to the 'answer to be returned to Professor Vambéry who has asked for a grant from Secret Service Money, a free railway pass, introductions etc., on the understanding that he is to visit India and preach loyalty to England and hatred of Russia – especially among the Mohammedans'. Godley had advised Cross 'that he had better have nothing to do with it', and asked, 'Do you approve?'[45]

One can see why. With his letter to Nawab Abdul Latif, which was published in *The Times of India*, Arminius had enclosed an article for the *Reis and Rayyet*, published by the great Calcutta journalist Dr Sambhu Chandra Mukherjee, with whom Arminius kept up a correspondence. Dr Mukherjee wrote to him regarding some corrections to the piece, 'which I hope improved the thing'. (He had not wished to publish at all but the Nawab had insisted.) Dr Mukherjee also wrote, more forcefully, to the journalist and former Liberal MP Edward Jenkins, who had been born in India. He noted that errors 'were almost inevitable in foreign publications when

---

45 Alder and Dalby, op. cit., 407–8.

writing about India'[46] adding that 'even Professor Vambéry has not been able to avoid it – he who is not only a great Orientalist but has travelled almost to the frontiers of India… He talks of coming out to India where he hopes to address the Mahomedans in Persian as if it were their own tongue. So far from Persian being one of the Indian vernaculars, none but the learned Mussulmans of the old clan know it and few of those who have read Persian can speak it or understand it when spoken. The Professor might just as well address a Mahomedan audience in Hungarian'.[47] It was perhaps lucky he never did get to India.

46 Ibid., 408.
47 F. H. Skrine, *An Indian Journalist: Being the Life, Letters and Correspondence of Dr Sambhu C. Mookerjee* (Calcutta, 1895), 282.

14

Royal Favour

By his own account, it was the publication of *The Struggle for India* in 1885 that brought Arminius an invitation to Windsor to meet Queen Victoria. He did not go there until 1889, although he had been a friend of the prince of Wales since their original meeting in 1865, and the queen may have known of him for as long. A letter in the Royal Archives to her from Disraeli, by then Lord Beaconsfield, suggests she had been asking about Arminius and the situation in Afghanistan. In the letter, dated 28 December 1879, after news of General Roberts' defeat of the Afghans at Sherpur, Disraeli wrote 'the news from Afghanistan is a great relief'. He 'agrees with the views of M. Vambéry on Central Asia and Afghanistan to a considerable degree', and considered 'his conclusions sound and unexaggerated', noting 'his local experience of the countries in question is large and various'. M. Vambéry was, he added, 'a Hungarian about 46 or 48 years'.[1] Queen Victoria had announced in an earlier letter to Disraeli, during the Russo-Turkish War, that she thought she would abdicate if the Russians reached Constantinople. They did and she did not, as Britain and other European powers intervened to limit Russian gains and save a depleted Ottoman Empire. To the prince of Wales, she had declared 'I don't believe that without fighting... those detestable Russians... any arrangements will be lasting, or that we shall ever be friends. They will always hate us and we can never trust them'.[2] The queen was a kindred spirit and Arminius found an appreciative audience in court circles. It enabled him to add an unimpeachable layer of royal favour to his

---

1 Royal Archives, Windsor, ref. VIC/MAIN/B/63/10.
2 Quoted in P. Hopkirk, op. cit., 379.

present and possibly his posthumous persona, and to become, long after his death, 'The Dervish of Windsor Castle'.

Arminius had met the prince of Wales in London on one of his earliest visits, and had then been invited to lunch at Marlborough House. Prince Albert Edward (entirely at home himself in French and German) was, Arminius wrote, fascinated by his fluency in a variety of languages, as well as by the story of his life and travels. Arminius, in turn, continued to be astonished by the prince's 'affability', compared with the European aristocracy he had encountered, and by his lack of prejudice towards those 'whose Jewish origin would have been depreciated by an everyday nobleman in Prussia and in other Continental countries'. His own friendship exemplified the principle in the royal circle of *non unde es, sed qui sis* – 'a man's individuality matters more than his origin'.[3] After lunching with the prince on one occasion, Arminius accompanied him to the inauguration of a London park and afterwards expressed astonishment that the prince had mixed with and spoken quite freely to so many people. Such a thing would not have happened in Hungary, he had said, and quoted the prince's answer: 'Well Englishmen must be treated differently. If I do not bow down to them, they will crawl up and scratch me in the face'. Arminius was delighted with this 'compulsory show of democratic tendencies' and observed that he had also witnessed the prince acting in the same way entirely of his own free will, 'sometimes to the dislike of the noblemen in his company'.[4] When the prince visited Budapest in 1873, the British consul-general in Budapest reported to the foreign secretary Lord Granville that he 'inspected the places and objects of interest... under the guidance of such experts as Count Longay ... President of the Hungarian Academy, and of Professor Vambéry, the Asiatic explorer'.[5]

The prince liked Hungary and visited again on his regular sporting tours in Europe. In 1885 he was in Budapest for the Hungarian National Exhibition, staying with Countess Karolyi, wife of the Hungarian ambassador to London. He was perfectly aware of the workings of Austro-Hungarian society, which meant he would not meet Arminius in the milieu in which

---

3 Sir Sidney Lee, *Edward VII: A Biography*, Vol. I (London, 1925), 356.
4 Alder and Dalby, op. cit., 310.
5 Lee, op. cit., 356.

he habitually moved, although he invited him to a large dinner party he was giving. When Arminius arrived, he was taken to the prince's rooms and thus it was arm-in-arm with the prince of Wales that he was introduced: 'Ladies and gentlemen, of course you know my friend, Professor Vambéry'.[6] That was not all. There are a number of versions of a story of the prince's 1888 visit to Budapest during Arminius' tenure as librarian of the Casino or Club of Magnates, a prestigious gentleman's club in Budapest, founded in 1827. When a dinner was given in his honour at the club, the prince asked Arminius if he would be there. Receiving the inevitably negative answer, he arranged to meet Arminius at the entrance to the club and, sweeping him through to the card-room, announced 'Professor Vambéry is an old friend of mine and I am so much looking forward to seeing him at the Club dinner...'[7]

On a later occasion, after Arminius had been made a member and was present at such a Casino dinner, the prince was required to make an impromptu speech of thanks and asked Arminius whether he should speak in French or English. Arminius wrote flatteringly in *The Story of My Struggles* of his astonishment when 'I saw him rise and deliver in most elegant and idiomatic French a speech which was a masterpiece of oratorical power', in which he praised Hungary and 'made happy allusions to the future in store for the chivalrous Magyars'. Prince and king, Edward VII epitomised perfect royalty in Arminius' eyes; he was 'of all the monarchs or Europe and Asia', the best-informed about other countries and nationalities, and his 'opinion was never influenced by difference in race or in religion'. He was 'a clever writer and a good orator', and 'proved his nobleness of mind' when he sent Arminius birthday wishes for his seventieth birthday via Francis Knollys, his private secretary. Birthday congratulations were endorsed a few days later on 18 March 1902 with a letter from Knollys to inform Arminius that the king had invested him with the CVO, 'as a mark of his appreciation of your having always proved so good and constant a friend to England, an as a token of his Majesty's personal regard towards you'.

---

6 Alder and Dalby, op. cit., 311.

7 This anecdote was quoted by Esmé Howard, who had heard the story from Arminius in his old age. Alder and Dalby give a more dramatic version, gleaned from a former student of Arminius, in which he was at home in bed when his presence was demanded by the prince. The next day, the prince of Wales visited him at home and thereafter the National Casino elected Arminius a member.

1889 brought something of a feast of royal encounters for Arminius, and another meeting that would add to the Vambéry legend. In 1888 he had returned to the Ottoman court and to Constantinople for the first time since that capital had been such a formative part of his life twenty-five years earlier. It appears that he had been invited by the sultan before,[8] but the railway from Budapest to Constantinople opened only in 1888, with a travel time of a mere forty-two hours, and became the route for Arminius' Turkish journeys for the next thirteen years. He had gone, on that first occasion, in company with his colleague and fellow member of the Academy, the Jewish-born priest Dr Vilmos Fraknói, on something of a wild goose chase. The famous library of King Matthias Corvinus of Hungary (r. 1458–90) was believed to have fallen into Turkish hands after the never-forgotten Hungarian defeat at the Battle of Mohács in 1526. The library had been largely destroyed, with its residue – 216 *Corvinas*, so-called, out of the possible original 2,000 volumes – distributed today across the world, but the legend of its survival in Constantinople had persisted.

Arminius had a nose for a lost library – rumours of the lost library of Bursa, that Eugene Schuyler had heard in Samarkand, may have informed his desire to purchase ancient manuscripts in that city. Did he now think his Constantinople contacts might lead him to a discovery that would once and for all confirm his international fame? The fate of the library had been explored exhaustively by the German archaeologist and Constantinople resident Dr Philipp Anton Dethier in the early 1860s. He had discovered a small number of potential Corvinian codices, but nothing previously unedited or unknown from other survivals, and had reported on his research to the Academy in Budapest.[9] It is likely that Arminius had known Dr Dethier in Constantinople before 1863, and why he thought he might find something new or neglected by the scholar who was the first director of the Constantinople Museum of Archaeology between 1872 and his death in 1881, Arminius did not say. The mission was reported in *The Times*[10] but is unrecorded in his

---

8 Alder and Dalby, op. cit., 391–2, from unpublished correspondence.
9 *The Times* (8 August 1864).
10 'A commission of six members of the Academy of Sciences is to start for Constantinople tomorrow with the interesting mission of exploring the archives in the Imperial palaces. The permission to conduct these investigations was obtained a few months ago by Professor Arminius Vambéry, who had reason to believe that the Imperial archives contained a great

autobiographies, beyond his remarking of his first return to Constantinople, 'I remained almost unnoticed, for after a space of thirty years only a few of my old acquaintances were left'.

Lack of more public notice did not preclude an audience at the Yildiz Palace with Sultan Abdul Hamid II and the beginning of a new relationship with a man Arminius had last met when the sultan had been a teenage boy. It seems improbable that the sultan would recognise Reshid Effendi as being his sister Fatma's French tutor many years before, but equally unlikely that he would not have enquired into the history of the man he now invested with the Grand Cordon of the Medjidieh Order for his services in disseminating 'a correct knowledge of the doctrines of Islam, so imperfectly known abroad'.[11] Abdul Hamid II had come to the throne in 1876 after the ninety-three-day reign of his brother, Murad. He had promised to promulgate the constitution Murad had intended – the fruit of the Tanzimat movement and of the endeavours of Arminius' old friend and student, now the grand vizier Midhat Pasha. Abdul Hamid had been described in the year of his accession by Lord Salisbury as 'a poor frightened man with a very long nose and a short threadpaper body', but he was an autocrat who had no intention of reducing his personal power with constitutional machinery. He ruled for thirty-three years until he was deposed in 1909. Both a moderniser and a *de facto* absolute ruler, he presided over the war with Russia, the slicing-up of his empire after the Treaty of Berlin, and its bankruptcy in 1881, leaving a vast debt owing to European powers. Arminius praised him on one hand for his 'many endowments', including a 'remarkable knowledge of European affairs', and described him as an 'ignoramus' and 'an incorrigible Arch-Turk' on the other. Later, much worse than that.

Abdul Hamid's repressive regime created growing unrest in Ottoman territories, and the horrific Armenian massacres of the mid-1890s gave him the nickname the 'Bloody Sultan' or 'Abdul the damned'. Meanwhile, the

---

many books and documents which belonged to Magyar kings and magnates, and which were carried off by the Turks during the wars with Hungary and during the long occupation of the Magyar kingdom. Professor Vambéry also hopes to discover documents which will throw more light on the history of the Byzantine Empire in its declining period. The Emperor has contributed 6,000 florins out of his privy purse towards the expense of the commission'. *The Times*, 21 September 1889.

11 *The Times* (8 August 1864).

European national representatives who ran the Public Debt Administration created new Turkish debts to European countries. They ate into Turkish political power but also supported the 'sick man of Europe' and the increasingly paranoid sultan for their own financial and commercial interests. On the same day in September 1888 that *The Times* reported Arminius' first audience at the Yildiz Palace, it also reported the hanging of one of the sultan's eunuchs. Arminius ascribed the delay in his royal audience to this 'unpleasant incident': the eunuch had shot another dead, leading to the discovery of a cache of arms in the palace, enough to disturb any monarch's sleep. Other reports that week of events in the Ottoman capital show the extent of international involvement in a bankrupt Turkey, with the sultan presiding over a meeting to arrange the terms of a loan from Deutsche Bank of one million Turkish pounds on the grant of an extension for the Scutari–Ismid railway line to the bank's representative. A couple of days later, the Russian grand dukes Paul and Sergei, sons of Tsar Alexander II, arrived on their yacht for meetings with the sultan, en route to a tour of Palestine and Syria.

Arminius was back in Constantinople in January 1889. By then, he wrote, memories had been revived, although his fluency in Turkish led to the assumption, among new acquaintances, that he was 'a Turkish renegade'. Thanks to his 'old connections… the problem was soon solved'. The Turkish newspapers published 'long columns about my humble person' and extolled the services he had rendered to Turkey. Arminius, the Turkophile and Turkish speaker, known in London, in Constantinople, and to the sultan, could now usefully re-invent himself as an expert informant and unofficial conduit between the Sublime Porte and London. This was a role for which his early Ottoman experience had made him almost uniquely qualified. Here too was a new means of thwarting Russia, and Arminius began making visits to Constantinople and to the sultan that went on until May 1901. He reported successively to Sir Philip Currie (later ambassador to the Ottoman Empire); to Sir Thomas Sanderson, his successor; and latterly to Charles Hardinge (later viceroy of India) in the same office. Arminius believed his relationship with the sultan to be unique and so it may have been, unencumbered as it was by diplomatic niceties and officialdom. He considered himself the first European known to the sultan who 'was equally at home in the East as in the West, familiar with the languages, customs, and political affairs of both parts of the world, and who, in his presence, was not stiff like the Europeans, but pliant like the Asiatics of the purest water'.

Furthermore, Arminius always wore his fez and greeted Abdul Hamid 'as an Oriental greets his sovereign'. The lessons of his youth and experience of diplomacy in Constantinople had remained with Arminius, and he was as much at home there as anywhere. It had been his first adult home and greatest source of education. Now, it was a place where he could bask in 'that old fairy-tale feeling' as he thought of the transformation between the extreme poverty of his early months in the city and his present situation. He was, he thought, a rarity indeed, a European who shared memories of earlier days with the sultan and had thereby created so easy an understanding that the monarch would dispense with court etiquette to meet him face-to-face and alone. When the sultan offered Arminius a cigarette and lit the match for him, the deal was, as it were, sealed. Arminius was 'quite overcome by the affability of the absolute Ruler' the Padishah, and 'as the conversation progressed the splendour and the nimbus of majesty disappeared', and he saw 'merely a Turkish Pasha or Effendi such as I had known many in high Stambul society'.

Arminius believed his comfortable situation with the 'Shadow of God' was due not only to his 'Asiatic' manners but also to his Hungarian nationality and the 'friendly feelings exhibited towards Turkey by Hungary during the late Russo-Turkish war'. He was known to be a Turcophile but, he wrote, the sultan had not heard of his philological and ethnographic studies. When Arminius presented a copy of his monograph on 'Uiguric' linguistics, Abdul Hamid expressed polite amazement at 'the existence of such ancient Turkish philological monuments'. He quoted some of the Turkish words and expressions that were in exclusive use in the Imperial household, and quite unknown outside it, which Arminius identified as Azerbaijani. Accurate or not, this identification of 'Turkoman linguistic remains' appealed to the sultan, who could use 'these monuments' as a validation of 'the unadulterated Turkish national character of the Osmanli dynasty'. That was a surprise. Arminius recalled that until recently the Turks had been rather 'ashamed of their Turkish antecedents', presumably favouring a Persian and Abbasid heritage as a better fit for the caliphate. Above all, he decided, 'the most valid reasons for the Sultan's attentions' were vested in 'the international character of my pen', and the notice his writing and public speaking received in

Britain. Arminius would undoubtedly have played up his influence with the British government. He was shortly to be dealt a trump card here. Before his second visit to Constantinople, in June 1889, Arminius had made another British tour. The seventh edition of his *Life and Adventures* and the third of his *Story of Hungary* had just been published, and he had been invited to Sandringham by the prince of Wales. He met Queen Victoria there in April, and was then invited to Windsor by her in May.

On 9 May 1889 Arminius gave a highly publicised lecture at Exeter Hall on the Strand that was calculated to appeal in Constantinople, in which he condemned British attitudes to the 'unspeakable Turk'. The Turks, he said, read the great English writers 'from Shakespeare to Herbert Spencer' although French literature had, at one time, been more fashionable. It was also quite untrue that the Quran forbade the study of science – on the contrary, religion and science were in better accord in Turkey than in Britain. He stopped short of claiming greater shared culture, but pointed out that it was to the detriment of British interests if British policy towards Turkey did not start with a better cultural understanding. Arminius had also met Foreign Office officials in London to report on access to 'his friend in Constantinople' and had opened channels of communication, at the sultan's behest, that placed him as an important go-between. Abdul Hamid, he wrote to the Foreign Office, thought a great deal of England's opinion, for 'in his innermost mind he was firmly convinced that England from motives of self-interest would be compelled to uphold the Ottoman State', even though the British had previously let him down by refusing a loan. In the Exeter Hall lecture, Arminius gave the sultan exactly what he wanted to hear when it was reported back to Constantinople.

Abdul Hamid also shared with Arminius a loathing of the Liberal government as personified by Gladstone, the overseer of the Anglo-Egyptian War of 1882 that had put an effective final full stop to Ottoman power in Egypt. Finally, Arminius' relationship with the prince of Wales 'carried weight' with Abdul Hamid. His invitation to meet Queen Victoria at Windsor induced the sultan 'to see in me something more than an ordinary scholar and traveller; in fact, he looked upon me as a confidant of the English court and government – two ideas which to him were inseparable, to whom he might freely and safely open his heart'. Arminius' letters, to Currie et al., are typical in their tone: informative and descriptive but biased, dictatorial, complaining, demanding, and, as time passed, disillusioned with both his Oriental and Occidental principals. Meanwhile, in October 1889, the kaiser entered the picture. He visited Constantinople 'to initiate that understanding between Germany and Turkey which was to bear fruit of peril to England'.[12]

On 25 April 1889 Arminius was at Sandringham and was presented to Queen Victoria by the prince of Wales. The queen's journal suggests that she was enjoying herself on her first trip to Sandringham since Prince Albert's death more than twenty-seven years earlier. She had been out in her donkey cart (a canopied chair, rigged to be pulled by a pony or donkey) on a 'fine, but very cold' afternoon with members of the family to view the estate, and had been delighted with what she had seen. The party for dinner was mainly family, the household, and a handful of local dignitaries, with Arminius the only real outsider. The queen found him

> ... a wonderfully clever man, who has travelled all over the East and gone through hair breadth escapes in Bokhara, Afghanistan and elsewhere, having disguised himself as a Dervish. He is a man of about 60 and speaks English perfectly well, also Persian and Turkish. He is an agreeable little man, profuse in expressions of admiration for England. He knows the Sultan well and said he was most kindly disposed to me personally. He also spoke a good deal of the poor broken-hearted Emperor and Empress of Austria and poor Rudolph.[13]

Arminius found Queen Victoria 'a little reserved at first', but, 'as soon as her clever brain had formed an opinion as to the character and disposition of the stranger, her seeming coldness was cast aside'. Walking next to her cart,[14] he began to talk about his adventures in Central Asia and 'her interest visibly increased'. To his astonishment, the queen 'not only retained all the

---

12 Lee, op. cit., Vol. I, 658.
13 Quoted in Alder and Dalby, op. cit., 312. On 30 January 1889 Prince Rudolph and his mistress, Marie Vetsera, had been discovered dead at his hunting lodge, Mayerling, outside Vienna, after an apparent suicide pact. How much, one wonders, had Arminius talked up his acquaintance with the emperor to the queen?
14 Pulled, he said by two donkeys. All the photographs of Victoria (and of donkey carts in general) show only one donkey in harness, but perhaps Arminius thought one was not good enough for a queen!

strange Oriental names, but pronounced them quite correctly, a rare thing in a European, especially in a lady'. One evening she also, he said, 'conversed with me for a long time about the East, chiefly about Turkey', and remembered all the Turkish ambassadors of the past half-century. The queen 'had more sense of the importance of strengthening British power in Asia than many of her noted ministers; and the Shah of Persia, on the occasion of his visit to Budapest, told me astonishing stories of the Queen's familiarity with Oriental affairs'. The queen showed Arminius her Hindustani written exercises, and her Indian servants were 'a living proof of the interest the Empress of India took in the establishment of British power in Asia'. When he saw the way 'these bearded Asiatics waited on a woman and, what is more, a *Christian* woman... I could hardly refrain from expressing my admiration. The knowledge that the most powerful sovereign in the world, who guides the destinies of nearly four hundred million human beings, stands before you in the form of a modest, unassuming woman is overwhelming'. When he saw the gilded 'presentations and assurances of devotion' from 'Asiatic potentates' in the Royal Library and their gifts in the treasury, he 'could never tire in my admiration of the power and greatness of Britain'.

On the second evening of Arminius' visit, the party for dinner was little changed: the only incomers being the earl and countess of Leicester. At 10 p.m., after dinner, the company went down to the ballroom where nearly three hundred people – 'all the neighbours, tenants and servants' – had assembled to watch a play presented by the company of the Lyceum Theatre, led by the actor-manager Henry Irving.[15] A theatre with scenery and backdrops had been made especially for the room, 'an exceedingly fine piece of miniature stage work', wrote Bram Stoker, Irving's business manager and friend. The programme, starring Irving and his long-term leading lady, Ellen Terry, was *The Bells* and the trial scene from *The Merchant of Venice*. Not exactly light post-prandial comedy but, Irving reported, 'I have never seen or heard a more enthusiastic audience within the bounds of decorum'.[16] The queen retired to bed at 1 a.m., after congratulating Irving and Terry, who then ate supper with the other guests and were introduced to Arminius. Irving was clearly fascinated and, whether or not Bram Stoker met Arminius

15 Queen Victoria's Journal for 25 April 1889.
16 Bram Stoker, *Personal Reminiscences of Henry Irving* (London, 1907), 375.

that evening, he became one of the 'interesting visitors to the Lyceum and the Beefsteak Room' to see the play and afterwards have supper with Irving, Stoker, and other members of their company.[17]

Neither Stoker nor Irving were strangers to celebrity. The lists of their guests at the famous first-night parties on the Lyceum stage are a catalogue of European and American society and success. The two men knew Richard Burton well, and Henry Stanley, and Stoker placed Arminius in the same bracket as a bold and unusual explorer with a remarkable story to tell. Arminius' greatest dramatic efforts were perhaps encouraged in this genuinely theatrical society. During supper in the Beefsteak Room on 30 April 1890,[18] after a performance of *The Dead Heart*, Stoker quoted the false dervish following in 'the track of Marco Polo' and wondered if 'when in Thibet he never felt any fear?' 'No,' Arminius answered, 'but I am afraid of torture, I protected myself against that however. I had always a poison pill fastened here, where the lappet of my coat now is. This I could always reach with my mouth in case my hands were tied. I knew they could not torture me, and then I did not care!' He was a wonderful linguist, Stoker wrote, and related having told the Empress Eugenie, when she had remarked on his walking so far for one who was lame, 'Ah Madam, in Central Asia we travel not on the feet but on the tongue'. Indeed so. Stoker was entranced. He and Irving would see Arminius receiving an honorary degree in Dublin two years later: 'On the day on which the delegates from the various universities of the world spoke, he shone out as a star. He soared above all the speakers, making one of the finest speeches I have ever heard'. He spoke of course 'loudly against Russian aggression – a subject to which he had largely devoted himself'. Stoker knew a thing or two about actors; this must have been quite a performance.[19]

His and the Vambéry names have been bracketed together ever since by those fascinated with Stoker's fabulous creation, *Dracula*. The ins and outs of Arminius' possible role as muse to the vampire's conception have been

---

17 Ibid., 238.
18 The Beefsteak Room (as opposed to the Beefsteak Club) was Irving's revival of the 'Sublime Society of Beefsteaks', the oldest surviving dining society in Britain. It was founded originally by John Rich, manager of the Covent Garden Theatre, in 1735, with a constant twenty-four members. When Irving revived it at the Lyceum, it had new rules to allow female guests.
19 Stoker, op. cit., 238.

exhaustively picked over; this book proposes to slip Dracula in at his possible beginnings as a temporary diversion from a surfeit of royalty. The vampire story for which Stoker remains famous today has generated what must be literally acres of written material and miles of celluloid, all encompassed now in terabytes of computer memory. The vampire count, judging by a quick search of recent academic papers on the subject, can be usefully moulded to fit any narrative from female hysteria and food, to the Venus flytrap plant and Victorian imperialism. In Christopher Frayling's preface to the 1993 Penguin Classics edition of *Dracula*, he notes, 'When Bram Stoker died in 1912, not a single newspaper obituary mentioned *Dracula* by name: today, the obituaries would mention little else'. In the intervening century, and especially since the 1970s, the literary-critical context of *Dracula* has shape-shifted beyond all recognition. In the 1950s Maurice Richardson famously called the text '...a kind of incestuous, necrophilous, oral-anal-sadistic all-in wrestling match'. Others have related it to civilisation and its discontents, the return of the repressed, sex from the neck up, homoeroticism, bisexuality and gender bending, reverse colonialism (the East getting its own back on the West), and 'a cosmic racial conflict between modern Anglo-Saxon stock and the 1,400-year-old bloodline of Attila the Hun'. Then there is the empowerment/disempowerment of women, the occult, and 'being strangled with red tape...' And so on.[20] Enough for anyone to get their teeth into. Most of it would have astonished Stoker and shocked the prudish Arminius quite dreadfully.

The vampire is a portmanteau invention inspired by multiple sources and coloured by the melodrama of the theatre that was Stoker's daily surrounding.[21] *Faust* and *The Dead Heart*, especially Irving's *Faust*, must have coloured many susceptible Victorian imaginations (and fuelled a few nightmares). Vampires had anyway been busily stalking the earth and the published page since the eighteenth century, and bloodsuckers and the undead had lurked in shadowy legend long before that. If Arminius, the great storyteller, found an appreciative audience in Stoker for the myths and folk tales of the

---

20 Christopher Frayling, 'Preface' in Bram Stoker, *Dracula* (London, 1993).
21 So far as this writer and non-Dracula expert is concerned, Jim Steinmeyer's 2013 book *Who was Dracula?* gives the clearest picture of Bram Stoker's invention. It includes Stoker's explanation that the novel was inspired by a nightmare after a 'surfeit of crab', and doubts much input from Arminius beyond the use of his name and persona. See *Who was Dracula? Bram Stoker's Trail of Blood* (New York, 2013).

bloodiest parts of real Hungarian history[22] – including Vlad (the Impaler) Dracula and the notorious Erzsébet Báthory, who bathed in virgins' blood and members of whose wider family were also Voivodes of Transylvania – then further supplemented with facts from his travels in the real world or inventions from 'Thibet', he may be placed as one useful source of inspiration to the author at a time when Stoker was gathering material for a story as yet unformed. Arminius does, after all, appear in the book, as himself. Dr Van Helsing remarks:

> I have asked my friend Arminius, of Buda-Pesth University, to make his record; and from all the means that are, he tells me of what he has been. He must, indeed, have been that Voivoide Dracula, who won his name against the Turk… The Draculas were, says Arminius, a great and noble race, though now and again were scions who were held by their coevals to have had dealings with the Evil One.[23]

Arminius' famous name was a good fit for a story set in Transylvania/ Hungary, but the use of the real professor of Buda Pest university does suggest some further role for him, not just in the story but in the making of the story. Did he speak the somewhat jangled English of Dr Van Helsing? Van Helsing was also probably a composite character and is considered by a number of commentators, including Frayling, to be more closely modelled on Max Müller, the great German-born philologist and Orientalist who was also an expert on religion and mythology. Müller had been teaching at Oxford since 1851, and Frayling believes he and Stoker were in written contact, although no record remains beyond a request to Irving, rather than Stoker, for a ticket for *Faust* in 1886.[24] Arminius or Müller might also have been the source of one of Count Dracula's discourses to Jonathan Harker

---

22 Arminius had researched Hungarian history for his *The Story of Hungary*, published in New York in 1886 as part of a series, *The Stories of Nations*. It is not a thrilling book, but it is readable, and some of the history might have made a good backdrop for Arminius' more theatrical story-telling in person.

23 Bram Stoker, *Dracula* (London, 1897), 264.

24 Clemens Ruthner, 'What's in a Name? The German-Speaking World and the Origins of Dracula', published as *The Shade and the Shadow, Proceedings of the Dracula '97 Conference*, held that year in Antwerp.

on Transylvanian history, when Dracula is described as having 'warmed up the subject wonderfully', but elsewhere the count's words are close to one of Müller's theories, too. Dracula speaks of 'we Szekelys', the same Transylvanian community as Alexander Csoma de Kőrös, who believed the Székelys had descended from Attila, and continues:

> we have the right to be proud, for in our veins flows the blood of many brave races who fought as the lion fights, for lordship. Here in the whirl-pool of European races, the Ugric tribe bore down from Iceland the fighting spirit which Thor and Wodin gave them... Here too, they found the Huns whose warlike fury had swept the earth like a living flame... What devil or what witch was ever so great as Attila, whose blood is in these veins?

And then:

> Is it strange that when Arpad and his legions swept through the Hungarian fatherland he found us here when he reached the frontier... And when the Hungarian flood swept eastward, the Szelekys were claimed as kindred by the victorious Magyars...[25]

Thus neatly potting the philological argument between Turkic and Finno-Ugric towards Müller's own 'Turanian' thesis.[26]

Stoker might have communicated with either or both of these philological contacts and conflated their arguments to create the count's narrative. Alder and Dalby go further and suggest that, while trawling for possible remnants of the Bibliotheca Corviniana, Arminius had come across the chronicles of Matthias Corvinus' Italian court historian Antonio Bonfini. These had been printed in 1543 and were believed to include unknown anecdotes about Vlad

---

25 Stoker, *Dracula*, 31–2.
26 Müller's theory of a 'Turanian' family of languages bracketed Finnic, Samoyedic, Turkic, Mongolic, and Tungusic languages together as the 'nomadic languages' spoken in Asia and Europe and separate to the other two families of Aryan and Semitic languages. Growing from this linguistic association, Hungarian Turanism identifies the Hungarian language and people with those of Asia – hence Arminius' own and other philological researchers' journeys into Central Asia and further east.

Dracul. Dracul had been held captive for twelve years by Matthias Corvinus but, despite rumours that have persisted over centuries of their contents, no such documents have ever come to light. It seems more likely that Arminius, never able to resist knowing best, but usefully so in this case, pointed Stoker in the direction of less esoteric guides to Hungarian history, folklore, and geography. Christopher Frayling wrote of Stoker finding the name 'Dracula' in a dull book about Wallachia and Moldavia, written by a retired diplomat, which he discovered in the Whitby Museum and Subscription Library during a wet family holiday in July–August 1890, when he had already made his first notes for a vampire story. Perhaps he also remembered Arminius mentioning the name?

Or not. The circle of conjecture is endless. If Arminius and Stoker corresponded, the letters have long since disappeared, like any to or from Müller. Now the reader can only turn the pages of *Dracula* again in search of Arminius' voice here or there, expounding facts or pet theories that may have been part of the fiction or fact of his conversations with Stoker, and with Irving (who was probably Stoker's greatest motivation for a story that would, he hoped, translate to the stage with the great actor in the leading role). It has been suggested that Arminius' shape-shifting abilities, his playing of different roles throughout his life, especially the exotic dervish, might have been another inspiration for Dracula the shape-shifter. That surely applies more obviously to Irving, who was at the centre of Stoker's life and who he imagined playing Dracula on the stage, the role being 'a composite of so many of the parts in which he has been liked'.[27] Dracula was not intended or expected to become either Louis Jourdan's beautiful and urbane vampire, or the more obviously monstrous Nosferatu of Max Schreck, but Irving was certainly closer in style and appearance to the imagined Dracula than he was to the real Transylvanian count who was Arminius' friend. Arminius stayed with Count Géza Kuun de Osdola, philologist, Orientalist, historian, and member of the Hungarian Academy, at his castle, Mintia, in Transylvania. Their extant correspondence mentions Arminius' other travels in Transylvania, so perhaps Géza Kuun was another source of Transylvanian folklore, even if Arminius' letters to his 'only Transylvanian

---

27 Bram Stoker, quoted in Steinmeyer, op. cit., 184.

friend' focus on more obviously scholarly interests.[28] But then again, Géza Kuun had been born in Sibiu, a town in Romania also known in German as Hermannstadt, where Stoker would locate the fictional lake of the same name and the 'Scholomance', the mythical school of black magic 'where the Devil claims the tenth scholar as his due'.[29] Count Géza Kuun the scholar was an improbable model for Dracula or the Devil's decimation, but he might have expanded Arminius' fund of local tales and thus one thing led to another...

A final supernatural note: in *The Dervish of Windsor Castle*, Lory Alder and Richard Dalby, who was a ghost story collector and anthologist, added as a postscript to the Vambéry/Stoker story a note on the publication of a 1956 book of ghost stories called *Cavalcade of Ghosts*. In the final story, 'The Riddle of the Thetford Vampire', the female vampire is 'the daughter of Arminius Vambéry, Professor of Oriental Languages at Pest University'.[30]

*

By Arminius' account he packed a lot into his two-night stay at Sandringham. His name appeared regularly thereafter in the Court Circular (which listed the activities of a far wider group of individuals than it does now). Arminius returned to Britain in April 1890 and was reported as a guest of the sultan in Constantinople with Madame Vambéry and their son, Rustem, in October that year. Arminius and Rustem were both decorated, with the second class of the Nichan-i-Chefakat and the Medjidieh fourth class, respectively. Did Arminius himself inform *The Times* about the visit? This sounds like his voice:

Professor Vambéry has been at Constantinople a week, continuing his examination of the Imperial archives and of ancient works relating to

---

28 They include Arminius' typical complaint in 1880 that the Academy had not asked his advice in the development of Géza Kuun's transcription and translation of the *Codex Cumanicus*, a thirteenth-century dictionary of Kipchak-Cuman with Persian and Latin. See Margareta Aslan, *Documents from the correspondence between Géza Kuun and Ármin Vámbéry* (Cluj-Napoca, 2013), 295–318.
29 Stoker, *Dracula*, 265.
30 Alder and Dalby, op. cit., 467.

Hungarian and Ottoman history. He has discovered some very interesting and valuable documents, the Sultan having graciously granted him per-mission to thoroughly search the reserved library in the Treasury, which no European has yet visited, and which contains works and documents several centuries old and so far never brought to light. Professor Vambéry returns to Pesth to give an account of his labours to the Hungarian Academy, which sent him on this important scientific mission.

In February 1893, there were reports that Professor Vambéry had broken his leg, falling on a slippery pavement. He was making a full recovery.

The Court Circular of July 1895 reported his presence at the Conserva-tive Club, with a group that included General Mikhail Annenkov, a hugely important figure in the Russian conquest of Central Asia. Annenkov had been involved in the taking of Bukhara, had been governor-general of Tran-scaspia, was a builder of the Transcaspian railway and had also played a part in the Panjdeh incident. There was also the Portuguese geographer Luciano Cordeiro; Clements Markham, president of the Royal Geographi-cal Society; Otto Irminger, the Danish Arctic explorer; the Belgian colonial officer Baron Dhanis, who served in the Congo and Africa; the French geographer Marcel Dubois; Oscar Neumann, a young German ornitholo-gist; and other notable European travellers. In June 1901 Arminius arrived in London to stay for a fortnight and to deliver a lecture in Sheffield on 'Russia's progress in Asia'. In 1902 he received his CVO, and in May the Court Circular reported his reception by the king at Buckingham Palace, after which Arminius gave an account of his second stay at Windsor in an interview to the *Pester Lloyd,* the leading German-language newspaper in Budapest.

Arminius revelled in his formal invitation to dinner and to stay the night at Windsor on 6 May 1889. He had, he pointed out, already received notice of the invitation in a telegram, 'as for political reasons, it was not thought wise to invite and do honour to the anti-Russian author without further reason – it would have seemed like a direct challenge to the Court at St Petersburg'. The diplomatic balm was an invitation 'to see the library and the sights of the Castle'. For himself he thought if the tsar could receive the great journalist W. T. Stead, pro-Russian friend and editor of Madame Novikov, there was no reason why the queen should not receive 'the representative of the opposite party'. He was received at Windsor by Sir Henry Ponsonby, the queen's private secretary,[31] and so came the moment when his birthday, inscribed in the queen's birthday book, became official. 'With the exception of this rather unpleasant but otherwise comical episode', Arminius wrote, 'my stay at Windsor was a most pleasant one'. The courtiers, 'whose acquaint- ance I made at lunch, vied with each other in their amiability to the foreign defender of British interests in Asia', but he was astounded when one of the higher officials, 'an ardent admirer of Mr Gladstone', spoke sharply about the prime minister, Lord Salisbury. 'Discretion', Arminius wrote, forbade him to speak more of Queen Victoria, to whom he sat 'next but two', at dinner that night, but he was much disposed to enlarge on his memories of other members of the royal family. His stays at Sandringham and Windsor that year added to his stock of stories and lost nothing in the telling.

After Queen Victoria's death in 1901, Arminius wrote of her heir, Edward VII, who 'showed me many marks of favour' and found 'greatly to my satis- faction, that the possession of a crown had caused no change in his character'. The CVO the king conferred on him, on his seventieth birthday in 1902, 'naturally caused a sensation abroad, and also at home, where Government had taken but scant notice of my festival'. The king, 'in spite of his exalted position does not allow himself to be influenced by difference in rank or religion', and was 'filled with the democratic spirit of our century'. To 'prove the truth of the proverb, "the apple never falls far from the tree"', Arminius told one of his well-glossed fables of the stay at Sandringham. Did he stay, as he said, in the absent Prince Albert Victor's rooms, next to those of his younger brother Prince George?[32] 'One afternoon', his story went, 'as I was occupied with my correspondence, I received an invitation from the Queen to join her in the garden; as I wished to wash my hands before going down, I rang several times for warm water, but no one came'. In the end, who should appear at the door to ask what he wanted but Prince George, who then 'disappeared, returning in a few minutes with a large jug in his hand, which he placed, smiling, on my washstand. Not at all bad, I thought for

---

31 Arminius referred to him as the Lord Steward, from whom his formal invitation had come, although that was in fact the earl of Mount Edgcumbe.
32 He was made prince of Wales on his elder brother's death, and came to the throne as King George V.

this poor Jewish beggar-student of former years to be waited upon by a prince! I have often laughed at the recollection of this incident and have since dubbed the future sovereign of Great Britain, "The Royal Jug-bearer"'. That story was re-told for years, syndicated in one after another newspaper across continents. It even appeared, in January 1914, after Arminius' death, in *The Elmcreek Beacon* of Elmcreek, Nebraska. In his journals at the time, Prince George himself noted only 'Professor Vambéry (Hungarian) came this afternoon, talked to him with Papa and Aunt Louise'. But there was yet more in Arminius' store of shining memories. When a gala dinner was given for the queen, Arminius was about to take in Princess Louise when the prince of Wales asked, 'Vambéry, why did you not put on orders?' At this stage Arminius did not have much in the way of orders to wear, but the princess spoke up: 'Why Papa, Professor Vambéry ought to have pinned some of his books on to his coat; they would be the most suitable decorations.' Tall tales apart, Arminius was right in saying that Edward VII 'understands the spirit of his times better than many of his brother sovereigns, and his popularity in England and America is a very natural result'.

On 20 May 1904, the Court Circular reported that Professor Vambéry had been received by the king at Buckingham Palace the day before. On the afternoon of 21 May, the king and queen went to Windsor where they remained for a week, though they continued to come into London for events at Buckingham Palace. It was a busy time of year, with courts and presentations. On his return to Budapest, Arminius gave an interview to the *Pester Lloyd* (another publication he had bombarded with articles and letters over the years) about this latest sojourn at Windsor. His visit is not reported in the Court Circular; nor does his name appear among the lists of court attendees over the next week or two. He may have been at Windsor again 'to visit the library', but Arminius always had a story to tell and if the facts did not suit his tale, that certainly didn't stop him. By this time, he had his CVO to wear as well as his Turkish orders, but the knee breeches that were a part of court dress were, he said, a different matter. The king had made them obligatory at court, but Arminius could not or would not wear them for fear of ridicule due to his small stature and lame leg. Instead, he told the *Pester Lloyd*, he had been allowed to wear his own trousers, the only man to do so. Were it true, there were others who would have viewed his trousered legs with envy. The king's strictures about knee breeches were so unpopular that they were generally given up except for state occasions. (The king is supposed to have enquired of Lord Rosebery, dressed one evening in trousers, whether he was part of the suite of the American ambassador? Not one of Arminius' stories, but one he might have liked to tell.)

His lame leg notwithstanding, Arminius, now seventy-two, told of a two-hour tour of Windsor with the king as guide and Field Marshal Lord Roberts in tow. Roberts, who was the same age as Arminius, almost collapsed with exhaustion, but not Arminius. (Lord Roberts VC, KG, KP, GCB, OM, GCSI, GCIE, KStJ, VD, PC, FRSGS, who had until that February been commander-in-chief of the forces, might also have been expected to have appeared in the various lists of court attendees that week, but he did not either.) The tour sounds highly improbable at the height of the season, when the king and queen were continually travelling between Windsor and Buckingham Palace, and there was one event after another, but Arminius expounded for the *Pester Lloyd* on the excellent servants' quarters in the castle, each room with its own bathroom, about which the king had commented, 'I am delighted to give my men all possible comfort, for good work requires good rest'. He expressed his greatest admiration for the dining room, set with plate 'all of pure shining gold', which he said took him back almost forty-five years to the memory of dining off similar gold plate at the Merasim Kiosk with Sultan Abdul Mejid – a truly fantastical vision for the clever but insignificant tutor he had been in those days. The castle now, Arminius said, was all 'dazzling, princely splendour', as opposed to the 'dark and sombre atmosphere' of his earlier visit.[33]

The Court Circular reported that the king gave a dinner party at Windsor on the night of 21 May – Arminius remembered that dinner at Windsor was at 9 p.m., a time, at home, when he would normally have been going to bed, but at Windsor his normal routine 'was always changed drastically'. When the king went to have his coffee and smoke a cigar after dinner with the guests with whom he particularly wished to talk, Arminius managed to stay awake to chat with him until well after midnight. He commented that the king never drank alcohol, not even wine, and that when he had been summoned to sit with him on successive nights, the messengers had been the prince of Wales on one night and Lord Roberts on the other. At dinner, Arminius said,

---

33 Alder and Dalby, op. cit., 322–5.

the king arranged for Hungarian tunes to be played in his honour. (The Court Circular reported the attendance of the Band of the Horse Guards.) Back in Budapest, Arminius showed his interviewer music programmes that included Brahms' *Hungarian Dances*, as well as menus for breakfast, lunch, and dinner. He also had postcards and photographs of the state rooms at Windsor, which had been open to the public since 1845. He was in his element, adding virtues to the king's person and words into his mouth: 'The English constitution, as you know, limits the influence on the monarch's part, nevertheless he succeeds tactfully in imposing his political point of view'. The king, as everyone knew, was responsible for the Entente Cordiale, agreed in April that year, and upon which Arminius had congratulated him. The king, he said, had replied, 'Just wait and see, Vambéry, the Russians will soon be finished as well'. Above all, Arminius praised the king's philo-Semitism, almost unique among European royalty. It was an irresistible dig at the Hungarian upper classes, underlined with the spectacular anecdote that when the king stayed with the prominent Jewish landowners the Sassoons to shoot, he ate kosher food. (The Sassoons and His Majesty would have been surprised – a menu for a dinner at Cannes in 1889, attended by Reuben Sassoon, his wife, and the prince of Wales, included both lobster and oysters.) Finally, the king had supposedly presented Arminius with a personally inscribed copy of *The Armoury of Windsor Castle*, which Alder and Dalby described as 'one of his most cherished possessions', although as a letter to John Murray makes clear, the book had in fact been sent to him while he was in London.[34]

There was a final postscript to Arminius' royal encounters of 1904. He had somehow discovered (probably because he had been preparing himself for royalty) that the grave of the princess of Wales's Hungarian grandmother was in need of restoration. The princess's grandmother, the daughter of another Transylvanian count directly descended from Arpad, had been Claudine Rhédey, known as the 'Wurttemberg Princess'. She and the duke of Wurttemberg[35] had fallen madly in love and were married morganatically since she was not of royal blood. She became Countess Hohenstein, and her son, the first duke of Teck, became Princess Mary's father. Claudine had been killed

---

34 Ibid., 322–4.
35 Ruler of the royal duchy of Wurttemberg, a long-surviving member of the Holy Roman Empire and a kingdom in its own right during the nineteenth century.

when her horse bolted into an advancing regiment of hussars at a review of her husband's troops, and her father had insisted on her burial among her ancestors in Transylvania at Erdoszentgyorgy (now Sângeorgiu de Pădure).

Arminius had written to Princess Mary from Budapest before his arrival in London.[36] He wrote again on 19 May after his reception at Buckingham Palace to say that he had the king's approval for a plan that would bring England and Hungary closer together. The grave needed a memorial plaque, and Arminius expressed the opinion that its restoration and the small expense required for continuing upkeep would achieve this happy result. Repairs would, he thought, cost about £20–30, and he would be delighted to be entrusted with the mission to arrange them. Back in Budapest in June, he wrote again, enclosing photographs of his family and, in July, of the Szent Gyorgy (Saint George) church where the grave was to be found. The correspondence, marked in the Royal Archives 'Correspondence with Professor Vambéry at

36 Royal Archives QM/PRIV/CC61/6/ 1–8.

Pest over my Grandmother's grave in Transylvania', ran on. Arminius took himself off to Rhédey Castle in September and supplied a description of the crypt in pedantic detail: the coffin, 'tied with copper bands', the separate heart of the countess, the question of taking up the floor (it might be 'very costly'), and whether the countess's coffin should be moved next to her father's. By 24 November, he was complaining that estimates for the work 'greatly surpass my expectations': 'Whenever there is a question of England and particularly the English Royal Family, people here and on the Continent in general are anxious to speak in big numbers.' He had, he wrote, mentioned the matter to the prime minister, Count Tisza, and to the bishop of the diocese which, he now believed, should undertake the repairs at 'a more favourable moment'.

It is unclear in the end who paid for what but, no doubt badgered by Arminius, someone did. A memorial slab, black Swedish granite with four bronze rosettes, was made, and Arminius undertook to translate the inscription into Hungarian. The princess had no idea of her grandmother's dates, which he supplied. When the weather allowed, he wrote, he would travel to see the slab fixed. The cost would 'not exceed £35–37 in spite of the distance from Budapest'. By March 1905, Arminius was sending 'heartfelt thanks' to Princess Mary for photographs he had requested from her 'to complete the ornament of this room'. He wrote in somewhat over-excited English, 'the studio of the quondam beggar adorned with the portraits of his august Benefactors furnishes on the one hand a bright and eloquent of [sic] Their Majesties', and their 'noble and high-minded feeling towards a humble writer, on the other hand it illustrates the extraordinary career of a man whom destiny has raised from the poorest origin to the highest pinnacle of Royal favour'. He was happy to have been able to 'render this insignificant service'. Finally, in April 1905, he sent a photograph of the memorial slab *in situ*, together with a genealogy of the Rhédey family and a note of the cost of £37, 'give or take a few shillings'. His royal photographs no doubt acquired extra provenance as time went on. In 1907 and still pursuing the spore of royal contact, Arminius sent Princess Mary news of the death of another Rhédey relative, of whom she had barely heard. She replied sending her deepest sympathy to the deceased's son and looking forward to seeing Arminius again in England.

Now seventy-five, he had made his final visit, but he continued to communicate with the king, latterly through Charles Hardinge at the Foreign Office, delivering gratuitous advice based on his view of the situation in

Turkey, and, as he hastened to point out, his close contact with political, social, and literary Turkey for more than fifty years. Edward VII was to die on 6 May 1910. 'Up to the end of his life, the King gave me proof of his sympathy, friendship, personal esteem', Arminius wrote. He underlined this friendship ('I, who was near to the King found him a man who was head and shoulders above his contemporaries'[37]) by contributing to Edward Legge's *King Edward in his True Colours*.[38] The book was supposed to balance obituaries that had emphasised the king's character as a 'man of the world'. As the *Graphic* noted a few days after his death, that appellation might not be 'the greatest praise to give to a clergyman or a dentist', but 'it is very nearly the highest praise you could give to a King'. When else indeed might an English king have been so happily described? 'William IV was a fool, George IV a fop, George III a farmer, and his two predecessors were impenitent Germans and William came to us from Holland'. King Edward had 'added to the roll of history ten years of as splendid and beneficent work as goes to the credit of any English Sovereign'. Not bad, you might think, but Arminius was particularly offended by the king's entry in the *Dictionary of National Biography* that also called him a man of the world and added that he 'lacked the intellectual equipment of a thinker and showed on occasion an unwillingness to exert his mental powers. He was no reader of books... He did not sustain a conversation with much power of brilliance; but his grace and charm of manner atoned for any deficiency of matter...'[39]

The *Pester Lloyd* published his piece, 'My Relationship with King Edward', prefacing it with the statement, 'It is well known that Professor Vambéry was on intimate terms of friendship with King Edward for over four decades: he is shattered by the news of his death'. Not so shattered, however, that he neglected to improve on the relationship. A eulogistic 'Appreciation' of the new King George and Queen Mary in *The Times* of 9 May from 'our correspondent' has Arminius' style blazoned all over it. His contribution to Edward Legge's book is even more graphically littered with himself, I, me. He described the late king's entry in the *Dictionary of National Biography* as 'the greatest possible calumny'. 'Not only', Arminius wrote, 'did I find him

37 Alder and Dalby, op. cit., 328.
38 Edward Legge, *King Edward in his True Colours* (London, 1912).
39 Alder and Dalby, op. cit., 328.

often reading serious works, but I know he mastered their contents, and frequently applied historical citations in support of his political views... if discretion did not bridle my pen, I could quote from his conversation passages destined to be given as advice to Sultan Abdul Hamid, which would justly astonish the most shrewd diplomatist'.[40] The piece in the *Pester Lloyd* re-ran Arminius' whole acquaintance with the king, the stories of his visits to Budapest and an implied wealth of lunches and royal stays across the decades. It underlined the excellence of the king's public speaking exemplified by the off-the-cuff speech given by him in French on Arminius' advice in Budapest, and another when he received Henry Morton Stanley at Marlborough House after his return from Africa. The duke of Edinburgh had been taken ill and was unable, at the last moment, to deliver the planned speech of welcome. Bizarrely, and most improbably, Edward is meant to have asked Arminius for 'two or three geographical proper names' in Africa. Thus armed, he had spoken, 'with as much cleverness and perfect knowledge as if he had... spent years in the Ruwenzori and among the pygmies'. Arminius finished, 'I beg to ask what Prince, what ordinary speaker would be able to accomplish a similar feat?' Edward Legge commented: 'If there is any gratitude in the British people, now is the time for them to express it to Arminius Vambéry!'[41]

What was the summit of Arminius' aspirations with regard to British royalty? Like so many of his social and academic ambitions, it seems he did not reach the heights he believed he deserved. He told his son, Rustem, that he might have become Sir Arminius, even Lord Vambéry, and Rustem, the second baronet – 'Sir Rustem and a member of the English aristocracy'. Rustem replied: 'I should prefer to be a university teacher – that is the title I should like to inherit from you'.[42] When Rustem's first son was born in 1905, Arminius thought he would confer a little royal stardust on his grandchild. He wrote to Prince George, then prince of Wales:

it is very natural that I cling with grateful attachment to your noble and glorious family... the only worthy reward I have found for all my

---

40 Ibid., 328–9.
41 Ibid., 329.
42 Ibid., 321.

sufferings was the Royal favour bestowed upon me by His Majesty, your Royal father, and by yourself, when yet in tender age… Anxious to keep up by relation of devotion and gratitude in my family, I beg leave from Your Royal Highness to give me the permission to name my grandchild George and to inscribe in the parish-register your Royal Highness as the God-father of the infant.[43]

Prince George said yes, allowing Arminius to write once again to give his 'most obedient and heartfelt thanks' for the 'extraordinary Royal favour… by which my humble family has been raised to the highest rank of honour and distinction attainable by a man of such poor antecedents and hard struggles as my life was connected with'. It ended, in Arminius' best 'Asiatic' style: 'you will always reap the benefits of your magnanimity and wisdom and I am sure the sum of your glory and happiness will never cease to shine'. As Alder and Dalby noted, Rustem and his wife Olga 'evidently had no choice over the name for their first baby'; if Arminius was a courtier elsewhere, he was a tyrant in his own castle.[44]

---

43 Ibid., 471–2.
44 Ibid., 472–3.

15

The Sultan

Arminius' 1889 international tour saw him back in Constantinople on 31 May. Sir Philip Currie showed gratifying interest in his activities regarding the 'present views' of 'your friend there', that 'very fickle and changeable person', the sultan, 'as to his country and the other Great Powers' and especially as to Russia.[1] Arminius wrote to Currie from the Hotel d'Angleterre[2] on 6 June after a dinner with the sultan at the Yildiz Palace. He reported that this had also been attended by the sultan's ADC, who had accompanied the Russian grand dukes on their Palestine tour,[3] and by Yusuf Riza Pasha, a statesman of 'pronounced Russian sympathies'. They were there, he considered, as diplomatic counterbalances to himself. After dinner he got his one-to-one interview with the sultan. The issue of the moment was Abdul Hamid's fortification of the Dardanelles with Krupp guns, thought by the British to be an attempt to keep them out after their humiliation of Turkey in Egypt.[4] Meanwhile, the defences to the Bosporus from the Black Sea were neglected and would allow easy access to a Russian fleet. The sultan was nervous of British designs, and less friendly to allies who he believed had already let him down over money and the annexation of Turkish terri-

---

1 Sinan Kuneralp, ed., *The Secret Reports of the Hungarian Arminius Vambéry to the British Foreign Office on Sultan Abdulhamid II and his Reign (1889–1909)* (Istanbul, 2013), 26. All correspondence in this chapter related to the Foreign Office's interest in the sultan is drawn from this text.
2 He was rather put out not to be staying in the palace itself, but he was the sultan's guest in the first European-style hotel in Constantinople, which had opened its doors in 1841.
3 Palestine was also part of the Ottoman Empire.
4 Egypt had been occupied by British forces in 1882 during the Anglo-Egyptian War and had become to all intents and purposes a British protectorate, much to the sultan's displeasure.

tory. Two days later, Arminius described defending himself against Abdul Hamid's suspicion that he was a British secret agent. He had told the sultan: 'I have absolutely nothing to do with the English Government, and I am not sent by anybody, I am not entrusted with any secret or covert mission...' He was there, he said, purely in the spirit of friendship and sympathy for both parties, to make peace between them, to explain misunderstandings and to remove the 'stumbling block for an entente cordiale', that is 'The Egyptian Question'. According to Arminius, the sultan then called him 'a godsend man', the only one 'capable to act as a disinterested mediator between me and the English', but even such a 'steady friend to my nation' could not clear up misconceptions relating to Egypt, the Bosporus, and Armenia.

The sultan, Arminius wrote, 'tried in vain to conceal his anxiety and his being terrorised by Russian influence'. He himself, however, had 'gained such a position with him, he is so fully convinced of the sincerity of my intentions, and above all he is so much afraid of the harm I could do him, if intentionally offended or slighted, that he took leave of me in a most friendly manner, and invited me to come next to Constantinople and to put up in the Palace, where two rooms will be kept especially for me'. The rest of the letter is a sort of job application for the role of unofficial mediator between the sultan and Britain. 'The Sultan is most anxious to re-establish his former relations of good friendship with England' and would 'hail with joy' an 'approach on the part of England' that might be engineered, in Arminius' words, before 'the reassumption of diplomatic intercourse and the re-opening of the Egyptian Question'. He went on to describe his relations with the sultan's ministers; those who had not known him thirty years earlier were 'jealous of my intimacy with the Sultan, and candidly avow, that there was never a foreigner and a Christian to whom the Sultan had shown such an amount of confidence. They say I have conquered him by my command over their language and literature...' This sounds very much like Arminius putting words into other mouths again, or telling Currie what he thought Currie would like to hear. Those, he said, who had known him since the days of Abdul Mejid 'alone have shown me frankness and sincerity, and with few exceptions, they are all favourably disposed towards England'. He proposed that he should not, for now, rouse the suspicion of the sultan 'by any act of excessive zeal for English interests' but instead 'instil in his mind drop by drop the spirit of my English policy'. Finally, Arminius gave a pen portrait of the sultan on which he would enlarge in the coming years: 'shrewd and clever', a 'tolerably good master of his language, without possessing the full command over the niceties and delicacies of this exceedingly difficult vernacular'. He was not well-versed in history or theological literature – 'indispensable in every well-educated Mohammedan' – and while interested in European politics, he was a procrastinator in the 'execution of his plans'. Arminius thought the 'superior qualities' of the then British ambassador, Sir William White, had gained the respect of the sultan despite the current coldness between their countries. Nevertheless, no representative of a foreign country, 'whatever be his abilities', would be able to cope with the 'excessive difficulties of the situation, considering that not only Oriental languages but full and perfect knowledge of Oriental life, habits and manners are required to obtain a desirable result'.

The European dragomans and interpreters, Arminius claimed, 'very rarely or never possess the Oriental mode of thinking and viewing things and persons in the special light of Orientals'. It was for this reason that a 'private agent, speaking Turkish exactly like a Turk and being in full possession of the peculiar mode of thinking, gesticulations, manners and habits of Orientals, will find much easier the way to the innermost feelings and thoughts of the Eastern sovereign than any however gifted, shrewd and accomplished European diplomatist...' Currie was already paying contributions to his travel expenses, and the letter quoted above set the tone for Arminius' long correspondence about Turkey with the Foreign Office, full of drama and warnings of tremendous crises, usually considered by the Foreign Office to be alarmist. For example, Arminius alluded to British 'difficulties with the Dervishes', meaning the continuing Mahdist state in Sudan, and laid the blame for such at the door of the sultan's 'incitation and encouragement' and 'multifarious plots and tricks'. He suggested the sultan was now fomenting revolt through other religious leaders, such as the sheikh of the Senussi dervish order in Kairouan. This was probably a matter of indifference to the British; Tunisia was a French protectorate and a dervish-led rising there was unlikely to impinge on the British Empire.

There were letters that ran into extensive reports, based on information gleaned in the Ottoman court and the Constantinople streets, or from conversations with the sultan. These were regularly tailored to, or garnished with Arminius' own opinions and interpretations. He freely delivered advice in general, about policy towards Turkey and sometimes far outside it, and there was always a larding of schoolmasterly hectoring when the British recipients of this counsel failed to act on his suggestions. There were also regular requests for payment for services rendered, or complaints of that payment being too meagre, but his profile was certainly being raised. On 20 June 1889 William Summers, Conservative MP for Huddersfield, asked the under-secretary of state for foreign affairs 'whether there is any foundation for the statement that Professor Vambéry had been on a special mission to the sultan at the request of Lord Salisbury [then foreign secretary], and if so whether he can inform the House what was the nature of the mission in question'. Sir James Fergusson replied, 'No Sir, the statement in question is without foundation.'

Lord Salisbury had met Arminius at the Foreign Office in April 1889, at a meeting almost certainly initiated by the latter. It would have been hard to refuse a friend of the prince of Wales, the famous and eminent Hungarian Orientalist, with a good story and a list of names to drop. Why indeed should Salisbury not be interested? That meeting may have inspired or rubber-stamped Arminius' new self-appointed role as conduit between the sultan and the British Foreign Office. It was never formalised and was always led by the opportunistic freelancer. As Alder and Dalby remark, after describing his 'Walter Mitty-like moments of flights of fancy' as 'a Hungarian Don Quixote, furiously tilting at windmills', Arminius trailed 'an elaborate red herring' in his memoirs.[5] He encouraged 'the rumours then prevalent, which made me out a secret political agent of England', by first pointing them out and then not quite denying them. In a confidential Foreign Office memo in 1891, Philip Currie wrote of the sultan, 'HM evidently believes Vambéry to be an English Agent, he no doubt does his best to make him think so...'

In its early stages, nuggets of information, carefully combed from the tangle of Arminius' correspondence, may have been of value, or been thought to be so. Their first recipients – Sir Philip Currie, later ambassador to the Ottoman Empire, and his successor, Thomas Sanderson – were kind, if not effusive. There was more concrete recognition of Arminius as a potentially important conduit of intelligence between the sultan and the British

---

5 Alder and Dalby, op. cit., 395.

government in the payment of the 'travel expenses' that he first requested in 1889, and which became a yearly stipend paid until his death. He was known to be a friend of the king (by then George V), as he had been of his father, and the annuity had become a habit which nobody would or could take responsibility for changing. In April 1890 Arminius wrote to Currie:

As to the rather delicate question of my expenses incurred in travelling and unavoidable baksheesh in the Palace, I shall ask £60. But you will easily understand that having shown myself disinterested hitherto, I am rather reluctant to bother you in that regard. If Lord Salisbury is willing to give me a round sum which would bring £50 or 60 a year, I would be fully satisfied, and I would never intrude for my whole life. It is a hard choice to ask remuneration for sympathies I have withstood hitherto valiantly in spite of the general belief of the whole world, but I am sorry to say that my efforts are frustrated by my poverty, of which I was always proud, but which nevertheless remains a stumbling block in my career. I dare say nobody will regard this as assistance, I ask, as a remuneration for a long and arduous work, which is acknowledged by every English man and by every civilised man of Europe and America.

I venture to write this knowing your noble hearted character, and I hope not to be misunderstood by you.

The letter was forwarded to Lord Salisbury with a memorandum from Currie. 'I would give Vambéry his money', Lord Salisbury wrote back in red ink, and continued to endorse such payments.

By 7 June 1890, Arminius was on what became an annual holiday to the village of Mühlbach in the southern Tyrol, after another visit to Constantinople. He wrote to Currie of the necessity of giving presents in the palace due to his arrival during the festival of Eid Bayram.[6] He had given a *toilette necessaire* to Süreyya Pasha, the first secretary, costing £36, and other gifts, amounting to a total of £74, for which he requested funds. He was pleased to finish his letter: 'My opinions and suggestions on the future doings of England I shall embody in my report and I hope you will do your best, that England should

---

6 Eid Bayram, known in Arabic as Eid al-Adha, is the Feast of Sacrifice and a traditional holiday when meat and other foods are distributed and gifts, particularly of sweets, are given.

secure the good opportunity and that my labours will not be thrown away'. Currie thought, 'he might have another £100', to be forwarded via Sir Arthur Nicolson, then consul-general in Budapest. And so the letters and reports continued. It is unlikely that Arminius' directives on British policy were ever much appreciated by Foreign Office officials and, as time went on, the replies from London express little more than polite interest in his reports. Later, under an impatient Charles Hardinge, they become terse and occasionally furious with the mischief-making of an indiscreet old man who thought his own opinions infallible. What the sultan thought of this odd, self-important little man, who was so linguistically gifted and claimed his friendship as well as the ear of the British king's and his government, no record remains.

Arminius' letter to Currie on 30 August 1889 brought news of another royal acquaintance revived. On 29 August *The Times* had reported from Budapest that 'Professor Arminius Vambéry, who has been acting as the Shah's official interpreter, greatly delighted His Majesty by making a speech in Persian when the Academy was visited. The Shah gleefully complimented the learned professor on his knowledge of a language so little spoken in Europe'. The shah of Persia, Naser al-Din, had already been in London on this, his third European tour. He had stayed at Buckingham Palace for a week and had then been entertained in great houses all over the country. Persia was of enormous commercial as well as strategic importance to Britain as she vied with Russia for concessions in railways, roads, agricultural, mineral, and other interests. For example, the Imperial Bank of Persia, the state bank, had opened in Tehran in January 1889 and was an important concession granted to the German-born British telegraphy and news entrepreneur Sir Paul Julius Reuter, who had his headquarters in London. Meanwhile the son of that renowned eccentric Central Asian traveller Joseph Wolff was now Sir Henry Drummond Wolff, the ambassador to Persia. His 'good-humoured skirmishes'[7] with Prince Dolgorouky, the Russian minister in Tehran, were the beginnings of a rapprochement between the rival powers that would lead to the formal division of their areas of interest in Persia in the Anglo-Russian Convention of 1907 – and their shared violation of Persian sovereignty.

In a letter to Currie, Arminius begged leave to 'submit confidentially to Lord Salisbury' details of his conversation with the shah on an excursion

---

7 Lee, op. cit., 685.

down the Danube, when his majesty had 'kept away from the crowd of ministers and dignitaries in the society of the Archduke Joseph and myself'. The archduke, formally the shah's host in Budapest, had, Arminius wrote, been 'mostly silent' while he had pushed Naser al-Din to discuss British railway concessions in Persia. Arminius did not hesitate to advise the prime minister: the shah, he said, was 'delighted with England' and persisting in an 'active and vigorous policy in Tehran' would ensure that Russia 'will not be able to attain her ends' with her own planned railway system. Arminius thought the shah 'a well-disposed man with the outer appearance of an Asiatic tyrant', and compared him with the sultan, who was outwardly more European but 'in his interior certainly more Asiatic and consequently less approachable'. Fifteen years later, in *The Story of My Struggles*, his account of the shah's visit to Budapest had lost nothing in the telling. The narrator informs us that the shah had been astonished by Arminius' 'speech in the Shirazi dialect and in true Oriental style', and had told Arminius that he had met no one who spoke Persian so idiomatically and so without an accent in the whole of Europe. Naser al-Din, Arminius remarked modestly, had written in his diary that even in Persia there were 'few orators who for elegance and force of speech could compete' with Arminius. He in turn was inclined to retain his favourable opinion of the shah although, by now, this was qualified. Arminius was amused in retrospect 'with the airs the Persian king put on'. He went about 'bedizened' with jewels, and 'although his dynasty had been founded by a condottiere of the lowest rank... he always wanted to parade the antiquity of his race' and was amazed 'that European counts, princes and dukes attempted to be on a familiar footing with him'.

Arminius leavened his description with several of the well-known stories that had circulated about Naser al-Din on his European tours. He had to keep his eastern potentates properly framed in their oriental otherness and peculiarity. In one of his last books, *Western Culture in Eastern Lands*, published by John Murray in 1906, Arminius would write of the 'excessive tyranny and cruel absolutism of these monarchs' as the 'chief causes of the rapid decline of the Moslem East'. By this time Arminius had re-embraced his dervish persona, or the possibility that he might be a dervish in disguise, for the eyes of pilgrims to the Gul Baba shrine in Budapest.[8] He also, as

---

8 The Gul Baba or 'Rose-father' tomb on a hill overlooking Budapest is the northernmost site

we have seen from his letter to Nawab Abdul Latif in India, waxed warmer towards Islam in later life as he took an increasingly dim view of Christianity and of religion in general. He was not a man of faith except when it suited him; few of his strongly expressed but butterfly opinions were pinned for longer than expediency demanded.

He thus repeated the tales that bracketed the shah neatly as 'this Oriental prince', while deploring the 'unjustly severe criticisms… of his Oriental manners'. It was, he wrote, 'only natural that he should commit occasional mistakes of etiquette, for what Western sovereign or prince when visiting at an Eastern court would not be guilty of similar blunders?' Arminius happily enlightened his readers on the etiquette that made Naser al-Din's loud belch after dinner with the German emperor and empress 'an expression of gratitude for the hospitality received' and which was always so acknowledged. As for throwing his asparagus stumps over his shoulder onto the floor at Marlborough House, the prince of Wales had politely done the same, 'so as not to shame his guest', and all present had followed suit. Arminius also hastened to point out that these anecdotes 'must be grossly exaggerated, for Nasreddin Shah never neglected to make strict inquiry into the customs of the lands he visited, and more than once I have given him information upon minor details'.

In 1900, after Naser al-Din's assassination in 1896, Arminius met his son and successor, Mozaffar ad-Din, in Budapest during one of his own three European tours. (This was the same crown prince whose investiture he had witnessed in Tabriz in 1862.) The new shah, Arminius wrote, 'hardly remembered our meeting', but he had 'carefully read the memoirs of his father's travels' in which Arminius' 'small personality had received most laudatory mention'.[9] On Mozaffar's arrival in Budapest, he had, Arminius reported, looked round the assembled dignitaries and demanded '*Vambéry kudjast?*' ('Where is Vambéry?') Arminius wrote to Sir Thomas Sanderson at the Foreign Office to report his appointment as interpreter and to send what he believed to be a 'highly important communication' for Lord Salisbury's

---

of Islamic pilgrimage in the world. It was restored in 1885 and again more recently. Gul Baba himself was a Bektashi dervish.

9 Naser al-Din's journal of his 1873 travels were famously translated and published in English. The journals from his later tours are less easy to track down, so the veracity of this claim has not been checked.

attention. This communicated exactly what the Foreign Office almost certainly already knew through its ordinary diplomatic channels. On the shah's return to Budapest after a visit to the sultan in Constantinople, Arminius wrote that he anticipated seeing him again and would 'try, as far as possible to be informed about his doings in the Turkish metropolis'. 'In the meantime', he was pleased to say, 'I have acquired the same position at the Persian court' as he had in the past 'on the Bosporus'. He was, typically, fully convinced that:

> through this position of mine I can be of more service to England and to the cause of our civilisation than many official diplomatists whose eyes very rarely get beyond the surface, and who are too frequently the victims of Oriental deception and duplicity. My only desire is that my reports should meet with the due attention of his Lordship, for it is no easy work to get out something from Oriental statesmen.

There were two further letters from Arminius to Sanderson about the shah, the first, in October 1900, 'as promised', on his return from Constantinople. It described the discussions that had taken place over the possibility of greater unity and religious understanding between Sunni and Shia rulers. Arminius promised to 'watch it assiduously' for 'the whole movement is undoubtedly directed against Russia and England'. After noting Sir Henry Mortimer Durand's unsuccessful tenure as British minister in Tehran and deploring the experiment of 'filling this post with Anglo-Indian officers',[10] he apologised for being too prolix in his reports. As a last word, he added his recommendation that Dr Hugh Adcock, the shah's British physician, be given a KCB: 'he is continually rendering great services to his country and he really deserves the honour'.

Dr Adcock did receive his knighthood in the 1901 New Year's Honours. Lord Salisbury's reply to Arminius, interpreted through Sanderson's polite pen, was nicely tempered. He thanked Arminius for his interesting account and Sanderson forwarded a draft for £50 in acknowledgment of his services, adding that he thought the Hungarian government, which had appointed

---

10 Durand (1850–1924) is better known for the Durand Line, the border established in 1893 between British India and Afghanistan.

Arminius to the position of interpreter to the shah, 'might come to your assistance, and save you from being a loser by the appointment'. It was, he wrote, 'scarcely a matter on which I have the right to express an opinion'. Arminius wrote again to Sanderson in April 1901 to report on news from Tehran, received 'owing to my personal connections with the leading court official and ministers of the shah'. The 'news' was court and street gossip that would have been well known to any of the international ambassadors in Tehran, and thence to those in London and St Petersburg, but Arminius saw a threat – although he was pleased to approve the new British consul-general in Tehran. Of him, he wrote, 'I daresay he will be up to his position and if supported by the Foreign Office, he can still turn the tide in favour of England'. (The new appointee, Sir Arthur Hardinge, was a fellow Russo-phobe who became British minister in Tehran and, later, after the founding of the organisation in 1923, an early member of the British Fascists.)

After the Foreign Office letters to Arminius were released, an article in the *Guardian* in 2005 described Arminius as one of the Foreign Office's first foreign agents, long before MI6 was established.[11] Talk of his Foreign Office 'handlers' in that article exaggerated his importance. At the time Lord Salis-bury called Arminius an 'alarmist' who 'had done more harm than good', and it is doubtful, from the answers to his long reports, that lesser offi-cials such as Sanderson thought differently. As a cog in the Great Game, encouraged all those years before by Charles Alison to keep his eyes open during his youthful dervish travels, Arminius had potential. His report on little-travelled regions, first to Alison, then relayed on to Lord Palmerston, was of interest, notwithstanding the British dampening and discounting of his fear and horror of Russia. By this point, however, if there was hope that Arminius' conversations in Constantinople might produce occasional useful information and occasional requests be made of him, there is little in the Foreign Office letters beyond standard expressions of thanks. There is no sense that they mattered, but there is some that officials were nervous of possible misunderstandings caused by this loose cannon.

In the 2005 article, the chief historian for the FCO described Arminius as 'a sort of near Eastern pimp'. His surviving letters to the Foreign Office

---

11 Richard Norton-Taylor, 'From Dracula's nemesis to prototype foreign spy', *The Guardian* (2005), accessed online 2 Oct. 2023.

do not do much to mitigate that judgement. Stripped of their egocentric frills, the reports from his nine visits to Constantinople and his meetings with the sultan between June 1889 and May 1901 add their mite to the story of empires at the end of the nineteenth century, but to describe them as 'reports' is hardly accurate. They add character to a picture of the Ottoman court, naming and portraying the ministers, favourites, servants, and foreign emissaries who circled the sultan. They are, however, so coloured by Arminius' own prejudices, so overlaid with the jumbled gloss of his own beliefs and opinions, and so punctuated with bull-headed advice that they are closer to popular journalism than dispassionate intelligence.

And on two occasions, Arminius was the bluffer bluffed. In 1892, as the Great Game played out among the peaks of the high Pamirs (the mountain range between Central Asia and what is now Pakistan), Arminius saw an evil design in a Russian expedition in that inhospitable region. (The Foreign Office meanwhile saw 'a fair prospect of an Agreement for an international commission for surveying and ultimately fixing the boundary'.) Currie begged that Arminius should not 'write to the press in an alarmist sense', but unfortunately that cautionary letter arrived simultaneously with the publication of Arminius' latest letter to *The Times*.[12] It was, luckily, an onomastic masterpiece, from which only the most determined reader might have ascertained fears of renewed Russian attempts on India from the thicket of historical and contemporary names. Arminius felt the need to enlarge on the 'alarming tenor' of the published letter in his next to Currie and to add notice of a visit from one Gholam Singh. Singh, Arminius wrote, was 'a Russian emissary', whose task was 'to convince the world of the superiority of Russian rule', a 'native of Djellabad and knows well India and the whole Mohammedan world'. He was a 'fanatic to the excess' and 'made no secret' of his connections to the sultan, the emir of Afghanistan, and the sharif of Mecca.

The Foreign Office, however, already knew of 'Singh' as a consequence of its involvement with 'the curious case of an Englishwoman turned Mahommedan and married to an Indian swindler who seems to make a trade of marrying foolish Englishwomen'. The husband in question was 'neither Gholam Singh nor an Afghan but a Hindu oculist who has taken the

---

12 Of 11 September 1892.

name of his master... He seems to be one of the greatest blackguards alive'. He was in fact one Eliahie Bosche, who had a wife in Lahore, and who had arrived in Plymouth with his employer Gholam Singh. There, Bosche had embarked on a name change and series of bigamous matrimonial adventures with British women that had taken him from Plymouth to Newcastle and on to Quebec and Constantinople, and left one putative wife 'in a lunatic asylum at Exeter without hope of recovery'. Arminius had been fooled but seemed quite unaware of the fact, reporting that Bosche – now Bux – was still in Budapest and was 'one of the most dangerous scoundrels', a speaker of Persian and Dari who Arminius intended to keep an eye on. He was again reporting to Currie on his 'excellent' relationship with the sultan: 'not the slightest doubt that he pays full attention to my reports and advice'. In his memoirs Arminius details examples of the sultan's favour, the sultan's band learning the Hungarian national anthem in his honour, presents of straw-berries, 'from the plants reared by the hand of His Majesty', and 'a peach of extraordinary beauty'. 'Interesting', was the dry comment in a Foreign Office memo of this date, '...but does not lead to any practical result'.

After recovering from his broken leg in the autumn of 1893, Arminius had received another interesting visitor. Señor Ximenes was, he wrote to the long-suffering Currie, a Spaniard who had spent three years in Russia and had travelled all over Central Asia. He now intended, Arminius reported, to travel through the Broghil Pass to the Pamir Mountains to build the highest mete-orological observatory in the world. This, Arminius considered, was 'certainly fit to arouse suspicion, the much more as the said traveller is in hand and glove with the leading personnel in Transcaspia... in a word with everybody in Turkestan and in St Petersburg who has to do with Central Asian politics'. Ximenes, as the Foreign Office knew well, was no more than another impos-tor who had in fact never been further than Tashkent, but somehow Arminius continued to get a 'tip' for such information from London. Currie, who must have been remarkably soft-hearted as well as endlessly patient, wrote to the foreign secretary, now Lord Salisbury's successor, Lord Rosebery, about the 'habit of giving him £100-£150 a year'. 'If you should think to continue this subvention which he has earned by his former advocacy of English views', he would forward to Arminius '£100 in a sealed envelope in notes'. At the end of March 1894, Sir Philip Currie had become ambassador in Constantino-ple and Arminius was writing to Sir Thomas Sanderson about the Armenian question and to announce his intention to stay with the sultan for three weeks in April. He would, he said, 'have the opportunity to impress upon the sultan the requirements of our policy in the East', and find out whether he had been 'enticed by the Franco-Russian machinations on the Bosporus'. 'For', he wrote blithely, 'however clever Orientals are, their plots are mostly so childish and ill-hidden that they rarely escape detection'.

That August, Arminius was in England and spent a week with his fellow philologist Professor Max Müller in Oxford. Despite their differing views on the Hungarian language, the two were close friends. (It was Max Müller's British diplomat son, William Grenfell Max Muller, who, in 1914 would send confirmation of Arminius' death to the Foreign Office.) Arminius had been invited to join the committee in the geography section at the annual meeting of the British Association for the Advancement of Science; and at Müller's house he now met H. H. Godwin-Austen, the great Himalayan explorer, mountaineer, and ornithologist, who had discovered K2, and Charles Doughty, the explorer of the Arabian deserts. He attended a garden party at St John's College, where the hugely popular Ashton's Blue Hungarian Band played Hungarian dance music, which Arminius no doubt considered a personal tribute. Back in London and ensconced in the United Service Club, he wrote to Sanderson regarding the possibility of instructions from Prime Minister Lord Rosebery before his next visit to Constantinople.

The hoped-for interview with Rosebery failed to take place so Arminius applied, via Sanderson, to the foreign secretary, Lord Kimberley, 'to give me the promised assistance for my next journey to Constantinople'. 'Sir Philip Currie', he wrote, 'has offered me funds but I do not like to take them from anybody but the Foreign Office'. Sanderson sent the letter on to Rosebery, asking, 'Shall I give him £100 and tell him that Sir Philip Currie and the Foreign Office are identical?' And adding, 'I suppose I must see him'. Lord Rosebery replied to the memo in the usual red ink, 'I pity you, I have seen him', and the £100 was duly sent. It paid for a long report with suggestions on 'England's policy', on Arminius' return from a six-week stay in Constantinople. In his first reference to the Armenian question and 'the rumour of recent atrocities in Mush',[13] Arminius advised 'the more the Armenians

---

13 Muş in eastern Turkey was the site of one of the first massacres of the Armenian population by Ottoman soldiers and Kurdish irregulars at the beginning of what became known as the

are supported by Europe, the greater becomes the danger which threatens them… for the scattered and isolated condition of these Christians makes every effective defence totally illusory under the present circumstances'. He ended by pointing out that the 'false and exaggerated report' of the German traveller Eduard von Nolde on 'the nefarious doings of England in Arabia' had been well-received by the sultan and remarked, 'The amicable arrangement with Russia, alluded to by Lord Rosebery, seems to me a sheer impossibility and I question the temporary value of such an understanding'.

Arminius was generally thought to be closer to the sultan than any other European. He certainly believed this to be the case at a time when Abdul Hamid's absolutist monarchy was increasingly beleaguered by revolutionary forces at home, soon to formalise as the Young Turks, and by international horror at the massacres of Armenian Christians between 1894 and 1897. Probably as a result of these events, and perhaps as a result of the enmity toward all Europeans of the sultan's close advisor, the Syrian Ahmad Izzet Bey Pasha al-Abid, Arminius suffered an apparent fall from grace after his visit of April 1896. By then the sultan was suffering from chronic insomnia and a persecution mania so uncontrolled that he shot and killed a small child, the daughter of a slave, who he had found playing with one of his guns. He was given to roaming the palace at night with a revolver in his hand, and its other inhabitants were instructed to keep strictly to their rooms for their own safety. Only Izzet Bey, formerly keeper of the imperial wardrobe, seemed able to calm the sultan, by reading to him, if necessary, all night. Arminius wrote of warning Abdul Hamid about Izzet Bey. He described, possibly fictitiously, the sultan's answer. Rolling up his sleeve and catching a large flea, the sultan said, 'You see how fat and lazy it is? Full of my blood. A new one would be hungry and take more'. And he put the flea back and rolled down his sleeve. It was Izzet Bey who was quoted as saying 'The only way of eliminating the Armenian question is to eliminate the Armenians themselves'.

For all his anecdotes and caveats, his 'eastern' gibes, and the opprobrium that came to more and more isolate Abdul Hamid, Arminius stood sentinel in his camp for many years. If his defence of the sultan was less fierce and

---

Hamidian massacres (named after Sultan Abdul Hamid II), and which were followed by the Armenian genocide during World War I.

more calibrated than his championship of Edward VII, it was sustained to an extent that made Arminius an apologist for actions that were condemned across the world. He admitted that 'great injustice and shocking cruelties have been committed by Kurds against the laborious and sober Armenians', but 'no doubt the reports circulated by Armenian patriots in England are greatly exaggerated'. He supported this statement by claiming (wholly mendaciously) of the Armenian regions of Turkey to 'know the country and its inhabitants from many years' practical experience, having been perhaps the only European who lived as a native amongst them'.

In 1895, he had written of the 'so-called Armenian question', and been 'sorry to state that the Armenians have been too much petted and that the sympathies shown to them are far above the compassion undeservedly felt for rebels against the authority'. He accused *The Times* and other British papers of 'gross mendacity' ('never has public opinion been misled in such a horrible manner'). The sultan, he said, had drawn his attention to England's role in fanning 'the fire of racial and religious hatred in Asia', and Arminius wrote in the press of the 'disastrous consequences of which England alone will be made responsible' and 'which will be utilised by England's watchful rivals in the East' – that is, Russia.

Sanderson wrote back calmly, 'making all allowance for exaggeration the actual facts are quite sufficient to justify the feeling', and hoped that 'the massacres now taking place will cease' and 'some serious attempt at good government and the administration of equal justice be made'. He could not encourage Arminius' intention of coming to England to give a series of pro-Turkish lectures which 'could only have the opposite effect to that which is desired'. Still, he had his supporters: Sir Ellis Ashmead-Bartlett, another Sheffield MP, invoked Arminius' name in parliament and his view of the dangers of attacks against the sultan, pointing out 'the advantage of having at that capital a representative who understood how to use political influence with the Sultan and his government'. Ashmead-Bartlett also maintained that matters in regard to Tokat, a largely Armenian town which had recently been the site of a massacre of over 700 people, were 'greatly exaggerated' and that matters in Armenia had 'very much improved'. The *Guardian* reported 'ironical cheers' and shouts of 'Tokat' as Ashmead-Bartlett made this statement, followed by 'laughter' and 'renewed laughter'.

What was going on in Arminius' mind at this point? Was it the irresistible

lure of royalty? Unconditional admiration for the Turks, Turkey, Constantinople? Loyalty towards a ruler who had embraced Reshid Effendi in his
Turkish costume? Or a deep-seated conservatism, a cleaving to the status
quo, the addicted craving of the outsider's soul for acceptance – or simply
the maintenance of a mutually advantageous relationship? Who now knows?
Arminius was certainly no cheerleader for the reform epitomised by the
Young Turks. He thought them 'far from being organised' in their early
incarnation and continued to doubt their success as late as 1908, as the Young
Turk Revolution spearheaded the Second Constitutional Era in Turkey and
the loss of the sultan's absolute power. In his final years, he did admit that
the Young Turks had put Turkey 'on the path of progress' and driven out the
'terrible reign of Absolutism', and was in turn admired by the new regime
for his championing of Turkey (and perhaps for his disinterest in the fate of
the Armenians who were no better fit in their nationalistic narrative than
they had been to its imperial predecessor). He cautioned:

> If the Near East is to continue to be what it has been for the last three
> hundred years, the wrestling ground for the intrigues of the diplomatic
> West, if by continuous and useless interference disorder is caused in the
> still loose joints of the constitutional structure... then all our hopes for
> better things will end in delusion.

But by then, the wind had changed again, and Arminius was playing his
last role as omniscient sage and oracle.

He dated his final breach with Abdul Hamid to the publication of a
booklet, *La Turquie d'aujourd'hui et d'avant quarante ans* in Paris in 1898.
The booklet had been written by Arminius in answer to the duke of Argyll's
Our Responsibilities for Turkey: Facts and Memories of Forty Years (1896), which
argued the case for British responsibility for the Armenians and the reform
of the Ottoman Empire and government. The duke, a liberal amongst Liberals during his long political career, promoted making terms with Russia and
amongst all European countries to bring down Ottoman Turkey, which he
described as 'perhaps the best existing representative of the Kingdom of Evil
upon Earth', protected for so long as a strategic British ally against Russia in
the East. Now, he wrote, it should be recognised that 'Russia is there and she
is there to stay'. Whatever the failings of her government and policies, Russia

had to be seen as a civilising force and 'one of the providential agencies in the progress of the World'. She should be worked with to attain 'security for life, industry and religion... in one of the fairest regions of the World, which for more than half a century we have been helping to keep down under a barbaric despotism which we know to be vicious, and corrupt'. If Arminius would never describe the Ottoman Empire in such terms, both he and the duke, liberal and conservative, wore matching cloaks of moral imperialism – their division was over the agents of its implementation. Arminius believed, he wrote to Sanderson, that his criticism in his booklet of the sultan's 'absolutist tendencies' and 'anti-reformatory bias' might even have put him in personal danger on his visit to Constantinople in 1898. The visits continued nonetheless, in 1899, 1900, and, lastly, in April 1901, by which time Arminius had found another potential cause.

16

A Jewish Homeland

Arminius' relationship with the sultan gave him his final role on the international stage as part of another great twentieth-century drama – the founding of the state of Israel. As always with his involvement in any cause, there are question marks, in this case over the level of his commitment to the Zionist cause and of his influence on the events that eventually led to the Jewish state. The story reads, as Alder and Dalby describe it, like 'the scenario of a movie epic'. The vast cast included 'two emperors, two grand dukes, a pope, a sultan', and princes, kings, politicians, diplomats, great writers, the poet laureate,[1] scientists, financiers, and 'a host of anonymous and dedicated extras'.[2] If Arminius' dedication was questionable and his role more ephemeral than has sometimes been suggested, greater merit did accrue to his name in this arena than in many another. (His finances benefitted too.) The eminent Palestinian historian Walid Khalidi places Arminius at the heart of negotiations with the sultan for the Jewish settlement of Palestine, and regards him as co-author, with Theodor Herzl, of the draft Charter of the Jewish Ottoman Land Company of 1901–2.[3] The draft was extensive in its ambition. The Zionist Congress had only been established by Herzl in 1897, and Zionism was hardly a cohesive and organised movement, but Herzl had a plan. It took advantage of Abdul Hamid's need for money and the Ottoman Empire's invidious foreign debt

---

1 The undistinguished Alfred Austin (1835–1913), appointed poet laureate in 1896 after the hiatus following the death of Tennyson.
2 Alder and Dalby, op. cit., 367.
3 Walid Khalidi, 'The Jewish-Ottoman Land Company: Herzl's Blueprint for the Colonization of Palestine,' *Journal of Palestine Studies*, 22/2 (Winter 1993), 30–47.

---

and, with his network of supporters and interested parties, Herzl believed his scheme could succeed.

By the time he met Arminius in 1900, that plan was well-advanced in theory but not in fact. Like his compatriot, the famous Professor Vambéry, Herzl had suffered from the pervading anti-Semitism in Europe, most shockingly realised in the Dreyfus trial in Paris in 1894, which he had attended as a newspaper correspondent. That shattering indictment of Jewishness itself, framed as a trial for treason, had been the catalyst that set his path towards a 'Jewish State' – the title of his 1896 pamphlet and statement of intent for a Jewish homeland. Herzl certainly looked the part of the 'spiritual father of the Jewish state': a vigorously youthful Old Testament prophet and charismatic leader, with a great black beard and dark visionary stare, dressed in elegant conformity and wearing expensive patent-leather shoes to suit the grandeur of his regular interlocutors.

Herzl knew of Arminius through their mutual friend Max Nordau. Nordau had also been born in Budapest but had spent much of his working life in Paris, where the Dreyfus affair had likewise compelled him towards Zionism. He was co-founder with Herzl of the World Zionist Organisation and was another luxuriantly bearded prophet-type. Arminius had been approached two years earlier in support of the Zionist cause but had shown little interest, and Herzl at first had thought him too old for active involvement. When they did finally meet, Arminius had been re-living his own experience of anti-Semitism through the writing of *The Story of My Struggles,* and proved to be more than ready to bolster the hopes and dreams of his new Zionist friend.

It is hard to believe that his Jewishness had suddenly trumped his careful agnosticism, expedient Christian conversion, or his most favoured persona as the great academic standing above questions of class or creed, but Herzl and Vambéry in some ways were a match. They both enjoyed being centre stage, while in private (in Herzl's case, in the five volumes of his revelatory diaries)[4] were dismissive or denigratory of many of their fellow players. If Arminius looked down on the inhabitants of the East as exemplified by

---

4 Theodor Herzl, *The Complete Diaries of Theodor Herzl,* Vols. I–V, ed. by R. Patai, tr. by H. Zohn (London; New York, 1960). All quotations from Herzl's diaries and correspondence are drawn from these editions.

those of Central Asia in the 1860s, Herzl stands accused of entirely ignoring the existing inhabitants of Palestine on his only visit there in 1898. Even his allies garnered his adverse critical notice, with the most notable exception of the kaiser (Herzl was greatly impressed by his 'truly Imperial eyes'). He would write of Baron Edmond de Rothschild – one of the important proponents of Zionism and financial supporter of early settlements in Palestine – that 'his intellectual mediocrity is distressing, but he is a man who is truly good and devoted to me'. Like Arminius, he had a well-tended sense of his own value as compared with almost anyone else, on one occasion describing a group of Austrian diplomats as 'these idiots of whose existence not a soul will any longer have an idea when my name will still shine through the ages like a star'.

The first Zionist Congress, held in Basle, Switzerland in August 1897, had defined its aims in the simplest but most epic terms: to create a home in Palestine for the Jewish people. It was a task of monumental and reverberating difficulty. In 1897 'Egyptian Palestine' was a contentiously dislocated part of the Ottoman Empire and was under British occupation. The archetypal imperial administrator, Lord Cromer, consul-general of Egypt, encouraged the Egyptian government's rejection of Herzl's schemes, leading Herzl to describe him as 'the most disagreeable Englishman I have ever faced'. Then his 1902 plan to colonise the region round Al-Arish in the Sinai Peninsula, near but not in Palestine, was rejected on grounds of the difficulty of allocating Nile waters in sufficient quantities to support it. This was followed by an offer in 1903 from the then British colonial secretary, Joseph Chamberlain, of 8,000 square kilometres of what is now Kenya – also deemed unsuitable, after investigation by a Jewish delegation. Another plan for settlement in Argentina had longer purchase and Mesopotamia was also considered. All these, however, were stopgaps. Nowhere could compare with Palestine, the land whose restoration to the Jews had also always been supported by Christian Restorationists as a pre-requisite for the Second Coming. And Palestine hinged on the sultan, who had not regarded Herzl's 1896 pamphlet with favour, telling Herzl's brilliant diplomatic advisor, the Polish count Philipp Michael de Newlinski, that 'he could never give up Jerusalem and that the Mosque of Omar [the only mosque in the old city of Bethlehem] must always be in the hands of Islam'.

Newlinski had been a young diplomat in Constantinople in the 1870s and had built up a network of contacts that took him into the presence and the favour of the sultan. After he left Turkey in 1880, he had worked as a journalist, and built up a matching European network worthy of even Arminius' envy. It enabled him to invoke friends from among fifteen cardinals, the pope, and the kaiser to Ferdinand of Bulgaria and King Milan of Serbia on Herzl's behalf. Herzl's plan, unadorned, was to barter Palestine from the sultan in exchange for buying off the Turkish debt with Jewish money. For that he needed the sort of personal access to the sultan that could bypass endless complicated and expensive negotiations. But the Turkish government understood this game far too well for the idealistic Zionists, at one stage contemplating the exchange of 70,000 square kilometres of Palestine for a 40-million-franc loan and the railway concession from the Mediterranean to the Persian Gulf. Herzl travelled to Constantinople with Newlinski in 1896 but all Newlinski's efforts could not gain an imperial audience for him. His meetings with the sultan's gatekeepers, high court officials such as the grand vizier Halil Rifat Pasha, resulted in little more than offers of empty promises in exchange for hard cash. Herzl's status was only saved in the eyes of his important international supporters by Newlinski's success in extracting tangible recognition for him from the sultan, when Herzl found himself awarded the Commanders Cross of the Medjidieh Order, yet even then the insignia was delivered unceremoniously in its box to his hotel room.

The sultan, in Herzl's view, was saving face in front of his courtiers, refusing to entertain him while privately offering conditions through Newlinski that included a loan of roughly £2 million and positive publicity for his Armenian policy. Herzl had seen the sultan as he drove past on his way to Friday prayers and described him as 'a shrivelled sickly man', but this was mild in comparison with the language he and Arminius would later use to describe him in their correspondence, and Herzl's own comparison of the Ottoman court – this 'anonymous band of bums' – to 'a tangle of venomous snakes. The weakest, sickest, and least noxious snake wears a little crown. But this army of snakes has such a peculiar structure that it looks as though its crowned head were the one that bit and poisoned everything'. Abdul Hamid himself he further described as 'this sultan of the declining robber empire' with 'the hooked nose of a Punchinello, the long yellow teeth with a big gap on the upper right. The fez pulled low over his probably bald head; the prominent ears "serving as pants-protector," as I used to say about such fez-wearers to my friends' amusement – that is, to keep the fez from slipping down onto the pants'.

In 1898, Herzl travelled to Jerusalem, arranging his journey to coincide with a visit by the kaiser. In his audience with that emperor, Herzl was 'fairly bewitched' by the 'remarkable, bold, inquisitive soul' he beheld and of whom he successfully requested intercession with the sultan in the Zionist cause. The kaiser fulfilled his promise, but his words fell on stony ground in the Yildiz Palace, and the dream of Palestine moved no further forward. Then Newlinski, on another path-smoothing, sultan-schmoozing visit to Constantinople in 1899, dropped dead of a heart attack. The avenue to Abdul Hamid narrowed and the Sublime Porte was obdurate in its public refusal to discuss Palestine, even if its officials continued to maintain their potentially lucrative contact with Herzl. The account in Herzl's diary of a conversation with the Ottoman diplomat Nouri Bey in 1900, shortly before he met Arminius, is just one example of the tone of the negotiations.[5]

Yesterday evening Nouri Bey came to see me. We dined in the salon adjoining my room... Nouri has an unpleasant rogue's face. The conversation at table was downright uncomfortable at first. I dragged it along over indifferent matters. Newlinski served as our *entree en matiere* [entry to the subject]. Nouri passed the hardest judgment on him, at first in guarded words. '*Appelons le le défunt* [Let us call him the deceased].' Newlinski,

---

5 Nouri Bey (1859–1937), who Herzl called 'a Viking in a frock coat', had a backstory to rival Arminius. Perhaps he had read the *Travels*. He was the illegitimate son of a Mälmo burgher, adopted by a tailor called Noring who married his mother and whose name he took. He had gone to Turkey aged nineteen and been employed as a tutor in high Ottoman circles; become involved in the Ottoman national library project; had access to the sultan's library; and set up as a businessman with ties to Bethel Henry Strousberg, the 'Railway King'. He had attempted to raise money in Sweden for the construction of the Baghdad railway, had converted to Islam, joined the Ottoman Ministry of Foreign Affairs in 1884, married an Ottoman princess, and was appointed Turkish consul-general in Rotterdam with the mission of spying on the Young Turks in Europe. Instead, he was won over to their cause, editing the satirical newspaper *Davul*, of which the sultan was a target. In 1901 he was charged and found guilty in Constantinople *in absentia* of high treason and sentenced to 101 years in prison. Thereafter, supported by his wife, who gave lectures on life in the harem, he roved Europe as a sort of professional enemy of the sultan. After the Young Turk revolution, he returned to Turkey and disappeared from the pages of history. See Barbara Flemming, *Essays on Turkish Literature and History* (Leiden, 2017), 190–202.

he said, had cheated me, had never brought my proposals to the attention of those in authority, but, on the contrary, had offered to spy on us. Mahmud Nedim had gone along with Newlinski in everything, *parce qu'il couchait avec sa femme* [because he slept with his wife].

The conversation grew more unguarded. Nouri said: '*Tranchons le mot, c'etait une sale canaille ce Newlinski* [Let's not mince words: this Newlinski was scum].'

… When Nouri saw that I was hesitating and beating about the bush, he made things easy for me and spoke openly, frankly, and cynically. 'There are people who want to make a buck. I'll get together a syndicate for you that will do the job at Yildiz. The Porte doesn't count at all. This man must get so much, that one so much. I'm on good terms with them all, because I always treat everyone correctly. Izzet Bey, for example, who is now out of favour, gets the same amicable treatment from me as before. I give him the same presents, etc. The man is too intelligent not to get back into favour again. Then he will be grateful to me for it.'

On 24 May 1900, Herzl noted a 'rather important alarm' – the newspapers had reported that Arminius was about to visit the sultan, and Herzl sent his long-time supporter and emissary, the Restorationist Anglican clergyman William Hechler (1845–1931), to enlist his assistance. In fact, Arminius had already left for Constantinople, where messages were sent to him immediately. Herzl's hopes were unaccountably raised that 'Schlesinger' (Arminius' codename) would somehow win over Abdul Hamid. 'Now I am waiting on tenterhooks. Could it be that we are close to the *dénouement*?' On the other hand, he dared not hope too much. 'Or shall we hear a categorical No from Yildiz?' The report came that 'Schlesinger' had received the latter answer. Whether it was a 'No' to the whole Palestine question or a 'No' to a meeting with Herzl was unclear. When Hechler went to visit Arminius on 17 June, back in Mühlbach, he reported that Arminius had never raised the matter with the sultan at all, at which Herzl immediately set off from Vienna to meet his new envoy for himself: 'Fourteen hours by fast train – and now, after a stay of only five hours, I am on my way back'. But he was seduced. He had been given the full Vambéry performance:

I have met one of the most interesting men in this limping, 70-year-old Hungarian Jew who doesn't know whether he is more Turk than Englishman, writes books in German, speaks twelve languages with equal mastery, and has professed five religions, in two of which he has served as a priest. With an intimate knowledge of so many religions he naturally had to become an atheist. He told me 1001 tales of the Orient, of his intimacy with the sultan, etc. He immediately trusted me completely and told me, under oath of secrecy, that he was a secret agent of Turkey and of England. The professorship in Hungary was merely window-dressing, after the long torment he had suffered in a society hostile to Jews. He showed me a lot of secret documents – though in the Turkish language, which I cannot read but only admire. Among them, handwritten notes by the sultan. Hechler he immediately dismissed brusquely: he wanted to be alone with me. He began: 'I don't want any money; I am a rich man. I can't eat gold beefsteaks. I've got a quarter of a million, and I can't spend half the interest I get. If I help you, it's for the sake of the cause.'

Arminius asked for every detail of Herzl's plan and told him that the sultan had sent for him to ask for his help in propagating better publicity for himself and his policies in the European press. He wondered if Herzl could help? Herzl 'gave an evasive answer'. Throughout the conversation Arminius 'kept getting back to the memorable events in his life which were indeed great'. It was through Disraeli, Arminius told him, that he had 'become an agent of England. In Turkey he began as a singer in coffee-houses; a year and a half later he was the Grand Vizier's confidant'. He could, Arminius told Herzl, stay at the Yildiz Palace any time and he ate from the same bowl as the sultan but 'he cannot get the idea of poison out of his mind. And a hundred other things, equally picturesque'. Herzl asked to call him 'Vambéry *bácsi*' ('little uncle') and asked him to write to the sultan to beg that Herzl should be received in exchange for 'a service in the newspaper world'. The meeting ended without a decision being made as to the next step and back on the train, again as recorded in his diaries, Herzl drafted a letter to Arminius:

Dear Uncle Vambéry,

The Hungarian word is good: *zsiddember* [a Jewish man]. You are one, so am I. That is why we understood each other so quickly and fully, perhaps even more on a human than on a Jewish plane, although the Jewish element is strong enough in both of us. Help me – no, us! Write the S. [Cohn – the sultan's codename] that he should send for me, 1) because I can help him with public opinion, 2) because my coming will improve his financial credit, even if he does not immediately accept my propositions. We can go into the details after the Congress, provided you come along and act as interpreter... you will do our cause a tremendous service if you obtain an audience for me now.

I understand what you intend to erect with your autobiography: a royal sepulchre. Crown your pyramid with the chapter: How I Helped Prepare the Homecoming of My People the Jews.

The whole of your memorable life will appear as if it had been planned that way.

Arminius replied that 'the business with the *mamzer ben nide*' ('the foully conceived bastard'), the sultan, could not be managed in writing, to which Herzl returned:

That doesn't sound comforting. You too are saying *yavash* [take it easy] like a born Turk. But I have no time to lose. There certainly is no need for your *mamzer* [bastard] to know that the matter is comparatively new to you. I think that 'after long thought and mature consideration' you could recommend this expedient and remedy to him as the best. You surely don't need to account to him for the number of *chibouks* [Turkish cigarettes] you have smoked and how many thousands of cups of coffee you have drunk in pondering this matter.

Your first word to me was that you were no *wonz-melammed* [imbecile of a teacher]. I really do look upon you as a man of action, as a man of my race which I believe capable of any amount of energy.

Disraeli once said to a young Jew: 'You and I belong to a race who can do everything but fail.'

My dear Vambéry *bácsi* we can do really everything, but we must be willing. Be willing, Vambéry *bácsi*!

From the way you have described your relationship with him I don't see why you shouldn't write Cohn and say: 'See here, send for that man.

He'll put an end to your *shlemazeln* [misfortunes]. Listen to him, take a look at him, and you can always throw him out afterwards.'

Herzl was desperate, and had persuaded himself that Arminius was the 'Open Sesame' who would get him past all the barriers to the sultan's inner chamber. He continued to appeal to the man he hoped Arminius was:

I would urgently request you to intervene with Cohn in whatever way you consider suitable, as quickly as you can, by telegram, if at all possible, and to tell him that what comes to him in this form is something highly useful to him.

Make him understand particularly that he will play a beautiful role if he takes in the homeless Jews. He will stand there as the benefactor of mankind, a generous man – and his benefaction will immediately bear interest and capital for him. Jewry all over the world will celebrate him. A *revirement* [sudden change] in the public opinion of the entire world! And at the same time he will have the gratitude of the other nations, those whom he has spared an influx of Jews. Surely all this is clear and true.

Herzl also wrote to Nouri Bey about his new approach to the sultan:

Our best-intentioned friends perhaps do not dare to come forward, though it is a matter of H.M.'s supreme benefit.

To fill in this gap I have tried to find something else and to make the request for an audience come from another quarter. At this moment I do not know whether that will be successful.

In August, the fourth Zionist Congress had taken place in London. Herzl believed it had been a great success and Arminius had sent him a 'reassuring letter', although by the time the two men met in Vienna in mid-September, Herzl was exhausted and beginning to have doubts about the efficacy of his *bácsi*. Arminius told him the same stories about himself all over again and assured him on his honour that the sultan would receive him by the following May. It seems suddenly to have dawned on Herzl that Arminius was making impossible promises 'about something that doesn't depend on himself'. By 1 October he was wondering if the whole matter had not 'fallen asleep again with him'. Requests from Nouri and other Turkish envoys for money continued to arrive and, without much real hope, he bargained over figures and timing and tried to raise huge sums of money as his cashbox 'hit rock bottom'. He still clung to the idea that if Arminius went to Constantinople 'the chances for our project would be favourable'. On 30 November reports came from Nouri Bey's fixer in Constantinople, Edouard Crespi, that Arminius had recommended Herzl's proposals to the sultan. The grand vizier, the first secretary, the minister of finance, and Izzet Bey were all thought to be in favour but now Herzl had to turn up in possession of the expected 'loan'. Crespi duly arrived in Vienna, on 3 December, to advise him on his best approach, in advance of the expected telegraphed summons from the sultan. Herzl described Crespi as a 'skinny, wax-yellow, black-bearded Levantine' with the appearance of 'a second or third-rate diplomat' but 'he calls a spade a spade, and speaks frankly about the people in power in Constantinople'. Crespi also supported Arminius' actions, which had 'done a tremendous amount of good', and said that his presence in Constantinople would 'be an enormous advantage' because he had 'access to the sultan at any time'. But the telegram failed to arrive and Herzl began to wonder if Crespi was no more after all than 'a Levantine braggart', who had come mainly to collect his 1,000 francs 'travel money' and to lobby for 'a lump sum for expenses and the like'.

In his diary, Herzl alternately writes of the negotiations using only the codenames or numbers given to the individuals involved, or forgets to use such subterfuge entirely in frank updates on progress – or rather the lack of it. Arminius' codename of 'Schlesinger', for example, was rarely used as their relationship continued and Herzl began to get better at recognising hollow promises. At this stage, he simply did not know who to trust. The Turkish position remained officially unchanged; meanwhile the Turkish ambassador in Berlin, Ahmed Tewfik, a relatively reliable official source, reiterated fears over Palestine to David Wolffsohn, Herzl's close associate and his successor as president of the Zionist Congress. The Turks, Tewfik said, would be happy to see Jewish immigration anywhere in Turkey except Palestine in case formal settlement was a precursor to an endeavour to declare an independent nation, as had happened in the Balkan states. Wolffsohn had replied that, if the Jews had been settled in the Balkans, they would still be Turkish because while the Balkan states had been able to break away with the aid of the great powers, the Jews had no other friends in the world other than the Turks. Unofficially, the horse-trading went on, with Crespi busy in Constantinople, pushing for confirmation to be sent to Izzet Bey by mid-December of an initial loan of £700,000, as this might be used as a bargaining chip for additional loans from other banks and consortiums jostling for access to Turkey. The grand vizier, said Crespi, would like to conclude a loan of £2–3 million.

Herzl wrote to Arminius on 19 December asking him to write the letter of endorsement that had been requested by Izzet Bey before he broached the subject with the sultan. He was looking forward to travelling with Arminius to Constantinople for face-to-face negotiations with that important official and, he anticipated, with the sultan himself. He hoped 'the journey in wintertime will not deter you'. Arminius wrote back with his own terms: a £5,000 commission if the deal was made on the £700,000, and a letter in confirmation. Herzl took this demand well. He must by now have been focused on the fact that the greater good was up for auction. He told Arminius that he had stipulated 'honoraria' for those 'outside our movement' who had 'a legitimate claim to material gratitude', and remarked that he had constantly used Arminius' name in the negotiations to legitimise his claim for commission. At the same time, Herzl reminded him that his 'true mission' was to 'help your old people with its self-redemption'. 'I regard you and your connections as a historic opportunity of the Jewish people', he wrote and requested therefore that Arminius should 'for goodness' sake write him this letter today rather than tomorrow'. By 28 December, the letter had been sent to the grand vizier and Arminius was in Constantinople alone. On 31 December Herzl wrote to him with what was essentially a prescription for blackmail: 'What I have in mind is that you immediately direct to Cohn a friendly warning in something like the following vein, though in your own words which will be more clever and more Turkish than mine'.

Arminius should, Herzl suggested, point out the assistance 'Cohn' had received from him personally and from the Zionists in general over recent years. Herzl had sent five doctors, at his own expense, to the theatre of the Greco-Turkish War of 1897, 'had your praises sung in his newspapers', and 'defended and propagandised for you'. The offer of the loan of £700,000, 'on terms far more favourable than the market ones', had been repaid with 'a slap in the face from a semi-official news agency', announcing the prohibition of the 'Israelites from entering Palestine, because the Zionist movement wants to set up the Kingdom of Judea. This is an absurdity. All the Zionists want to do is to settle the country of Palestine under your sovereignty, with peaceful workmen who are too unhappy elsewhere'. Now, 'since the Jews have nothing to hope for from you, you no longer have anything to expect from them…' More than that, Herzl threatened, he would induce 'his most powerful financier friends… to grant you no more loans when you most urgently need them'. Unless, he said, the sultan sent for Herzl immediately, he would 'make incalculable trouble for him'.

Herzl also warned Arminius, 'Don't you believe, my good *bácsi*, that this is only a trick. If I have no invitation from Cohn by January 15th, I shall carry out what I have said above. This is my decision'. On 4 January 1901 Arminius reported delivery of Herzl's message to the sultan with doubts as to its effect. Meanwhile emollient messages came from Crespi in Constantinople, regarding favourable Turkish intentions towards the Zionists, that were promptly belied by German newspaper reports of Turkish feelings of 'the utmost violence against the movement'. On 18 January Herzl wrote to Arminius to tell him that the deadline for 'this small loan' – the £700,000 – had passed. He was somewhat embarrassed in front of his financiers but an eleventh-hour demand from the sultan's various agents in Constantinople for much higher *baksheesh* on the deal had been the final straw.

That was not, however, the end of things. There were other 'different and larger' financiers in the wings, ready to manage 'our great project'. Nevertheless, by March, supported as he was by the great, the good, and the extremely rich across Europe, Herzl's plan for Palestine was foundering on Turkish obduracy. In his diary he wrote 'I am now industriously working on *Altneueland*.[6] My hopes for practical success have disintegrated. My life is no novel now. So the novel is my life'. But the melodramatic moment passed and the parley continued. In April, Arminius went to Constantinople again with 1,000 gulden, travelling expenses supplied by Herzl after a loan from Viennese supporters. Herzl was not optimistic: Crespi had continued to make bold promises from Constantinople and now hinted at double-dealing on Arminius' behalf,[7] even as he played the part of the old man's secretary or

---

6 *The Old New Land*, Herzl's Utopian novel, published in 1902.
7 Reading Herzl's puzzled account of the opaque messages coming both from Crespi and from

messenger. Arminius was in Constantinople for three weeks, returning on 8 May to Budapest to be met from the train, which was an hour late, by Herzl, Rustem, and Rustem's wife, Olga: 'With a volley of oaths, this grand old man of 70 stepped from the train. The train shed resounded with his thunderous voice because no porter was at hand'.[8] Rustem and Herzl carried his baggage to Herzl's carriage and, when the younger Vambérys had departed, Arminius delivered his news. The sultan was ready to receive Herzl. But this good news was hedged with perplexing conditions. The sultan, Arminius said, was 'plumb crazy and a robber'. Herzl must not speak to him of Zionism, 'that is a phantasmagoria, Jerusalem is as holy to these people as Mecca', although 'Zionism is good nevertheless – against Christendom'. 'You must', Arminius said, 'gain time and keep Zionism alive somehow'. When Herzl asked if the sultan had made any remarks about him, Arminius claimed, 'he doesn't even know your name'. (Later Herzl would wonder how that statement squared with earlier comments from the sultan on the Basle conferences and himself and his refusal to see the Zionist leader, but at the time Arminius the storyteller still had him in thrall.) On 10 May Herzl began his diary entry 'On the Orient Express. Somewhere in Serbia'. He was on his way to see the sultan at last. The day before, he had broken his journey from Vienna to get last-minute instructions from Arminius in Budapest. The meeting had been difficult. Arminius had been 'less friendly' than usual and had completely lost his temper when the conversation had turned to the question of promised shares of the commission to the Turkish fixers such as Nouri Bey, officials at the Yildiz Palace, and Crespi. 'He was furious. For three weeks he had toiled and slaved, and now others were to reap the fruits.'

Two days later, Arminius was painting an alternative narrative of his three weeks in Constantinople to Sir Thomas Sanderson: the sultan's present 'implacable hatred' of England, the deterioration in the country generally, current palace politics, and a hundred other matters; but he included not one word about Zionist hopes, of which Sanderson would have been generally aware, or of his own role in that imbroglio. He mentioned Herzl only

---

Arminius regarding the situation in Constantinople, it is hard not to imagine the two were working together to reap the greatest possible rewards from the situation.

8 Others had remarked on Arminius' voice: 'like a foghorn'. See Alder and Dalby, op. cit., 380.

once in his own English writings, when describing the meeting with the sultan in which he had introduced the Zionist leader, a flat contradiction of his assertion to the latter that the sultan did not know his name. He had, he wrote, 'to use all kinds of pretexts to disarm the sultan's apprehension. He was fond of the Jews,[9] he knew that Jewish colonisation in Palestine would serve as a counterpoise against the steadily intruding inimical Christians and would strengthen his rule in Syria'. 'But', Arminius wrote, 'it nevertheless cost me days and days of persuasion ... and when he ultimately acceded to my wish and agreed to receive Dr. Herzl, he did so under the condition that I must leave Constantinople at once... Now I am quite at a loss to discover the reason of his command and I shall probably never know it'.

Was Arminius justifying not being present when Herzl met the sultan so that he could not be blamed if things went wrong? Might he then turn any failure to his advantage against his rivals? Was he simply no longer welcome or, as he had implied to Sanderson in 1898, safe in Constantinople? That assertion seems doubtful given his continuing visits after that date, but perhaps by 1901 he had indeed finally blotted his copybook irredeemably with the sultan or his court. Much later, in 1907, he reported the Turkish hand of friendship was extended to him once again but no further visit ever took place. Herzl was naïve in his dealings with Arminius but Arminius must have seemed to provide a more comprehensible route into the Yildiz Palace than Crespi, Nouri Bey, and all the other opportunistic obstacles in officialdom. And Herzl was careful always to remind his *bácsi* of the great cause in which he was engaged. In his own case, the exhausting campaign had almost buried the original spirit of his dream, and it finally killed him. After Herzl's unexpected death in 1904, Arminius went quiet on the subject of a Jewish homeland, although he stayed in touch with David Wolffsohn, advising him on the bribery of relevant Ottoman officials and, in the absence of the fabled charter for Palestine, to accept lesser concessions. This compromise was rejected by Wolffsohn. In August 1907, however, as the eighth Zionist Congress took place in The Hague and another visit to

---

9 This was true. The Jews in Turkish imperial service were generally staunchly opposed to Herzl's Jewish State, which they saw as a threat to their comfortable and secure lives in Constantinople. He could look for little support in their direction and was aware of the Turkish Chief Rabbi's enmity.

Constantinople was mooted, Arminius was suddenly much in evidence in the German and American Jewish press.

In December 1906 he had assured Charles Hardinge, then permanent under-secretary at the Foreign Office, that he would 'not visit the capital as long as sultan Abdul Hamid is alive', but in March 1907, he wrote again to report a despatch from Abdul Hamid. The sultan, he said, wished to 'acquaint me of some important plans of his'.[10] To Wolffsohn he wrote, 'it may be that there is an opening for a new dialogue. It is possible that the prospects are better than in Herzl's time'.[11] Wolffsohn believed the invitation was due to his own visit to Constantinople earlier in the year, but Arminius was certain that, once again, Turkish financial troubles had pushed the sultan to revisit a potential source of funds, and Arminius was easing himself into a final role as champion of his Jewish brethren, if not precisely of the Zionist dream. An interview from the Viennese *Neue National-Zeitung*, with 'The famous Orientalist, Professor Vambéry', was quoted in full in the *Jewish Outlook* of Denver, Colorado. In it, Arminius 'emphatically denied that he had been baptised … On the contrary, he declared that it was his greatest pride to be a Jew and to belong to the people which was the embodiment of everything that was noble, humane and elevated'.

Another interview by the *Brooklyn Eagle* was syndicated to the *American Israelite* on 29 August 1907. 'One of the most talented Jews of his time, who has played an important part in the very inception of the new political Zionism' and who was a 'friend and advisor to the sultan', was able to report that the sultan was 'a great friend of the Jews but his love for them is not un-influenced by his own interests'. As for mass Jewish immigration into Palestine, the professor could not encourage it at present, mainly on grounds of lack of security against marauding Bedouins. Instead, he said, 'we must have patience and wait for a favorable moment', and 'so long as my influence will stand for weight with the sultan, I am myself ready to defend before him the Zionist movement'.

On 13 May 1901 Herzl, in company with Wolffsohn, was back in the Hotel Royal in Constantinople, where he had last stayed with Newlinski, and was waiting once again on the sultan's pleasure. Crespi had turned up as

---

10 Kuneralp, op. cit., 94.
11 Alder and Dalby, op. cit., 387.

well, a cringingly scheming Uriah Heep, nervous of securing his payment as the hotel manager spread rumours of the double-dealing that had caused Arminius to throw the man out and another, a swindled Frenchman, to slap his face. Herzl magnanimously concluded that it was cheaper to keep Crespi on the payroll than to have him as an enemy. His guide to Constantinople on this occasion was a Dr Wellisch, another Hungarian Jew turned Turkish official, who had been recommended by Arminius and was presumably sympathetic to the Zionist cause. After an abortive first visit to the palace, they went sightseeing and then they waited, and waited, for a summons to the sultan. It came on Friday 17 May, when they attended the Friday *selamlik* and Herzl, on his own, penetrated the inner chamber to meet Abdul Hamid. The sultan behaved with considerable grace, telling Herzl courteously that he was a regular reader of his newspaper, *Neue Freie Presse*, although, as Herzl knew, he did not speak German. He spoke of the friendly relations between Turkey and Austria and 'rejoiced to hear that the Emperor Franz Joseph was well', and more of the same.

Herzl stuck to the script prescribed by Arminius and carefully avoided mention of Zionism. Instead, he garlanded Abdul Hamid with the gratefulness of the Jewish people for their good treatment at his hands and 'lamented the injustices we experience throughout the world'. When the sultan replied 'I am and always have been a friend of the Jews', Herzl came indirectly to the point. When Professor Vambéry, he said, had informed him that His Majesty would receive him, he had thought of the story of Androcles and the lion. Might, he wondered, his Majesty be the lion, 'and perhaps I am Androcles, and maybe there is a thorn to be pulled out?' Asking if he could speak plainly, Herzl named that thorn as the public debt and his belief that he could remove it so that 'Turkey would be able to unfold afresh its vitality, in which I have faith'. For two hours, as the court interpreter translated, the sultan and the petitioner built and shared in their castles in the air and Herzl concluded 'I had spun the threads the way I wanted'. If Herzl was brought back to earth by the thicket of outstretched hands awaiting *baksheesh* as he left the palace and by Crespi's reappearance on his arrival at the hotel, he was 'calm as always, in success'.

The success was short-lived. There followed several days' worth of efforts to gain a second audience with the sultan, endlessly frustrated by court officials at his design. A yellow diamond set in a stick-pin arrived for Herzl as a token of friendship and by 21 May he was on his way back to Vienna, bearing only an impression of the sultan as 'a weak, cowardly but thoroughly good-natured man... in whose name a rapacious, infamous, seedy camarilla perpetrates the vilest abominations'. On 29 May he met Arminius who characteristically declared his achievements 'tremendous', and believed 'we shall have the Charter this very year'. He suggested that Herzl should draw up a draft which he would submit to the sultan in secrecy for his signature and for which Herzl promised him '300,000 guilders and a eulogy in world history'.

Arminius went to London in June and Herzl waited. But by August, to his surprise, in his correspondence with Herzl, his *bácsi* was preaching revolution in the Porte and the overthrow of Izzet Bey, with himself as replacement secretary or perhaps even the overthrow of Abdul Hamid. A few days later Arminius undermined both men further in a letter to Sanderson. The byzantine backstory to all this lay in the murky waters of Ottoman rivalries and enmities, exacerbated by fluctuating foreign agency in the end days of empires, and is now lost to view. Herzl stuck to the matter in hand, the charter, and looked forward to good news from Arminius on his expected visit to the Yildiz Palace, but that visit never happened. He continued to ask Arminius' advice and, with remarkable loyalty, to report events to the old man. As he found himself heading down one dead end after another in the international labyrinth that surrounded the dream of a Jewish state, Arminius was only one among many who made promises to him and then broke them. It is hard to see, as Alder and Dalby asserted, that Arminius' efforts 'paved the way'[12] towards the establishment of that state with the Balfour Declaration, four years after the man's death. Whatever his real intentions, in their implementation he did little more than join the crowd muddying the waters for their own ends.

---

12 Ibid., 388.

17

The British Pensioner

Arminius' physical absence from Constantinople after 1901 did not stop him communicating with Sanderson in London every snippet of information he could glean from his sources there, in Budapest, and elsewhere, about the situation in Turkey. His letters were full of advice about Turkey and Britain in relation to Russia, France, and Hungary, and his growing suspicion of the kaiser's relationship with the sultan but, as always, Russia headed his list of enemies. In October 1896, shortly after the successful visit of the new Tsar Nicholas II to Britain, 'Professor Vambéry's Opinion' on the Armenian question had appeared in *The Aberdeen Journal.* The prime minister, Lord Salisbury, was then feeling his way towards the more harmonious relationship with Russia that would eventually evolve into entente. More immediately, in concert with public opinion over the Armenian massacres, Salisbury believed Russia might be party to efforts to force reform on the sultan. Arminius' opinion strongly condemned 'the attacks made by Englishmen upon the sultan', blamed the situation in Armenia on British 'intermeddling', and was highly sceptical of any Anglo-Russian agreement. There was, he said, 'no likelihood of abatement' of the rivalry between Britain and Russia in the East. He was wrong and he was appalled by the rapprochement between the two countries, formalised in 1907. He wrote to Hardinge, 'You will be astonished that I withhold my opinion about the Anglo-Russian convention. Well, I do not like it at all. You have paid too high a price for a temporary peace, for such it is, and the humiliation undergone will not enhance British prestige in Asia'.[1]

---

1 Foreign Office correspondence quoted in this chapter is drawn from Alder and Dalby, op. cit., and material from the National Archives.

It is remarkable that the well-mannered veneer of the Foreign Office did not crack more obviously than it did as the opinions of the 'Orientalist and Asiatic explorer, so well-known in England' were disseminated in newspapers across the world. Internal memos attached to Arminius' correspondence give a clearer picture of the official view, but there is only one letter to him, from Charles Hardinge in January 1909, when boredom or irritation give way to fury. Arminius, now in his late seventies, had swum in deep waters at a time when the endless quadrille of the European powers that had brought Russia, France, and Britain together in the Triple Entente remained fragile, and German power was on the rise in alliance with Austria-Hungary. The unscrupulous machinations of the German–Hungarian foreign minister of Austria-Hungary, Baron Alois Lexa von Aehrenthal (1854–1912), further threatened that Anglo-Russian alliance. In 1908 Aehrenthal annexed Bosnia-Herzegovina from its Turkish suzerain as a diamond jubilee present for his emperor, Franz Joseph, of whom he was a favourite. Almost simultaneously, the ruling prince of Bulgaria, 'Foxy' Ferdinand of Saxe-Coburg Gotha, declared independence for Bulgaria from Turkey.[2] As Aehrenthal attempted to make side deals with the Russian foreign minister Alexander Izvolsky, Europe teetered. Knowing of Arminius' relationship with Edward VII and believing in his influence in Britain, Aehrenthal now attempted to co-opt Arminius, 'with the intention to use my pen in the interests of assuaging the anti-Austrian feeling in England'.

Arminius wrote to Hardinge in November 1908 to report a conversation with Aehrenthal. The baron had flattered him by asking his advice and had expressed astonishment regarding 'the vehemently inimical language' of the British press against its old ally, Austria-Hungary. He had mined Arminius for information and beguiled him with his 'frank and open language'. Arminius had been so far emboldened, in the report of the meeting sent to Hardinge, to mutter about divided loyalties, 'fraught with moral dangers' and (predictably) likely to entail 'serious material losses' to himself. In the same letter, he had also advised caution with regard to the Young Turks, whose revolt that summer would eventually result in the reinstatement of the constitution in

---

2 Arminius had met the prince in Sofia en route from Budapest to Constantinople in 1900 and had then carried the prince's oath of feudal fidelity to the sultan. The prince was already planning the independence of Bulgaria.

Turkey with the sultan as a constitutional monarch. Aehrenthal knew of or believed Arminius' own estimation of his position in Britain and his relationship with the king. He must have expected the old man's refusal formally to brief on behalf of Austria-Hungary. Arminius would have risked his relatively steady Foreign Office income and undermined the position he held in his own and in popular, if not official, estimation, as an orchestrator of international relations and an expert on events in the regions on which he had built his reputation. Whatever the baron understood of this self-appointed role, he succeeded in encouraging Arminius' public engagement with the issues in play, and thus his interference in international relations at an extraordinarily delicate moment. And whatever Foreign Office officialdom thought of Arminius in general, it was aware that his reputation continued to ensure him an audience. That made his unbridled airing of opinions, informed by partial understanding and dubious information from parties with opposing interests, distinctly dangerous.

In December Arminius wrote again to Hardinge. He had decided, 'as far as I can judge from a distance, things do not look so dark and so hopeless' in Turkey. He was, he said, 'in direct communication with the Constantinople Committee of Young Turkey, who always appreciated my efforts to bring on a friendly feeling between England and Turkey'. This 'favourable position of mine', he wrote, he intended to use 'in the interest of good understanding between Turkey and Austria'. To that end he advised 'something ought to be done to belie such gossip spread by the German press in order to exterminate all sympathies for England'. His next letter, on 5 January 1909, was in reply to one from Hardinge taking him severely to task after a lecture Arminius had given in Budapest on 18 December, which had been reported in *The Times*. Arminius had alleged that Russia and Britain had been plotting against the Balkan interests of Austria-Hungary during the highly publicised and important meeting between Edward VII and Tsar Nicholas II at Reval in June 1908, the meeting that had set the royal seal on the 1907 entente. It was an extraordinarily dangerous rumour, and one in which Hardinge himself was implicated, as the minister in attendance and representative of the British government during the king's two-month-long, friendship-building tour of European countries that summer.

Arminius apologised and passed the blame to Aehrenthal. Could he have doubted 'the words of a state minister enjoying the confidence of the sovereign of my country?' He had also, he wrote, not been correctly reported; he had in fact qualified his statements by saying, 'I speak of the events on the assertion of the highest authority', and assured Hardinge 'my audience understood perfectly that I am repeating the words of our Minister for Foreign Affairs'. He had also claimed that the Liberal MP Noel Buxton, a man of causes that included the Balkans, had instigated a boycott against Austro-Hungarian goods to protest the annexation of Bosnia-Herzegovina. Hardinge's answer on 11 January was excoriating. He accepted Arminius' statement 'although it was quite easy for you to have ascertained from the Embassy in Vienna or the Consul General in Budapesth whether the statements made to you were true or not. Coming from you, such misstatements have had a very mischievous effect which it is impossible to correct'. It concluded, 'If it should occur again, I shall be reluctantly compelled to reconsider our relations to each other'. Arminius could not 'refrain from expressing my astonishment at the very severe criticism' and hoped Hardinge would 'give a proper estimate of the difficulty in which I find myself and not find too much fault with my behaviour'. At the time Hardinge had more important things to deal with (in his memoirs, Hardinge named Aehrenthal as one of the four men most responsible for World War I[3]), but Arminius was in company with dangerous men, and a lesson had to be given. By mid-February 1909 Arminius would report to Hardinge 'in spite of my sincere intentions to mitigate the enmity between the two leading states of Europe, I find my effort a quite hopeless one and I must keep aloof from any participation'. Hardinge, shortly to go as viceroy to India, must have been hugely relieved. Arminius' last letter to Hardinge, in March, begged 'leave to forward a paper which I thought necessary to write in order to dispel the much spreading beliefs of the imminent danger which threatens England's position in India' and closed 'I am afraid my criticism of the Anglo-Russian agreement was not totally wrong'.

Arminius had first requested a regular allowance from the Foreign Office during his summer trip to Britain in 1894, to which the prime minister, Lord Salisbury, had then reluctantly agreed after an intercession from the prince of Wales. Sanderson in his role as the permanent under-secretary of state

---

3 See Lord Hardinge of Penshurst, *Old Diplomacy: The Reminiscences of Lord Hardinge of Penshurst* (London, 1947).

for foreign affairs had sent the money in notes to the Athenaeum, where Arminius was staying, and a simultaneous note to Lord Salisbury:

I have paid Professor Vambéry his £120… If he goes talking to the Prince of Wales about it, all London will know. Shall I give him a caution that any payments he receives must be kept absolutely private? I am afraid that as a foreigner he could not receive a pension from the Civil list for his writings and travels – otherwise that would be a better plan than these payments.

At the time Arminius had thanked Sanderson, adding optimistically, 'I nevertheless feel satisfied for I have no doubt whoever will be at the head of the Foreign Office no one will have any cause to discontinue the payment of a modest honorarium'. He was right. Foreign Office officials found the occasional gold in his straw, were irritated or entertained in varying degrees by their informant's presumption, and the payments continued. Lord Salisbury insisted 'he cannot make any pledge as to the allowance being annual' but Sanderson promised 'to bring the question of the gratuity before him each August or September on receiving a simple reminder'. Sanderson saw some value in Arminius' correspondence and thought a steady pension might mean control of Arminius' more impulsive actions, and that 'He would probably give up going to Constantinople… and [without] we should get little or no assistance from him'. Arminius continued to pursue the pension through Sanderson, 'trusting the Government will dispense me of the inconvenience to beg every year'; and Lords Kimberley, Rosebery, and Salisbury, as successive foreign secretaries, continued to scribble on the back of his letters 'Make usual payment of £120', to which occasional supplements were added for 'expenses'.

In May 1904, when Arminius was in London to be received by the king at Buckingham Palace, he wrote to Sanderson on Windsor Castle headed paper. Sanderson had arranged a meeting for him with the prime minister Arthur Balfour, and Arminius followed up with a letter. Arminius must, by then, have seemed like the relic of another age. Direct channels to the sultan were closed but he pointed out it had been forty years since 'I began to lay before the British and Continental public my experiences regarding the political situation in Central Asia, putting a particular stress upon the danger, which might threaten Great Britain by the continual encroach-ment of Russia in Turkestan'. His 'literary activity' had not enriched him, he wrote, and he 'must turn for assistance to the country to which I devoted all the talent and energies of a long life'. It was 'not greed, but sheer necessity' that compelled him now to request 'an annual stipend of £250 till the end of my life'. The Foreign Office, led by Lord Lansdowne as foreign secretary, gave in. It was the easiest line of defence when officials feared that efforts from the king on the old professor's behalf might lead to disclosures of his activities over the years. They also clearly hoped that the pension might be some sort of lever to stop Arminius causing them embarrassment and were prepared to go to considerable trouble to arrange an annuity of about £140, which would add to, rather than replace, his habitual £120 yearly payment to give him more than the requested £250. There was also a £200 grant for the translation of his new book, *Western Culture in Eastern Lands*, in Lans-downe's devout hope that it would not be 'too antagonistic to Russia'.

Arminius, inevitably, pushed his luck, attempting to have the annuity vested in his son, Rustem, no doubt thinking that it might thus continue after his own death. This idea was firmly dismissed on the grounds that an Act of Parliament forbade the setting up of annuities for foreigners unless they were also householders. This highly unusual situation was further complicated by Arminius' lack of a birth certificate or, as an alternative, a certificate of baptism – or one at least that he was prepared to show. In whichever way the term 'secret agent' is defined and whether applicable or not to Arminius' information-gathering activities, he had all the instincts of the undercover operative to hide his real self for his best advantage. This time his best advantage also suited the Foreign Office, and, without the relevant formal documentation, the evidence of Arminius' age and career was accepted by George Hervey, comptroller general of the National Debt Office, for an annuity of £140. It was paid out at the rate of £70 in January and in July on the presentation by Arminius of a 'certificate of existence' each time. This he found extremely irksome, but he sent Sanderson his newly published *The Story of My Struggles* by way of thanks, and in turn received the Foreign Office payment intended as insurance for a judicious translation of *Western Culture in Eastern Lands*.

The book's publication by John Murray involved new correspondence with John Murray IV, who had inherited the publishing house from his father, Arminius' original publisher. Arminius had remained in touch with the publishing house over the years, requesting books to be sent to him and offering reviews of others. Hallam Murray, John IV's brother, had in turn requested a catalogue, in 1903, from the Hungarian National Museum, which Arminius promised and then failed to send on grounds that the Italian old masters in which Murray was interested were not in the museum. Instead, he sent a paper on the Emir Habibullah of Afghanistan, which he hoped might be published in the *Monthly Review.* The Murrays had not published Arminius since *Travels,* but he opened the batting over his new book while he was in London in 1904 by requesting that they receive and despatch to him in Budapest the 'luxurious edition of *The Armoury of Windsor Castle*', signed and sent to him by the king, and 'for which I have no room in my modest luggage'. He did offer to pay the cost of postage. A year later he sent the manuscript of *Western Culture in Eastern Lands,* asking for a 'small honorarium' of £120 as he felt the subject to be of enough current interest for the cost of the book to be easily covered.

However, his remark that this would be his last book and thus its publication by John Murray would mean their bookending of his writing career proved to be a mistake. Mr Murray had taken exception to the mention in *My Struggles* of the 'comparatively modest sum' he had made from it, the blame for which Arminius had placed at John Murray's door. John Murray IV considered his remarks 'highly derogatory to my father'. Arminius travelled old ground again: 'the privations of life', 'extraordinary struggles', 'pressing poverty', dangers, and then the wonderful reviews for *Travels* and 'the greatest disappointment in my life'. Surprisingly, John Murray IV still took the new book and the instructions from its author as to revisions (from which Arminius excused himself due to his deteriorating eyesight) and the desired speed of its printing. He assured Murray that he was undertaking 'a patriotic work' in 'proving to the world that England's civilising work in Asia is far above that of Russia' and that the book would be read by 'enlightened politicians all over the world'.

The *Globe* 'cordially recommended the volume' to those 'interested in the history of Eastern approximation to the culture of the West'.[4] Others were as complimentary: the review of the book in the *Tablet* on 2 June

---

4 As reviewed on 2 April 1906.

1906 noted Professor Vambéry's acknowledgement of good work done by Russia in Asia, and his nod to Foreign Office strictures. It continued to his conclusion that 'a nation scarcely emerged from infancy... which is held fast in the bonds of a despotic absolute monarchy' could not compare with 'a politically free nation, occupying a higher cultural level', that was 'enhanced by the sincerity and reliability of English officials'. Arminius' evidence, the reviewer decided, was 'based on concrete facts and knowledge' and delivered with 'fullness and telling force'. One review struck a rather more tempered note: if his opinions 'afforded Professor Vambéry a fresh excuse for blowing his own trumpet, we are all good-natured enough to hope that he may live to do it for another 40 years, since no one is hurt by it, while he is evidently pleased'.[5] *The Story of My Struggles* meanwhile was a roaring success, running into three editions in London and a paperback edition, but boycotted in Germany where Arminius' recent anti-German articles had made him an enemy.

On his retirement in 1905 Sanderson, prompted by Arminius, wrote a memo on 'Professor Vambéry: History of F O allowance to him & method of payment'. He added a note that Arminius was asking for an increase in the annuity to £250. Arminius followed up his gift of *My Struggles* to Hardinge with a request for £150 to cover its translation into French and German and was reminded that he had already received a translation fee. Astonishingly, the money was then granted personally by the new foreign secretary, Sir Edward Grey, who would remain in office until 1916. The payment was accompanied by another note, stating that this would be the final payment connected with the book, and Arminius promptly returned to his complaint over the certificate of existence, which he considered an indignity. 'I doubt whether the Government is aware of my work done in India in furthering the British sympathies of the Mohammedans', he wrote, adding, 'it is unfair to extol my own services, but it is the result of strenuous and persistent work and I cannot leave it unmentioned'.

In July 1910 Esmé Howard, who had befriended Arminius during his posting as consul-general in Budapest, wrote to Hardinge regarding his concern about letters from the Foreign Office and members of the British government held by Arminius. Hardinge had already been adding 'please

---

5 *Homeward Mail from India, China and the East* (14 August 1905).

regard this letter as private' to all his correspondence with Arminius, but Howard had been informed by 'a friend of Vambéry's' that 'the old gentleman owing to advanced age was getting indiscreet'. Howard thought the letters should be acquired, possibly in exchange for some honour to mark Arminius' forthcoming eightieth birthday. The Foreign Office opinion was that money might be the answer, although Sir Edward Grey considered it 'delicate ground'. Grey's private secretary William Tyrrell shouldered the problem after Hardinge left for India, and he received another letter from Howard in November. He had broached the subject of the letters with Arminius and it had not gone well. 'He blazed up at the idea, said that nothing would induce him ever to show them to anyone and that if he ever felt himself ill he would call for me or my successor and hand them over in a sealed packet for transmission to the Foreign Office'. In the event of his death, Arminius had added, his son (who, Howard noted, was 'a Professor here and I believe a very good fellow') would have instructions to do the same. Howard considered that Arminius saw the letters as 'a sort of hostage for the regular payments of his allowance' from the government. Arminius, he wrote, 'does not disguise his feelings about our entente with Russia' but 'I make it a rule not to enter into any discussions with him'. The old professor was 'not a bad sort but tremendously self-centred and vain'. That, Howard wrote, was 'perhaps not unnatural in a man who has really done a great deal'.[6]

In December Howard reported a visit from Dr Ferdinand Leipnik, editor of the *Pester Lloyd*. Leipnik, generally described as a historian and entrepreneur, and who had probably been the original 'friend of Vambéry's', almost certainly had some sort of covert relationship with the British himself,[7] one that resulted in a liaison role between Austria-Hungary and Britain. Arminius had spoken to Leipnik about the letters and Leipnik had advised

6 Alder and Dalby, op. cit., 454–5.

7 Today he appears as a somewhat shadowy figure who played an intermediary role between the British and Austria-Hungary during and after World War I, by which time he was living in The Hague, resulting in his occasional misidentification as Dutch. He wrote *A History of French Etching from the 16th Century to the Present Day*, published by the Bodley Head in 1924. After he left the *Pester Lloyd*, Esmé Howard noted that he 'was too detached from fashionable nationalisms [...] and too ironical in the expression of his opinions of them and their prophets to be "popular" as a journalist'. He must have been most refreshing in the times in which he lived.

him to hand them back, 'since it was impossible to tell into whose hands they might not accidentally fall'. Leipnik endorsed Rustem as 'absolutely trustworthy' but the Foreign Office was nervous, especially as Arminius had recently insisted to Leipnik that he had received an entirely fictitious letter from Sir Arthur Nicolson, Hardinge's successor as permanent under-secretary, on the subject of the Foreign Office's fears. Leipnik was not surprised; he had 'felt sure the old gentleman was romancing', and he thought that he might persuade Arminius to hand the letters over in confidence that his annuity would continue. In 1911 a solution was reached. Arminius wrote to Nicolson via Howard asking to be relieved 'of the onerous task to beg annually twice for the sum the Foreign Office has decreed as a reward for the service I have rendered for more than 40 years'. Howard, who was about to leave for a new posting in Berne, told Nicolson 'he would like the money to be paid to him half yearly through the British Embassy at Vienna. He would prefer this to having it done through the Consulate here – why I don't quite know'. Howard thought it would be 'an excellent thing, as I am really rather nervous about some of the letters'. Howard, like so many others who had put up with Arminius' foibles through the years, must have had a soft spot for the old man. He went on to wonder 'whether on his 80th birthday, he could be given an honorary degree at Oxford. It would please him immensely'.

Nicolson wrote to Arminius on 10 January 1911, hoping 'to be able to arrange matters in a manner which will meet our wishes' and 'glad to hear that you agree with us that it would be prudent to let us have the letters which are in your possession'. Two days later, his private secretary, Lord Errington, went to the National Debt Office 'to endeavour to come to some arrangement by which the Foreign Office can meet the wishes expressed by Professor Vambéry'. The red tape was not easily laid aside. The comptroller general, Mr Turpin, had dealt with 'aged persons' who 'refused to furnish Life Certificates' before. Normally no payments were disbursed to them under this circumstance and the money was allowed to accumulate, presumably until they were persuaded of the lesser evil. Under pressure, Errington disclosed to Turpin 'certain of the circumstances which prompted our request' and Turpin agreed 'to take upon himself the responsibility of waiving a Life Certificate', on condition of formal assurance from the Foreign Office that Professor Vambéry was still alive. Arminius remained reluctant to give up the letters, but on 19 January he handed all but one of the seventy-seven to Howard, who carried them to London. The last letter he described as 'of a private and confidential character' and it has never reappeared; but the full stop to Arminius' intelligence career came on 4 March 1911 in the form of a secret eight-page memorandum: *Payments to Professor A Vambéry from Secret Service Funds*.

Alder and Dalby quote Sir Stephen Gaselee, keeper of the papers at the Foreign Office from 1920 until his death in 1943, in summing up Arminius as 'one of the greatest Turkish scholars of the nineteenth century; a strong friend of this country and a bitter enemy of Russia', and as a 'useful source of information' who 'had the ear of the sultan'. That judgement might just have passed muster with Arminius. The historian Harold Temperley, who met him in 1909, dismissed him as a 'Great Charlatan',[8] after Arminius had attacked the British Liberals whom he had always mistrusted. (At his most vainglorious, he claimed his lectures had brought down Gladstone's government in 1885.) Temperley was right. Arminius' personal relationship with the sultan and access to international informants rarely delivered more than those slivers of information to the Foreign Office that officials might have had from less complicated sources. Their doubts, often proven, over the veracity of his claims were outweighed by the ingrained habit of accepting and paying for his intelligence, and by the aura of untouchability vested in his relationship with Edward VII and in his entrée in the Yildiz Palace. As the historian Antony Best pointed out, as 'an unofficial agent of empire, his exhaustive accounts of his dealings with Abdülhamid and his detailed analyses of Ottoman politics are probably of more service to today's historians than they ever were to his contemporaries in Whitehall'.[9]

During the years of Arminius' involvement with Turkey, letters, papers, pamphlets, and books poured undiminished from his pen. He was interviewed regularly for articles that were syndicated across the world and especially in the USA. His output during this last period of his life most importantly included his two-volume biography, *The Story of My Struggles*, and, as we have seen, Murray published *Western Culture in Eastern Lands*.

---

8 Quoted in John Fisher and Antony Best, eds, *On the Fringes of Diplomacy: Influences on British Foreign Policy 1800–1945* (Oxford, 2011), 81.
9 Ibid.

Then there was *The Story of Hungary*, commissioned by T. Fisher Unwin in London, which came out in 1886, as part of their *Story of the Nations* series. It was translated into other languages and had good international sales just as its author was getting into his stride with the Foreign Office. (In Hungary, Arminius wrote, 'it was never appreciated' and was generally ignored.) Other later publications included a booklet in 1891 dedicated to the Persian ambassador in Vienna: *Aus dem Geistesleben persischer Frauen*;[10] *Freiheitliche Bestrebungen im moslimischen Asien*;[11] and *The Growth and Spread of the Magyars* (1895). The last returned to the question of Hungarian ethnogenesis, but none was translated from its original language.

There were other works. *The Travels and Adventures of the Turkish Admiral Sidi Ali Reis, in India, Afghanistan, Central Asia, and Persia during the Years 1553–1556*, a lengthy title for a translation of the *Mirat ul Memalik* or 'Mirror of the Kingdom', was published by Luzac in London in 1899. It is a travelogue that might almost have been written three centuries later by a player in the Great Game. Notes on words and phrases the translator found obscure are often prefaced with 'must be', 'perhaps', 'maybe from the Italian', or markers saying 'unintelligible', and the geography of India was clearly not the translator's special subject. In 1904, *Le Peril Jaune* ('The Yellow Peril' – not the only publication with that title) was dedicated to Lord Lansdowne, then British foreign secretary. It was a pro-Japanese, anti-Russian publication at the time of the Russo-Japanese War, and recommended an Anglo-German alliance in Asia. In 1911 Arminius also translated the Uzbek epic *Jusuf und Ahmed* from the Khivan dialect. His final book, written in Hungarian and never translated, and published posthumously in 1914 with a preface by Rustem, was, suitably, a study of Hungarian-Turkish relations.[12]

By 1911, Arminius was an old man out of step with a fast-changing world. He took a dim view of the situation in England, governed once again by the hated Liberals, and with a prime minister, Asquith, who he must have seen as a dangerous radical. As he wrote to John Murray, 'I cannot conceal from

10 'From the Spiritual Life of Women', inspired apparently by an eighteenth-century manuscript Arminius had discovered discussing the literary work of Persian women. Alder and Dalby name it as *Mazmai Mahmudi*.
11 'Endeavours for Freedom in Moslem Asia', published in Berlin in 1893 but never translated from German.
12 *A Magyarsag Bolcsojene* (Budapest, 1914).

you the uneasiness I feel in viewing the sad change which has taken place in your country. The present party in power is ruining the prestige of England all over the world and the former pride of mankind has become the laughing stock of the nations. That is not *my England,* which I could revisit'. His England had, however, helped to provide for the comfortable life he now lived in Budapest. The payments for his services to the Foreign Office over twenty years amounted to more than £5,000. It is impossible to say if that was fair payment for the time he had put in on a job he had invented for himself, regardless of the value of his production. The only certainty is that the old mountebank himself, on his high horse, would have considered it a pauper's wage had it been ten times that figure.

18

The Last Act

Lory Alder (who was Arminius' great niece) and Richard Dalby, authors of *The Dervish of Windsor Castle*, were able to interview Rustem Vambéry's son Robert as well as others with first-hand or only once-removed memories of Arminius in his final years. More than forty years after their book was published, they and their publishers, the husband-and-wife team of Bachman & Turner Ltd., are long gone. Richard Dalby died relatively young, in 2017, not long before I first encountered the dervish in Uzbekistan. Arminius Vambéry's family line ended with Robert, his elder brother, George, having died of paratyphoid aged twenty-three in 1928. *The Dervish of Windsor Castle* is, therefore, the nearest thing to a primary source for Arminius' final days, beyond the cold lists of his published articles, biographical entries in encyclopaedias and works of reference, the medals and honours he received, and records of various gala or jubilee events marked by photographs and more press coverage.

His international fame and, by this time, his comfortable circumstances, do not seem to have given him much pleasure. He was disillusioned by the modern world, and his influence on the great events of his lifetime was, in the end, negligible, but his admirers did not know that. He was a celebrity but that was not enough either. He was 'bitter and irascible... cantankerous and resentful, inclined to harbour a grudge for years and with the proverbial long memory of an elephant never to forget a slight, real or imaginary'.[1] His conviction that he had been somehow done out of the bigger rewards and most glittering of prizes soured his final years. He could not rest even on

---

1 Alder and Dalby, op. cit., 468.

those laurels that he had deserved. What did he think if he took stock of his life? Did it matter to him that much of his fame was founded in what today would be apostrophised as fake news? Did that grate against his fine perception of himself and disturb his *amour propre*? Or is it always someone else's fault when a life has not quite reached its self-prescribed heights?

Writing about Arminius Vambéry, my growing irritation as I uncovered the overlay of fabrication in his life – the exaggeration, story-telling and straightforward untruthfulness – has influenced my view of a man who was certainly exceptional. The backwards view from a different age may have led to some unfair judgements. I might have found his egregious self-invention more entertaining and easier to disregard if we were not so beset by mendacity in public life today, and, truth be told, if it had displayed the devil-may-care dishonesty of the best fictional villains, enjoyed by its perpetrator above all. Instead, the dissatisfied young man, although he had triumphed in the eyes of many, became a pompous and disagreeable old man. A character as described even by himself with whom it is hard to empathise and whose complaints cloud the attractive image of the excited young adventurer, bursting with youthful *chutzpah*, setting out into the world, swimming hard to stay afloat and, by his wits, reaching secure landfall. Arminius had an extraordinary life, however fraudulently embellished.

There were plenty in his lifetime who believed his mythology and took him at his own estimation. As Alder and Dalby wrote, 'stories about Vambéry circulated in all corners of the Moslem World'. The adventurous traveller R. B. Cunninghame Graham[2] 'found himself talking one night to a Persian who was enthusing about the great "Bamborah".' The Persian, it turned out, had met Arminius in Budapest. The Persian said:

> large hearted was this Bamborah, and speaking Persian, a Christian dervish, knowing all the East, having read all books, explored all countries, mastered all sciences and learning; the friend of kings, for had not the Sultan Abdul Hamid (whom may god preserve) sent him a ring of 'diamond' worth a thousand pounds?

---

2 Cunninghame Graham (1852–1936) travelled in Morocco disguised as a Turkish sheikh, was a radical Liberal MP, co-founder of the Scottish Labour Party with Keir Hardie, and first president of the Scottish National Party.

Cunninghame Graham reported 'he himself had been shown that ring by "Bamborah"' as 'they sat discoursing in his hospitable house'.[3]

I have no doubt that Arminius made the journey through Central Asia that launched him into public life and imagination. I also have no doubt that the danger to him in that admittedly highly dangerous part of the world was exaggerated by 'the male Scheherazade'.[4] Accidents might always have happened: a sandstorm; a robbery with violence; lack of water; an everyday accident or a knife in the back just because. The more picturesque possibilities of death at the hands of the khan of Khiva, the emir of Bukhara, or the slave-trading Turkmans of Central Asia were greatly reduced, possibly entirely removed, by the untouchable talisman of the sultan's *tugra* much more than they were by any dubious dervish disguise. Arminius' embrace of the dervish persona was not much more than skin-deep in any case. He might have got away with playing the holy fool in some circumstances, but plenty of those he met were suspicious of his identity. They may simply have thought it safer not to explore their suspicions if the strange foreigner sheltered in the long shadow of the sultan. And who knows what tale Arminius wove when he presented himself, armed with the passport of the caliph, to the religious zealots who ruled in the khanates? Haji Bilal, his friend and companion on his Central Asian journey, who visited Mecca and Medina again in the 1870s, was said to have remained convinced of Arminius' Muslim identity. Arminius wrote, 'He even asserted that if I had adopted an incognito at all, it was decidedly rather in Europe than in Asia, and that my Christianity was apocryphal'. That too was the storyteller's story, but it is unlikely that Haji Bilal would have believed the bearer of the *tugra* to be other than a respectable messenger of Islam – whatever his idiosyncrasies.

There were always doubters and Arminius could never resist making a good story better. The 'hospitable house' in Cunninghame Graham's tale was a spacious first-floor apartment in 19 Ferenc Jozsef Rakpart[5] on the Pest side of the Danube embankment, not far from the university. He had previously lived on the same street in a flat at Number 33, but it was unmodernised, with the lavatory on an outside landing. Arminius of course scattered star-

---

3 R. B. Cunninghame Graham, *Mogreb-el-Acksa: A Journey in Morocco* (London, 1898), 168.
4 Alder and Dalby, op. cit., 468.
5 Now Belgrad Rakpart.

dust over his family's removal from this inconvenience: Lord Curzon, he said, came to call on him in the flat and found him in bed with a chill from cold nocturnal visits to the loo – he immediately reported the situation to Queen Victoria, who was horrified: 'What! A friend of mine living in such miserable conditions! He must move at once!' Money was sent to Budapest, something between £250 and £400, to be supposedly greeted by Arminius exclaiming, 'A flat at this price? Why I could not find one in the whole of Budapest if I tried'.[6]

In fact, he had moved only some years after the queen's death. The new apartment was in a new building, close to the old and with the same grand view of the Danube and the Gellért Hill. It had five rooms and a large bathroom, reputedly where Arminius also stored papers and magazines. He insisted on carrying many of his possessions himself from one flat to another, saying he could not trust his secrets to other hands, and was said to have announced, aged seventy-five, 'I believe there is no man as strong as myself'.[7] The little lame figure with his unrequited hunger for gold and recognition, who must indeed have been strong to overcome his handicap as well as he did, begins in imagination to resemble a sort of Nibelung. Number 19 Ferenc Jozsef Rakpart later became the German Legation, and then the office of the Hungarian Association of the United Nations. It was under renovation when I visited at the end of 2019 and now seems to consist of short-term rental apartments. A plaque on the outside wall says, 'In this house lived Arminius Vambéry 1832–1913, World-famous Orientalist, Explorer of Central Asia, Outstanding scholar of Turkish philology, Member of the Hungarian Academy of Science. Budapest City Council 1974.'

He must have been gratified by his haul of international honours and medals. He needed no longer to rely on his books alone for decoration, even if he still hankered for that improbable British knighthood. Now the insignia of the CVO from Edward VII sat beside that of the Austrian Knight of the Imperial Order of Leopold, the Italian Order of St Maurice and St Lazarus, his Turkish Grand Cordon of Medjidieh, the Persian Order of the Lion and the Sun, the Order of Notre Dame de Guadalupe,[8] and another

---

6 Ibid., 475.
7 Ibid., 478.
8 A Mexican order presumably in the gift of the Hapsburgs.

gold medal from Emperor Franz Joseph.[9] In 1906 he received the Order of the Sacred Treasure from the emperor of Japan, in recognition of his pro-Japanese stance during the Russo-Japanese War of 1904–5. In 1907 he was made an Honorary Fellow of the Royal Society of Literature in London, and on 10 October 1910 the Hungarian Academy celebrated the fiftieth anniversary of his membership. He was presented with a jubilee diploma and, *The Times* noted, 'received congratulatory visits from large numbers of Hungarian scientists and public men' as well as telegrams from all over the world. A subscription had been opened to found a Vambéry scholarship in philology. On 19 March 1912, Arminius celebrated his 'official' eightieth birthday and *The Times* ran a piece to acknowledge his public standing and venerable age. His pupil Gyula Germanus remembered the Vambéry apartment as being filled with students for the occasion and the great and good of Budapest coming to offer their congratulations while Arminius tried to ration the cognac, telling his servants, 'Go easy there, the guests don't need so much, a little will do…'[10]

The old man continued to write for and to the newspapers on his pet subjects, even if he increasingly found himself on the wrong side of arguments with beginnings in places and policies he no longer understood. There was a refutation in *The Times* of 22 December 1908 of those dangerous statements that had so infuriated Charles Hardinge. His inaccurate statements on the boycott of Austrian goods by the Young Turks 'caused considerable amusement, not unmixed with annoyance' in Constantinople.[11] He was pleased to congratulate the British government on its appointment of Syed Amir Ali as the first Muslim member of the Privy Council, 'for it denoted the happy turn in the relations of Great Britain with her Mahommedan subjects and with Islam in general',[12] but irritated readers of *The Times* by misrepresenting Russian opinion on the value of the Trans-Persian railway in 1912.[13] In those final years, the Professor Vambéry who appeared in the American

---

9 Alder and Dalby described this as the 'Grand Gold Medal' – it may have been membership of the Order of Franz Josef, a jubilee medal in 1908, or some other civilian Imperial Austrian order.

10 Alder and Dalby, op. cit., 482.

11 *The Times* (2 January 1909).

12 *The Times* (3 February 1910).

13 *The Times* (27 August 1912).

---

newspapers was more often Rustem, who had achieved his ambition to be a university professor as well as becoming a well-known lawyer and criminologist. (Many of those newspapers also noted that Rustem's eldest son, George, was the godson of King George V.) Rustem, however, had married his wife Olga in opposition to his father, who had not attended the wedding and who had refused to help the couple financially. When his grandsons arrived, he mellowed enough to begin to invite the family for supper and Sunday lunches. Robert Vambéry remembered that they had to bring all their own food and drink, but there were interesting things to play with in his grandparents' flat and each boy was allowed to take a penny from a plate of small change. In particular there were 'many ornate gold cigarette cases decorated with precious stones, gifts from the rich and powerful'.[14] When the war came in 1914, they were sold by weight and the proceeds invested in land mortgages that were paid off afterwards in almost worthless inflated money.

Rustem was not his father's son for nothing. He also held strong opinions, less transmutable than many of his father's. He loathed the Nazis and the Hungarian Communists in turn. His absolute opposition to injustice and exploitation led to difficulties in his court cases, and he became known as 'the Hungarian Voltaire' for his challenges to all sides of a case and often to the judge on grounds of reason, tolerance, and liberalism. Reputedly it was said 'if you want to lose your case let Rustem Vambéry defend you'.[15] Among his notable clients in the 1920s he defended Matyas Rakosi, later Stalinist leader of Hungary, against the prosecution of the Fascist regime under Regent Miklos Horthy. Rakosi must have been a good deal easier to defend then than he would have been later in his career but, at that time, the cause he espoused was the lesser of two extremes, for which he went to prison for fifteen years. Rustem was also an advisor to the British Legation in Budapest and, as part of a delegation of Hungarian liberals and socialists to the first British Labour government in 1929, addressed two committee meetings at the House of Commons. To escape the Nazis, he and his family moved to the USA in 1938 where he was already well known as an academic and lecturer. He became Hungarian minister to the USA in 1947 but resigned only a few months later in disgust at the behaviour of his own government, and

---

14 Alder and Dalby, op. cit., 473.
15 Ibid., 495.

became a naturalised American. He died on the New York subway of a heart attack in October 1948 leaving Olga and his surviving son, Robert.

In his old age Arminius became almost a tourist attraction for foreign visitors. Curmudgeon he may have been but Gyula Germanus remembered those random workmen on the Danube embankment, whose ears were filled with the old professor's fantastical life stories. He loved an audience, and must have been delighted when the journalist C. Townley Fullam visited him in the 'beautiful spacious room' that was his library. Townley Fullam was a contributor to the American periodical *The Forum* and to others in the USA and Britain. He wrote about the emergence of the Magyar race in an odd piece in 1916 that makes the reader wonder which highly coloured details in fact came from Arminius' version of the dim and distant past.[16] Captain Bernard Granville Baker, soldier, artist, writer, and author of *The Walls of Constantinople* (1910), was another visitor; he described Arminius in *The Danube with Pen and Pencil* as 'a man who loves Old England as intensely as he loves his own fair country'. He 'welcomes travelling Britons, giving them freely of the treasures of his well-stored mind'.[17] The Austrian artist Marianne Stokes and her English husband Adrian met Arminius when they were writing their book about Hungary, one that is illustrated most strikingly with Marianne's unique and beautiful portraits. Adrian wrote, 'it was most gratifying to hear the old gentleman – with the freshness and enthusiasm of a young man, though not without an astute criticism now and again – speak in praise of England and in recognition of the kindness and appreciation he had received there'.[18]

Arminius had not lost the art of telling people what they wanted to hear. It is no wonder that Esmé Howard became nervous of his discretion, in respect of the British Foreign Office and his letters, in front of all these and more admirers of mixed nationalities and loyalties. There was a constant correspondence from all over the world. Arminius wrote 'worst of all the poor international writer fares at the hands of the Americans. The number of autograph collectors is astonishing'. They were, however, 'kind enough

16 C. Townley Fullam, 'The Birth of a Nation', *The Forum*, 55 (1916), 419.
17 Captain Bernard Granville Baker, *The Danube with Pen and Pencil* (London, 1911), 154.
18 Adrian Stokes and Marianne Stokes, *Hungary: Painted by Adrian and Marianne Stokes* (London, 1909), 268.

to enclose an American stamp or a few cents for the reply postage'. Some of the requests were bizarre – he reported one American surgeon asking for photographs of his tongue, 'that from its formation he may draw his conclusions as to my linguistic talent'.

If foreign visitors fawned on him in his old age, the view of his compatriots was often less amicable. His old student and now enemy, Goldziher, voiced an opinion with more venom than most others. In 1900 he wrote 'after a long hiatus I again visited the Dervish today. With the old age of this evil adventurer, the evil of his soul grows'. Arminius infuriated him by talking of 'the high value of money' and the quarter or half a million *kronen* he had earned 'but not with science. Science is shit... In Hungary one needs no science. Do you think I earned my fortune with Science? Ha, ha, ha, I received an annual salary from the English Queen and from the Sultan, for political matters. England has now increased my salary by 50 pounds sterling a year. This is science'.[19] In 1905, just after Goldziher had finally been appointed a full professor at the university, he saw Arminius again. 'I again met the limping liar on the street... And he let loose some of the many vilenesses with which his black liar's soul is filled.'[20] It was a complicated relationship. Arminius may have tried to help Goldziher over the years, but it had always seemed to the latter to be a condescending, back-handed effort that, if anything, damaged his chances. He believed that Arminius was a liar and a fake, whose success was based on trickery and that coloured every other aspect of their relationship. In slight mitigation for Arminius in an opinion with which I largely agree, Goldziher was also a bitter man, who had struggled to achieve less than he deserved.

One of Arminius' final visitors, shortly before his death in 1913, was Abdu'l-Bahá (1844–1921), son of Baha'u'llah, founder of the Baha'i faith in Persia. Exploration round this final turn in the rabbit warren of Arminius' religious belief (or lack of it) comes only to a literal dead end, but in the time he had left, Arminius somehow managed to secure himself an enduring place in Baha'i legend. Did Arminius, one cannot help wonder, remember his dismissive view of the Bàbis, all those years ago in Persia, when he passed by the site of

19 See Raphael Patai, *Ignaz Goldziher and his Oriental Diary: A Translation and Psychological Portrait* (Detroit, 1987), 43–4.
20 Ibid.

their massacre? He would no doubt have told Abdu'l-Bahá a different story. Ties grew between Bahaism and Zionism, and the Baha'i World Centre is now in Israel, where Bahaism, persecuted in Persia and the Ottoman Empire, finally found a resting place in Haifa, but that came much later. Arminius' involvement with one was unlikely to have led him to the other. In the years before World War I, the search for religious truth embraced new philosophies and made celebrities of their leaders. Abdu'l-Bahá had become well known in Europe and the USA during his journeys in the West, and his arrival for the first time in Hungary was celebrated by the great, the good, and the curious, including Arminius' pupils Ignaz Goldziher and Gyula Germanus.

There are, as expected, mixed stories of Arminius' meeting with Abdu'l-Bahá. Arminius appears to have been too unwell at the time to attend public occasions, and the two probably met at his house, where 'he still took every opportunity to offer his views on developments in Eastern and Middle Eastern politics' and, legend has it, 'had also been following the movements of the Master'. Arminius told Abdu'l-Bahá, 'For many years have I been following your teachings, and ever longed to meet you. I admire more than anything your supreme courage, that at this advanced age you have left everything and are travelling all over the world to spread your humane principles'.[21] Rustem reported the 'deep friendship' between his father and Abdu'l-Bahá, and Arminius has sometimes been called the first Hungarian Baha'i. More verifiably, it was Rustem who espoused Bahaism and wrote the preface to the first Baha'i book to be translated into Hungarian in 1933.[22] Before his early death, Rustem's eldest son George took instruction from Martha Root, a Baha'i 'Hand of the Cause', who claimed Queen Marie of Rumania as the first royal Baha'i.[23]

21 "Abdu'l-Bahá and Professor Árminius Vámbéry', *The Journey West* (2013), accessed online 2 Oct. 2023.

22 J. E. Esslemont, *Bahá'u'lláh and the New Era*, with a preface by Rustem Vambéry and Martha Root (Budapest, 1933).

23 Abdu'l-Bahá was head of the Baha'i faith from 1892 to 1921, and described the Hands of the Cause as those who should 'diffuse the divine fragrances, to edify the souls of men, to promote learning, to improve the character of all men and to be, at all times and under all conditions, sanctified and detached from all earthly things. They must manifest the fear of God at all times by their conduct, their manners, their deeds and their words'. Martha Root was an American writer and teacher of the Baha'i faith who travelled all over the world. The last Hand of the Cause died in 2007.

Arminius once again placed himself centre stage for posterity. He is quoted as telling Abdu'l-Bahá, 'I hope to hear from you. Please, when you return to the East, send me the Writings and Treatises of your Father, and I will do everything to spread them in Europe. The more these principles are spread, the nearer will we be to the age of Peace and Brotherhood'. After his departure from Hungary, Abdu'l-Bahá sent Arminius the gift of a carpet and received a letter of thanks that is a masterpiece of Vambéryiana and 'outshone Oriental hyperbole'.[24] It was submitted to *The Egyptian Gazette* by an associate of Abdu'l-Bahá's in Egypt for publication ten days after Arminius' death, and was later reproduced in the Baha'i newsletter, *Star of the West*. Both letters are reproduced unexpurgated here as part of the predella to Arminius' life.

To the Editor *"Egyptian Gazette."*

Sir: – In view of the recent death of that distinguished scholar and Orientalist, Arminius Vambéry, I feel that the subjoined letter, sent only a few weeks before his death to Abdul-Baha (Abbas Effendi), becomes a historical document of worldwide interest and importance. This hitherto unpublished letter I am happily permitted to make public.

Written in Persian its exquisite diction and courtesy reveal how thoroughly this wonderful scholar inherently understood the heart of the religious East and how fully he sympathised with all truly noble aims. To many Vambéry was perhaps known only as a brilliant and indefatigable anthropologist and researcher into hidden origins; to others, who know the infinite complexities of life and thought in the Near East, he meant a great deal more. His strenuously active life comprised more knowledge based on experience than is generally to be found in the career of three ordinary diplomatists. His linguistic attainments were remarkable, for he spoke and wrote over fifteen languages.

Naturally his judgment on men and things was therefore remarkable for its penetrative accuracy and shrewdness and for four years he worked as special adviser to the ex-Sultan, Abdul Hamid. A particularly hard youth, fought in such bewildering surroundings as Turkey, Persia and the Balkans, gave him unequalled opportunities for observation and study.

---

24 Alder and Dalby, op. cit., 482–3.

Concerning religious philosophy he could enter into discussions with the best and especially on Islamic theology, whether Persian or Arabian, he spoke with an intimate and immediate knowledge that inspired great respect among the learned mullahs. Many are the biographical sketches that have appeared on this extraordinary genius from time to time in European reviews and now many more will be surely presented; but it may be doubted whether any will reveal the inner soul and high aspirations of this scholar at a ripe old age as do the contents of the following communication. We seem to feel the glow of a flame that flashed out from the heart of one who had always searched to find a great truth, a compelling conviction, and that this glad experience had finally been accorded and he was satisfied.

The memorable meeting between Abdul-Baha and the professor took place in Buda Pesth last April where the great Bahai Master met with an ovation on the part of scholars, Orientalists and social reformers. On the return of Abdul-Baba to Egypt he wrote to Vambéry, sending him a gift, and the following letter was the reply. For the information of those who are unfamiliar with Eastern expressions I may add that the style is, in Islam, only adopted by the religiously learned and only used towards a supremely great teacher or leader.

Believe me, yours, etc.,

J. STANDARD.
Ramleh, September 22

LETTER TO ABDUL-BAHA FROM PROFESSOR VAMBÉRY

I FORWARD this humble petition to the sanctified and holy presence of Abdul-Baha Abbas who is the centre of knowledge, famous throughout the world and beloved by all mankind. O thou noble friend who art conferring guidance upon humanity, may my life be a ransom to thee!

The loving epistle which you have condescended to write to this servant and the rug which you have forwarded came safely to hand.

The time of the meeting with your excellency and the memory of the benediction of your presence, recurred to the memory of this servant and I am longing for the time when I shall meet you again. Although I have travelled through many countries and cities of Islam, yet have I never met so lofty a character and so exalted a personage as your excellency and I can bear witness that it is not possible to find such another. On this account, I am hoping that the ideals and accomplishments of your excellency may be crowned with success and yield results under all conditions; because behind these ideals and deeds I easily discern the eternal welfare and prosperity of the world of humanity.

This servant, in order to gain first-hand information and experience, entered into the ranks of various religions; that is, outwardly I became a Jew, Christian, Mohammedan and Zoroastrian. I discovered that the devotees of these various religions do nothing else but hate and anathematize each other, that all these religions have become the instruments of tyranny and oppression in the hands of rulers and governors and that they are the causes of the destruction of the world of humanity.

Considering these evil results, every person is forced by necessity to enlist himself on the side of your excellency and accept with joy the prospect of a fundamental basis for a universal religion of God being laid through your efforts.

I have seen the father of your excellency from afar. I have realized the self-sacrifice and noble courage of his son and I am lost in admiration.

For the principles and aims of your excellency I express the utmost respect and devotion and if God, the Most High, confers long life, I will be able to serve you under all conditions. I pray and supplicate this from the depths of my heart.

Your servant,

VAMBÉRY.[25]

Ill health or not during April 1913 when Abdu'l-Bahá was in Budapest, Arminius was well during that summer and staying near Vienna. But in early September he was suffering from the symptoms of arteriosclerosis. On 13 September he wrote to Rustem:

---

25 'Professor Vambéry and the Bahai Religion', *Star of the West*, 4/17 (1914), Bahai.works, accessed online 2 Oct. 2023.

My dear son! I am feeling very ill. Again I suffered the whole night and did not close an eye. Yesterday I took two powders, I was more or less alright during the day, but so much more terrible was the night. I am near to Despair. Tell the doctor this.

Your unhappy father.

On 14 September he was busy again, dictating letters to Rustem for friends in England. That night he died in his sleep. The telegraphs, letters, and wreaths from all over the world, from academics, friends and acquaintances, emperors and princes, flooded into Budapest. The Archduke Joseph sent a telegram on behalf of Franz Josef; and only the Hungarian government 'failed in its official duty to convey the sorrow of the nation' to Arminius' widow and their son.[26] Count Tisza, the prime minister, and Arminius had fallen out (not that he ever intended to find common ground with the sort of Hungarian society that was exemplified by Tisza). Tisza, in line with his philo-Semitic policy of appointing Jewish advisors and ministers to his government – highly unpopular in anti-Semitic circles – had in fact attempted to honour Arminius by making him a privy councillor. Under these circumstances Arminius might have felt honoured, but that elephantine memory for the sticks and stones thrown at him during his life did not allow for graciousness to the likes of the aristocratic Tisza, and he turned the honour down. Tisza took this insult personally and had not forgotten it by the time Arminius died.

According to Alder and Dalby, Arminius had refused any suggestion of a grand public funeral. Whether it would have been offered, given Count Tisza's feelings, is another matter. For all his status abroad, the majority of Hungarian academia and society at home was unenthralled by the Vambéry myth and in some cases, such as the influential Goldziher, positively contemptuous of his achievements. Acclamation did come from one surprising source, however. When old General Görgey heard of the death, he asked his daughter to make a wreath out of the flowers in his garden. At the funeral in Kerepesi Cemetery, attended only by family and a few friends, she stepped forward to lay forget-me-nots and other flowers at the graveside. Arminius

---

26 Alder and Dalby, op. cit., 485.

was being hailed as a Hungarian hero by another controversial Hungarian hero.[27]

The obituary writers in Britain and all over the USA dug into the files of their newspapers and revamped the many biographical pieces already written about Arminius. They focused always on his friendships with royalty and his linguistic abilities and were exhaustive but clichéd; what else was there to say? In due course, the periodicals and reviews caught up and wrote the same things at slightly greater length. The widespread and instant effusions of the Anglophone press were followed by more quizzical obituary pieces in the newspapers of Austria-Hungary. The *Pester Lloyd* noted Arminius' fame in Britain, commenting that 'it took a long time for his fame abroad to reach his native country'. It wondered if he had died too early or too late. Some of his political prophecies had been proved wrong – or might they still come to pass? Another article praised him for his retired life in Budapest and his preference for his homeland when he had been so feted abroad. It once again listed his languages, grown to include 'at least twenty French and as many Turkish dialects'; recalled how he had indeed astonished an audience at Geneva by speaking in the local patois; and described him as an exemplary teacher and a friend of great men, his house a focal point for foreign visitors of importance.

Less standard was the information that the 'Rector Magnificus' of the university had issued a special announcement on Arminius' death, and that the Hungarian Geographical Society, of which Arminius was a founder member, had called a special meeting to honour his memory. It had also laid a wreath on his coffin. Count Paul Teleki, its general secretary, later became professor of geography at Budapest University and prime minister. They were odd fellow associates – like Tisza, Teleki came from the powerful aristocratic background most despised by Arminius – but in some respects they stood on common ground. Teleki was known for his anti-Semitism and, as prime minister, in 1920 brought in the first anti-Jewish law to Europe after World War I. (As prime minister for the second time in 1939 he pushed another anti-Jewish act, which forbade Jews from working

---

27 General Görgey was famous for his brilliant leadership of the Hungarian National Army against Austria in 1848 but was later accused of treason for surrendering to the Russians and was not rehabilitated for many years.

in almost any position of influence and was responsible for further measures against the Jews leading to terrible loss of life.) Immediately after World War I, however, the opinions he expressed of Hungarian Jews were wholly in line with Arminius' own and those of so many others for whom their Jewishness had become entirely blended into their sense of Magyar national identity and affiliation.[28] Meanwhile, on 25 October 1915, Ignaz Goldziher was the mistaken choice to give the memorial lecture for Arminius at the Hungarian Academy. 'Today', he wrote in his diary, 'I gave my memorial speech about Vambéry in the academy. On all sides great applause. Thus I carried out this sour task in a decent manner. The chapter of my biography entitled "Vambéry" is now closed'.[29]

Arminius would have been delighted with his posthumous press and honours, or he might have thought 'bah, humbug' to valueless words. The *Neue Freie Presse,* for which Herzl and Nordau had both worked, only acknowledged Arminius' death in its edition on 18 September, remarking 'As is generally known, the Orientalist Arminius Vambéry who died the day before yesterday achieved special fame in England as a daring explorer and clever politician, and after his first lecture at the [Royal Geographical Society]... became the man of the day'.[30] The *Royal Geographical Journal* described the 'name of Vambéry' as a 'household word in connection with Asian matters', but for 'an earlier generation'. It took C. Townley Fullam to reach the heights of hyperbole with his 'Recollections of Professor Vambéry' for the *Westminster Review:*

'The last great Englishman is low' – Tennyson
Vambéry is dead. The man who ought to have died of torture with his boots on and in the full light of day set out upon his last adventure peacefully, as a child in sleep. But he never did regard the proprieties.
Hungary has not been too prolific of great men. Her Homeric Age is so recent a phenomenon that of the famous five – Széchenyi, Kossuth, Deák, Görgei and Andrássy, one Görgei still lives, and one, Andrássy was

---

28 Teleki committed suicide when pushed by the Nazi regime to support Germany's invasion of Yugoslavia in 1941.
29 Patai, *Ignaz Goldziher,* op. cit., 44–5.
30 All quotes from the German press are taken from their translation in Alder and Dalby.

younger than Sir A R Wallace. The less easy it is to understand the attitude of many cultured Magyars whose opinions usually count. They considered Vambéry to be 'over-rated'.

Vambéry was certainly not a Cromwell but he had more than that commander's indomitable will. He had not the mad enthusiasm of Loyola, but he accomplished more, crippled as he was, than did that General in his own proper person. He had not the physical proportions of Burnaby, but the Guardsman must have succumbed before half the work had been accomplished. Nor was he, in the nature of things, a Hester Stanhope, but even the Queen of the Desert, dared not have penetrated, by stealth, the camps which Vambéry stormed in the light of day. Indeed, if one ransacked the whole range of fiction, from the days of one-eyed Calenders [the 'Qalandar' of the *Arabian Nights*] to those of de Rougemont, if one pass in review the long roll of honourable adventurers, – Peterborough, Clive, Paul Jones, Cochrane, Stanley, J F X O'Brien, and Disraeli, one could scarcely make of the total combination a more startling picture than that furnished by the career just closed.

A Little Jewish boy – it was no light drawback to be a Jew in Hungary – an emaciated cripple, hungry and despised, yet invincibly buoyant, tramping the weary way to school in all weathers, in all physical discomfort, there to encounter the scorn of the Christian, and what was incalculably worse, the contemptuous pity of the better disposed.[31]

The end of Arminius' association with Britain came with the certified copy of his death certificate, sent on 8 April 1914 from the Register of Deaths in Budapest, with a translation by the British diplomat Sir William Max Muller. On 16 April a note came from the Commissioners for the Reduction of the National Debt 'in regard to the expiry of the annuity' on the life of Professor Arminius Vambéry. But what of memorials? In the UK there is that street in Woolwich, near Plumstead Common. It was in fact named for Arminius long before his death, at the suggestion of his champion of the 1880s, Charles Marvin, who lived nearby. In a letter to the *Kentish Independent* on 21 September 1889, he put forward to the Plumstead Board that a new road should be named after the famous Hungarian, who had

---

31 C. Townley Fullam, *The Westminster Review*, 180/5 (1913), 525–30.

visited his house, 'to show that Plumstead at least was not unappreciative of the numerous services Vambéry has rendered to England'. He noted the acknowledgement of those services by the queen and the prince of Wales and considered the 'title simple and well-known'. He objected in any case to the present 'inappropriate and uncouth' suggestion of 'Heavitree' as a road name on grounds that it would be corrupted to 'Evytree... or some such abomination to the cultured ear'. Alder and Dalby also record a British trawler named *Vambéry*. It was arrested several times in the 1930s for illegal fishing in Icelandic waters. In Hungary, after World War I, entirely correct rumours of Arminius working for a foreign government put his name into disrepute, but by 1954 he was rehabilitated enough to have his image on a stamp, in the series of eight 'Great Hungarians', with minarets and a camel in the background. The Hungarian Academy issued a Vambéry Armin medal for outstanding linguistic merit, and in 1970 his wooden grave marker was replaced by the red granite headstone that stands today. In 1974, the memorial plaque was placed on the wall of his former house.

Much more recently, the end of Communist rule in Hungary and a new

nationalism have re-instituted Arminius Vambéry as an important Hungarian. He has been the subject of several academic papers and the excellent exhibition of his life in Budapest in late 2019 introduced him to a new audience. It was able to draw on those papers and photographs that had been preserved by Rustem and Robert Vambéry in America, in addition to engravings, photographs, and stories from Arminius' biographical works. Robert had first moved to Berlin in 1926 and then to Paris, emigrating finally to the USA, like his parents, in 1938, where he taught drama at Columbia University before retiring to California. He was a librettist and dramaturgist who worked closely with Kurt Weill and Bertolt Brecht, and left his papers to John Fuegi, professor at the University of Maryland and Brecht's biographer. They are now in the university library. The Hungarian Academy also holds a collection of valuable Turkish, Persian, and Arabic documents that were Arminius' original collection from his travels, as well as others later donated by Rustem. In the USA and Britain, *The Dervish of Windsor Castle* and old copies of Arminius' biographical works are occasionally swept of their gathered dust by those interested in the more obscure nineteenth-century travellers into Central Asia, but the name of Arminius Vambéry is almost unknown. I discovered only one person as I set out to write this book, one of those with the necessary *Wunderkammer* mind without recourse to Wikipedia, who had ever heard of him. Does that matter? Not in the least; but the storyteller's life was quite a story.

> *One Dervish to another. What was your vision*
> *of God's presence? I haven't seen anything,*
> *but for the sake of conversation, I will tell you a story.*

Jalaluddin Rumi

List of Illustrations

Bibliography

The first part of this bibliography includes the full publication details of those works cited most frequently. The second part, 'Further Reading', gives details of other works consulted by the author (and also given in the footnotes), for the reader who wishes to explore more of the life and times of Arminius Vambéry.

Alder, Lory, and Dalby, Richard, *The Dervish of Windsor Castle* (London, 1979)

Eastwick, Edward B., *Journal of a Diplomat's Three Years' Residence in Persia* (London, 1864)

Hopkirk, Peter, *The Great Game: On Secret Service in High Asia* (London, 1990)

Mandler, David, *Arminius Vambéry and The British Empire: Between East and West* (Maryland, 2016)

Marsh, H. C., *A Ride Through Islam* (London, 1877)

Patai, Raphael, *The Jews of Hungary: History, Culture, Psychology* (Detroit, 1996)

Schuyler, Eugene, *Turkistan: Notes of a Journey in Russian Turkistan, Khakand, Bukhara, and Kuldja*, Vol. I (London, 1876)

Vambéry, Arminius, *The Coming Struggle for India: Being an account of the encroachments of Russia in Central Asia and of the difficulties sure to arise therefrom to England* (London, 1885)

———, *The Life and Adventures of Arminius Vambéry: Written by Himself* (9th edn., London and Leipzig, 1914)

———, *The Story of My Struggles* (New York, 1904)

———, *Sketches of Central Asia: Additional Chapters on My Travels, Adventures and on the Ethnology of Central Asia* (Philadelphia, 1868, reprinted New York, 1970)

Further Reading

'An Indian Officer', *Russia's March towards India* (London, 1894)

Abbott, Sir James, *Narrative of a Journey from Heraut to Khiva, Moscow, and St Petersburgh During the Late Russian Invasion of Khiva* (London, 1843)

Algar, Hamid, '*Tarîqat* and *Tarîq*: Central Asian Naqshbandîs on the Roads to the Haramayn' in Alexandre Papas, Thomas Welsford, and Thierry Zarcone (eds.), *Central Asian Pilgrims, Haj Routes and Pious Visits between Central Asia and the Hijaz* (Berlin, 2012)

Amanat, Abbas, *Pivot of the Universe: Nasir-al-Din Shah Qajar and the Iranian Monarchy, 1831–1896* (London, 1997)

Baker, Captain Bernard Granville, *The Danube with Pen and Pencil* (London, 1911)

Baumer, Christopher, *The History of Central Asia: The Age of Decline and Revival*, Vol. 4 (London, 2018)

Burnes, Alexander, *Travels into Bokhara*, ed. Kathleen Hopkirk (London, 2012)

Conolly, Arthur, *Journey to the North of India: Overland from England, through Russia, Persia, and Afghanistan* (London, 1834)

Couliboeuf de Blocqueville, Henri de, *Gefangener Bei Den Turkmenen 1860–1861*, tr. Renate Pfeifer (repr. Nuremberg, 1980)

Curzon, George, *Russia in Central Asia and the Anglo-Russian Question* (London, 1889)

Denison Ross, Edward, *Jewish Travellers* (London, 1930)

————, *Both Ends of the Candle* (London, 1943)

Eldridge, C. C., *England's Mission: The Imperial Idea in the Age of Gladstone and Disraeli, 1868–1881* (London, 1973)

Esslemont, J. E., *Bahá'u'lláh and the New Era*, with a preface by Rustem Vambéry and Martha Root (Budapest, 1933)

Evans, Professor John L. (ed. and tr.), *Mission of N. P. Ignatiev to Khiva and Bukhara in 1858* (Newtonville, MA, 1984)

Fox, Edward, *The Hungarian who Walked to Heaven* (London, 2001)

Glazebrook, Philip, *Journey to Khiva: A Writer's Search for Central Asia* (London, 1992)

Green, Abigail, *Moses Montefiore: Jewish Liberator, Imperial Hero* (Cambridge, MA, 2012)

Krämer, Gudrun, Matringe, Denis, Nawas, John, and Rowson, Everett (eds.), *The Encyclopaedia of Islam Three Online*, https://referenceworks. brillonline.com/browse/encyclopaedia-of-islam-3

Herzl, Theodor, *The Complete Diaries of Theodor Herzl*, ed. by Raphael Patai, tr. by Harry Zohn (Vienna, 1960)

Herzl, Theodor, *The Old New Land* (n.p., 1902)

Holmes, William Richard, *Sketches on the Shores of the Caspian* (London, 1845)

Hopkirk, Kathleen (ed.), *Central Asia Through Writers' Eyes* (London, 1993)

Howard, Douglas A., *A History of the Ottoman Empire* (Cambridge, 2017)

Howard, Esmé (Lord Howard of Penrith), *Theatre of Life: Life Seen from the Stalls* (London, 1936)

Johnson, Major E. C., *On the Track of the Crescent: Erratic Notes from The Piraeus to Pesth* (London, 1885)

Kavanagh de Boulger, Demetrius Charles, *England and Russia in Central Asia* (London, 1879)

Koerner, Andràs, *How They Lived: The Everyday Life of Hungarian Jews, 1867–1940* (Budapest, 2015)

Komoróczy, Gèza (ed.), *Jewish Budapest: Monuments, Rites and History* (Budapest, 1999)

Kuneralp, Sinan (ed.), *The Secret Reports of the Hungarian Arminius Vambéry to the British Foreign Office on Sultan Abdulhamid II and his Reign (1889–1909)* (Istanbul, 2013)

Lee, Sir Sidney, *Edward VII: A Biography* (London, 1925)

Lewis, Bernard, *The Emergence of Modern Turkey* (3rd edn., Oxford, 2002)

Lord Hardinge of Penshurst, *Old Diplomacy: The Reminiscences of Lord Hardinge of Penshurst* (London, 1947)

Mackintosh-Smith, Tim (ed.), *The Travels of Ibn Battuta*, (London, 2002)

Maclean, Fitzroy, *To the Back of Beyond* (London, 1974)

Malleson, Colonel G. B., *Herat: The Granary and Garden of Central Asia* (London, 1880)

Mansel, Philip, *Constantinople: City of the World's Desire, 1453–1924* (London, 1995)

Marsh, H. C., *A Ride Through Islam* (London, 1877)

Marvin, Charles Thomas, *The Russians at the Gates of Herat* (New York, 1885)

Marvin, Charles Thomas, *Merv: The Queen of the World; and the Scourge of the Man-Stealing Turcomans* (London, 1881)

Mirfendereski, Guive, *A Diplomatic History of the Caspian Sea* (New York, 2001)

O'Donovan, Edmond, *The Merv Oasis: Travels and Adventures East of the Caspian During the Years 1879–81* (London, 1882)

Papas, Alexandre, *Thus Spake the Dervish: Sufism, Language, and the Religious Margins in Central Asia, 1400–1900;* tr. Caroline Kraabel (Leiden/Boston, 2019)

Paston, George, *At John Murray's: Records of a Literary Circle 1842–1892* (London, 1932)

Patai, Raphael, *Ignaz Goldziher and his Oriental Diary: A Translation and Psychological Portrait* (Detroit, 1987)

Rawlinson, Major-General Sir Henry, *England and Russia in the East: A Series of Papers on the Political and Geographical Condition of Central Asia* (London, 1875)

Richmond, Steven, *The Voice of England in the East: Stratford Canning and Diplomacy with the Ottoman Empire* (London, 2014)

Rodenbough, Brigadier Theophilus F., *Afghanistan and the Anglo-Russian Dispute* (New York, 1885)

Roth, Joseph, *The Radetzky March* (London, 2013)

Schuyler, Eugene, *Turkistan: Notes of a Journey in Russian Turkistan, Khakand, Bukhara, and Kuldja*, Vol. II (London, 1876)

Sharify-Funk, Meena, Dickson, Rory, and Shobhana Xavier, Merin, *Contemporary Sufism: Piety, Politics and Popular Culture* (Abingdon, 2018)

Siegel, Jennifer, *Endgame: Britain, Russia and the Final Struggle for Central Asia* (London, 2002)

Skrine, F. H., *An Indian Journal: Being the Life, Letters and Correspondence of Dr Sambhu C. Mookerjee* (Calcutta, 1889)

Stephens, John Lloyd, *Incidents of Travel in Greece, Turkey, Russia, and Poland*, Vol. I (New York, 1853)

Stoker, Bram, *Dracula* (London, 1897)

————, *Personal Reminiscences of Henry Irving* (London, 1907)

Stokes, Adrian and Marianne, *Hungary: Painted by Adrian and Marianne Stokes* (London, 1909)

Thubron, Colin, *The Lost Heart of Asia* (London, 1994)

UNESCO, *History of Civilizations of Central Asia, Vol. V: Development in Contrast: from the sixteenth to the mid-nineteenth century* (Paris, 2003)

Vambéry, Arminius, *Sittenbilder aus dem Morgenlande*, tr. Barbara Schwepcke for the author (Berlin, 1876)

Walikhanov, Shoqan Shynghysuly, *The Russians in Central Asia* (London, 1865)

Warburton, Sir Robert, *Eighteen Years on the Khyber* (London, 1900)

Wawro, Geoffrey, *A Mad Catastrophe: The Outbreak of World War One and the Collapse of the Habsburg Empire* (New York, 2015)

Wright, Denis, *The English Amongst the Persians: Imperial Lives in Nineteenth-Century Iran* (London, 2001)

Index